Universe and Inner Self in Early Indian and Early Greek Thought

EDITED BY RICHARD SEAFORD

EDINBURGH
University Press

Edinburgh University Press is one of the leading university presses in the UK. We publish academic books and journals in our selected subject areas across the humanities and social sciences, combining cutting-edge scholarship with high editorial and production values to produce academic works of lasting importance. For more information visit our website: edinburghuniversitypress.com

Edinburgh University Press Ltd
The Tun – Holyrood Road
12(2f) Jackson's Entry
Edinburgh EH8 8PJ

Typeset in 10.5/13 Times New Roman by
Servis Filmsetting Ltd, Stockport, Cheshire

A CIP record for this book is available from the British Library

ISBN 978 1 4744 1099 1 (hardback)
ISBN 978 1 4744 1100 4 (webready PDF)
ISBN 978 1 4744 1101 1 (epub)

Contents

Acknowledgements v
Notes on contributors vi
Abbreviations ix

Introduction 1

1 The common origin approach to comparing Indian and Greek philosophy 12
Nick Allen

2 The concept of *ṛtá* in the *Ṛgveda* 28
Joanna Jurewicz

3 *Harmonia* and *ṛtá* 40
Aditi Chaturvedi

4 *Ātman* and its transition to worldly existence 55
Greg Bailey

5 Cosmology, *psyche* and *ātman* in the *Timaeus*, the *Ṛgveda* and the *Upaniṣads* 71
Hyun Höchsmann

6 Plato and yoga 87
John Bussanich

7 Technologies of self-immortalisation in ancient Greece and early India 104
Paolo Visigalli

8 Does the concept of *theōria* fit the beginning of Indian thought? 118
Alexis Pinchard

9 Self or *being* without boundaries: on Śaṅkara and Parmenides 134
Chiara Robbiano

10 Soul chariots in Indian and Greek thought: polygenesis or diffusion? 149
Paolo Magnone

11 'Master the chariot, master your Self': comparing chariot metaphors as hermeneutics for mind, self and liberation in ancient Greek and Indian Sources 168
Jens Schlieter

12 New riders, old chariots: poetics and comparative philosophy 186
Alexander S. W. Forte and Caley C. Smith

13 The interiorisation of ritual in India and Greece 204
Richard Seaford

14 Rebirth and 'ethicisation' in Greek and South Asian thought 220
Mikel Burley

15 On affirmation, rejection and accommodation of the world in Greek and Indian religion 235
Matylda Obryk

16 The justice of the Indians 251
Richard Stoneman

17 Nietzsche on Greek and Indian philosophy 265
Emma Syea

Bibliography 279
Index 303

Acknowledgements

The astonishing similarities between early Indian and early Greek thought have long attracted great interest, but seldom the collaboration that is required for a real advance in explaining them. This volume contains most of the papers delivered at a conference at the University of Exeter in July 2014, as part of the project 'Ātman and Psychē: Cosmology and the Self in Ancient India and Ancient Greece'. The conference, and the project as a whole, were funded by the Arts and Humanities Research Council, to which we are most grateful. The conference consisted of days of lively discussion between Indologists, Hellenists and others: interdisciplinary discovery at its best. Another outcome of the project will be a monograph by myself.

I would like to thank Richard Fynes for his help with Sanskrit, and Edinburgh University Press for their enthusiastic efficiency.

Richard Seaford
Exeter, January 2016

Notes on contributors

Nick Allen qualified in social anthropology at Oxford, after studying classics and medicine, undertaking fieldwork in Nepal. From 1976 to 2001 he taught Social Anthropology of South Asia at Oxford, publishing on the Himalayas, kinship theory and the Durkheimian Tradition. Since the 1980s he has also worked on Indo-European Cultural Comparativism.

Greg Bailey, formerly reader in Sanskrit, is an Honorary Research Fellow in the Program in Asian Studies, La Trobe University, Melbourne. He has published translations and studies of the *Gaṇeśa Purāṇa*, Bhartṛhari's *Śatakatrayam* and books on the god Brahmā, early Buddhism, contemporary Australian society and many articles on Sanskrit literature.

Mikel Burley is Associate Professor of Religion and Philosophy at the University of Leeds. His publications include *Classical Sāṃkhya and Yoga: An Indian Metaphysics of Experience* (2007), *Contemplating Religious Forms of Life: Wittgenstein and D. Z. Phillips* (2012) and *Rebirth and the Stream of Life: A Philosophical Study of Reincarnation, Karma and Ethics* (2016).

John Bussanich is Professor of Philosophy at the University of New Mexico. He co-edited with Nicholas D. Smith *The Bloomsbury Companion to Socrates* (2013). He is the author of *The One and its Relation to Intellect in Plotinus: A Commentary on Selected Texts* (1988) and of articles on Socrates, Plato and the Neoplatonists. Other research interests include comparative philosophy, and philosophy and mysticism in South Asia.

Aditi Chaturvedi is a doctoral candidate in Philosophy at the University of Pennsylvania, writing a dissertation on the role of *harmonia* in Plato's metaphysics and ethics.

Alexander S. W. Forte and **Caley C. Smith** are doctoral students at Harvard University. Alexander's dissertation is on metaphor in the Homeric poems. Caley's dissertation examines mimetic performance in the Ṛgveda and its implications for the social project of the early ritual and the redaction of the text.

Hyun Höchsmann has studied philosophy, art history and literature at the Ludwig-Maximilians Universität in Munich and the University of London. She has taught at the Juilliard School of Music, the American University in Cairo and East China Normal University in Shanghai. Her publications include *On Chuang Tzu* (2001), *On Philosophy in China* (2003) and *Zhuangzi* (2006).

Joanna Jurewicz is a professor in the Oriental Studies Department of Warsaw University. She uses an interdisciplinary methodology of philology and cognitive linguistics to analyse ancient Indian texts. She is the author of *Fire and Cognition in the Ṛgveda* (2010), of *Fire, Death, and Philosophy. A History of Ancient Indian Thinking* (2016) and of many articles.

Paolo Magnone teaches Sanskrit Language and Literature at the Catholic University of the Sacred Heart as well as Oriental Religions at the Higher Institute for Religious Sciences (both in Milan). His research interests include thematic studies in the epico-purāṇic literature; the philosophy of the *Upaniṣad*s and Sāṃkhya–Yoga in the light of the commentators; comparative studies in Ancient Greek and Indian philosophical thought.

Matylda Obryk is a visiting professor of Classics at the Northeast Normal University in Changchun, China. After studying classics and philosophy in Kraków and Jena, she obtained a PhD from the University of Cologne, with a dissertation published as *Unsterblichkeitsglaube in den griechischen Versinschriften* (2012).

Alexis Pinchard is 'professeur agrégé' of philosophy at the Lycée Militaire d'Aix-en-Provence (France) and associate member of the CNRS, UMR 7528 'Iranian and Indian Worlds'. His PhD dissertation was published as *Les langues de sagesse dans la Grèce et l'Inde anciennes* (2009). His research focuses on the connection between ancient metaphysics, ancient soteriology and comparative linguistics.

Chiara Robbiano is Assistant professor of Philosophy at University College Utrecht. Her PhD dissertation (Leiden) on Parmenides was published as *Becoming Being* (2006). She publishes her work on comparative and ancient philosophy in *Philosophy East and West*, *Ancient Philosophy*, and elsewhere.

Jens Schlieter studied Philosophy, Tibetology / Buddhist Studies and Comparative Religion in Bonn and Vienna. He is Professor of the Systematic Study of Religion at the Institute for the Science of Religion, University of Bern (Switzerland). His contributions comprise method and theory in the study of religion, comparative philosophy and Buddhism in India, Tibet and the West.

Richard Seaford is Emeritus Professor of Ancient Greek at the University of Exeter. His publications include many articles; commentaries on Euripides' *Cyclops* (1984) and Euripides *Bacchae* (1996); and *Dionysos* (1996), *Reciprocity and Ritual* (1994), *Money and the Early Greek Mind* (2004) and *Cosmology and the Polis* (2012). His current project is a monograph comparing early Indian with early Greek thought.

Richard Stoneman is an Honorary Visiting Professor at the University of Exeter and Chairman of Westminster Classic Tours. His books include *Alexander the Great: a life in legend* (2008) and (most recently) *Xerxes: a Persian Life* (2015). He is currently writing *The Greek Experience of India from Alexander the Great to Menander Soter*.

Emma Syea is currently completing her doctoral studies in Philosophy at King's College London. Her research examines Nietzsche's philosophy of mind, specifically his views on self-knowledge and self-deception.

Paolo Visigalli's work explores the interplay between language ideologies, hermeneutic techniques and the production and renegotiation of textual meaning. He received a PhD in South Asian Studies from the University of Cambridge. His current research focuses on etymological theories and practices in Hindu and Buddhist texts, in Sanskrit, Pali and Chinese. He is currently teaching at Fudan University, Shanghai.

Abbreviations

AiĀ	*Aitareya Āraṇyaka*
AiB	*Aitareya Brāhmaṇa*
AV	*Atharvaveda*
BG	*Bhagavad Gītā*
BSB	Śaṅkara, *Brahmasūtra-bhāṣya*, in E. Deutsch and R. Dalvi (eds), *The Essential Vedānta: A New Source Book of Advaita Vedānta*, Bloomington, 2004.
BU	*Bṛhadāraṇyaka Upaniṣad*
ChU	*Chāndogya Upaniṣad*
DK	H. Diels and W. Kranz (eds) *Die Fragmente der Vorsokratiker*, 6th edn, Berlin, 1951.
DL	Diogenes, *Live of the Philosophers*
FGrH	F. Jacoby (ed.), *Die Fragmente der Griechischer Historiker*, Berlin and Leiden, 1923–58.
KaU	*Kaṭha Upaniṣad*
KauU	*Kauṣītaki Upaniṣad*
KU	*Kena Upaniṣad*
MaiU	*Maitrāyaṇīya/Maitrī Upaniṣad*
MuU	*Mundaka Upaniṣad*
RV	*Ṛgveda*
ŚB	*Śatapatha Brāhmaṇa*
ŚvU	*Śvetāśvatara Upaniṣad*
TĀ	*Taitttirīya Āraṇyaka*
TaitU	*Taitttirīya Upaniṣad*
TB	*Taittirīya-Brāhmaṇa*
TS	*Taittirīya Samhitā*
TU	*Taittirīya Upaniṣad*
YS	*Yoga Sūtra*

Introduction

How are early Greek and early Indian thought similar? And how do we explain the similarities? These questions can contribute to the current debate about the so-called Axial Age, in which – it is claimed – various civilisations were in the first millenium BCE transformed, intellectually and ethically, in ways by which we are still defined.

There is general agreement neither on the dating of the Axial Age nor on which civilisations count as manifestations of it. The focus of this volume is mainly (but not exclusively) on the period from about 800 BCE to Alexander's crossing of the Indus in 326 BCE. In this period we can say that philosophy is to be found in both Greece and India, provided that 'philosophy' is defined not by rationality, which is in a sense ubiquitous, but rather by understanding the universe as a systematic whole that lacks any fundamental role for the personal agency of deity. Of course in neither culture was this a majority view. It is certainly not the only possible definition of philosophy, and we might even prefer to call it proto-scientific rather than philosophical. But it defines a phenomenon of considerable intellectual and historical significance, and distinguishes Greece and India (and China) from the other societies that are often regarded as manifesting the Axial transformation: Israel and Iran.

The belief just described as defining 'philosophy' is one of many shared by Greece and India in this period. Allen finds a basic pentadic *structure* in various contexts in both Greek and Indian texts. The development of *abstraction*, as a prerequisite for philosophy, is traced as early as the *Ṛgveda* by Jurewicz in the instance of *ṛtá* – 'cosmos, order, truth' – a concept that is then compared with Greek *harmonia* by Chaturvedi. Other shared 'philosophical' beliefs are monism (the belief that everything is in fact a single entity, for which see Seaford, Robbiano, Obryk), and the idea that understanding the (sometimes explicitly incorporeal) inner self or soul (*psuchē*, *ātman*) is central to understanding the universe and vital for human well-being.

This last theme runs through most of the chapters. Linguistic aspects of the development of *ātman* are discussed by Bailey. The close relation, in both cultures, between the inner self and the totality of existence (Höchsmann) is a basis for the practices that in both cultures seek transcendent wisdom, immortality, or liberation from the cycle of births and deaths (Bussanich, Visigalli). Even the well-known distinction of motivations for contemplating the universe (salvation in India, wonder in Greece) is partially dissolved by Pinchard. An even closer relationship of subject (knowing) with Being produces for both Parmenides and (much later) Śaṅkara a monism that has positive psychological and ethical implications (Robbiano). Psychological and ethical implications are at the heart of the elaborate image of the inner self as a chariot, which famously occurs in both cultures (Magnone, Schlieter, Forte and Smith, Höchsmann). The development of the inner self is in both cultures affected by the *interiorisation* of the cosmic rite of passage (Seaford). Another such belief (about the inner self) exclusive in this period to Greece and India is ethicised reincarnation, the sources of which are discussed by Burley.

Most of this (the main exceptions are *Ṛgveda* and Śaṅkara) falls within the period from about 800 to 326 BCE. A longer perspective is adopted by Obryk, who applies to both cultures the threefold typology of religions that consists of affirmation, rejection and accommodation of the world. The Greek views of Indian justice discussed by Stoneman were produced both before and after Alexander crossed the Indus. And we conclude with a sample of reception: Syea explores Nietzsche's positive evaluation of both Greece and India as embodying alternatives to Christianity.

How are the similarities in thought to be explained? There are three possibilities: (a) a shared Indo-European origin, (b) influence (in one direction or the other, or by diffusion from a third source), and (c) parallel autonomous development. These three kinds of explanation, which are not necessarily mutually exclusive, all appear in this volume. (a) is more likely for basic structures of narrative and thought (Allen) than for philosophy as defined above, which does not appear in the earliest texts (*Ṛgveda*, Homer), whereas (b) is more likely (and sometimes certain) after than before Alexander crossed the Indus. Espousal of (b) or (c) prompts the question – no more than touched on in this volume – of the conditions that allow or promote their occurrence. A good case to think with is the famous image of the inner self as a chariot: Magnone inclines to assign it to (b), but Schlieter inclines to assign it to (c), which is favoured more confidently by Forte and Smith.

This volume takes its place in a long history from antiquity onwards – vividly presented by Halbfass (1988) – of thinking about the similarities and differences between Greek (or European) and Indian thought. Many recent contributions are listed in the consolidated bibliography at the end of the volume. As an example of what a single scholar can achieve one might single out the flawed but impressive synthesis by McEvilley (2002). Our volume is distinctive (though not unique) in that its chapters were discussed at a conference by a mixture of Hellenists with informed interest in India and Indologists with informed interest in Greece. The vastness of the subject requires this kind of approach. Further, the volume appears at a stage in the advance of globalisation at which it has become unprecedentedly implausible – however much the practice continues – for any culture to assume its own (implicit or explicit) metaphysical assumptions to be a standard to which other cultures should aspire. This lends interest and urgency to discussion of the origins of such differences, and to the burgeoning debate about the Axial Age. Did the Axial transformations occur in each civilisation independently? How and why did they occur? Do we now require, as some have suggested, a second Axial Age, and how could it occur? Our volume may be considered a small contribution to the fascination of understanding where our various civilisations have come from, but also – indirectly – to the question of where they are going.

What follows is a summary of each of the chapters.

Ancient similarities between Greeks and north Indians – in their institutions, poetic phraseology, myth and epic – have been attributed to their shared Indo-European origin. A contribution to this perspective is made here by Allen, who focuses on two kinds of similarity. Firstly, he sets out a series of correspondences between two journey narratives, the journey to the next world in the *Kauṣītaki Upaniṣad* and the journey of the Homeric Odysseus from Ogygia to Phaeacia. Despite the obvious differences, the number of similar details (he counts twenty-five), in roughly the same order, is too great to be coincidental. His second kind of similarity between the two cultures is based on the shared 'trifunctional ideology' that Georges Dumézil attributed to their Indo-European origin (the three functions are – roughly speaking – sovereignty, physical force and production). However, Allen finds both the total of three and the category of social function, adequate though they may be for a well-functioning society, too restrictive for a *worldview*. Accordingly he favours the replacement of Dumézil's triadic structure with a pentadic one, in which the triad acquires at the bottom what is *undesirable* and at the top something *transcendent*. This pentadic structure is found in various kinds of context. From India Allen focuses on the ontological classification of five pentads of *tattvas* elaborated by the philosophy known as Sāṃkhya, and from Greece on the set of five elements. Finally, the two kinds of similarity intersect: the journey narratives manifest pentadic patterns, and the Sāṃkhya schema contains an evolutionism that gives it a narrative quality.

Jurewicz emphasises *abstraction* as a key component in the development of philosophy in India. Whereas Havelock (1983) related the origin of Greek philosophy to the advent of literacy, Jurewicz argues that the development of the capacity for abstraction is attested already in the earliest Indian text, the *Ṛgveda*, many centuries before the advent of writing in India. This issue is important, she claims, not only for Indology but also from the more general point of view of philosophy seen as a human endeavour, not limited to the European tradition. In contrast to the earliest European philosophy, which is preserved only in fragments, the Vedic tradition is a rich source for the beginnings of human philosophical inquiry. The understanding of metaphor provided by cognitive linguistics reveals mechanisms by which the concrete is used to express the abstract. In particular, she shows how in the *Ṛgveda* the Sanskrit word *ṛtá*, which may be used of an abstract and metaphysical concept ('cosmos, order, truth'), derives in stages from the fundamental concrete experience of herding cows, as well as from the experience of other fundamental concrete realities such as the dawn, rivers and ritual. Experience is transformed in order to create abstraction that is conducive to philosophy.

Chaturvedi begins from the observation of Emile Benveniste that, for the Indo-Europeans, the idea of 'order' is 'the foundation, both religious and moral, of every society', and that the importance of this notion is shown in the considerable number of lexical forms derived from the root *H_2er* (to fit, to arrange). She discusses two of these forms – the Greek *harmonia* and the Sanskrit *ṛtá*. She analyses hymns from the *Ṛgveda* and the fragments of Philolaus, Empedocles and Heraclitus, with the aim of uncovering the extent to which they play similar roles in their respective cosmologies. She first discusses *harmonia* and *ṛtá* as cosmological principles, showing how both involve a harmonic regulation of opposites, and then focuses on the moral applications of these principles. She concludes that, at the most abstract level, *harmonia* and *ṛtá* are principles of order that stand for the dynamic fitting together of disjointed entities. The fitting together takes place in nature, the macrocosm, and in human life, the microcosm; furthermore, it involves adaptations *between* microcosm and macrocosm.

Bailey notes that the central concept of the *ātman*, so crucial for refining the nature of personhood in the *Upaniṣads* and beyond, is still not understood in its full epistemological and ontological contexts. In part this is because it is 'ungraspable and unthinkable', leading many teachers in the *Upaniṣads* to give their own take on it. He proposes no magic solution to its comprehensibility in the older *Upaniṣads* (sixth to fourth centuries BCE), but rather begins from the proposal that the people who composed these texts – like those who composed the early Jain and Buddhist texts – were brilliantly skilful at defining existence as a fundamentally negative condition. Given that worldly existence, with its social, cultural, political and economic spheres, remains the problem to be confronted, how is the connection between the ontologically complete *ātman* (Brahmā) and the ontologically incomplete *manas/śarīra*, the physical world of the senses and the mind, argued for and maintained? In order to illuminate the certainty with which the link – even if ontologically true or false – had to be made, he focuses on some passages of cosmological/cosmogonic import from the *Bṛhadāraṇyaka Upaniṣad*, where a contrast is made between the two verbs *as* and *bhū*, both conveying a different ontological sense of 'being' and 'becoming' as they apply to the *ātman* and the Brahmā. It is by use of these verbs that the entrance of the *ātman* into the world of imperfect existence is described. In addition, attention is focused on the Sanskrit prefix *vi*, which indicates difference and diffuseness, in defining the ontological development of the *ātman*. Finally he contextualises this within the kinds of socio-economic structures that background a shift in the stress on particular ontological categories, and questions whether the sixth–fourth centuries BCE were really periods of radical change, as scholars have often suggested.

Höchsmann describes how the conceptions of universe and soul in *Timaeus*, *Ṛgveda* and the *Upaniṣads* converge and overlap but do not coincide. While the *Ṛgveda* (10.129) invites conjectures regarding a plurality of universes, the *Upaniṣads* affirm that there is one universe, as *ātman* is identified with *brahman*, the eternal totality of all that exists. The cosmology of the *Timaeus* integrates the open-ended view of the origin of the universe in the *Ṛgveda* with the certainty of the *Upaniṣads*. In the *Ṛgveda* and the *Upaniṣads* there is (as in subsequent Indian cosmologies) an ethical conception of the cosmic order, but *cosmogony* seems morally and aesthetically neutral: in contrast to the *Timaeus*, there is no motivation to create a cosmos endowed with beauty and goodness, no eternal paradigm of supreme goodness. Their anthropomorphic cosmogony is distinct from the mathematical structures and the ordered harmony of the cosmogony in the *Timaeus*. But all three regard the universe as a hierarchically organised and interrelated system in which order (*ṛtá* in the *Ṛgveda*) prevails. In both *Timaeus* and the *Upaniṣads* cosmology is the prerequisite for self-knowledge (of *psyche* and *ātman*) and ethics. Such knowledge is in *Timaeus* both metaphysical (of *dēmiourgos*, eternal model for the universe, and forms) and empirical (the *psyche* experiences the order and harmony of the planetary movements corresponding to the laws of musical harmony). As for the *ātman*, it encompass all that is encountered in existence. The *Timaeus* and the *Upaniṣads* both lay the foundations for moral realism, the view that moral values, principles and actions have objective validity beyond individual preferences, cultural norms and social institutions. The knowledge of *ātman* and *psyche* has theoretical and practical significance. Interpretive analyses of *ātman* and *psyche* as the constant and enduring self throughout persistent change can increase our understanding of personal identity and continuity of consciousness.

Bussanich presents fresh approaches to Plato's conception of wisdom and the means to attain it by comparison with South Asian yoga traditions. Despite important differences, Plato, classical Vedānta, Yoga and early Buddhism all seek transcendent wisdom and liberation from the cycle of births and deaths. On the basis of homologies between cosmos and psyche in which the hierarchy of consciousness mirrors the structure of reality, these traditions promote cognitive and affective practices whose aim is to remove external accretions to the self and the delusion and suffering they bring in their wake through the attenuation of desire and thought. Vedānta and classical Yoga espouse withdrawal of the senses (*pratyāhāra*), meditation (*dhyāna*), concentration (*dhāraṇā*) and meditative absorption (*samādhi*). Early Buddhism promotes calmness meditation (*samatha/śamatha*), whose goal is *samādhi*, and insight meditation (*vipassanā/vipaśyanā*), whose goal is wisdom (*prajñā*). There is evidence in the Platonic dialogues for analogies to South Asian meditative praxis which enables the soul to ascend the hierarchy of states of consciousness. Comparison of these practices raises questions about the similarities and differences between South Asian and Platonic conceptions of wisdom and the means to attain them. Are the highest states of knowledge in Plato non-conceptual? Is the interdependence of the intellectual/analytical insight and non-cognitive 'cessative' meditations in South Asian yoga found also in Plato?

Visigalli explores the idea, present in both ancient Greece and early India, that immortality can be achieved through some structured methods. Borrowing and adapting Michel Foucault's (1988) notion of the technologies of the self, he calls such methods 'technologies of self-immortalisation'. While Foucault is concerned mainly with the exploration of how these technologies of self-caring and self-knowledge produce a certain self-understanding, Visigalli explores how composite psychophysical practices are aimed at producing a post-mortem immortal self. First, building on Sedley's (2009) discussion of different kinds of immortality in Plato, he examines the theme of self-immortalisation through the practice of philosophy in Plato's *Timaeus*. Then he explores the ritual construction of an immortal self (*ātman*) in the ritual of the construction of the fire altar (*agnicayana*). In doing so, he focuses on the interplay of ritual actions and the attendant ritual speculations. Finally, he poses some questions about immortality, and considers how the Indian and Greek evidence invites different answers.

Pinchard challenges the common view that, unlike Greek speculation, primeval Indian thought about the whole universe (in the *Upaniṣads*) was not strictly theoretical but mainly aimed at salvation. Husserl, for example, held this view. But this contradistinction is not valid because certain Greek philosophers linked the intimate experience of eternity, which really breaks the power of death, with the true *theōria* in order to define a complete way of life (it is more explicit in Plato and Aristotle, especially at *Nicomachean Ethics* X, 7, but it may be present in some Pre-Socratic thinkers too), while in India wonder may also be viewed as the first motive leading to the disinterested search for truth about metaphysical principles (cf. Aristotle *Metaphysics* A1). Such personal names as Satyakāma (*Chāndogya Upaniṣad*) have to be interpreted literally. Indeed the absolute reality, the *brahman* itself, is desire, but desire for itself. It is not just a thing. Hence to unite personally with the *brahman* implies keeping the desire for truth alive. The cult of selfhood typical of Indian philosophy is very different from a restricted selfishness, and the disinterestedness of the theoretical attitude cannot be restricted to Greek thought alone.

Robbiano presents the argument, shared by Parmenides and Śaṅkara, that boundaries between human individuals and between things are 'epistemologically weak', because they are not real but superimposed by humans. Parmenides, Śaṅkara and Descartes would agree on being certain of 'being' in some sense, but would differ when asked to specify of what being they are certain. Descartes, embracing Aristotle's assumption that predicates must belong to a substance, would say that the being of which he is certain belongs to a thinking substance or a soul. But Parmenides and Śaṅkara would argue that being does not belong to any substance: any entity we might regard as the subject or owner of being is produced by custom, by which we superimpose boundaries on being, which is fundamentally undivided. What leads Parmenides and Śaṅkara from the certainty of being to the certainty of *undivided* being is their shared foundational conception of knowing, according to which it is impossible to *know* anything other than being. It follows that we cannot know any boundary, since we cannot know any second being, and therefore no knowledge is possible of any boundary allegedly separating the two. With no knowledge of a first boundary, no other boundary can be regarded as trustworthy; consequently no knowledge can be claimed of the many things, separated by unreliable boundaries. The step from the impossibility of knowing anything other than being to the lack of reality of any second being might look like a fallacy, taking an unwarranted step from epistemology to ontology. However, for the conception of knowing and being that entails their identity, there is no fallacy. Finally, the metaphysics of undivided being might facilitate *experiencing* the lack of boundaries, yielding 'unshakenness' and invulnerability (Parmenides), compassion and liberation (Śaṅkara).

Magnone discusses the intriguing similarity between the allegories of the soul chariot in Plato's *Phaedrus* and in the *Kaṭha Upaniṣad*. The similarity has been pointed out – if not thoroughly investigated – by several scholars, with varying assessments that are largely dependent on each individual scholar's assumptions concerning various issues: the bare possibility or degree of likelihood of contacts and influences between early Greek and Indian thought, the significance (or otherwise) of the intercultural comparative endeavour, or indeed the methodological soundness of even positing the question in the almost complete absence of pertinent historical documentation. Because assessments are thus heavily influenced by theoretical assumptions, the chapter begins with some methodological considerations in order to define the grounds, scope and limits of the attempted comparison, also drawing on the methodological discourses of other related fields, like mythology and folklore. Then a review of the relevant texts of the *Phaedrus* and the *Kaṭha Upaniṣad* sets out both the congruencies and the discrepancies in the treatment of the chariot allegory. A summary reference to the results of a detailed survey of kindred passages in both literary traditions (presented by Magnone elsewhere) helps to demonstrate that the allegory of the soul chariot is integral to Upaniṣadic thought in a way that is unparalleled in Greek thought, thus supporting the conjecture of diffusion in a westward direction. Finally, the chapter will briefly discuss the paramount difference – i.e. the conspicuous absence of the idle passenger in the *Phaedrus* allegory vs. his centrality to the allegory of the *Kaṭha* – and its significance as a theoretical watershed between Upaniṣad-based Indian and Plato-influenced Greek philosophy.

Schlieter uses theoretical work on metaphor to argue that in both Greece and India the danger, intense experience and various uses of chariots were a source domain for a dynamic 'anthropo-therio-technological metaphor' for the interpretation of various abstract domains. Chariots were not only depicted as vehicles of gods such as the sun (*helios*, *sūrya*, *kāla*), i.e. symbols of cosmic stability, but also used as symbols of royal power and social prestige (in the *Iliad*, Vedic hymns, and poetic literature). As for chariots as metaphors for the mind or soul and its liberation, Indian influence on pre-Alexandrian Greece is, although highly unlikely, theoretically possible, since the absolute chronology of the *Upaniṣads* is still disputed. But the striking similarities follow a certain logic, given that a somewhat similar use of chariots (both actual and metaphorical) in the respective traditions had already been established. There are subtle but important differences in the Greek and Indian chariot metaphors for the inner self – e.g. the passenger able to leave the chariot at a final destination, a difference discussed also by Magnone. Cognitive analysis of chariot metaphors may bring out those (sometimes hidden) philosophical preconceptions prevalent in abstract domains such as the 'mind', the connection of 'body and mind', the relationship between the 'rational' and the 'emotional' part, or the relation between a 'steering mind' and the 'Self'. Finally, in late antiquity, which saw the end not only of the light and fast chariot but also of a certain ideal of embodied self-mastery, it seems that chariot imagery was no longer fully 'functional'. The Buddhist use of chariot imagery in the Indian, and the Christian use in the late antique tradition may each be a final allegorical phase producing a rigorous deconstruction of the chariot (ride) and its symbolic force for visualising the mind, Soul and liberation.

For Forte and Smith the genealogy of the chariot imagery in both Greece and India is best explained not by influence but through local intertexts: the *Iliad* and the Vedas respectively. For the Greek material their main concern is not with Plato but with the chariot journey described by Parmenides. The concentration of similarities between *Iliad* 23 and the text of Parmenides suggests that he is engaging specifically with the chariot race during Patroclus' funeral games, which also serves as a source of philosophical material for Empedocles and includes the *locus classicus* for Socratic ἐπαγωγή. The chariot in *Kaṭha Upaniṣad* is a metaphor for the sacrifice, specifically the fire altar; its imagery is a redeployment of the chariot imagery and narrative setting used in the earlier *Kaṭha Brāhmaṇa*. They argue that understanding the metaphysics of the *Katha Upaniṣad* is only possible when contextualised as a component of a hieratic canon. Once these commitments are recognised, it becomes apparent that Parmenides' poem and the *Kaṭha Upaniṣad* have distinct antecedents and discursive agendas.

Seaford proposes as a similarity between the two cultures, around the middle of the first millennium BCE, the *interiorisation* of ritual, specifically the cosmic rite of passage (sacrifice in India, mystic initiation in Greece). The internal or mental performance of the ritual, or the adoption of its terminology and structure to describe intellectual transition, tends to replace its actual performance. In India this development issues from the discernible *individualisation* of the sacrifice. Conflict, reciprocity (voluntary requital) and group are marginalised; the power of the ritual tends to become invisible and automatic; merit is accumulated by the individual; the object of the sacrifice becomes the self; and finally everything is absorbed into the individual self. In the same period in Greece the language and structure of the ritual of mystic initiation are used by Heraclitus, Parmenides and Plato to describe the *intellectual* progress of the individual. In both cultures this interiorisation is connected to the advent of monism and of the all-importance of the inner self. As for the causes of the development, it is proposed that an important factor in both cases was the advent of a general means of exchange. *Monetisation* can be correlated with various features of interiorisation (and of monism): money unites all goods, individualises, bestows a sense of (unified) interior power, and replaces conflict and reciprocity with power that is invisible, automatic and individually accumulated.

Burley begins by presenting the 'ethicisation' thesis developed by the anthropologist Gananath Obeyesekere. According to this thesis rebirth beliefs with only minimal ethical features evolved into *karmic* beliefs that regard one's future life as being conditioned by the ethical quality of one's current life. Though applying primarily to South Asian traditions, this thesis also bears upon ideas of transmigration in ancient Greece. Underlying both Obeyesekere's analysis and other speculative views is the assumption that a metaphysical conception of rebirth is logically and chronologically prior to any ethical outlook that accompanies it. But this assumption is challenged by Catherine Osborne, who argues that the ethical outlook of certain Greek philosophers generated their transmigration theories. Elucidating and critically engaging with Obeyesekere's and Osborne's work, this chapter not only disrupts the aforementioned assumption but also questions whether there must be an order of priority between metaphysics and ethics at all. A viable alternative is that worldviews involving rebirth comprise both metaphysical and ethical dimensions, neither of which is prior to the other. An implication of this latter view is that talk of a transition from *non*-ethicised to ethicised conceptions of rebirth should be replaced by considerations of the transition from one kind of ethically imbued conception to another.

Obryk applies to both cultures the typology of religious movements created by Roy Wallis (world-affirming, world-rejecting and world-accommodating religions). In Indian philosophy we may compare the scheme *karma*, *jñāna* and *bhakti*. In Greece the world-affirming type could be seen in both the *polis* religion, with its immanent gods and rituals, and the practice of magic. This corresponds in the Indian typology to *karma* (action), which involves the mechanistic process of controlling the world and environment by means of sacrifice (*yajña*) and ritual (*karma-kāṇḍa*). When frustration arises from apparent lack of success in controlling the world, then *jñāna* (science) appears, striving to find a transcendent monistic supreme power behind the world of occurrences. This parallels Wallis's world-rejecting type, which can be found in Greek thought and practice as the philosophical search for the primordial principle. Thirdly, there seems to be a reconciliation of the ritualistic and philosophical approaches to religion and worldview in the theurgy of Iamblichus and (partially) much earlier in the individual development of Socrates' religiosity. This corresponds to the *bhakti*/*upāsana* strand (loving service or devotion): transcendence is understood to be fully independent of worldly presumptions and the world, and what is in the world is used for the service of this transcendent but personal divinity. This corresponds to Wallis' world-accommodating type.

Stoneman investigates the report that Ctesias (early fourth century BCE) 'claims that the Indians are very just people; he also describes their customs and manners'. What were the sources of Ctesias' information? What did he mean by 'justice'? Was he correct in ascribing these qualities to the Indians? Did Greek δικαιοσύνη/δίκη correspond to an identifiable Indian term? Did Greek reports of India provide information about Indian reality or are they merely an *interpretatio Graeca*? These questions are set in the context of Greek comments on Indian society from Homer and Scylax of Caryanda to Onesicritus, Megasthenes and the Alexander Romance. The main components of the Greeks' idea of Indian justice may be summarised as 'honesty', non-violence, piety, and the avoidance of usury, theft, adultery and drunkenness, as well as respect for authority. These overlap with Greek definitions of justice, not least in the form elaborated by Plato (in the main social justice). In some respects – e.g. absence of slavery and non-violence – Indian 'justice' seems to resemble Greek utopian ideas, as developed by Plato but also in Hellenistic writers, Cynic philosophers and parts of the Alexander Romance. Greek assertions can be compared with Indian texts that include not only the *Ṛgveda* and the *Upaniṣads* but also texts that were written down later than Ctesias (and even Megasthenes), such as the *Arthaśāstra*, *Dharmasūtras* and *Laws of Manu*. Most of what the Greeks believed about Indian society and its justice can be shown to be true, though they sometimes misunderstood what they observed or were told. The Greek texts are more reliable than has sometimes been supposed, and the information in the Alexander Romance and Onesicritus is more up-to-date than that in Ctesias or even Megasthenes; much depended on who the authors' informants were.

Syea brings us into modernity. The arresting and intriguing parallels which exist between Greek and Indian philosophy did not go unnoticed by Friedrich Nietzsche, who spoke of 'the wonderful family resemblance of all Indian, Greek, and German philosophising' (*Beyond Good and Evil* 20). Nietzsche's works provide us with a useful prism for exploring these similarities. In *On the Genealogy of Morality*, Nietzsche demonstrates how values which emerge in cultures are driven and supported by physiological, psychological and sociological trends. This genealogical method complements the notion of parallel autonomous intellectual development in ancient India and ancient Greece, as it suggests that similarities would emerge, should certain conditions obtain in both cultures. In particular Nietzsche was interested in how the *agonal* spirit surfaced in the warring *poleis* of ancient Greece, and how this came to imbue Greek literature and philosophy – we need only think of Homer's *Iliad*, Hesiod's two Erises and Heraclitean strife. It is suggested that this agonal culture could also be extended to the city-states of ancient India, where it also filtered through to philosophical writings – epics like the *Mahābhārata* and the *Rāmāyaṇa* explicitly place discussion of self, state and normativity against a background of conflict. The chapter examines how Nietzsche found in these cultures viable models of self and state, suggests that these models were born out of an agonal context, and proposes that Nietzsche came to see 'Greek' and 'Indian' as *modes of being*, which informed his own ideas on normativity, providing him with an alternative to the Christian slave morality he so despised.

1

The common origin approach to comparing Indian and Greek philosophy

Nick Allen

Can a comparison between Indian and Greek philosophies abstract from history? Most scholars would agree that to isolate philosophical positions from the socio-cultural history in which they were formulated is artificial and problematic, but the question then becomes what sort of history is needed. Of course the Vedas were preceded by the Indus Valley civilisation and Homer by the Mycenaeans, but such precursors cast little light on philosophy and can be left to other specialists. So histories of Sanskrit thinking usually start with the *Ṛgveda*, much as their Greek equivalents start with Homer. No doubt many scholars take for granted that no other style of history is or ever will be feasible.

The assumption is paradoxical, however, since, as languages, Sanskrit and Greek have histories that go back well before the Vedas and Homer. For two centuries philologists have been writing their own sort of history, embodying many of their findings in the starred forms they attribute to the Indo-European protolanguage (usually dated to the fourth millennium BCE). This history involves semantics as well as phonology, and the well-known work of Benveniste (1969) studied the vocabulary of Indo-European institutions. Equally well-recognised are Calvert Watkins (1995), who applied a similar approach to the history of Indo-European poetical phraseology, and Martin West (2007), who in addition tackled some particular constructs found in Indo-European myth and epic.

More immediately relevant is the vast corpus of comparativism produced by Georges Dumézil (1898–1986), much of it addressing the Indo-European 'trifunctional ideology'. Leaving the functions till later, I emphasise the word 'ideology', which Dumézil defines in various ways. Depending on viewpoint, it can be defined 'either as a means of exploring material and moral reality or as a means of ordering the capital of ideas accepted by the society'. It was 'at once an ideal and a way of analysing and interpreting the forces that ensure the smooth running of the world (*le cours du monde*) and the life of men'. Trifunctionality was 'the framework (*cadre*) of a system of thought, an explanation of the world, in brief a theology and a philosophy, or, if you like, an ideology'.[1] Elsewhere he puts in parallel the words mythology, theology and ideology as meaning respectively the collection or catalogue of myths, of gods and of governing ideas (*idées directrices*).[2] Thus, although he does not use the term, in talking of an Indo-European ideology Dumézil is postulating a proto-philosophy lying behind the thinking of these early literate societies. If one wants to situate Sanskrit and Greek philosophy within history, here is an historical approach that possesses a considerable literature and at least merits serious consideration.

Many factors have contributed to the relative neglect of Dumézil's approach. Obstacles internal to the oeuvre include its sheer bulk (some seventeen volumes published or reissued after 1966 – the year he saw as opening his *phase du bilan*, his 'summing up period'). The books are not particularly repetitive, and their range of reference makes considerable demands on the serious reader. I would add that the correlational type of ideology is postulated without explicit reference to anthropological literature on classification, and thereby risks appearing odder than it is;[3] also that (as we shall see later), the trifunctional schema by itself is too narrow to constitute a plausible ideology. External obstacles include the conservatism of academic disciplines, criticisms by opponents of cultural comparison and controversies among its practitioners, and the play of fashion.[4] But the difficulties and objections can be overcome and Dumézil-style work continues.

Much of this comparativism explores the survival of the ideology in different contexts – socio-structural, legal, mythic, ritual and so on, but Dumézil never claimed that the Indo-European cultural heritage could be reduced to manifestations of trifunctionality – indeed he protested against such reduction.[5] Much scope exists for comparison of narratives to which the functions are not immediately relevant, and this is how I shall start: the conceptual simplicity of the argument makes it an appropriate opening to the empirical part of the paper. If the units of a Sanskrit story, one after another, resemble the units of a Greek story, and the resemblances are unforced and persuasive, then the more numerous the resemblances the stronger the case for common origin. Logically, to

1 Respectively Dumézil 1958: 18–19, 1968: 15, 1979: 79–80.

2 Dumézil 1986: 19; a meaning of ideology that he describes as 'very humble'.

3 Allen 2000: 39–60.

4 Here is an outspoken but not unrepresentative opinion: 'Wide-ranging comparison has consistently disappointed. Books of Lévi-Strauss, Dumézil and Eliade now sit beside those of Max Müller and Frazer as cautionary examples. They consistently misrecognised products of their own imagination and desire (human mind, tripartite ideology, homo religiosus) for objects having historical, prehistorical and/or transhistorical actuality' (Lincoln 2012: 100).

5 Dumézil 1981: 34.

compare Sanskrit and Greek manifestations of a hypothetical ideology is a more complex undertaking.

Otherworld journeys

The relation between this world and other worlds has been a traditional philosophical issue pertaining to cosmology and eschatology, but it is a relation that is often spatialised and presented as a journey: an obvious instance is Er's return journey to the other world, narrated at the very end of Plato's *Republic*. However, of the two journeys we shall compare, only the Sanskrit one is straightforwardly cosmic and eschatological. The *Kauṣītaki Upaniṣad* is among the five early *Upaniṣads* that were written in prose and are probably pre-Buddhist. Like some others of the five, it is an anthology of 'material that must have existed as independent texts', before being put together by one or more editors.[6] The material that concerns us (KauU 1.2–7) is one such unit of text or pericope. It tells us what happens to the souls of the dead, and is preceded (1.1) by a scene-setting account of why Citra Gāṅgyāyani (doubtless a king) came to be teaching a Brahmin.

To summarise *Kauṣītaki Upaniṣad* 1.2, all who die go to the moon, which is the door to the heavenly world. The moon asks the soul 'Who are you?', and those unable to answer correctly turn into rain and fall to earth for rebirth, in higher or lower forms depending on their behaviour and knowledge. Breaking into verse, the text gives the correct answer, and those who know it are allowed to proceed on the path of the gods. Our concern is primarily with this *devayāna* (as distinct from the *pitṛyāna*, the path of the fathers or ancestors).

In 1.3, the knowledgeable soul traverses the worlds of Agni, Vāyu, Varuṇa, Indra and Prajāpati, before reaching that of *brahman* or Brahmā (the neuter abstraction and the masculine deity often merge in Sanskrit, which lacks capital letters, and Olivelle writes only the former). Nothing further is said about the first five, but the passage through the final world (Brahmāloka) is presented initially as a summary. The phrase *sa āgacchati*, 'he arrives at', introduces each one of the ten locations, which are then given a shorter or longer comment. Brahmā is the end-point of the journey.

The Greek comparandum picks up the voyage of Odysseus after he leaves Ogygia and follows him until his first night in Alcinous' palace (*Od.* 5.282–7.347). Vast and obvious differences separate the two travellers. Odysseus is an epic hero from ancient times, but within the story he is very much alive. The

[6] Olivelle 1996: xxxiv, = 1998: 11. The 1996 paperback lacks the Sanskrit text, with its variant readings and scholarly conjectures, but otherwise hardly differs from the 1998 monograph. I rely heavily on Olivelle, but when glossing Sanskrit terms have made selective use of Monier Williams' *Sanskrit-English Dictionary*.

Vedic figure is nameless since he represents any Upaniṣadic contemporary who knows the answer to the moon's question; and he has certainly died. However, our focus will be less on the travellers than the journey.

1. The lake Āra. 'He crosses it with his mind, but those who go into it without a complete knowledge drown in it.' Compare the wily and tenacious Odysseus who, despite nearly drowning in the storm sent by Poseidon, succeeds, with the help of other deities, in completing his sea-crossing from Ogygia to Scheria. The Sanskrit word for the lake is *hrada*, 'a large or deep piece of water, lake, pool (only rarely applied to the sea)', but commentators compare the name Āra with Ara, one of two seas (*arṇava*) situated in the world of Brahmā (ChU 8.5.3–4).

2. The watchmen Muhūrta, who flee from him. The name refers to a duration of about forty-eight minutes, but neither the reading nor the meaning is clear and I defer discussion.

3. The river Vijarā ('Ageless'), which he crosses with just his mind. The comments here are substantial (fifteen lines in the translation), but only need selective treatment. Having crossed the river, the traveller shakes off his good and bad deeds (respectively onto the relatives he likes and dislikes), then proceeds freed from them. Compare the unnamed river or River God, who helps Odysseus exit from the sea, and into which the hero then throws or drops his buoyancy-aid-cum-headdress. He had received it from the goddess Ino, who had requested its return, which the river duly performs (5.346–51, 459–62).

The scene shifts for a moment to Brahmā (presumably in his palace). The god knows that the soul has reached the river, and instructs five hundred nymphs (*apsaras*) to go there quickly and welcome him. Each group of a hundred carries something different: garlands, lotions or ointment (*āñjana*), cosmetic powders, clothes and fruit. The beloved Mānasī (from *manas* 'mind') and her twin or counterpart Cākṣuṣī (*cakṣus* 'eye, seeing, sight') bring the flowers they have picked, and three additional females are named. The welcome party adorns the traveller with Brahmā's ornaments, and he proceeds.

After Odysseus lands and falls asleep on a hillock, the scene shifts (6.1–84). Wanting to help the hero return to Ithaca, the goddess Athena visits Alcinous' palace. Taking the form of Nausicaa's friend and age-mate (*homēlikiē*), the daughter of Dymas, Athena gives the sleeping princess the idea of making a laundry trip to the mouth of the Scherian river; her father should arrange transport. In the morning Alcinous cheerfully agrees, and a mule wagon is loaded not only with laundry but also with supplies of food, drink and olive oil for bathing. Nausicaa sets off on it, accompanied by her age-mate and maid-servants. The females do not know that they will meet and help Odysseus, and Athena intervenes again to bring this about. The princess ensures that the hero receives oil for his bath in the river, then clothes, food and drink, and advises him on the journey to the city.

The shared features are as follows: exit from river and the discarding into it of something no longer needed; scene-shift; deity's initiative to encourage or help the traveller; involvement of the palace owner (so Brahmā parallels Athena *plus* Alcinous); journey by a group of young females; their supplies, which include oil, clothes and edibles; their paired leadership (two twins or age-mates); meeting of females and traveller beside river; beautification of traveller by females (he acquires adornments or clothes). Moreover, of the three other named celestial females, two, Ambā and Ambālī, are paired as Jagatī (possibly a reference to heaven and earth): compare the two beautiful handmaidens who sleep on either side of the entry to Nausicaa's bedroom (6.18–19).[7]

The next five Vedic locations have in common their almost cursory treatment. A measure of unity is also provided by a feature discussed later, but for now we need only the Greek comparanda.

4. The tree Ilya. Compare the poplar grove, sacred to Athena, situated within shouting distance of the city (6.291–4, 321–2), where Odysseus is to leave the maidens and wait for a while. The grove, with its environs (spring, meadow, park, vineyard), is the only topographical feature mentioned by Homer between the water-meadow and the lofty city walls.

5. The plaza (*saṃsthāna*, 'urban public place') Sālajya. Compare the agoras that Odysseus admires in the Phaeacian capital (7.44, cf. 6.266).

6. The palace Aparājita ('Invincible'). Compare the dwelling or palace of Alcinous (his *dōma*, *dōmata* or *domos*).

7. The doorkeepers Indra and Prajāpati, who flee from him. Compare the immortal and ageless dogs made of gold and silver by the god Hephaestus, and stationed as guards on either side of the entrance to the palace (7.91–4).

8. The hall Vibhu ('Extensive'). Compare the hall (*megaron*, 6.304) in which the royal couple sit, together with other Phaeacian nobles.

The two remaining locations are again treated in parallel.

9. The throne Vicakṣaṇa ('Radiant, Far-shining'). Nothing is said about anyone sitting on it. Instead, the paired components of the throne – front legs, back legs, lengthwise supports and side-supports – are correlated with pairs of named *sāman* chants, and the whole throne is identified with wisdom. Ignoring all this, simply compare the object with the throne of Alcinous (6.308), and with the silver-studded *thronos* next to it, which the king's favourite son vacates for Odysseus (7.162, 167–71). At just this point Odysseus is described as 'wise and crafty-minded' (*daïphrōn*, *poikilomētēs*, 7.168).

10. The couch or bed Amitaujas ('Of unlimited power'), which is life-breath

[7] The third, Ambikā, is mentioned simply as another nymph. Discussing the journey, Ruben (1947: 226–31) remarks on what a beautiful story it could be if only Citra were not so wooden (*hölzern*). Did Ruben have the *Odyssey* in mind?

(*prāṇa*). The component parts again receive correlates (only two of the pairs are linked with particular *sāman* chants), but instead of eight parts there are thirteen, and the extra ones include the longitudinal and transverse strings, two layers of bedding and a pillow. Compare the bed on the portico where Odysseus sleeps after talking to the royals (7.335–8, 345): it is covered with three layers of bedding and the bedstead is described as 'pierced' (*trētos*) – 'in order to take the cords that served as mattress'.[8]

The traveller mounts the couch on which Brahmā is sitting, is questioned by the god, gives satisfactory philosophico-religious answers, and is accepted into the god's world (1.6–7). Here ends the first section (*adhyāya*) of this *Upaniṣad*, and the next one, unrelated to the scene set in *Kauṣītaki Upaniṣad* 1.1, is not about dead souls. The pairing of the new arrival and his host, who must be sitting side by side on the couch, finds a parallel of sorts in the pairing of Odysseus and the royal couple: the text moves directly from the former, sleeping on the portico, to the latter, sleeping in an inner chamber (346–7). These two lines conclude book 7.

However, to find a comparison for Brahmā's questioning of the new arrival, we must turn back to the Greek throne room (location 9). After the Phaeacian nobles have dispersed, Queen Arete puts the first question asked of Odysseus: who is he and from where (7.238). Brahmā opens his interview with the same question, 'Who are you?'; Sanskrit *ko 'si* and Greek τίς εἰς are etymologically cognate. Neither respondent offers anything so banal as a name, parent or place of birth, but even so they both quickly gain the questioner's approval. Brahmā says his world is now the traveller's. If Odysseus decides to stay, Alcinous offers him marriage to Nausicaa and a respectable place in Phaeacian society (7.311–15).

So far the focus has been on comparing the journeys location by location, but the locations can also be compared in groups. Roughly speaking, the first three are watery and peripheral; the next five are transitional and move towards a centre; the final two form a climax.

The three watery locations: The Vedic lake and river parallel the Greek sea and river, but we offered no Greek comparison for the second location, that of the watchmen Muhūrta, who flee. If one accepts Olivelle's translation of the uncertain text, one seeks a parallel in the watery section of the Greek; but the only other location identified by agents rather than objects is the seventh, that with the two doorkeeper gods, who also flee (same verb: *apa*, 'away' + √*dru*, 'run, hasten, flee'). One therefore looks for agents who might have blocked the traveller's progress, but do not do so. Poseidon sees Odysseus from a distant mountain (5.282–3), gives him a hard time during the storm, watches him

[8] Hainsworth 1998: 340.

suffer until he starts swimming, and then departs for his own palace, lashing his horses.

The transitional locations: In the Sanskrit these are held together by references to the senses. At the tree the soul is permeated by Brahmā's fragrance (implying smell), at the plaza by the god's flavour (taste), at the palace by his radiance (vision). This sequence forms the start of a standard rising hierarchy of senses which ends with hearing, and the last quality to permeate the soul (at the hall) is Brahmā's *yaśas*, his glory or fame; so perhaps here, in this oral culture, fame is linked with hearing; and perhaps too, though the text does not say so, the remaining sense, namely touch, correlates with Indra.[9] In any case, with the radiance (*tejas*) from Brahmā's palace compare the radiance (*aiglē*, 7.84) from the palace of Alcinous. Moreover, the first transitional location in the Sanskrit sees the start of the sequence of senses, and in the Greek marks the hero's separation from Nausicaa's party and a new phase of his journey. Henceforth, as Odysseus moves from nature to culture, the locations he comes to are associated only with human artefacts and deities.

The climactic locations: These are both items of palace furniture on which humans can place themselves, whether to sit or lie. One or other is the site of the final host-traveller conversation, and the second forms the end of a significant textual unit.[10]

In concentrating on Brahmā's world, we have ignored the soul's earlier post-mortem travel. Like everyone who dies, he begins by going to the moon, where his knowledge enables him to escape from the round of births and deaths on earth and to take the more desirable path of *devayāna*. Compare Odysseus, whose qualities of character enable him to avoid drowning along with his crew after the visit to Thrinacia (12.416–19), so that he can do as he wishes and return eventually to wife and family. But between leaving the moon and reaching Brahmāloka the soul comes to (*āgacchati* again) five other worlds. In the sequence Agni-Vāyu-Varuṇa the first two theonyms mean Fire and Wind, and the third is a god of waters. With the traverse of the world of Wind, compare Odysseus' double visit to the isle of Aeolus, Controller of the Winds (10.1–76).

These two pre-Brahmāloka rapprochements are somewhat weakened by the fact that in Odysseus' life story the separation from his crew comes after his visit to Aeolus, rather than preceding it. Within Brahmāloka this sort of objection applies only to the conversations at the climax locations. Otherwise, locations and events follow the same order in the two stories: the tree Ilya resembles the poplar grove not only *qua* arboreal but also in that the tree/grove appears after

9 The sequence smell-sight-hearing-taste-manual action appears in KauU 1.7.

10 The timing of the *devayāna* is indeterminate, but the palace bed on which Odysseus ends his first day in Scheria contrasts with the outdoor bed of leaves on which he began it.

the river scene and before the plaza/agora. The positional similarity reinforces the intrinsic similarity.

The similarities relevant here are those that can reasonably be understood as deriving from an Indo-European (or at least Greco-Aryan) protonarrative, but it is difficult, and probably unnecessary, to formulate rules for recognising such a similarity and for deciding whether or not it is outweighed by the differences, which of course can always be found. Even so, and without claiming any precision, one can ask roughly how many rapprochements we have found for the Brahmāloka journey. Including the groups of locations, but ignoring positionality and a few relatively weak comparisons (e.g. Poseidon as watchman, Nausicaa's paired beautiful handmaidens, Odysseus' wisdom at location 9), I estimate more than twenty-five. This degree of similarity, bearing both on structure and details, cannot plausibly be explained except by some common origin.

I hope then to have persuaded readers both that Citra's dry eschatological doctrine is cognate with the epic adventures in Homer, and that comparativism based on linguistic common origin need not be speculative, superficial or neglectful of philological detail. Some may still worry that our *Upaniṣad* was written down too late in the history of Sanskrit literature to have retained narrative content that bypassed the earlier Vedas – copious as they are; but such worries overlook the dimension of secrecy in the transmission of the Vedas, and also rest on a historiographic prejudice. In fact, previous work along similar lines provides reassurance: the *Mahābhārata*, written down perhaps half a millennium after our *Upaniṣad*, also contains much narrative that is cognate with Homer and that bypassed earlier Sanskrit literature.

In particular, the Great Epic narrates several otherworld journeys, and notably one by its central hero: Arjuna goes to heaven to visit his divine father Indra in his palace in the city of Amarāvatī (from *amara*, 'immortal'). His journey too is cognate with that of Odysseus to the palace of Alcinous, and a fuller study of the Brahmāloka journey would benefit from this additional comparison.[11] Moreover, the comparison can also be extended to the internal journey of the yogin, directed towards the mental state of *kaivalya*, and to the progress of the Buddha to Enlightenment.[12] The Upaniṣadic eschatology belongs to a family of narratives that includes not only epic adventures but also spiritual undertakings;

[11] At the river Vijarā the text compares the soul shaking off his deeds to a man driving a chariot who looks down at its two wheels and sees nights and days, good deeds and bad ones, and all the pairs of opposites. Compare Arjuna's views from the celestial chariot that takes him from the Himalayas to heaven (3.43.26ff., 3.164.40ff. in the Critical Edition). The theme of the traveller being tested by a deity is clearer in the Sanskrit epic than in the Greek.

[12] Allen 1998, 2005a.

and as we shall see, codifications of Hindu philosophy include yoga among their six categories.

Philosophy and the functions

Dumézil saw Indo-European ideology as made up of three components: the first function (F1) related to sovereignty, the sacred and wisdom; the second (F2) to physical force; the third (F3) to fecundity and wealth. Full formal definitions can be found in Dumézil,[13] but these succinct indications will suffice here. Though an important manifestation of the ideology is in the ideal division of labour in society – into the descending hierarchy of priests, warriors and producers – social structure is, as we noted above, only one of the many contexts in which the same pattern occurs. But even at this point in the argument, worries may arise. Supernatural assistance, reliable defence, a flourishing economy – all these are desirable, even necessary, for a well-functioning society, but are they sufficient basis for a worldview? Do not ideologies typically have a place for what is undesirable and devalued – phenomena like demons, death, pollution and enemies?

To make a long story short, already in 1961, the Rees brothers, analysing the fivefold sacred geography of Ireland, proposed in effect that Dumézil's model – useful, indeed essential, as far as it went – needed to be expanded from three categories to five,[14] and I have long argued that they were right. We need not only an extra category at the bottom of the hierarchy, but also a readjustment at the top. We can leave priests and their specialised wisdom in F1, but sovereignty needs a separate category relating to transcendence, totality and creation. The new categories, bracketing the old, sometimes hang together, and for this reason among others, I label them respectively F4- and F4+ (the minus and plus referring to negative and positive valuation). The model as a whole I label 'pentadic'.

The pentadic ideology has shaped so much of Indian life and thought that the choice of starting point is difficult. One option would focus on social structure, citing the brief myth of origin of the *varṇas* in the *Puruṣasūkta* (RV 10.90.11–12) and relating it to caste, while another might start from Vedic sacrifice, the theme that dominates the Brāhmaṇa texts.[15] Yet a third could follow the Reeses and open with the spatial schema of centre and cardinal points. However, for specifically philosophical thought the obvious choice is Sāṃkhya.

The medieval classification of orthodox Hindu philosophies mentioned above organises its six 'views' (*darśanas*, from *dṛś*, 'see') into pairs, and couples Sāṃkhya with Yoga. Sāṃkhya is widely regarded as the first of the six to have

13 Dumézil 1958: 18–19.

14 Rees and Rees 1961: 118–39.

15 See respectively Allen 2007 and Allen 2015.

been systematised, and was immensely influential on the others – it provided yoga with its metaphysical assumptions. The name, from *saṃkhyā*, 'reckon up, enumerate, calculate', already suggests the developed theory, which lists twenty-five principles or realities (*tattvas*), and can be read as supplying an ontology both for the cosmos and for individual psycho-physiology.[16] Thus Puruṣa, the first *tattva* in typical lists, can be read both as an update of the creative Puruṣa of *Ṛgveda* 10.90 and as *puruṣa*, 'man, human being, person'. The theory is emphatically soteriological and dualist. The aim is to recognise the fundamental difference between *puruṣa* and *prakṛti* ('nature or Nature', which covers all the remaining *tattvas*), and by doing so to bring 'the adherent to the condition of isolation (*kaivalya*) or release (*mokṣa*)'.[17]

Whereas yoga starts from the pluralistic here-and-now and works towards *kaivalya*, Sāṃkhya, starting from the holistic and abstract, moves towards the plural and concrete, by laying down processes of evolution or emergence. But the emergence of *tattvas* is not presented simply as a sequence; the list is structured into five sets of five. The first pentad, too complex for a truly satisfactory discussion here, contains three successive evolutes from *prakṛti*, including *ahaṃkāra*, roughly 'the ego' (from *aham*, 'I', cognate with Latin and English *ego*, and *kāra*, 'maker'). From this ego-principle evolve three of the remaining four pentads: the senses, the organs or capacities for action, and the subtle elements. It is as if they were three successive sets of quintuplets, born to one father, for the last member of one pentad precedes the first of the next, but does not emanate it. The final pentad, the gross elements, emerges from the subtle ones.

The twenty-five-*tattva* doctrine as presented in the *Sāṃkhyakārika* is relatively late (fourth century CE or later), and specialists have studied earlier texts in the hope of working out its development. An interesting phrase occurs in the oldest *Upaniṣad*, in a discussion of the nature of *brahman*. In *Bṛhadāraṇyaka Upaniṣad* 4.4.17 Yājñavalkya says that within *brahman* are established *pañca pañcajanā ākāśaśca*, which Olivelle translates as 'the various groups of five, together with space'. He thinks that 'the repetition of *pañca* is meant to indicate an indeterminate number of such groups', and cites some possible instances; but he recognises 'five groups of five' as an alternative rendering.[18] Anyway, whatever the verdict in this case, developed Sāṃkhya offers a pentad of pentads, and we need to consider the higher-level set as well as the five lower-level ones.

At the lower level the first five *tattvas* seem to have conflated several

16 Wanting to maximise the philosophical coherence of Sāṃkhya, Burley 2007 attacks the cosmological reading, but I mainly follow Larson 1979. Both books include a text and translation of the *Sāṃkhyakārika*.

17 Larson 1979: 13.

18 Olivelle 1998: 520.

different ideas, but pentadic theory focuses on the relation between *puruṣa* and *prakṛti*, and the composition of *prakṛti*. Puruṣa is contentless consciousness, inactive and detached, yet at the same time fundamental. It is close to and observes, even enjoys, *prakṛti*, which covers not only materiality but also much that Westerners would label 'mental'. While *puruṣa* is a masculine word and *prakṛti* feminine, the two are not presented as relating sexually. Nevertheless, the implicit maleness of Puruṣa, combined with his otherness relative to Nature in general, makes him a potential representative of the transcendent category F4+. Prakṛti is complex: she or it has two conditions – unmanifest and manifest, and is composed of three 'qualities' (*guṇas*, literally 'strands'). Extraordinarily widespread in ordinary life, as well as in philosophy, the *guṇas*, which are not *tattvas*, form a descending hierarchy: *sattva*, *rajas* and *tamas* were characterised by Dasgupta as intelligence stuff, energy stuff and mass stuff.[19] Despite Dumézil's doubts and a weakish argument regarding *tamas*, the triad can be taken to represent F1–2–3; and the fourth *tattva*, the ego-principle, associated with devalued 'self-conceit', can represent F4-. This interpretation is presented by Allen,[20] and if it is on the right lines, the third *tattva* (*buddhi*, 'intelligence') and the fifth (*manas*, 'mind') must be extrinsic ideas included for one reason or another.[21]

The other pentads are more straightforward. The second and third derive from the ego-principle in its *sattva* mode, the fourth from the same principle in its *tamas* mode. The second coheres neatly with the fourth: hearing, feeling, seeing, tasting, smelling correspond to sound, touch, form, taste, smell. The third, the organs of action, also corresponds more or less – speaking, grasping, walking around, making love, excreting.[22] The fifth lists the elements as we normally understand the word.

The set of five pentads form a descending hierarchy with a one-three-one structure. The first pentad, with its internal complexity, contains the really fundamental *tattvas* and can be construed as transcendental and creative (F4+). The middle three all derive from the ego-principle, but are themselves ranked by their order and links to the *guṇas*. Their shared origin sets the core triad apart from both the first and the fifth pentad, and the latter, derived from the fourth, is removed from the first by one additional step. But the collective labels for the second and third pentads, *buddhīndriyas* and *karmendriyas*, derive from *buddhi*

[19] Dasgupta 1922: 242, 244.

[20] Allen 1998: esp. 181–7.

[21] Thus *manas* not only fills out the first pentad but also, taken with the second and third pentad, constitutes 'the group of eleven' (*tattvas* 5–15). Note too that the derivatives of the ego-principle are structured as 1+4, i.e. *manas* plus four pentads.

[22] Manu (2.89–92), claiming to present the eleven in their proper traditional order, roughly reverses the order in his *karmendriya* list, which moves from anus to ear.

(same root as in the 'Buddha'), and *karma*, 'action' (from *kṛ*, 'make, do'). So these pentads fall under F1 (wisdom) and F2 (dynamism). Just as the immaterial *puruṣa* outranks the partly material *prakṛti*, so the subtle elements outrank the more material gross elements, even if the devaluation is positional and implicit rather than overt.

Admittedly, the subtle elements (*tanmātras*, 'only that much, rudimentary') are not clearly linked to the definition of F3. Their position in the hierarchy is the one so often associated with fecundity and wealth, but here any such association is indirect (via the *guṇas*) or absent. Nevertheless it is reasonable to construe the upper-level pentad as reflecting the pentadic ideology. The ideology provided the framework within which those who devised Sāṃkhya operated creatively. The argument must be looked at as a whole; one cannot expect every manifestation of the ideology to conform perfectly to the model.

At the lower level we shall now concentrate on the fifth pentad: space, wind, fire, water, earth. The list corresponds reasonably well to the second and fourth: space to hearing and sound, wind to feeling and touch, fire (providing light) to seeing and form, water to tasting and taste, earth to smell. The ordering of the elements is the standard Indian one, already found in the *Upaniṣads*. 'From *ātman* (arose) space, from space air, from air . . .' (TaitU 2.1); but after earth the list continues with plants, food and man. Elsewhere (ŚvU 2.12, 6.2), the standard order is reversed, but the pentad appears as an isolated whole.

Let us follow the standard order. *Ākāśa* means 'space, ether, sky', and in philosophy 'the subtle and ethereal fluid supposed to pervade the universe and to be the peculiar vehicle of life and sound'. Wind – air in motion – is akin to breath. Fire covers the sun as well as fires maintained by humans; within the list it is anomalous in normally requiring fuel. Water of course includes rain. Earth (*pṛthvī*), feminine as a noun and female as a goddess, can be related within its pentad to *ākāśa* taken as sky, but within the whole schema it relates to *puruṣa*, the first *tattva*; very roughly, the list views the cosmos from above downwards, but other hints of hierarchy appear in the trend from whole to part, abstract and rarefied to concrete, and male to female. More precisely, the two extremes stand apart from the core, again illustrating the one-three-one pattern. In a geocentric universe earth is static, and space has nowhere to go, while the intervening triad are all mobile: they blow, spread or rise, and flow.

It has long been known[23] that the Greeks recognised the same list of elements but reversed the standard order of the second and third: ether, fire, air, water, earth. The one-three-one pattern seems to be present in the cosmogony of the sixth-century Pherecydes:[24] Zeus, Khronos and Khthoniē (Earth) are primal,

[23] E.g. Deussen 1999: 189.
[24] West 1971: 1–27.

and from his seed Khronos made fire, wind and water. There follows a distribution among five cosmic nooks (*mukhos*, 'recess').

In any case, the Greek sequence accords precisely with pentadic theory. Ether, like *ākāśa*, pertains to totality (F4+). Fire is central to sacrifice in Greece – consider its place in Hesiod's origin myth (*Theogony* 535ff.) – no less than in India, where Agni is sometimes the priest of the gods; and in a cosmic context its place in religion (F1) outranks its role in domestic human nourishment (which would imply F3). Wind exerts force (F2), especially in storms. Water is essential for the flourishing and fecundity of humans, but no less for that of agricultural plants and animals – the source of wealth (F3). Earth here falls under F4- by virtue of its position, but no doubt for other reasons too, such as its acceptance of polluting corpses; in other contexts its fertility may place it under F3.

In his comparison of Greek and Indian philosophy McEvilley explores the elements but neglects the possibility of common origin.[25] In criticising this neglect, I presented a fuller account of the relation between elements and functions, including some evidence from Zoroastrianism.[26] However, I hope enough has been said here to render it plausible that, despite the minor difference in standard order, both Indian and Greek lists manifest the pentadic ideology.

It would be interesting to explore the correlations between elements and senses, but all I can offer here is a note on the rank of the 'transcendent' sense and its relation to the orality that for so long dominated these early cultures. Most Hindu traditions allot ultimate philosophical authority to the Vedas, and the Vedas are *śruti* ('hearing, ear, sound' – the texts were originally 'heard' by sages). Among the many meanings of *brahman* are 'pious effusion or utterance, prayer, the Veda', but 'the most sacred sound in the whole Veda' is the often-used monosyllable *oṃ*, which can even stand for *brahman*.[27] Compare the Pythagorean notion of the harmony or music of the spheres; but also the *akousmata* (from *akouō*, 'hear'), the curt oral maxims so significant to the movement that they served to label one of its subgroups (the *akousmatikoi*).

The elements provide one clear bridge between Sāṃkhya and early Greek philosophy, but it is not the only one. Among the lesser-known texts of the anthropologist Marcel Mauss (whose first academic post was as a Sanskritist) is his 1911 article 'Anna-Virāj'.[28] Virāj, often linked with food (*anna*), is a

25 McEvilley 2002: esp. 300–10.

26 Allen 2005b. I take the opportunity to amplify a remark on p. 66 of the article. Many Pre-Socratics proposed an *arkhē*, a 'basic source or principle of all things' (Graham 2010: 18). Thales favoured water, Anaximenes air, Heracleitus fire; and Anaximander's *apeiron* ('the boundless or infinite') corresponds to F4+. According to Aristotle, no philosophers regarded earth as an *arkhē*, but Xenophanes may perhaps have done so (Graham 2010: 117, 131).

27 Killingley 1986: 14.

28 Mauss 1969, vol. 2: 593–600.

cosmogonic figure, sometimes male, sometimes female. Presented in *Ṛgveda* 10.90.5 as both the child and the parent of Puruṣa, Virāj was seen by Renou[29] as the female principle, 'a sort of primitive Śakti', and her sex is also noted by Jamison and Brereton.[30] But Virāj is also the name of a metre characterised by verses of ten syllables (5+5); and as an adjective *virāj* (from *rāj*, 'reign') means 'ruling far and wide, sovereign'. In seeking to link these various attributes Mauss cites *Chāndogya Upaniṣad* (4.3.8), which identifies the metre with the highest throw in dice, namely ten (presented as 5+5). As he notes, and as is well known, the names for the throws of the four-sided dice are the same as the names of the *yugas*, the four eras of cosmic time; the throws 4, 3, 2, 1 form a series of decreasing value, as do the homonymous eras. At first sight we are dealing with quartets. But Mauss suggests that some forms of dicing allowed a winner-takes-all score of 1+2+3+4 = 10. In other words, via the dice, he is connecting a cosmogonic female with arithmetic or numerology, and at the same time recognising a fifth entity that is totalising and transcendent. As we noted, the very name 'Sāṃkhya' points to numerology, and clearly 'Anna-Virāj' deals with Sāṃkhya-like ideas.

In Greece the combination of numerology, ontology and soteriology points us to Pythagoras and his tradition (the attribution of mathematical thinking to the sixth-century founder can be doubted). The Pythagorean tradition greatly valued the tetractys, a name for the sum of the first four numbers. Regarding it as the kernel or epitome of reason, the adherents referred to it in their most solemn oath,[31] and presented it visually as a triangular array of ten pebbles (the 'perfect triangle'); one pebble at the top, then two, then three, with four in the bottom row. They also used the pentagram or five-pointed star;[32] and pentagons, which can be made by joining the points of the star, form the surfaces of only one among the five regular solids, namely the dodecahedron, which was said to symbolise 'the sphere of the all' (Plato *Tim.* 55c). Whether or not the Pythagoreans connected these various manifestations of fiveness, I suppose that in all cases the number somehow related to the old ideology.

On the other hand, pentadic theory is only superficially about five (or ten) being a sacred number among Indo-European speakers. Basically it is about the manifestation of an ideology having five compartments, and provided each compartment has only one representative (which is not always the case), five will appear as specially favoured. No doubt various natural factors have contributed to the picture – the five (or ten) digits, the number of readily distinguishable senses, the five true planets then known, the fact that an individual has a back,

29 Renou 1956: 98, 247–8.
30 Jamison and Brereton 2014: 1538.
31 Burkert 1972: 72, 186–7.
32 Burkert 1972: 176.

front and two sides. But such factors can hardly have given rise to the ideology, which is more likely to have originated in a society having five clans.[33]

In practice, 'fours' are often more salient than 'fives'. India has four *varṇas*, Vedas, *yugas*, *puruṣārthas* (values); Greece often lists only four elements, and the term 'tetractys' alludes to four, not five. Influenced by such facts, certain comparativists have seen quintessences and the like, not as representing an F4+, but (often) as in a sense secondary, as a superadded summary.[34] An Africanist anthropologist, van Binsbergen (2012), perceives rightly that study of the elements must one day go beyond Indo-Europeans (and the relatively well-known Chinese five-element theory), and particularly attacks Eurocentric emphasis on Empedocles' recognition of four elements.[35] Certainly fours are prominent. However, those who look for representatives of F4+ will often find them. When Empedocles referred to his quartet as *rhizōmata* ('roots'), he, and his predecessors, were surely aware that roots spread out from a central trunk or stem.

Concluding observations

The otherworld journeys and the pentadic sets exemplify different aspects of the ideological tradition shared by Indian and Greek philosophers, but they do not represent any deep-lying divide within the Indo-European heritage. The journey stories often manifest pentadic patterns, in whole or part: as we saw, the transitional locations correlate with at least three of the five senses, and among the five worlds that the soul traverses before reaching Brahmā's, three are linked with the mobile elements. The tenth and final location is characterised with a compound of *a-mita*, literally 'not measured'; compare the *arkhē* of Anaximander, whose *a-peiron* is literally 'what lacks an end'. The evolutionism implicit in the Sāṃkhya schema gives it a narrative quality comparable to that of the genealogies in Hesiod's *Theogony* (and in certain passages of the Sanskrit epic).

The chapter has argued that comparisons of Indian and Greek philosophy need to recognise the importance of the Indo-European cultural heritage that they share, but this does not imply rejection of other historical approaches. Greek contacts with West Asia (especially Iran), as favoured by Martin West, must be relevant to certain topics such as astrology. As for Richard Seaford's interest in urbanisation and monetisation, it is *a priori* implausible that such massive social changes had zero impact on philosophising. In the language of biological anthropology, whereas Seaford pursues homoplasty (similarities arising from similar

33 Allen 2012.

34 Pierre and André Sauzeau 2012: esp. 55–62.

35 But he ranges so boldly across continents and ages that, as he recognises, few are likely to follow his theories.

selection pressures), pentadic theory pursues homology (similarities resulting from common origin); and like the biologists, we need both. I only claim that those thinkers who innovated did so within, or at least in the light of, the pentadic ideology, in whatever forms it had reached them.

2

The concept of *ṛtá* in the *Ṛgveda*

Joanna Jurewicz

In this chapter I will discuss the problem of the beginning of abstract thinking as it is attested in the *Ṛgveda*. It is an ancient Indian text from the fifteenth to the thirteenth centuries BCE, composed in Sanskrit. Its final redaction was done probably in the seventh century BCE. The *Ṛgveda* (similarly to other early Indian texts) was composed and transmitted orally for centuries. Its earliest known manuscript is dated to the eleventh century CE.

In his paper 'The Linguistic Task of the Presocratics' Havelock (1983) reconstructs the beginnings of abstract concepts in Pre-Socratic philosophy. He shows how the concepts of dimension and space, body and matter, void, change, motion, etc., were created. He claims that the beginning of abstract thought is connected with the beginning of literacy. He shows how the Pre-Socratics used their earlier oral tradition, how they extended the meanings of words and broke the rules of traditional syntax in order to produce more abstract meanings.

My analysis will show that the way chosen by the Pre-Socratic philosophers is not the only possible way of creating abstract concepts. Moreover, my claim is that abstract thought is not necessarily connected with literacy because, as I have just mentioned, the early Indian texts were composed and transmitted orally.

The most general definition of the abstract concept is that it is a concept that does not refer to any concrete experience. We do not find many such concepts in the *Ṛgveda*. The main instances are *sát* (being/truth), *ásat* (non-being/untruth) and *ṛtá*, which is translated as 'truth, order, cosmos'.[1] (For *ṛtá* see also Chaturvedi in this volume.) While *sát* and *ásat* appear rarely and mostly in abstract contexts, *ṛtá* often appears in contexts which evoke concrete concepts connected with everyday life experience. For example, we can read about its horn, milk, udder, womb, etc. The expressions 'horn of truth' or 'udder of cosmos' sound strange,

[1] Mayrhoffer (1992) translates it as 'Wahrheit, Übereinstimmung, (Welt-)Ordnung'. For difficulties in translation of this word see Witzel 2014.

but the concept denoted by the word *ṛtá* must be such as to justify them. What is also intriguing is that the word *ṛtá* is the past participle of the verb *ṛ*-, 'to go', and literally means 'something that has gone'.

In order to understand the Ṛgvedic concept of *ṛtá*, I will use the methodology of cognitive linguistics, which investigates the problem of how people create meaning and make the world meaningful for them. The main assumption of cognitive linguistics is that thinking is motivated by experience coming from our bodies and environment, both physical and cultural. Thinking is manifest in signs, and so analysis of signs can lead us to the understanding of thought and of its experiential motivation.

Cognitive linguistics proposes models of mental operations which are reflected in signs. One of these models is conceptual metaphor.[2] It is a model of thinking which operates between two concepts. It enables thinking about one concept in terms of another. The concept that provides its categories is called the source domain, and the concept which is conceived in its terms is called the target domain. For example, in the Indo-European languages, cognition is conceived in terms of seeing: seeing is the source domain, cognition is the target domain.[3] Since conceptual metaphor reflects itself in language, we can meaningfully say: *I see what you mean*, when we understand someone else's thought (cognitive metaphor analysis is also used by Schlieter in this volume).

This metaphor is used in everyday thinking elaborated in, for instance, art and advertisements. It is also elaborated in philosophy. For example, in his definition of intuition, Descartes writes: 'Intuition is the undoubting conception of an *unclouded* mind, and springs from *the light of reason* alone.'[4] Within the frames of this metaphorical thinking, reason is conceived in terms of a lamp and possibilities of cognition are conceived in terms of possibilities of seeing. One of these possibilities is light, another is lack of a cloud covering the object. In the source domain, if there is light but the object is covered, we cannot see it. In the target domain, if reason works properly, but the mind does not, there is no intuition.

Usually, the complex concepts are conceived with the aid of various source domains. Cognition is such a concept: another way of conceptualising it is to conceive it in terms of grasping, as in the sentence 'Now I have grasped your point.'[5]

2 For conceptual metaphor cf. e.g. Lakoff and Johnson 2003, Lakoff 1993, Lakoff and Turner 1989.

3 Sweetser 1990.

4 Quoted after Lakoff and Johnson 1999: 394.

5 For other examples of English conceptualisation of thinking and mind see Lakoff and Johnson 1999: 235ff.

Using this methodological tool, I will show how the abstract concept of *ṛtá* was created and understood in the *Ṛgveda*. I will also show that reconstruction of the experience which motivates the way towards abstraction allows us to understand much more about the target concept. Finally, I will argue that translations of *ṛtá* as 'truth', 'order' or 'cosmos' obscure the semantic core of this concept. Since the full analysis of the usages of *ṛtá* would go beyond the scope of the present paper, I will only analyse some examples of the genitive use of the word *ṛtá*. Similarly to cognition, *ṛtá* is a complex concept and is conceived in various terms. I will focus on its conceptualisation in terms of a cow.

Before proceeding I must say a few words about the Ṛgvedic concepts of world and man.[6] The world is a manifestation of reality conceived in terms of fire (*agní*), which in creation manifests its opposite aspects. One of them is conceived as fiery, the other is conceived in terms of Soma. The Sanskrit word *sóma* refers to a plant[7] from which juice was prepared and offered in fire during ritual. The juice and its divinised form are also called by this name. During ritual the juice was poured into the fire and drunk by the priests. It produced supernatural effects such as (the Ṛgvedic poets claim) omniscience, the ability to fly, and immortality.[8] The poets believed that during ritual gods come to the earth and men fly up to the sun where the supernatural effects of Soma could be realised. Thus sacrifice was a sphere where earth and sky unite beyond time and space. Moreover, it was the ritual which set the cosmos in motion. The kindling of fire made the dawn appear. The Somic juice, poured into fire, became the rising sun.

For the Ṛgvedic poets, the prototypical cow is a moving cow. This was motivated by their semi-nomadic life, which was divided between periods of migration (*yóga*) and settling (*kséma*).[9] The Sanskrit word *yóga*, used to denote the first period, literally means 'a yoke', which betrays one of the main occupations of Ṛgvedic society, namely breeding cattle. During the periods of migration, cattle travelled with people in search of new pastures. The moving cow in terms of which *ṛtá* is conceived is not mentioned explicitly but is evoked metonymically *via* the concepts of path (*pánthā/páth*) and track (*padá*). It is important to note that in northwestern India, during the times of the *Ṛgveda*, the paths and roads were made by the tracks of living beings or chariots and carts. At least, we do not have any archaeological evidence for paths made in a different way.

The use of the word *ṛtá* in the genitive case with the concept of path and track is the most frequent of all its usages in this case. The poets create the image

[6] I have presented them in full length in Jurewicz 2010.

[7] It not known what kind of plant it was. For possible identifications see Wasson 1968, Falk 1989, Oberlies 1999, Stuhrmann 2006.

[8] Jurewicz 2010: 171ff.

[9] Oberlies 1998: 333ff.

of the agents who follow the tracks of a cow that went away and disappeared. The agents following the cow are dawns, rivers, fire, Soma and thoughts. It is important that all of them are conceived in terms of cows and bulls in the *Ṛgveda*, and this conceptualisation is conventionalised. So in the source domain, the poets create images of cows and bulls following the path of a leading cow which, marching in front of the herd, is invisible for those who follow it. The analysis of this source domain will allow me to reconstruct the meaning of *ṛtá* in these contexts and its modes of conceptualisation. I will then briefly show how other parts of the cow's body are used in the conceptualisation of *ṛtá*.

1. Dawn

> *eṣā́ divó duhitā́ práty adarśi jyótir vásānā samanā́ purástāt* |
> ***ṛtásya pánthām*** *ánu eti sādhú prajānatī́va ná díśo mināti* || (1.124.3)[10]
>
> The Daughter of Heaven has appeared opposite, dressed in light, in the same way [as the others], from the east. She follows **along the path of truth (*ṛtá*)**, straight to the goal. Like one who knows the way, she does not confound the directions.

If the recipient activates the conceptualisation of dawn in terms of a cow, he will create the image of a cow which follows the path made by a leading cow. The recipient can easily evoke the image of the herd of cows, taking into account that dawns are usually presented as plural in the *Ṛgveda*. These are the terms in which the appearance of the morning light is conceived: it appears in the nocturnal sky in the same way as cows appear in the pasture.

In this stanza, the concept of dawn is activated *via* the epithet 'the daughter of heaven' (*divó duhitā́*). It triggers the recipient to evoke another conceptualisation of the dawn in terms of a young woman who in this context can be interpreted as a cowherdess. People universally conceive natural processes in terms of actions performed by agents.[11] In the source domain, the cowherdess makes the cows go to the pasture. In the target domain, the personified dawn creates morning light in the dark sky. As the personified agent of the appearance of morning light, dawn is divinised as the goddess. The cowherdess also follows the path of a leading cow which went out to the pasture for the first time by itself.

Within the frame of this metaphoric conceptualisation, *ṛtá*, conceived in terms of the leading cow, is the first dawn which appeared during creation.

10 All translations of the *Ṛgveda* are from Jamison and Brereton 2014.

11 For example, we say *The wind has closed the window.*

2. Rivers

yéna síndhum mahī́r apó ráthām̐ iva pracodáyaḥ |
***pánthām r̥tásya yā́tave** tám īmahe* || (8.12.3)

[That] by which you impel the great waters forth to the Sindhu like chariots to travel **the path of truth (*r̥tá*)** – for that we beg.

The Sanskrit word for water, *áp*, is always used in plural in the *R̥gveda*, and waters are conceived in terms of cows. So in the source domain the poet creates the image of a cowherd who makes the cows follow the path left by the leading cow. In these terms there is conceived the flow of rivers from their sources along their river-beds to reach the river Sindhu. *R̥tá*, conceived in terms of the leading cow is the first river which made the river-beds for all other rivers. In this stanza, the personified agent who makes the rivers flow is the god Indra, to whom the whole hymn is devoted.

3. Ritual

Fire created in the morning ritual
idám u tyán máhi mahā́m ánīkaṃ yád usríyā sácata pūrviyáṃ gaúḥ |
***r̥tásya padé** ádhi dī́diyānaṃ gúhā raghuṣyád raghuyád viveda* || (4.5.9)

Here is the great face of the great ones [= Sun], which the ruddy cow [= Dawn] followed (as it went) in front.
She [?] found it shining hidden in the track of truth (*r̥tá*), going quickly, quick-streaming.

The stanza comes from the hymn to fire (Agni). In the first hemistich, the dawn is conceived in terms of a reddish (*usríyā*) cow.[12] In the source domain, the cow is presented as finding something which quickly moves. In the *R̥gveda*, fire, when it is kindled, is conceived in terms of a little calf which agrees with the experience evoked in the source domain: a cow finds a calf.[13] Conceptualisation of fire in terms of being found agrees with the R̥gvedic thinking about fire and the experience of its kindling. Fire was kindled in fire-sticks where, as it was believed, it was hidden. In the stanza, it is the dawn which kindles fire but the recipient understands that the intention of the poet is to present a simultaneity of earthly and cosmic processes: fire is kindled when the dawn appears. As I have

[12] Since such a qualification of cows is very common in the RV, we can presume that real cows possessed by the R̥gvedic poets had this kind of colour.

[13] This conceptualisation is very much elaborated in RV 1.164 to conceive of cognition (Jurewicz forthcoming).

already mentioned, the Ṛgvedic poets were even more bold in their ontological assumptions: kindling of fire during sacrifices made the dawn appear.

Since speech is conceived in terms of fire and words are conceived in terms of cows in the *Ṛgveda*, the recipient can also understand that the stanza presents the appearance of speech in the morning. This also agrees with the experience: the ritual kindling of fire and preparation of Somic juice was accompanied by recitation of Ṛgvedic stanzas. Within the frames of the conceptualisation activated in the stanza, *ṛtá*, conceived in terms of the leading cow, is the first kindling of fire and first recitation.

Fire created by people in the morning
táṃ yajñasā́dham ápi vātayāmasi ***ṛtásya pathā́*** *námasā havíṣmatā* (1.128.2ab)

The one who sends the sacrifice to its goal along **the path of truth (*ṛtá*)**: we make him our familiar with reverence accompanied by oblations.

This verse also comes from the hymn to fire, which is described as one that makes the sacrifices successful. I would agree with other translators of the *Ṛgveda* who interpret it as presenting the poets who kindle the fire along the path of *ṛtá*.[14] This interpretation is more justified both on the ground of the syntax of the sentence and on the ground of the logic of the image created by the poet. Fire is conceived in terms of a calf/bull which is expected to follow the path left by the leading cow. The recipient may create the image of herds of bulls if he activates conceptualisation of flames of fire in terms of bulls. The agents of this activity are men. *Ṛtá* is the first flame of fire which appeared in the world.

Path between the earth and the sun
ábhūd u pārám étave ***pánthā ṛtásya*** *sādhuyā́* |
ádarśi ví srutír diváḥ || (1.46.11)

And the path of truth has come into being to lead the right to the far shore. The course of heaven has appeared.

The Ṛgvedic poets believed that there is a uniting element between the earth and the sun which is activated during sacrifices and which enables the ritual union of the sacred and profane spheres. This element is conceived in terms of a path[15] which appears in the morning and is marked by the rising sun. As already mentioned, the sun is conceived in terms of a bull in the *Ṛgveda* and if the recipient activates this conceptualisation, he will see the logic of the image built in the hemistich. The path made by the leading cow is every day followed by the rising

14 Witzel and Gotō 2007, Elizarenkova 1989, Renou 1964.

15 There are other concepts for Soma such as tree and plant. In more general terms, it is the *axis mundi*.

sun, and by men and gods in ritual. Here, the cosmic change is conceived as having no personified agent. *Ṛtá* is the first sunrise.

Streams of Soma
rā́jā síndhūnām pavate pátir divá ***ṛtásya*** *yāti* ***pathíbhiḥ*** *kánikradat* | (9.86.33ab)

The king of rivers, the lord of heaven, purifies himself. He proceeds along the paths of truth, ever roaring.

In the source domain, the image of a neighing stallion/a roaring bull is created which follows the paths left by the leading cow.[16] The target domain consists of two concepts. The first one is the appearance of the proper form of the juice during its preparation. The second one is the god Soma who appears during the ritual. *Ṛtá* is the first act of preparation of Soma and the first appearance of the gods during ritual.

Thoughts at the beginning of supernatural cognition
índrāgnī ápasas pári úpa prá yanti dhītáyaḥ |
ṛtásya pathíyā *ánu* || (3.12.7)

Indra and Agni! From our [ritual] work our insights go forth toward [you] along **the paths of truth (*ṛtá*).**

Within the frames of the metaphor activated in this stanza, thoughts are conceived in terms of cows which follow the track of the leading cow. The gods Indra and Agni are the agents who cause the thinking of men. *Ṛtá* is the first true cognition.

The climax of supernatural cognition
kánikradad ***ánu pánthām ṛtásya*** *śukró ví bhāsi amṛ́tasya dhā́ma* |
sá índrāya pavase matsarávān hinvānó vā́cam matíbhiḥ kavīnā́m || (9.97.32)

Ever roaring along the path of truth, gleaming you radiate across the domain of the immortal one [the sun?]. Providing the means for exhilaration, you purify yourself for Indra, spurring on your own speech with the thoughts of the poets.

In the source domain, a horse or a bull follows the path left by the leading cow. In these terms, Somic juice is conceived. However, it is presented as illuminating 'the domain of what is immortal' (*amṛ́tasya dhā́ma*). Since cognition is also conceived in terms of illuminating in the *Ṛgveda* (as by Descartes), the recipient understands that the juice, when it is drunk, causes supernatural cognition. The

[16] That the concepts of the bull and the stallion overlapped can be seen in that both can be called by the same name (*vṛ́ṣan*) and their sound is denoted by the same verbs (*krand-*, 'to neigh', *rud-*, 'to roar').

object of this cognition is conceived in terms of the abode where immortality may be realised.

However, the recipient is also prompted to activate one more target domain of the bull/horse which is the sun. As we have seen, the sunrise is conceived in terms of a bull following a path made by the leading cow (1.46.11). Moreover, as has also been already stated, the Ṛgvedic poets believed that Somic juice poured during morning ritual into fire became the rising sun. Within the frames of this belief, in ritual men follow the same path after the bull, in terms of which the Somic juice transformed into the rising sun is conceived. Thus conceived, it is the causative agent of the supernatural cognition and is divinised. Men were also conceived in terms of bulls, so the image is very coherent. Here, *ṛtá* is the first sunrise and the first cognitive realisation of ritual.

We can see how the experience is used to express very abstract concepts. All the concepts, conceived in terms of the leading cow which went away, are the processes: the first appearance of dawn, the first sunrise, the first outflow of the first river, the first ritual with its frames and actions: the first kindling of fire, the first preparation of juice and its first cognitive results. Taking into account that ritual performed by men sets the cosmos in motion, we can generally understand *ṛtá* as the creative act during which everything happened for the first time. Reality manifested itself in all these processes – as burning fire and the dawn, as Somic juice and the rising sun, and as the cognitive agents, gods and men who will be able to repeat these processes for ever. It is difficult to find any European philosophical concept which could render this meaning in one word, as the Sanskrit word *ṛtá* does. The Ṛgvedic poets, to make this abstract concept more understandable, conceptualised it in terms of the leading cow which is far away, at the front of the huge herd, but people know that it is somewhere and follow its tracks. Conceptualisation of various elements of the world in terms of cows and bulls allows the Ṛgvedic poets to express many processes in terms of this one image.

It is important to note that not every concept could be conceptualised in terms of bulls and cows. As we have seen, they are the agents of the processes crucial for the Ṛgvedic poets, the processes which could be seen as life-giving.[17] They are connected with the appearance of light and water in the cosmos and with ritual in its social and psychic dimensions.

4. The general meaning of the concept of cow

So the concept of cow is a very general concept in the *Ṛgveda*. Its generality allowed the poets to construe general statements:

[17] I call them defining events in Jurewicz 2010.

> *útsa āsā̃m paramé sadhástha* ***ṛtásya pathā́*** *sarámā vidad gā́ḥ* || (5.45.8cd)
>
> At the fountainhead of them [= cows], in the highest seat, Sarama found the cows along **the path of truth (*ṛtá*).**

Sarama is a mythical bitch that is presented in the *Ṛgveda* as leading the poets. This concept also probably comes from the experience of cowherds who use dogs. The bitch is presented as following a path left by cows and as finding them. The cows are found in their highest seat (*paramé sadhásthe*) and at their fountainhead (*útse*).

As I have already mentioned, the Ṛgvedic poets believed that Soma poured into fire became the rising sun. The sun was conceived then in terms of a fiery receptacle filled with Soma. When the sun reaches its zenith, Soma which filled it becomes most perfect. Men who reach the sun in ritual can drink it, which strengthens their supernatural state. At the same time, it was also believed that Soma flows down from the sun in the form of rain.

So the target domains are as follows. The first one is streams of Soma in the sun. The second is thoughts which appear in the mind of man exalted by Soma. The third is streams of rain. Since Soma in the sun could not appear without ritual which preceded it, the recipient is prompted to unfold the whole cosmic cycle which begins with human activity. *Ṛtá* is conceived in terms of the first cow which is now traced by Sarama. The meaning of *ṛtá* in this context is very abstract. It is the first creative action which resulted in sunrise and rain.

5. How *ṛtá* was understood

I will now discuss some other implications of the conceptualisation of *ṛtá* in terms of a leading cow that went away. The poets present themselves as those who guard the tracks of *ṛtá* (10.5.2). In RV 9.73.6d it is stated that 'evildoers do not traverse the path of truth (*ṛtá*)' (*ṛtásya pánthāṃ ná taranti duṣkŕ̥taḥ*).[18] As the tracks of cattle are hidden from outsiders, in the same way the poets hide knowledge about reality. It belongs only to them. If an outsider finds it, it will be seen in terms of theft of cattle and evaluated as morally bad.

As we have seen, in most of the stanzas a divinised agent of the process or activity is mentioned. The gods in the *Ṛgveda* are called cowherds (*gopā́*).[19] This conceptualisation implies that they guard everything that is conceived in terms of cattle, beginning with *ṛtá* and ending with men. Moreover, the concept of gods links the abstract concept of reality acting on itself with everyday human

[18] The enemies of the poets are qualified as morally bad in the RV (Jurewicz 2010: 65ff.)
[19] E.g. 1.1.8, 5.63.1, 6.49.15, 9.48.4, 10.8.5.

life. Conceived in terms of cowherds, gods lead men in their ritual activity in the same way as the cowherds safely lead their herd:

> ***ṛtásya*** *mitrāvaruṇā* ***pathā́*** *vām apó ná nāvā́ duritā́ tarema* || (7.65.3cd)
>
> By your **path of truth (*ṛtá*)**, Mitra and Varuna, we would cross over difficulties, as [we would] waters by a boat.

In the source domain, the poets are presented as following the path of the leading cow. In the target domain, they repeat the first creative activity. The recipient understands that the gods have already repeated this activity. Putting this in terms of the source domain, they went along the same path as the leading cow. Conceptualisation of gods in terms of bulls strengthens the coherence of this interpretation. Men are the next herd of bulls which follows the path. Since, as I have mentioned above, in the time of the *Ṛgveda* paths were made by the tracks of those who left them, the more people and animals went along them, the better the path was. Walking on such a path is the source domain for a good life.[20] Thus seen, *ṛtá* is not only the first creative activity but also the condition of the good life for men.

Conceptualisation of *ṛtá* in terms of the leading cow that went away also implies that it is not present in the world. However, other usages of the genitive case of this word show that it can be partially perceived. Manifestations of *ṛtá* in the world are conceived in terms of manifestations of parts of the cow's body.

The link which unites sky with earth is conceived in terms of a cow's horn (*ṛtásya śṛ́ṅgam*, 8.86.5), which is extended when the sun rises. The sun is conceived in terms of a cow's udder from which milk can be milked by men in ritual (*ṛtásya dhā́rāḥ sudúghā dúhānāḥ*, 7.43.4[21]). The fuel of fire which is clarified butter is conceived also in terms of cow's milk (*ṛtásya páyas*, 1.79.3, 3.55.13). The milky streams of *ṛtá* are mentioned in many stanzas (*ṛtásya dhā́rā*, e.g. 1.844, 5.12.2, 7.43.4, 9.33.2). The ritual place where fire is kindled and Somic juice prepared is conceived in terms of a cow's womb from which calves are born (*ṛtásya yóni*, e.g. 1.65.3, 3.1.11, 3.62.13, 9.64.20). In the following stanza, the back (*sā́nu*) of *ṛtá* is mentioned:

> *ṛtásya sā́nāv ádhi cakramāṇā́ rihánti mádhvo amṛ́tasya vā́ṇīḥ* || (10.123.3cd)
>
> Having stridden onto the back of truth (*ṛtá*), the voices lick at the immortal honey.

20 This conceptualisation of happiness in terms of a good journey on the chariot can be seen in the later Sanskrit term for happiness which is *sukhá*. In the RV this word is used only in reference to a chariot which has a good axle. Such chariots made the journey good.

21 See Jurewicz 2014.

This stanza is a good example how concrete experience is used and transformed in order to express the metaphysical and ritual content. The concept of voices metonymically[22] activates the concept of people who sing during ritual. The context implies that they are conceived as being in the sun. As I have just mentioned, the sun is conceived in terms of the cow's udder in the *Ṛgveda*. This conceptualisation is evoked *via* the concept of licking honey. Honey corresponds to milk which flows from the udder and is identified with Soma in the *Ṛgveda*. Thus the people are conceived in terms of calves which drink milk from a cow's udder.[23]

However, the experience is transformed in the stanza. The recipient is also prompted to create the impossible image of people who sit on the back of a cow and, at the same time, are calves which drink milk from the udder. In these terms, the climax of their supernatural cognition under the influence of Soma is conceived. The impossibility of the image expresses the impossibility of this state which goes beyond the everyday limits of human life.

The concrete source domain gives a clear structure to the target domain. In terms of the back of the cow, the borderline sphere between the manifest and unmanifest aspects of reality is conceived; this sphere is reached with supernatural cognition. The manifest aspect of reality is conceived in terms of the body of the cow. The unmanifest aspect is conceived in the negative terms of something which is not the cow and cannot be cognised.

Within the frames of this conceptualisation, the word *ṛtá* refers to the whole manifest aspect and is often used in the *Ṛgveda* with this meaning. At first glance, it may seem contradictory to the conceptualisation of *ṛtá* in terms of the leading cow which went away, as analysed above. A closer look, however, reveals the coherence of the thinking of the poets who masterly transform their everyday experience in order to express their metaphysical assumptions.

In more general terms, *ṛtá* can be understood as energy initiated in *illo tempore* and constantly active in cosmic processes and human ritual actions. I would argue that the most important feature of *ṛtá* understood as energy is its order, which is realised in time on the cosmic level and in ritual on the human level.[24] Manifestations of this energy in the world are conceived in terms of the parts of a cow's body. Its existence is known on the basis of inference, which is conceived in terms of following tracks left by the cow. This energy can be cognised and experienced directly in supernatural cognition, which is conceived in terms of

22 Conceptual metonymy is another model of mental operations analysed in cognitive linguistics, see Lakoff and Johnson 2003.

23 The climax of supernatural cognition is also conceived in terms of drinking from a spring which is on the sun, e.g. 1.154.5.

24 *Ṛtá* is also conceived in terms of a chariot (e.g 3.2.8, 4.10.2, 6.55.1, 7.66.12). The concepts of a chariot and its parts are elaborated in RV 1.164 to present manifestation of reality in time and speech (the most important part of ritual) (see Jurewicz forthcoming).

reaching the cow's back. From this place, not only the whole cow can be seen but also the whole herd it leads. The unmanifest source of energy is uncognisable.

It seems that the concept of *ṛtá* has no counterpart in Greek philosophy. The concept of energy, which can be used as one of its counterparts, narrows the meaning of *ṛtá*, and the same is true of its other translations mentioned at the beginning of this chapter. In the mind of the recipients of the *Ṛgveda*, this word activates the whole complex of metaphysics together with the condition of man. Its conceptualisation in terms of the experience connected with cowherding allows the poets to precisely express subtle aspects of a single but multileveled reality.

We can see that abstract concepts can be conceived in concrete terms without loosing their abstractness. Just the opposite, the clear and simple structure and scenario of the source domain is mapped onto the target domain in a way which highlights the aspects of the abstract concept without pulling it into concreteness. The Ṛgvedic evidence proves this. Moreover, it shows that the ability for abstraction was part of human thinking even in the most ancient times known to us. Taking into account that the *Ṛgveda* continues a rich Indo-European poetical tradition,[25] we can infer that this ability appeared much earlier. It is also worth adding that the attempts of the Pre-Socratic philosophers, analysed by Havelock, aimed at creating abstract concepts that reified experience. I have shown that the Ṛgvedic poets looked for such conceptualisations which could preserve their dynamic vision of reality.

[25] Watkins 1995.

3

Harmonia and *ṛtá*

Aditi Chaturvedi

As has been noted by Émile Benveniste (1969: 99–101), 'order' is an extremely important concept for Indo-Europeans and is represented by, inter alia, Greek '*harmonia*', Sanskrit *ṛtá*, Avestan *aša*, and Old Persian *arta*, all of which descend from the same PIE root – **H2er*- (to become adjusted, to fit).[1] However, as Franklin has pointed out, the importance of order to Indo-Europeans is often discussed in light of the connection between *arta* and *ṛtá*.[2] It is surprising that there have been scarcely any accounts of the striking similarities between *harmonia* and *ṛtá*, and my aim in this paper is to shed some light on that affinity.[3] *Harmonia* was an important cosmological and ethical concept for Heraclitus, Empedocles and the so-called Pythagoreans; *ṛtá*, on the other hand, is considered by many

1 I have followed Benveniste's (1969: 99–101) lead in assuming that *ṛtá* derives from the same root as *harmonia* – *ar2* (to fit or adapt), which is a phonological descendant of the PIE **H2er*. It has also been claimed that it derives from *ar1* (to move); this is the view of Oldenberg (1888) and Apte (1942), for instance. *ar1* and *ar2* are homophonous, but syntactically different. Both these roots are falsifiable and it is beyond my scope here to offer justification, apart from the fact that a considerable majority of scholars – including Bergaigne (1883), Grassman (1875), Renou (1949), Dumézil (1954), Dandekar (1967), Benveniste (1969) and Malamoud (1989) – assume that *ṛtá* derives from *ar2*. In any case, I am in keeping with Gonda's (1977: 142) view that 'any etymology is by definition a hypothesis and as such never unchallengeable, always liable to constant revision', and that 'prehistoric roots . . . are not real words but abstractions of our making considered to symbolize in a brief formula what some related words have, formally and semantically, in common'. Accordingly, I use etymology merely as a starting point and not in order to make substantive arguments.

2 Franklin 2002: 1.

3 John Curtis Franklin's (2002) paper is one of the very few to discuss this connection in any detail. Even Benveniste who, in his discussion of '*themis*', points out that the Greek *arariskō* comes from the same root as *ṛtá* (1969: 100), does not mention *harmonia* in this context.

to be the quintessence of Vedic philosophy. I argue that both these terms can be understood as abstract concepts of order, and I rely on evidence from the *Ṛgveda* and from the fragments of Heraclitus, Empedocles and Philolaus in order to do so. (For *ṛtá* see also Jurewicz in this volume.)

The first pressing problem concerning both terms is that they are not easily translatable. A cursory glance at any lexicon will demonstrate the vast range of meanings that *ṛtá* has; and *harmonia* isn't nearly as straightforward as most present-day translators have taken it to be – indeed much is lost in unhesitatingly translating it as 'harmony'. Accordingly, I will begin with an overview of the various meanings of each of these terms before turning to the Ṛgvedic hymns and Pre-Socratic fragments in order to offer a conceptual comparison between the two.

Harmonia

I would like to begin with a brief note on the etymology of '*harmonia*' ('*harmoniē*' in the Ionic Greek dialect). The abstract suffix 'ia', (*-i̯ə̯*) is added to a conjectural theme **ar-mn*, which itself presumably comes from the PIE root **H2er-* (fit).[4] *Harmonia* does not, of course, mean what contemporary music theorists define as 'harmony'; indeed, as the other words that derive from this root suggest,[5] the earliest uses of *harmonia* are not even specifically musical. For Homer, in whose works we find the first extant occurrence of the word, the primary meaning is 'physical joining' together of planks of wood.[6] In the same corpus, though, we already encounter a more abstract meaning in the *Iliad* (22.255–6), where *harmonia* stands for 'covenant' or 'agreement'.

Hesiod (*Theogony* 933) describes the goddess Harmonia as the daughter of Aphrodite and Ares. Lasus of Hermione's fragment 702 contains the first extant use of *harmonia* in reference to the realm of music.[7] In Pindar's odes, we find mention of the goddess Harmonia[8] in addition to *harmonia* as a musical mode.[9] From these early uses, we can see that the notion of *harmonia* entails the

4 Ilievski (1993) traces the roots back to Linear B. He claims that the dialectical basis of the noun *(h)armo* and the verb *harmozō* can be explained only by phonetic rules according to which the inherited IE vocalic nasal -mn- developed a reflex -mo-.; the verb is a technical term and, he claims, there is no doubt that the noun *harmonia* is derived from this verb.

5 These include verbs like *harmozō* (fit together) and *arariskō* (join together) and nouns like *harma* (chariot), *arithmos* (number), *artus* (bond) and *arthron* (joint).

6 Cf. *Odyssey* 5.247–8; 5.361–2.

7 Δάματρα μέλπω Κόραν τε Κλυμένοι' ἄλοχον μελιβόαν ὕμνον ἀναγνέων Αἰολίδ' ἀμ βαρύβρομον ἁρμονίαν.

8 *Pythian Ode* 3.87–92; 11.7–12.

9 *Nemean Ode* 4.44–9; *Pythian Ode* 8.67–75.

preexistence of two or more disjointed entities, usually in a state of tension – as is exemplified by the mythical figure who is the product of the goddess of love and the god of war. To borrow from Finney, we can understand *harmonia* as a 'reconciliation of opposites, a fitting together of disparate elements, whether in music, universe, the body politic, or the body of man'.[10] For the later Greeks, *harmonia* comes to stand for order – and, as we will see, a particular kind of order – in the universe as well as many other domains, including mathematics, psychology, ethics, poetics and music.

For Heraclitus, *harmonia* was a central cosmological principle whereby opposites were in the proper relation to one another. Empedocles described it as a principle of balance working alongside love (*philotēs*) and strife (*neikos*). It was of supreme importance to the Pythagoreans as well – they regarded *harmonia* as the orderly fitting together of sound and considered that the good of the human soul consisted in 'grasping and assimilating to that order'.[11] I will offer a more detailed discussion of Pre-Socratic conceptions of *harmonia* in what follows. For now, let us turn to *ṛtá*.

Ṛtá

The substantive *Ṛtá* has been commonly translated in English as 'truth', 'order' and 'law', in French as '*verité*', '*ordre*' and '*loi*', and in German as '*Wahrheit*', '*Weltordnung*' and '*Gesetz*'. Yet none of these – individually or taken together – suffice to properly capture the sense of the word. The *Ṛgveda* alone contains over four hundred instances of the noun *ṛtá* as well as its adjectival form, occurring in a variety of contexts, in hymns dedicated to different deities.

In the Böhtlingk *Wörterbuch* (1928), *ṛtá* as an adjective was defined as 'ordered, right, righteous, brave, efficient, true'; as an adverb, it meant 'rightly, correctly, properly, strongly'; finally, as a substantive, it could mean: 'a) fixed order, determination, decision, b) order in sacred matters, sacred custom, statute, pious work, divine law, faith as the epitome of religious truth, c) the right, truth (especially religious truth), and the right path'. Apart from this array of possible meanings, one of the remarkable things about *ṛtá* is the richness of imagery associated with it – a path (*pantham ṛtásya*),[12] a seat (*ṛtásya yonī*,[13] *ṛtásya sadan*[14]), a wheel (*cakram ṛtásya*[15]) and a stream (*dhārām ṛtásya*[16]), to name but a few.

[10] Finney 1973: 388.
[11] Barker 1989: 6.
[12] RV 1.46, 65, 79, 124, 128, 136; 3.12, 31; 5.45, 80; 6.4; 7.44, 65; 10.66, 70
[13] RV 3.62; 4.1.
[14] RV 1.84, 164; 3.55; 4.21, 42; 5.1; 7.53.
[15] RV 1.164.
[16] RV 1.67; 5.12; 7.43.

As we can see, it is by no means so straightforward a term that a single translation could do it justice.[17] My goal is merely to highlight its various senses before attempting to ascertain whether these can be subsumed under some more general principle. Perhaps one way of arriving at a somewhat coherent understanding of a term with so many different senses is by regarding *ṛtá* as a single principle with manifestations in various domains – indeed, much the same could be said for *harmonia*. Gonda puts it well when he describes *ṛtá* as 'that untranslatable term which may be approximately described as the supreme and fundamental order-and-reality conditioning the normal and right, natural and true structure of cosmos, ritual and human conduct'.[18] In this passage, Gonda describes the domains of *ṛtá* as the cosmos, ritual and human conduct; we could say, on the other hand, that the domains of *harmonia* include the cosmos, human conduct and the human soul. Both *harmonia* and *ṛtá* could be understood as principles of order and balance that have different manifestations in these different domains. In the remainder of this chapter, I will explore the extent to which this hypothesis is tenable. I hope, in the process, to shed more light on the precise nature of this 'order'.[19]

One of the most striking similarities between *harmonia* and *ṛtá* is the manner in which they serve as regulating principles in the cosmos. The universe, for both the *ṛṣi*-s of the *Ṛgveda* and for the Pre-Socratic philosophers, is made up of opposing principles – night/day, hot/cold, mortal/immortal, etc. – and it is imperative that these opposing principles be kept in the proper relation to one another, for it is this state of balance that constitutes a well-ordered universe. I contend that *harmonia* and *ṛtá* are the keys to the maintenance of this relationship, for the Pre-Socratics and the Vedic *ṛsi*-s respectively: there is ample evidence for this claim in the fragments of Heraclitus, Empedocles and Philolaus, as well as in several hymns of the *Ṛgveda*. Let us first take a look at the role of opposites and dualities before turning to a discussion of how *harmonia* and *ṛtá* regulate these.

Opposites

Various hymns, including the famous *Nāsādiyasūkta* (RV 10.129), mention primal waters preexisting anything animate.[20] They are prior to the One (*tad*

17 *Pace* Lüders (1959), who claims that *ṛtá* is identical to '*Wahrheit*'. For more on why Lüders' claim is problematic, see Gonda 1977: 137–8.

18 Gonda 1972: 109.

19 I should note, at the outset, that I will not be comparing *harmonia* and *ṛtá* in all their domains of application – there will be no further discussion of the ritualistic role of *ṛtá*, for instance, nor will I talk about the structure of human souls; my focus will be on the natural domain and its connection to the moral one.

20 It is difficult to isolate a unified cosmogonical account in the *Ṛgveda*, and I rely on reconstructions, such as those of Brown (1942), when I discuss Ṛgvedic cosmogony.

ekam) in RV 10.129 and to all the Gods (RV 10.121, 10.80), presumably including the cosmic craftsman, Tvaṣṭṛ. In general, the primal state is one in which the basic opposites that define the cosmos as we know it have not yet come into existence – there is no night/day, midspace/heaven, or death/deathlessness (RV 10.129.1–3). Most importantly neither the *sat* (being) nor the *asat* (non-being) existed then (RV 10.129.1). The cosmos could not have existed without opposing principles, and it is these very principles that underlie reality. In the *Ṛgveda*, as in the fragments of Empedocles, the cosmos as we know it only comes to exist when there is some degree of differentiation.[21] In an Empedoclean universe dominated entirely by love (*philotēs*), as described in 31 DK B27 for instance, everything is homogeneous; all mortal things have a 'double passing away' (B17) – complete separation (the rule of strife) causes things to pass away, but so too does the coming together of all things (the rule of love) because of the absence of recognisable masses like earth, air, fire and water (B38): oppositional forces form the very fabric of the cosmos.

The *Ṛgveda* abounds with descriptions of opposing principles. I have already mentioned the fundamental pairs present in RV 10.129 – being/non-being, night/day, death/deathlessness and midspace/heaven. To these we can add darkness/light (RV 10.129) and heaven/earth (RV 10.190). Dyaus (Sky) and Prithvi (Earth) are the parents of the gods; the gods themselves are broadly divided into Devas and Asuras and the struggle between them incarnates the struggle between opposing principles. Indeed, the very names of some gods stand for abstract principles of opposition. Consider, for instance, the Ādityas and the Dānavas. As Brown points out, their names are derived from those of their mothers – Aditi and Dānu

[21] Compare Empedocles 31 DK B27 with RV 10.129.1:

ἔνθ' οὔτ' ἠελίοιο διείδεται ὠκέα γυῖα
οὐδὲ μὲν οὐδ' αἴης λάσιον μένος οὐδὲ θάλασσα·
οὕτως Ἁρμονίης πυκινῶι κρύφωι ἐστήρικται
Σφαῖρος κυκλοτερὴς μονίηι περιηγέι γαίων.

Here are distinguished neither the swift limbs of the sun nor the shaggy might of the earth, nor the sea; but equal from every side and without end, it stays fast in the close covering of *harmoniē*, a rounded sphere rejoicing in his circular solitude. (31 DK B27)

nā́sad āsīn nó sád āsīt tadā́nīd
nā́sīd rájo nó víomā paró yát
kím ā́varīvaB kúha kásya śármann
ámbhan kím āsīd gáhanan gabhīrám

The nonexistent did not exist, nor did the existent exist at that time.
There existed neither the airy space nor heaven beyond.
What moved back and forth? From where and in whose protection? Did water exist, a deep depth? (RV 10.129.1, tr. Jamison and Brereton 2014)

respectively, the first standing for 'boundless, infinite' and the second for 'bonded, restrained'.[22] The opposition can also be observed in respect to their functions: the Ādityas are associated with creative forces and the Dānavas with destructive ones.

While several Pre-Socratic philosophers describe opposites as fundamental principles in the cosmos, nowhere is this more apparent than in the fragments of Heraclitus, who describes a range of opposites, such as immortal/mortal (22 DK B62), death/life (B62, B48), pure/impure (B61), waking/sleeping (B88), cold/hot (B126), dry/wet (B126), and young/old (B88). Philolaus of Croton, a so-called Pythagorean, describes the limiting (*ta perainonta*) and the unlimited (*ta apeira*) as the two fundamental metaphysical principles in his account of the cosmos (44 DK B1, B6). The basic cosmic principles according to Empedocles are love (*philotēs*) and strife (*neikos*), forces of attraction and repulsion that are engaged in an eternal struggle. We can see opposing principles in his four roots or elements (*rhizōmata*) as well – water/fire and earth/air, the former representing cold/hot and the latter representing dense/rare.[23]

This brief survey demonstrates the fundamental role played by opposing principles in both Ṛgvedic and Pre-Socratic cosmologies. Yet, what is common to both is also the *necessity* of these opposing principles and the strife between them. The cosmos cannot exist in the absence of these principles, and the pre-cosmic state is characterised by a lack of differentiation. However, it is not enough for these opposites to merely exist in the absence of some principle of regulation. I suggest that *ṛtá* is an ordering principle for the Rgvedic cosmos much as *harmonia* is an ordering principle for the Pre-Socratic one.[24]

Order in nature

In the *Ṛgveda*, the *sat*, the sphere of being and life, is regulated by *ṛtá*. The *sat* is opposed to the *asat*, which is ruled by *anṛtá* (lacking in *ṛtá*). We can learn more about the characteristics of the *asat* from RV 7.104. There is material opposition between them, since the *asat* is dark and dry whereas the *sat* is full of moisture and light – the conditions necessary for life. As I mentioned earlier, *ṛtá* is associated with images of paths, waters and light. *Sat*/*ṛtá* and *asat*/*anṛtá* also stand in moral opposition – RV 7.104 tells us that an evil person is to be relegated to the

22 Brown 1942: 90. '*Aditi*' is formed from the privative '*a*' and '*diti*' whose root is '*da*' (to bind; to fetter). '*Dānu*' comes from the same root as '*Aditi*' – *da* – and is a primary derivative with the suffix *-nu*. Cf. Brown 1942: 90–1.

23 Empedocles (31 DK B21) explicitly describes the sun as hot ('ἠέλιον . . . θερμὸν') and water (rain) as cold ('ὄμβρον . . . ῥιγαλέον). Cf. Aristotle *On Generation and Corruption* 314b–15a.

24 I refer only to the Pre-Socratic cosmologies I have discussed above. Anaximander, for instance, described this principle of regulation as justice (*dikē*) rather than *harmonia*.

asat, ruled by *anṛtá* and that the fate of such a person is destruction (*nirṛti*). The evil person is also described as one who strengthens by the darkness (*tamovṛdh*) associated with *anṛtá* whereas the gods are often described as being strengthened by *ṛtá* (*ṛtávṛdh*) and, what is more, born in it (*ṛtájāta*).

In general, various gods are associated with *ṛtá* and *sat*. Agni, Indra, Mitra-Varuṇa and Soma are the primary deities associated with *ṛtá*. Seventy-eight of the hymns to Agni, thirty-five to Indra, forty-two to Soma, fifteen to the Aṣvins (the twins), and nine to Uṣa (dawn) mention *ṛtá*. Agni is often described as being the 'first-born of *ṛtá*' (*prathamajā́ ṛtásya*; RV 10.5), 'true to *ṛtá*' (*ṛtāvana*), and as the 'guardian of *ṛtá*' (*ṛtásya gopah*). Lüders conceives of Varuṇa's primary role as being the master of *ṛtá*:[25] he is said to spread out the cosmos, with its three realms, by means of *ṛtá* (RV 4.42)[26] and is even said, at one point, to take its form (RV 1.180, *ṛtápsu*). Indra is described as resting on the seat of *ṛtá* along with the Maruts (RV 4.21) and he, too, is a protector of *ṛtá* and born in it (RV 7.20, *ṛtapā́ ṛtejā́ḥ*). Indra, Varuna, Mitra and Aryaman are all said to grow strong through *ṛtá* (RV 7.82). Indra is also 'yoked to *ṛtá*' (*ṛtāyuj*, RV 6.39) when he is destroying Vala. The gods are responsible for maintaining *ṛtá* as the dominant principle – Mitra, Varuṇa and Agni are all guardians of *ṛtá* (*ṛtásya gopah*), and they (the Ādityas) also grow strong through it (RV 2.27, *ṛtenāditya mahi*). At RV 7.66, we are given a slew of descriptions for Mitra-Varuṇa: true to *ṛtá* (*ṛtāvan*), born in *ṛtá* (*ṛtājata*), strengthened by *ṛtá* (*ṛtávṛdh*), and haters of *anṛtá* (*anṛtádvis*). This last epithet serves to heighten the contrast between *ṛtá* and *anṛtá*. Furthermore, we can see from the cosmic roles assigned to the gods that their proper domain is *sat* whereas Paṇis and Dānavas have their domain in *asat*.

Beyond these associations, we also find two myths in the *Ṛgveda* – that of the Indra-Vṛtra battle and that of the Paṇis (RV 10.108) – which demonstrate the urgency of threats to this *ṛtá*. According to RV 10.108, the Paṇis, demons who live in the sky, steal various treasures from the Angirases – horses, cows, dawn and her rays, ritual fire, the sun, and the path of light and day. Srinivasan highlights that these are all items essential to the performance of the sacrifice and this sacrifice is crucial because it strengthens *ṛtá*.[27] Eventually, the priests, in alliance with Soma, Indra, Agni and Bṛhaspati, are able to have these treasures released and to proceed with the *ṛtá*-strengthening sacrifice. The battle between Indra and Vṛtra (whose name aptly means 'encloser') has as its consequence the creation of the cosmos as we know it.[28] Like the Paṇis, Vṛtra had bound various necessities

[25] Lüders 1959: 28–40.

[26] *ṛténa putró áditer ṛtā́vā/utá tridhā́tu prathayad ví bhū́ma* (RV 4.42.4).

[27] Srinivasan 1973: 44.

[28] The Indra-Vṛtra battle is described in various hymns and I rely on Brown's (1942) synthesis in my discussion.

of the cosmos – waters and the sun, for instance. Indra releases the waters and the waters, in turn, give birth to the sun. Indra's acts of creation after the defeat of Vṛtṛa involve the separation of the *sat*, which comes to be ruled by *ṛtá*, from the *asat*, ruled by *anṛtá*.

However, as Srinivasan points out, neither of these creation myths can be considered to formulate a literal cosmogonic account.[29] Instead, the main issue raised in both is the difficulty entailed in preserving the *ṛtá*-governed *sat*. It is also significant that neither *asat* nor *anṛtá* disappear (RV 2.24). There is still some darkness below the earth (RV 5.32, 8.6), where the *rakṣasas* (demons) are believed to dwell. *Ṛtá* predominates, strengthened and maintained by gods and men, but both these accounts – that of the Paṇis and that of Indra-Vṛtṛa – emphasise its precarious state. There exists a harmonic balance between *sat* and *asat* as well as between the other opposing principles and realms.

We have already seen how the existence of oppositional principles is necessary for creation. For the universe to be in an ordered rather than chaotic state, there needs to be some kind of arrangement between these oppositional principles. In the *Ṛgveda* (as well as in the Pre-Socratic fragments) such an arrangement entails predominance of one principle over another without the eradication of the other. The goal is not an equilibrium between opposites, but a state wherein they are in the proper proportion to one another. It is *ṛtá* that controls the transformation, the balancing and the adjustment of forces in a state of tension. *Ṛtá* is not 'order' in the sense of a 'cosmic blueprint'; it is, rather, a *dynamic* principle of order, regulating the constant struggle between the oppositional forces that are the very fabric of the cosmos. I now attempt to show how *ṛtá* and *harmonia* regulate the opposites and, in so doing, highlight yet more important aspects of these concepts and points of resemblance between them.

Although oppositional phenomena and principles play an important role in Ṛgvedic cosmology, I am not claiming that the Vedic *ṛṣi*-s believed that there were neat groups of opposite principles in reality, since RV 10.129 claims that everything emanated from a single principle. *There are* apparent opposites, but these are all closely interconnected and interrelated because of *ṛtá*. In this respect, there is a strong resemblance to Heraclitus' cosmology.

Heraclitus believed that nature (*physis*) loves to hide (B123) and that for this reason the knowledge of this nature was not easy to acquire, even if the account (*logos*) is common to all creatures (B2). He also claimed that the hidden *harmonia* was superior to the obvious one (B54). I contend that this hidden *harmonia* refers to the underlying metaphysical organisation of the world, which consists in the balance and interconnection of all apparent opposites, some of which I have mentioned above. Further, we are told that 'it is wise to agree that

[29] Srinivasan 1973: 55.

all things are one' (ὁμολογεῖν σοφόν ἓν πάντα εἶναι, B50). Such a claim might seem less enigmatic if we understand it to mean that there is an inherent harmonic connection between opposites. This unity of Heraclitus' opposites can be understood as the *harmonia* of these opposites wherein '*harmonia*' isn't just a synonym for 'unity' but a particular principle of order. For Heraclitus, night/day and winter/summer are regarded as one (B57, B67), and, in light of his views on *harmonia*, we could understand this to mean that such natural phenomena are regulated by the principle of *harmonia*. In the *Ṛgveda*, too, the days and the seasons are the clearest example of the way in which *ṛtá* regulates natural phenomena.

Mitra-Varuṇa and Aryaman, the Ādityas, who are described as the charioteers, guardians and strengtheners of *ṛtá* (RV 7.66), are the ones who establish the day, the night, the year and month (RV 7.66.11). The *ṛtá*-possessing Mitra-Varuṇa are responsible for bringing the year to completion (RV 7.61). Recall, also, that nights and days and years are said to come about only after *ṛtá* and *satya* were born out of the initial heat (*tapas*) according to the cosmogony in RV 10.190. Uṣa (the dawn) is true and obedient to *ṛtá* (RV 5.80.1; RV 1.123), moves according to it (RV 7.75), resides in the seat of *ṛtá* (*ṛtásya sadan*, RV 4.51), and has her horses yoked to it (RV 4.51). Varuṇa, master of *ṛtá*, is also supposed to have prepared the path of the sun and the stars (RV 1.24). At one point, dawn and night are described as the mothers of *ṛtá* (RV 1.142, 5.5); at another point, sky and earth are described as its parents (RV 6.17, 10.5). The terrestrial rivers, too, are true to *ṛtá* (*ṛtávarī*, RV 3.33, 4.18) and the sun is even described as the wheel of *ṛtá* (RV 1.164.11).[30] In general, all the major natural phenomena are related to *ṛtá*, and *harmonia* played a similarly important role in the natural order described by Empedocles and Philolaus.

We know from Diogenes' *Lives* (DL 8.85) that Philolaus of Croton was supposed to have written a work entitled *On Nature* (Περὶ Φύσεως), that this work began with the claim that nature is made up out of limiters and unlimited, and that both entities need a third to come upon (*epigignein*) them in order for the cosmos to exist. This third entity is *harmonia* (44 DK B1, B6). The world-order as a whole as well as all the individuals within it are regulated by *harmonia*.

Empedocles, too, recognised the importance of *harmonia* even though we

[30] *duvā́daśāraI nahí táj járāya*
várvarti cakrám pári dyā́m ṛtásya
ā́ putrā́ agne mithunā́so átra
saptá śatā́ni viṃśatíś ca tasthuḥ

Twelve-spoked, the wheel of *ṛtá* [= the Sun] ever rolls around heaven – yet not to old age. Upon it, o Agni, stand seven hundred twenty sons in pairs [= the nights and days of the year]. (RV 1.164.11, tr. after Jamison and Brereton 2014.)

have limited evidence for this. According to him, the universe consists of four elements being controlled by the cosmic principles of love, which unites the elements, and strife, which forces them apart. In the final stage of cosmic development, love causes all things to come together (31 DK B35) – there is complete unity of the elements in the form of a homogeneous sphere, while strife is left completely outside the sphere (B17, B27). Empedocles describes the current situation as being one where love predominates but strife nonetheless offers enough resistance to prevent all things from becoming homogenised; some elements are mixed and some are not. When strife prevails, however, there is a complete separation of the elements (B35). Love integrates living organisms while strife disintegrates them (B20).

However, *harmonia* holds everything in a fixed proportion. Consider for instance B96:

> ἡ δὲ χθὼν ἐπίηρος ἐν εὐτύκτοις χοάνοισι
> τὰς δύο τῶν ὀκτὼ μοιράων λάχε Νήστιδος αἴγλης,
> τέσσαρα δ' Ἡφαίστοιο· τὰ δ' ὀστέα λευκὰ γένοντο
> Ἁρμονίης κόλλῃσιν ἀρηρότα θεσπεσίῃσιν.

> Earth in well-made melting pots got two parts of glittering Nestis, out of its eight parts, and four from Hephaestus; white bones were produced, joined by the divine glue of *harmoniē*.

This fragment is remarkable as one of the earliest instances of *harmonia* being used in a case of explicitly numerical proportion – bones are made out of earth, fire and water in a numerical ratio. Here, *harmonia* stands for mixing in a particular proportion – there is balance and not complete unity or merging and, in this, it is importantly different from love. It entails a proper fitting together of discrete entities that nonetheless retain their original identity and don't simply blend into one another.

Fragment B23 also provides us with an image of how *harmonia* regulates and, indeed, creates all of nature as we know it:

> . . . οἵτ' ἐπεὶ οὖν μάρψωσι πολύχροα φάρμακα χερσίν,
> ἁρμονίηι μείξαντε τὰ μὲν πλέω, ἄλλα δ' ἐλάσσω,
> ἐκ τῶν εἴδεα πᾶσιν ἀλίγκια πορσύνουσι,
> δένδρεά τε κτίζοντε καὶ ἀνέρας ἠδὲ γυναῖκας
> θῆράς τ' οἰωνούς τε καὶ ὑδατοθρέμμονας ἰχθῦς
> καί τε θεοὺς δολιχαίωνας τιμῇσι φερίστους·

> and so when they take pigments of various colours in their hands, mixing them in *harmoniē*, some more, some less, [and] from them prepare forms resembling all things, making trees, men, women, beasts, birds water-nourished fish, and long-lived gods foremost in honours.

When read in conjunction with B21, this fragment likens the work of painters with their pigments to the effects of love and strife on the four elements – Empedocles even uses dual forms to describe the work of the painters (*meizante*, *ktizonte*), which emphasises their analogy to love and strife. However, love and strife alone are not enough – they need to mix pigments in order to bring about creation in accordance with *harmonia*. From what we know, the painters' task did not involve blending different pigments to create new colours, but rather juxtaposing (four basic) different pigments in order to create realistic depictions – so 'mixing in *harmoniē*' most likely meant mixing in an ordered and fitting way.[31] In the cosmos as we know it, love and strife are optimally balanced such that existence comes about by means of *harmonia*, partly mixed and partly unmixed, since the prevalence of either extreme would result in the destruction of our world.

Order in human life

We have seen how *harmonia* and *ṛtá* play an exceedingly important role in the natural world and are responsible for its orderly functioning. Another significant – and closely related – point of comparison lies in the relationship that human beings bear to the principles of cosmic order. It is the case, with both *ṛtá* and *harmonia*, that ordinary human beings are not immediately able to distinguish and recognise them, and both the Ṛgvedic and Pre-Socratic writers assert the value of this ability. Indeed, in the Greek tradition, perfection of the human soul consists in comprehending the cosmic order and living in accordance to it.[32] In the *Ṛgveda*, both men and gods live in the realm of *ṛtá*, but only the latter are able to recognise it. Most of the hymns that mention *ṛtá* emphasise its connection to the gods, and some mention that they know and hate *anṛtá*. Mitra-Varuṇa lives in the house of *ṛtá* and fights the hated *anṛtá* (RV 7.60.5, 7.66.13), and Varuṇa is described as the king who is able to discern *ṛtá* from *anṛtá* (RV 10.124.5). On the other hand, the Vedic *ṛṣi*-s have to implore the gods to reveal to them the difference between the two:

31 For more on ancient painting, cf. Sections III. 29–44 from *The Natural History* by Pliny the Elder. See also Kranz 1912, Bruno 1977 and Struycken 2003.

32 I have limited myself to a discussion of *harmonia* in Pre-Socratic writings. However, the remarkable account in Plato's *Timaeus* (90b6–d7) is worth mentioning, especially since it represents ideas that many have taken to be Pythagorean. The universe has a harmonic structure and motions that are proper to this structure; the human soul initially has this same structure and motion, but these are disturbed when the human soul is first embodied. It is only by attending to the *harmonia* in this world that we can bring disordered human souls to their initial harmonic order. This restoration of order to the soul is what happiness and the best life consists in.

> *amī́ yé devā́ sthána*
> *triṣú ā́ rocané divā́ḥ*
> *kád va ṛtáṃ kád ánṛtaṃ*
> *kúva pratnā́ va ā́hutir.*

> You gods, who are yonder in the three luminous realms of heaven –
> What is *ṛtá* for you, what is *anṛtá*? Where is the age-old offering for you?
> (RV 1.105.5, tr. after Jamison and Brereton 2014)

This hymn expresses the anxiety of a Vedic *ṛṣi* about the maintenance of the cosmic and the earthly order. He begins by describing both kinds of order and then expresses his fears about them being upheld. The verse above expresses his fears concerning his lack of insight into *ṛtá*. This insight is important because it allows him to act in accordance with *ṛtá* and thereby to strengthen and uphold it.

Two hymns describe the *ṛṣi*-s who have managed to attain this knowledge. RV 10.71 describes the degrees of mastery of sacred speech (*vāc*) attained by the *ṛṣi*-s. This mastery is needed in order for them to perform Soma rites, which in turn strengthen *ṛtá*. Not everyone is able to understand the sacred speech in the same way – some, who supposedly hear, do not truly hear, but hear in vain (RV 10.71.4, 6). All the *ṛṣi*-s have the ability – by sensorial means – to grasp the sacred speech, but not all have the quickness of mind needed for this task (RV 10.71.7). Sensory imperviousness to *ṛtá* is also mentioned in RV 4.23.8, where the hymn to *ṛtá* is said to have the power to open even deaf ears. Being receptive to *ṛtá* and being able to grasp it is the ultimate goal of any mortal, and this is something that some *ṛṣi*-s are indeed able to do. The path for the enlightened *ṛṣi*-s who seek *ṛtá* is thornless and easy (RV 1.41.4). In the hymn to Bṛhaspati mentioned above (RV 2.24), *ṛṣi*-s are described as possessing *ṛtá* and perceiving *anṛtá* (*ṛtā́vānaḥ praticákṣyānṛtā*); they are thus able to aid in the battle against Vala and in the upholding of *ṛtá*. As Mahoney puts it:

> Vedic sages ... understood Ṛtá to be the inherent universal principle of balance and concord, a dynamic rule or order in which all things contribute in their own unique way to the smooth running of the cosmos as a whole. If they were aligned with Ṛtá, therefore, all things would be true to their own given nature and, in so doing, would properly express their particular function in that intricate and delicately aligned system of order.[33]

Ṛtá regulates the cosmos and the divine realm but also regulates the human realm and dictates human conduct, since the highest kind of human life involves understanding *ṛtá* and being aligned to it. Much the same is true of *harmonia* for the Pre-Socratics.

---

[33] Mahoney 1998: 48.

Heraclitus chastises human beings for being unseeing and unhearing (B1). In echoes of some hymns from the *Ṛgveda*, humans are described as hearing like the deaf and being 'absent while present' (B34). Nonetheless, Heraclitus claims that the true metaphysical structure of the world is available for anyone who searches for it properly even though the search is a difficult one and often yields little.[34] According to him, the *logos*, which has strong connections to *harmonia*, is eternal, although men fail to comprehend it (B1).[35] Like unskilled *ṛṣi*-s and laymen, most people are unable to distinguish the hidden structure of the universe.

As I mentioned earlier, Heraclitus' hidden *harmonia* might refer to the hidden metaphysical structure of the universe. From this, we may infer that only someone who truly listens to the *logos* will be able to progress from a mere perception of the obvious *harmonia* to the knowledge of the true *harmonia* that governs nature. In the words of Kahn: 'The concept of *harmonie* as a unity composed of conflicting parts is thus the model for an understanding of the world ordering as a unified whole. And it is the comprehension of this pattern in all its applications that constitutes wisdom.'[36]

***Harmonia* and *ṛtá* as dynamic and ontologically independent principles**

Having examined how *harmonia* and *ṛtá* similarly function as principles of order, governing both nature and human life, I will end with two claims about the nature of these principles. I argue that, in the Ṛgvedic as well as the Pre-Socratic texts considered in these pages, *harmonia* and *ṛtá* can both be understood as a dynamic principle of order as well as ontologically independent from any divine entity. We can perhaps better understand the first claim by paying attention to the striking imagery in Heraclitus' fragment about the *harmonia* of bow and lyre:

> οὐ ξυνιᾶσιν ὅκως διαφερόμενον ἑωυτῶι ὁμολογέει· παλίντροπος ἁρμονίη ὅκωσπερ τόξου καὶ λύρης.
>
> They do not comprehend how a thing agrees at variance with itself; it is a *harmoniē* turning back on itself, like that of the bow and the lyre. (B51)

34 χρυσὸν γὰρ οἱ διζήμενοι γῆν πολλὴν ὀρύσσουσι καὶ εὑρίσκουσιν ὀλίγον. Seekers after gold dig up much earth, but find little (22 DK B22).

35 I have argued in an as yet unpublished paper for the relationship between Heraclitus' concept of *logos* (word, account) and that of *harmoniē*, and it is beyond my scope here to offer a complete explanation of this relationship. We can understand the *logos* as the account of the world, and this account would consist in a description of the metaphysical organisation of the world. I contend that, for Heraclitus, *harmoniē* is the principle that organises the world.

36 Kahn 1979: 200.

The bow and the lyre are the key to understanding how two or more things that are in a state of tension can nonetheless agree. We can understand this *harmonia* as the sound created when tense strings come together to create consonance – they create 'harmony' in the musical sense. But the common translation of 'attunement' doesn't fully capture the meaning of *harmonia*. Both bow and lyre illustrate the unity of entities in tension on account of their shape as well. They are similarly constructed and contain at least one string that is in tension. The tension between string and frame in both the bow as well as the lyre shows how something being stretched apart also comes together in a productive way. Both the duality and the unity of opposites is clearly brought out in this fragment as is the importance of balance. In a remarkable coincidence, the *Ṛgveda*, in a hymn to Bṛhaspati, also provides us with an image of a *ṛtá*-possessing bow:

ṛtájyena kṣtájyen bráhmaena pátir
yátra vátra prá tád aśnoti dhánvanā
tásya sādhvīr íādhv yābhir ásyati
nṛcáknāag dṛ́śáye kárśáyeāag b

The lord of the sacred formulation, with his swift bow whose string is *ṛtá* – where he wishes, there he reaches. To him belong the straight flying arrows [= the hymns] with which he shoots – [arrows] to be seen, drawing the gaze of men, and whose womb is the ear. (RV 2.24.8, tr. after Jamison and Brereton 2014)

In this hymn, Bṛhaspati is described as slaying Vala with his bow and arrow. The string of this bow is described as '*ṛtájyena*', which can be translated as '*ṛtá*-strung' or 'one whose string is *ṛtá*'. As with the Heraclitean fragment, we can see how fittingly the image of the bow illustrates the manner in which *ṛtá* balances and orders.

It is also notable that both *harmonia* and *ṛtá* seem to be ontologically independent from any divinity. In the *Ṛgveda* (10.190), *ṛtá* and *satya* ('what is; the truth') are born out of the primordial heat (*tapas*) and prior to the Vedic divinities. I have already cited the various instances of the gods being referred to as 'born in *ṛtá*' – they uphold it and reside in it and even strengthen it, but they are not responsible for its creation. The same is true of *harmonia*. Philolaus took it to be an independently existent principle that supervenes upon the existent limiters and unlimited; Heraclitus did not think that either men or gods had anything to do with the established natural order; and within Empedocles' system, love, strife and *harmonia* are responsible for the creation and destruction of all other entities.[37]

[37] Franklin also notices the parallels between *ṛtá* and *harmonia* in this respect and, in addition, points out that *ṛtá* is 'remote and impersonal . . . but provides the ordered context in which all personal experience becomes meaningful' (2002: 7).

Conclusion

Harmonia and *ṛtá* both refer to the regulation of cosmic principles as well as natural phenomena. Furthermore, they play an important role in regulating human conduct, since the best human life consists in living in accordance with these principles. I have also argued that they resemble each other in being dynamic principles of order that occupy a central place in their respective systems while remaining ontologically independent from any divinity. There still remains much to be said about the connection between the two: for instance, a discussion of the relations between *harmonia* and *logos* on the one hand and *ṛtá* and *satya* on the other could prove fruitful. The present investigation has also been limited to the hymns of the *Ṛgveda* and to the fragments of three Pre-Socratic thinkers, and we could learn yet more about these terms by including other corpora. For the present, though, I would like to conclude that at the most abstract level, *harmonia* and *ṛtá* are principles of order that stand for the dynamic fitting together of disjointed entities. The fitting together takes place in nature, the macrocosm, and in human life, the microcosm; furthermore, it also involves adaptations *between* microcosm and macrocosm.[38]

Acknowledgements

I would like to express my gratitude to the audience at the 'International Conference on Cosmology and the Self in Ancient India and Ancient Greece', held at the University of Exeter in July 2014. This chapter also owes much to the helpful comments of Deven Patel, Robin Seguy and Pushkar Sohoni.

[38] Renou describes *ṛtá* as 'le résultat des correlations, le produit de l'adaptation', de l'agencement' entre le microcosme et le macrocosme' (1949: 266). The same holds true for *harmonia*.

4

Ātman and its transition to worldly existence

Greg Bailey

What can we say about a concept like the *ātman* when its principal feature is its apparent indefinability and impersonal nature? Initially we could do worse than utilise Jurewicz's definition of the term, based mainly on Ṛgvedic sources: 'This word is used to denote the essence of an entity, the whole body (which ensures personal identity and existence), its most important parts, which are the head (which ensures personal identity and existence – here and in the afterworlds) and the breath (which ensures the existence of a living being)'.[1] But moving on to the *Upaniṣads*, the final texts in the Vedic corpus, we find a systematisation and an impersonalism in the conceptual development of the *ātman* idea. We are confronted in the *Upaniṣads* with what individual teachers say about it, rather than what it is, because what it is defies easy description in words and this has to be taken as the axiomatic commencement point for any study of it.

In looking at the possible origin of the idea of such an essence, we could draw upon Proferes, who has recently argued for ideas of universal sovereignty, associated with the sacred fire[2] of the household, clan and tribe, where the *rājā*'s fire combines the parts with the whole. It becomes a political metaphor that could be used to develop a metaphysical idea of unity within diversity. For Proferes,

> The identity of the king with his dominion and, ultimately, with the cosmos can be shown to have directly informed the early *Upaniṣadic* discourse on the nature of the

1 Jurewicz 2007: 130.

2 See Proferes 2007: 31, 'The fire is produced in each far-flung household separately, and yet is present among them all simultaneously. As such, it marks the presence of a central power, . . . it serves to bind together the distinct members of the greater polity and affirm a common unity.' And: 'What was more revolutionary, however, was the uncoupling of the ideological underpinnings of the rite from its social context, and the concomitant generalisation of the values expressed through the rite to all twice-born males, regardless of political status' (2007: 136). Jurewicz 2007 is also important here, focusing on the essentiality of fire to life and identity, but does not suggest a political subtext.

> absolute and the means to achieving spiritual freedom. The evidence is found in the substantial number of *Upaniṣadic* passages in which metaphors of sovereignty are employed in immediate connection with the identification of the macrocosm and microcosm.[3]

He gives a series of examples from the two earliest *Upaniṣads*, in order to argue that it is the sense of 'unlimitedness' associated with Vedic ideals of freedom that becomes disconnected from theories of kingship and translated into a metaphysical idea of freedom from all limitations. This is necessarily impersonal and abstract, but at the same time universal in applying to a definition of personhood.

In this chapter I attempt to explore how the *ātman* enters the world or relates to the world of limitations, where the word 'world' designates everything ontologically different from the *ātman*, and 'relates' refers to how it can know things outside of itself, usually by means of the senses (also part of the world of limitations). Ontologically, *ātman* and world, consisting of psychological and physical constituents, are conceptual opposites. Yet strenuous efforts are made to describe how the *ātman* interacts with the world, most of these descriptions phrased in strongly assertive language,[4] and in highly elliptical sentences, all showing the conceptual difficulties involved in using language to define a concept that seemingly defies language. What seems to have happened is that a belief in some kind of entity existing beyond temporal and spatial limitations was asserted, then logical consistency required exploration of how it might be known by what was ontologically separate from it and, in turn, how it managed to cognise that which was separate from it.

Definitions of the *ātman*

There are a range of explanations/paraphrases of the *ātman* given in *Upaniṣads* of differing time periods, and the later their date of composition, the more and more Sāṃkhyan ideas seem to have infiltrated into the teaching of the *ātman*'s entry into the world.[5] In the *Bṛhadāraṇyaka* and the *Chāndogya Upaniṣads* we are given fragments of cosmogonic myths – largely demythologised in relation to their Vedic antecedents and their Purāṇic successors – where the *ātman* is sometimes depicted as the beginning point in the creation process. I have used these first because they genuinely attempt to account for the *ātman*'s entry into the world and simultaneously present definitions of the *ātman*.

In a brisk reading of the *Bṛhadāraṇyaka* and the *Chāndogya Upaniṣads*, I have totalled up thirty-four definitions of the *ātman*. We could argue whether or

3 Proferes 2007: 143.

4 See Gren-Eklund 1978.

5 Of which the best example is found in MaiU 6.17–30.

not these are definitions, descriptive paraphrases or metaphorical statements, and the very number of definitions/paraphrases may signify the difficulty in using language to describe such an ethereal concept, one that seemingly needed first to be experienced intuitively, then taught. Additionally, and a direct consequence of this, it signifies that different teachers – abridged versions of whose teachings are collected in the extant *Upaniṣads* – had their own understandings of what this concept may have meant to them. In truth, when it is defined or paraphrased it is usually in terms of negative theology or in positive terms – where the criterion is complete liberation from all the limitations of the material world – such that it is said to be 'the immortal' (*amṛtá*).

Here is a famous passage summarising the *ātman*'s incapacity to be known:

> About this self (*ātman*), one can only say 'not–, not—.' He is ungraspable, for he cannot be grasped. He is undecaying, for he is not subject to decay. He has nothing sticking to him, for he does not stick to anything. He is not bound; yet he neither trembles in fear nor suffers injury . . .[6]

These qualities are seemingly all physical – though 'ungraspable' could be perceptual – as they contradict everything that could be said about the body and so are contrary to all the conditions of the material and psychological world. Yet, many other paraphrases go beyond this in attempting to explain how something quite the opposite from the material/psychological participates in it. In the Sanskrit the negative definition is communicated in the first three lines by opposition between passive verbs, and negative gerundives and one negated nominal form, then one negative participle form and two finite verbs in the present tense, both having an intransitive sense. It is as if such language is utilised so as to present the *ātman* as having no agency of its own, but this may be intended only to distinguish it from what does have agency, even where this absence of agency will be contradicted in other Upaniṣadic passages.

Additional to this are some single sentences from the same *Upaniṣad*, all repeating this very same clichéd expression, but adding some useful contextual interpretations: 'so indeed, my dear, this self has no distinctive core and surface; the whole thing is a single mass of cognition' (BU 4.5.13).[7] And:

[6] *sa eṣa neti nety ātmā* |
agṛhyo na hi gṛhyate |
aśīryo na hi śīryate |
asaṅgo na sajyate |
asito na vyathate |
na riṣyati | (BU 3.9.26 = BU 4.2.4; 4.5.15) (Olivelle 1998: 101)
Unless otherwise indicated all translations are from Olivelle 1998. Where I write 'following Olivelle', it means I have modified his translation.

[7] *evaṃ vā are 'yam ātmānantaro 'bāhyaḥ kṛtsnaḥ prajñānaghana eva* |

> This self, you see, is imperishable; it has an indestructible nature (*avināśī vā are 'yam ātmānucchittidharmā*[8] BU 4.5.14). For when there is a duality of some kind, then the one can see the other, the one can smell the other, . . . and the one can perceive the other. When, however, the Whole has become one's very self (*yatra tv asya sarvam ātmaivābhūt*), then who is there for one to see and by what means? . . . Who is there for one to touch and by what means? Who is there for one to perceive and by what means? (*kena kaṃ spr̥śet tat kena kaṃ vijānīyāt*). By what means can one perceive him by means of whom one perceives this whole world? (*yenedaṃ sarvaṃ vijānāti taṃ kena vijānīyāt*). About this self (*ātman*) one can only say . . .[9]

An ontological quality is given here for the self and a question of how it can be perceived is raised. In both cases they are expressed in terms of a negation of 'empiricist' ways of knowing, except for the positivity implied in the *ātman*'s indestructible nature. A distinction is drawn between the pronoun *asya* and *ātmā*, but it is unclear whether this pronoun refers to the agent who is capable of knowing through the senses – as it is elsewhere in the *Upaniṣads* – or whether the neuter *sarvam* designates the *ātman*/*brahman* with all the other worldly elements separated from it. The final question, involving the repetition of two interrogatives, implies that the *ātman* may be a conceptual 'object', given that *kam* is in the masculine accusative.[10] But I wonder if these two interrogative sentences are rhetorical, even if not composed in the normal rhetorical style? Because, the answer Yājñavalkya gives is simply to restate the idealised definition of the *ātman*. I also note the repetition of the prefix *vi* in *avināśī*, and three times when used with *jñā*. Given that it often conveys the sense of distinction between things, this usage may have been deliberate as a means of emphasising the difference between the *ātman* and everything else.

In *Br̥hadāraṇyaka Upaniṣad* 2.5.14–15 we are presented with an equally elliptical paraphrase – in no sense is it a definition – of the *ātman* and its connection to the world.

> This self (*ātman*) is the honey of all beings, and all beings are the honey of this self. That radiant and immortal person (*puruṣa*) in the self and the radiant and immortal person (*puruṣa*) connected with the body (*ātman*) – they are both one's self. It is the immortal; it is *brahman*; it is the Whole.
>
> This very self (*ātman*) is the Lord of all, the king of all beings. As all the spokes are fastened (*samārpitāḥ*) to the hub and the rim of a wheel, so to one's self (*ātman*)

[8] Would it be possible to read a double meaning in this compound indicating that the *ātman* cannot be analysed?

[9] Olivelle 1998: 129–31.

[10] It is not possible to determine if *kena* is masculine or neuter. If it were the former, to what would it refer? If we read further Yājñavalkya recognises there is a problem here: *vijñātāram are kena vijānīyād ity*: 'Look – by what means can one perceive the perceiver?' (Olivelle 1998: 131).

are fastened all beings, all the gods, all the worlds, all the breaths and all these bodies (*ātman*).[11]

These two prose passages form a virtual conclusion to a fairly lengthy section where the visible physical features of the world, as well as *dharma*, truth and humanity, are declared to be the honey of all beings. And as there has to be some kind of summing up, so here it is given in our quoted verses. What does 'honey' mean here? Essence? And should we give it more precedence than the other listed components? Additionally, is the *ātman* simply one amongst a number of high-profile concepts that are being listed as part of the larger universe? Even if everything 'real' can be reduced back to the *ātman*, all of the other elements of the physical, psychological and cultural universe still have to be recognised for what they are.

The *puruṣa* concept emerges here, with a virtually direct identification between it and the *ātman*. This is further suggestive that the *puruṣa* is the *ātman* in the world – a point taken up below.[12] It is into the *ātman* that the various categories of things are attached, not into the person, but what kind of relationship is this? The root √*ṛ* may have the sense of 'attach to, fall down into, fix on to', but surely the use of the prefix *sam* is important here. It connotes a sense of collectivity within the framework of an emerging unity, such that it is their connection with the *ātman* that provides them with a sense of unity.

Yet another definition conforms more to the absolute ontological distance between *ātman* and other:

> 'The self within all is this self of yours.'
> 'Which one is the self within all, Yājñavalkya?'
> 'He is the one who is beyond hunger and thirst, sorrow and delusion, old age and death. It is when they come to know this self that Brahmins give up the desire for sons, the desire for wealth, and the desire for worlds, and undertake the mendicant life.' (BU 3.5.1)[13]

As often, emphasis here is placed on everything the *ātman* is not, while telling us what the *ātman* is. It does, however, suggest that the negative elements, both emotional and physical, which define the world are so well known that they can be fully understood even where they are reduced to single code words. By implication they point us towards what the *ātman* might be.

Finally, I cite a passage where there are listed some definite positive characterisations of the *ātman*, which also point out how it may interact with the world in functioning cognitively:

[11] Olivelle 1998: 73.
[12] Two other places where *puruṣa* and *ātman* are juxtaposed are ChU 8.7.4 and 8.12.3.
[13] Olivelle 1998: 83.

> 'But when both the sun and the moon have set, the fire has died out, and the voice is stilled, Yājñavalkya, what then is the source of light for a person (*puruṣa*) here?'
> 'The self (*ātman*) is then his source of light. It is by the light of the self that a person sits down, goes about, does his work, and returns.' (BU 4.3.6)
> 'Which self is that?'
> 'It is this person (*puruṣa*) – the one that consists of perception (*vijñānamayaḥ*) among the vital functions (*prāṇa*), the one that is the inner light within the heart. He travels across both worlds, being common to both. Sometimes he reflects, sometimes he flutters, for when he falls asleep he transcends this world, these visible forms of death.' (BU 4.3.7)[14]

Once again the *puruṣa* is placed in apposition with the *ātman*, but consisting of *vijñāna* it is given a clear cognitive function and it could even be argued that its function as the inner light also has an epistemological implication. But its qualification as *antarjyotiḥ* ('inner light') needs also to be noted, as the contrast between inner[15] and outer seems to define the relationship between *ātman* and *puruṣa* even where they seem ontologically identical. Thus its entry into the world will always be perceptual.

Cosmogony/cosmology as the *ātman*'s entry into the world

The well-known cosmogonic description found at *Bṛhadāraṇyaka Upaniṣad* 1.4.1ff. offers a very rich conceptualisation of the *ātman* and its emergence into individuality.

> In the beginning this world was the self alone[16] having the form of a man. He looked around and saw nothing but himself. At first he said, 'Here I am.' From that the name 'I' came into being. Therefore, even today when you call someone, he first says 'This is I' and then states whatever other name he may have.[17] (BU 1.4.1)[18]

There are some significant lexical forms descriptive of the creative process here which recur elsewhere: the use of the verbs √*as* and √*bhū* together, occurrence

[14] Olivelle 1998: 111.

[15] Cf. BU 1.4.8; contrary is 2.5.19 declaring *brahman*/*ātman* to be outside of space and time; and 3.7.2–23 where the *ātman* is the *antaryāmin*, the 'inner-controller', who is different from everything but is still influential in governing worldly behaviour.

[16] I have modified Olivelle's (1998: 45) translation of this as 'a single body'.

[17] *ātmaivedam agra āsīt puruṣavidha* |
so 'nuvīkṣya nānyad ātmano 'paśyat |
so 'ham asmīty agre vyāharat |
tato 'haṃnāmābhavat |
tasmād apy etarhy āmantrito 'ham ayam ity evāgra uktvāthānyan nāma prabrūte yad asya bhavati |

[18] Following Olivelle 1998: 45.

of the prefix *vi* and use of personal pronouns to indicate the *ātman* and the 'I'. In some measure these are associated with a juxtaposition of masculine and neuter, where *ātmā* and *puruṣavidhaḥ* ('having the form of a man')[19] seemingly stand in apposition with the neuter *idam*, telling us that the *ātman* did not exist by itself, that it was a totality of all that existed physically and epistemologically. I take the imperfect *āsīt* as indicating not that this was just a primordial state, but that it was one potentially constant, beyond change. Yet the *ātman* here seems simultaneously to be in the created world. This is the only conclusion that can be drawn from the occurrence of the masculine compound *puruṣavidhaḥ*, where the prefix *vi* indicates a sense of distinction/modification as it does elsewhere in the *Upaniṣads*.[20] Hence I conclude that the *ātman* is already in some modified state, even in a cosmological passage such as this, where it is a question of the principles unfolding in primordial creation.

Even though in a modified state already, further development is required and this is described in the second line. The self, in the masculine, begins to cognise. Both verbs *anuvīkṣya* and *apaśyat* have the primary sense of knowing by seeing, implying some physical capacity, but both can also have the secondary sense of 'to perceive'. *Anu* and *vi* may imply that he looked behind and sideways, and it is surely significant that *vi* occurs here, pointing to a movement away from the idea of a unified self. But when he has looked around – his first act – he sees – his second act – nothing other than the self. *Anyat*, 'other', is in the neuter as opposed to the masculine demonstrative pronoun *so* at the beginning of the line, almost mirroring the juxtaposition of *ātmā* and *idam* in the previous line. Is this *ātman* also *puruṣavidhaḥ*? One would assume so as its identity has already been established in the previous line.

The process of modification is continued in the next two lines: 'At first he said, "Here I am." From that the name "I" came into being.' But why does he say 'Here I am'? There seems to be no connection between his realisation of his isolation and his statement of individuality. Yet there are significant repetitions. Two pronouns *so* and *aham* are being used here, in a manner common in Sanskrit where apposition of third and first person pronouns places emphasis on the identity of the person being described, as reflected in Olivelle's translation. Use of *asmi* ('I am') also invites comparison with the first line of the passage, though it is in the present indicative, signifying direct speech as opposed to the narrative

19 The same compound occurs at TU 2.2–5, MaiU 6.34.

20 And in earlier Vedic texts. Cf. Smith 1989: 62, 'The creation myths we have considered, then, may also be understood as the tracing of the transition from *sarva* to *viśva*, a transformation from a perfect unity without parts to a defective totality. Another step in the metamorphosis is required for true cosmos: the reintegration of the totality (*viśva*) into a constructed whole, a composed unity of parts the texts call *samāna*.'

imperfect defining an originally existing state. The words *asmi* with the quotative particle *iti* designate a speech act of naming, thus giving further definition to the *ātman* which existed as a person and now has a kind of psychological and linguistic identity. Further, there is repetition of the preposition *agre* ('at first') and the use again of the prefix *vi* in *vyāharat*, both strengthening the sense of creation through establishment of difference.

The fourth line confirms the sense of individuality, created by naming, that is already implied in the second line where he, the *ātman* as a man, sees nothing other than the *ātman*. This perception has now become self-conscious (*asmi*) by being given a name, and 'from that', that is, from the statement of the first person pronoun, the name I arises or 'becomes', where the word 'becomes' (*abhavat*) indicates a change of state already implied by the three-fold repetition of *vi*.

As this passage proceeds the word *ātman* is not used. Instead the third person pronoun he (*sa*) continues to be found as a substitute and 1.4.2–3 confirms that he is a knowing agent as he becomes the subject of verbs such as 'to fear' and 'to like', both used to indicate that they require an object, though none is present for the *ātman*. They simply extend the range of actions of perception exercised right from the time where he exists in the form of a man.

Much of what follows for the next five prose sections elaborates on the process of creation as separation and distinction, and at the beginning of 1.4.7 develops this as a general principle:

> At that time this world was without real distinctions (*avyākṛtám āsīt*); it was distinguished (*vyākriyata*) simply in terms of name and visible appearance – 'He is so and so by name and has this sort of an appearance.' So even today this world is distinguished (*vyākriyata*) simply in terms of name and visible appearance, as when we say, 'He is so and so by name and has this sort of appearance.'[21]

I am not confident the translation 'real' can be justified, because the occurrence of *āsīt* seems to be signifying a primordial state of the kind described in 1.4.1. Again there is repetition of the prefixes *vi* and *ā*, analogous to *vyāharat* in that same section, and in a similar semantic usage, *vy/ā√kṛ* can also designate the act of making declarations. The *ātman* thinks itself into consciousness and existence, both only making sense when there are distinctions enabling it to differentiate itself from objects, with it as the knowing subject. The juxtapositions of third person pronouns of masculine and neuter gender exemplify this, as does the use of *aham* to indicate the individualising process.

As this cosmology proceeds it morphs more and more into a definition of the *ātman*, and exposes the difficulty in defining it. Because, we are told that:

[21] Olivelle 1998: 47.

> Penetrating this body up to the very nailtips, he remains there like a razor within a case . . .[22] People do not see him, for he is incomplete (*akṛtsno hi saḥ*) as he comes to be called breath when he is breathing, speech when he is speaking, sight when he is seeing, hearing when he is hearing, and mind when he is thinking. These are only the names of his various activities (*tāny asyaitāni karmanāmāny eva*).[23]

Certainly this is a description of the *ātman* in the world, specifically as it is when it is *puruṣavidha*. The point is that he is all these things, not just one and so defies description simply in terms of designation. As such

> A man who considers him to be any one of these does not understand him, for he is incomplete within any one of these (*akṛtsno hy eṣo 'ta ekaikena bhavati*). One should consider them as simply his self (*ātmā*), for in it all these become one. This same self (*ayam ātmā*) is the trail (*padanīyam*) to this entire world, for by following it one comes to know this entire world . . .[24]

As such the *ātman* in the world is perceived as functioning somehow through the senses, while bypassing the danger that it could be identified with any of the individual senses by the assertion that they constitute a unity in the *ātman* itself, that it has no wholeness/completeness when identified with any one of them. Completeness does not imply a spatial or ontological limitation, but it does contradict any idea of the *ātman* being limited, which it would be if it were identified with a single sense. I note here that *bhavati* is used in describing its incompleteness and their unity in it, as this involves a perceptual awareness of correct ontological status. Whilst the *ātman* may have a permanent status that would be designated by the use of √*as*, its entrance into the world is a product of discovery by those who would seek to know it and in that sense involves a changed apprehension, hence the idea of becoming (*bhavati*).

As this cosmology proceeds it transfers its attention to *brahman* and uses language already seen with the *ātman* when it enters into the world or 'into a state of existence' we might say: 'In the beginning Brahmā was (*āsīd*) this, one alone. Being that one, he did not develop (*vyabhavat*)' (BU 1.4.11). Use of √*as* suggests primordiality beyond time, contrasting with the entry into time, exemplified by the occurrence of the prefix *vi* before √*bhū*. Then it proceeds in a quite different manner from the cosmology involving the *ātman*, because for no

22 Cf. Gren-Eklund 1978: 92, 'In this passage the notions of *nāman* and *rūpa* in the context only prepare for the idea of the presence of *ātman* in everything. *sa eṣa iha praviṣṭa ā nakhāgrebhyo* has been unanimously interpreted as referring to *ātman*. In an analysis this may be corroborated by the *sa eṣa*, not only a reference to somebody through *sa* but to an *eṣa* – somebody who should be known (more or less) totally, not so much through the preceding text but by given continual attention.'

23 Olivelle 1998: 47.

24 Olivelle 1998: 47.

stated reason it creates the *kṣatra*, the *viś* and the *śūdra*. Following this it creates *dharma* and a brief discussion about the four classes ensues.

Then, as if deliberately continuing the cosmological theme, another cosmology begins in 1.4.17: 'In the beginning this world was only the self (*ātman*), only one. He desired: "May I have (*syād*) a wife, then I can father offspring." Then he desired, "May I have (*syād*) wealth, then I can perform rituals."' I note in the first sentence a close similarity with 1.4.1: *ātmaivedam agra āsīt puruṣavidhaḥ*, with substitution of *eka eva* for *puruṣavidhaḥ*, where the words *eka eva* are suggestive of the *ātman* in a state of absolute isolation, having undergone no modification along the lines of a *puruṣavidhaḥ*. Yet the verbs which follow: √*kam*, √*jan* and √*kṛ* very much define the activities of a *puruṣa*, certainly not of the *ātman* in its pure form, if, in fact, it is ever in its pure form.

The next line beginning *tasmād apy etarhy*[25] brings this teaching up until the present day in declaring that without offspring or wealth a man is incomplete (*akṛtsnaḥ*).[26] These expressions occur only in this section of the *Bṛhadāraṇyaka Upaniṣad*. They are significant in juxtaposing the condition/state of the primordial with the condition/desire of a person living in the world where social and cultural expectations come into play, and because they raise the very idea of completeness and incompleteness in respect of the *ātman* and the person. Both are seen to be complete or incomplete in their own way and either of these could be perceptual or ontological, or both at the same time. Here is the text of 1.4.17:

> So even today when one is alone, he wishes, 'May I have a wife, then I can father offspring, may I have wealth, then I can perform rituals.' As long as he does not obtain any one of these[27] he considers himself to be quite incomplete. Here is his completeness: the mind alone is his self (*ātmā*); his speech is his wife; his breath is his offspring; his sight is his human wealth, because through his eye he finds that; hearing is divine wealth, because through his ear he finds that. His self (*ātmā*) is certainly the ritual, because through his self he performs the ritual. He is this fivefold sacrifice, he is this five-fold animal, he is this five-fold man, everything whatever that is five-fold, that all does he gain who knows this.[28]

To summarise, this final section begins with the *ātman* in the form of a person and ends with it consisting of five components, enabling it to function in the world and so providing a completeness it would lack if it consisted only of

[25] Variants also occur in the following passages in the BU: 1.4.1; 1.4.7; 1.4.10; 1.4.17.

[26] *akṛtsno hi saḥ prāṇann eva prāṇo nāma bhavati* |
vadan vāk paśyaṃś cakṣuḥ śṛṇvañ chrotraṃ manvāno manaḥ |
tāny asyaitāni karmanāmāny eva |
sa yo 'ta ekaikam upāste na sa veda |
akṛtsno hy eṣo 'ta ekaikena bhavati |

[27] Olivelle 1998: 51, 'either of these'.

[28] Following Olivelle 1998: 51.

one of these components. Such a seminal passage still does not tell us, or point towards, what the *ātman* might be when no qualification is added to it.

Individuation as the *ātman*'s entry into the world

Each of the passages analysed in the previous section arguably contributes to our understanding of the relationship between *ātman* and the created world. Further illustrative of its entrance into the world as both a knowing and experiencing being are some passages analysed here.

> If (*cet*) a person (*puruṣa*) truly perceives (*vijānīyāt*) the self,
> knowing 'I am he';[29]
> What possibly could he want,
> Whom possibly could he love,
> That he should worry about this body? (BU 4.4.12)[30]

> Who has found, fully understood that the self
> has entered into this dense body,
> He is the maker of everything, because he is the maker of everything,
> He possesses the world, and he certainly is the world. (BU 4.4.13)

Though taken out of context both passages are highly instructive. In the first instance the relationship between the *puruṣa* and the *ātman* is countenanced again, the *puruṣa* being portrayed as different from the *ātman* whilst also being identical with it. *Ātman* as direct object, implied *puruṣa* as subject of the verb, *ayam* as a third person pronoun laying emphasis on the implied *aham* in *asmi*, and *puruṣa* as standing in apposition or contrast with *ātmānam*. That the *puruṣa* declares itself to be 'I am he', seemingly connotes the idea of some kind of bounded entity, at least conceptually speaking, because fundamental emotions are denied. But once the *puruṣa* knows this, does it mean that the *ātman* ceases to be a direct object, such that the *puruṣa* does as well?

Yet, as the next verse (*yasyānuvittaḥ pratibuddha ātmāsmin saṃdehye gahane praviṣṭaḥ*) tells us, this is only part of the question. For also required is an understanding that the *ātman* has entered into the body, the body which is a 'dense jumble', as Olivelle's translation captures it beautifully. Three verbs are used here and each is prefixed. Of these, *anu√vid* implies 'looking behind' and finding, whereas *prati√budh* must designate the 'full understanding' that comes from the 'finding', the self is the object of these verbs, and the remainder from *asmin* onwards is the predicate of the self. I assume the relative pronoun designates the *puruṣa*, because as the agent of the discovery and subsequent

[29] Why not 'this' instead of 'he' for *ayam*?
[30] Olivelle 1998: 123.

understanding of the *ātman* in the world, the provisional distinction between it and *ātman* is maintained. The participle form *praviṣṭa* is also used at 1.4.7 in a precisely similar meaning,[31] and tells us that the *ātman* has entered into the body, which, as *saṃdehya* suggests, is a collocation of components. It does not tell us how it has entered.

But in the final line of 4.4.13 we are told of the consequence of fully understanding this: *sa viśvakṛt sa hi sarvasya kartā tasya lokaḥ sa u loka eva*. Repetition is seemingly used here for emphasis, but I wonder if there is a Vedic ritualistic vestige in the implied reference to a person creating his own world? *Kartā* is used in the middle *Upaniṣads* to designate the person with the ego who believes he/she is a unity and whose psyche blocks him from knowing the *ātman*. In this case, though, the sentence seems to be saying that the *ātman* creates its own world, or has the potential to do so, when the *puruṣa* has recognised that it is the *ātman*, and has entered the world of which it is ontologically not a part.

Yet another passage throws light on the *ātman*'s creative capacity and therefore on its entry into the world in an individualised form:

> As a spider sends forth itself by its thread, and as tiny sparks spring forth from a fire, so indeed do all the vital functions (*prāṇa*), all the worlds, all the gods, and all beings spring from this self (*ātman*). Its hidden name (*upaniṣad*) is 'The real behind the real', for the real consists of the vital functions, and the self (*eṣa*) is the real behind the vital functions.[32] (BU 2.1.20)[33]

Initially, in the first analogy the spider is the subject, acting intentionally though its action may be intransitive, whereas in the second there appears to be no agent, even if it is not a passive construction. Rather the verbs seem also to function intransitively. The correct meaning seems to be that the spider moves upwards/outwards by means of its thread, whereas the sparks just move up, almost as though without motivation. Then the same verb (√*car*) is used to designate how the fundamental components of the world emerge from the *ātman*, almost without motivation. In saying this, is the author attempting to say that the *ātman* in the world enters the world or creates it, without some motivating agency? Secondly, the prefix *vi* comes into play again in the two instances where it is a case of intransitive action, perhaps strengthened by the occurrence of *vi* in *viṣphuliṅgā* ('sparks')? But if this is a case of modification, it seems different from that found in *Bṛhadāraṇyaka Upaniṣad* 1.4 where it applies to verbs associated

31 Cf. also ChU 6.3.2–3.

32 *sa yathorṇavābhis tantunoccared yathā agneḥ kṣudrā viṣphuliṅgā vyuccaranty evam evāsmād ātmanaḥ sarve prāṇāḥ sarve lokāḥ sarve devāḥ sarvāṇi bhūtāni vyuccaranti |*
tasyopaniṣat satyasya satyam iti |
prāṇā vai satyaṃ teṣām eṣa satyam ||

33 Following Olivelle 1998: 63–4.

with cosmology. Thirdly, there is the use of pronouns in conjunction with the word *ātman*: *asmād . . . tasya . . . eṣa*, 'from this', 'of him', 'he', in contrast with the quantifying pronoun *sarve*. This replicates what we find everywhere in the *Upaniṣads*, but it may have no extra significance since *ātman* is a masculine word, and any referent behind the pronoun itself can be difficult to locate, possibly deliberately so.

Beyond this, we can ask what it means to say that the components of the world spring up, because this is not equivalent to *sṛj*, 'to create', as developed in the earlier cosmogony studied? Though identifiable parts of what constitute the worlds emerge from the *ātman*, nothing concrete is said about the *ātman* itself, presumably because it is pure subject rather than object. Even the qualification that it is *satyam* ('real/truth') does not help in elaborating its meaning, as *satyam* is as equally difficult to discern in this chapter as is *ātman* itself.[34]

Archaeological sidelines

Here I shift tack quite dramatically by asking how the material/social conditions of the time might have influenced thinking about *ātman* and *brahman*. If there is a direct continuity within Vedic thought, including the *Upaniṣads*, does this mean the apparent, substantially changing, socio/political/economic conditions after 600 BCE had no impact on the intellectuals who developed these theories and taught them? That is, if there really were substantial changes apart from the emergence of the second wave of urbanism, resting on an increase in agricultural production that had probably been occurring since 1000 BCE. The more and more I read the archaeological material, the more and more I become sceptical of arguments attributing the development of fundamentally innovative philosophical concepts as being responses to sudden shifts in material and cultural conditions. Where such shifts did occur they seemed to be gradual from 1000 BCE onwards, if not earlier. Kenoyer gives an excellent summary of the transitional period from '1300/1000 B.C. to approximately 600/300 B.C.':

> The process of transition can be summarised as follows. First, the Harappan socio-ritual elites had lost their legitimation, and the vast regions that had once been integrated were split into different localised polities. Second, other cultural groups in the Gaṅgā-Yamunā Doab, who had been on the periphery of the Indus Tradition, began to build up regional networks of alliances, probably based on kin related hereditary elites. These elites controlled land and cattle and eventually specific villages became centres of ritual and political power. Some of these villages began

34 Though compare Gren-Eklund 1978: 96, '*satyam* is not only the "real", "the true", but had originally rather to do with "the sum-total", the manifestable as well as the manifest, all that might be an object of man's thought'.

> to control the trade of important resources such as iron and other minerals as well as agricultural produce. Over time we see the emergence of competing towns that become the capitals of new regional polities that are referred to as *janapada*. These *janapadas* were eventually integrated through political, economic and military action under Magadhan, and eventually Mauryan rule.[35]

Most of the archaeological work done over the past three decades which is pertinent to the areas where this summary is relevant simply buttresses what Kenoyer writes without allowing us to put names or faces to the emerging polities and hosts of small villages that provide the agricultural and productive base for these developments. The impression given is one of gradual change in an extended period of slowly increasing production and general prosperity, though with emerging class differences, which would have had implications for the distribution of wealth. Only after about 500 BCE does money seem to begin to play a significant role. Yet it is this kind of extra intellectual framework that is often attributed as the cause of the dramatic expansion in the exploration of ideas about the nature of personhood. Rather than climactic changes in socio-economic conditions, the climactic changes were most marked in the realm of thought.

We have to bear in mind that the people who developed and taught these ideas about ontology were not the poor and the struggling (about whom we know virtually nothing); they were the more materialistically well off. Whilst it is often the case that revolutions begin with the disaffected middle class, why would their concerns have been expressed metaphysically rather than materially? Nor should we think there was no economic or political mobility at this time. We know that a number of the governing kingdoms were neither Brahmin nor Kshatriya. And it may be, as Brian Black implies, that the Brahmins were using speculations around the *ātman* theory to define themselves as a particular class, perhaps different from and/or overlapping with the Vedic *śākhas*.[36] This then would define them as religio-spiritual specialists an important part of whose identification was knowledge of the esoteric nature of the *ātman*, just as previously they had emerged as custodians of the highly scholastic workings of the ritual and the micro-macro cosmic resemblances it evoked. But if this were a mode of ascribed status recognised by others, there is little evidence in the texts to support it. However, the idea that the Brahmins were utilising claims to possession of specialised knowledge is given support in the early Pali texts where

[35] Kenoyer 1995: 234–5. See also Singh 2013: 278; Coningham 1995: 72; Chakrabarti 1999: 260.

[36] Black 2007: 27, 'Taken together, the dialogues tell brahmins how to receive a proper education, achieve fame, attract students, receive patronage, get married, and have male children, thus indicating that achieving selfhood is closely related to achieving the status of a brahmin.'

there occur consistent attacks on the pretentiousness of Brahmins based on their claim to received wisdom.

Concluding speculations

What Richard Seaford wants to ask is why certain conceptions of the person developed, under what conditions and motivated by what.[37] Such questioning involves both psychological and material factors, if not metaphysical ones, though we tend to assume the latter depend substantially on the former. In the Indic context the word *ātman*, the focus of our study, is found in the earliest Sanskrit literature and likely only assumes its later denotation as 'the permanent self' in the early *Upaniṣads*. Does this suggest the likelihood of genetic development given a concept of personhood, even if just a reflexive pronoun was known in pre-Upaniṣadic literature? Does it mean the idea came from outside of the Vedic/Brāhmaṇa intellectual pool, as implied in Bronkhorst's (2007) work?

Even if these questions can be answered in a manner that might be regarded as in any way satisfactory – and they cannot – this still does not tell us why the idea of an *ātman* that is beyond time and space and virtually beyond definition was developed in the first place. Even before probing into this question, it must be acknowledged that the huge body of Buddhist and Jain literature, also speculating heavily on this question, constitutes a kind of intellectual weight that cannot be avoided. It is here that Bronkhorst's work becomes important. Yet it is primarily as a brilliant theory of change that the Buddha's teachings become fundamentally significant at an intellectual level. Change and causality, both important themes in the *Upaniṣads*, dominate early Buddhist psychology and metaphysics. But the *ātman* is beyond change and causality, or so it seems, like any absolute concept found in early Indic thought. Even so, change there is and transformation, not to forget modification, only not for the *ātman* itself.

What would cause serious and well-trained minds – operating in a highly competitive environment – to allocate so much effort to refining a concept of the person that seemingly defies all empirical experience?[38] Maybe it was because unexplained death at a young age was such a prevalent feature of the world from the tenth–fourth centuries BCE, death caused by natural causes and internecine warfare.[39] Would this though have spilled over into sophisticated theories of

[37] Seaford 2004: 12: 'the emergence of multiplicity from unity in cosmology is premonetary (in Hesiodic mythical cosmogony), but the advent of money transforms the unity into a general and increasingly abstract, impersonal (non mythical) unity that continues to underlie apparent multiplicity'. Cf. also pp. 175, 212, 247, 257 and esp. p. 298.

[38] See ChU 8.7.1–8.12.6.

[39] This is highly speculative because we have virtually no empirical evidence on the basis of which we can draw firm conclusions.

change, motivated it is true by the belief in multiple births? Was death such a profound change that it gave rise to Upaniṣadic and Buddhist metaphysics associated both with *loka* and *nirvāṇa*? Certainly the question of overcoming death is thematically central in both Vedic and early Buddhist literature.

In the final analysis the connection between the development of money as concept and practice and the development of metaphysical notions of an abstract unity underlying phenomenal appearances needs to be tested in the ancient Indian context. My inclination is that the answer may be found in the *Mahābhārata* – though considerably later than the oldest *Upaniṣads* – because there money seems not to be often distinguished from more general senses of wealth, and yet the *ātman* theory is accepted as a given. This may reflect its 'warrior' concern for wealth as material goods, cattle and horses, rather than money, but it may also be a sign that the influence of monetised economies on ancient Indian ontologies has already been determined previously, and the transitional period is not reflected in later texts.

5

Cosmology, *psyche* and *ātman* in the *Timaeus*, the *Ṛgveda* and the *Upaniṣads*

Hyun Höchsmann

> I see that I am about to receive a complete and splendid banquet of discourse. (Plato *Timaeus* 27b)

'A feast of reason' – cosmology in the *Timaeus*

Anticipating 'a complete and splendid banquet of discourse', Socrates prompts Timaeus to begin his narration about 'the knowledge of the nature of the universe' after calling upon the gods, 'as custom requires' (27b).[1] To launch the 'discourse about the universe' with the epic convention of the invocation of the gods places Timaeus' description of the origin and the nature of the cosmos in the realm of poetic invention – the realm of *muthos*.[2]

Timaeus explains that we cannot know the cause of the creation of the cosmos with certainty and that his transmission is only a probable story (*eikōs muthos*, 29c–d). Why is the origin of the cosmos difficult to ascertain and the pattern on which it is built unknowable? For Plato it is not because, as Heraclitus remarked, 'nature loves to hide itself' (B123). If Plato contended that he had some privileged way of knowing the origin of the cosmos, he would be enlisted in the ranks

1 I am indebted to Richard Seaford for his insightful comments on this chapter

2 Cornford (1997: 31): 'The *Timaeus* is a poem . . . There are two senses in which the *Timaeus* is a myth or story (*muthos*, cf. Frutiger, *Mythes de Platon*, 173ff.): [in the first place] no account of the material world can ever amount to an exact and self-consistent statement of unchangeable truth. In the second place, the cosmology is cast in the form of a cosmogony, a "story" of events spread out in time. Plato chooses to describe the universe, not by taking it to pieces in an analysis, but by making it grow under our eyes.' Since, as Cornford states, for Plato, 'To find reality you would do better to shut your eyes and think', we might say that Plato makes the universe grow in our *minds*.

of a mystic.[3] But the cosmos Plato envisages is a formidable construct of reason. In *How Philosophers Saved Myths* Luc Brisson elucidates Plato's presentation of Timaeus' discourse as both *eikōs muthos* and *eikōs logos* as follows: 'And this is because the dialogue is a discourse on the constitution of the sensible world, that is the "image" or "copy" of the intelligible world.'[4] As Brisson notes, Plato contrasts (29b3–c3) the true discourse and a credible discourse in terms of their corresponding subjects, the model (*paradeigma*) and its copy (*eikon*). Timaeus' discourse is a description of the physical world of becoming which cannot be known with certainty.

The starting point of Plato's cosmology (27d–28a) is the distinction between *being* ('that which is always real and has no becoming') comprehensible by rational understanding and *becoming* ('that which is becoming and is never real') perceived by the senses. The first question regarding the world ('heaven or the world – let us call it by whatever name which would be adequate for it') is then:

> Has it always been or has it come to be, starting from some beginning? (28b)[5]

Clearly, the world has come to be 'since it can be seen, touched and has a body and all such things are sensible'.

Desiring goodness, beauty and harmony

> Desiring that all things should be good, and, insofar as it is possible, nothing imperfect, the *dēmiourgos* took all that is visible – not at rest, but in discordant and unordered motion – and brought it from disorder to order since he judged that order was in every way better. (30a)

Desiring to make the best universe from a model, *paradeigma*, with the available material in the 'receptacle' of the material, *khōra*, the *dēmiourgos* builds the

[3] Einstein (1954: 262) writes in 'Scientific Truth': 'Certain it is that a conviction, akin to a religious feeling, of the rationality or intelligibility of the world lies behind all scientific work of higher order.' Wittgenstein, in his construction of the logical universe in the *Tractatus Logico-Philosophicus*, which opens with the resounding proclamation, 'Die Welt ist alles, was der Fall ist' (The world is all that is the case), verges on mysticism when it comes to cosmological considerations: 'It is not how things are in the world that is mystical, but that it exists. To view the world *sub specie aeterni* is to view it as a whole – a limited whole. Feeling the world as a limited whole – it is this that is mystical' (1995: 6.44–5).

[4] Brisson 2004b: 28. For further expansion on the topic of *eikōs muthos*, see Brisson and Meyerstein 1995 and Burnyeat 2009. Johansen (2004: 54–5) explains that the description of the sensible world shares the imperfections of the sensible world itself.

[5] Citations from the *Timaeus* are adapted from Cornford 1997. I am grateful to Richard Seaford for his suggestions and corrections regarding the translations.

cosmos as a living being as it is the most beautiful. He makes one unique cosmos and not multiple universes since a part is less complete compared to the whole (31a–b, 33a–d).[6]

The true cause (*aitia*) of the coming to be of the cosmos is the desire of the *dēmiourgos* that all things should be good, 'insofar as it is possible'. This qualification foreshadows another factor operating in the process of ordering the pre-existing material.

> The generation of this world was a result of a mixed combination of necessity (*anangkē*) and reason (*nous*). *Nous* overruled necessity persuading it to guide the greatest part of things that become towards what is best. (48a)

As Brisson and Meyerstein explain, 'A cause, called *anangkē*, perpetually resists the order the demiurge attempts to introduce in the world.'[7] *Anangkē* is an 'errant cause', a recalcitrant and an intractable feature of the *khōra*, within which 'all that is visible' is found. From the contents of the receptacle the *dēmiourgos* separates out four 'kinds', fire, air, water and earth. With triangles as the fundamental units, he constructs regular solids as the figures for the primary elements (53c–55c).

The soul of the universe and the divine part of the individual soul are made by the *dēmiourgos*. The world soul is made from a harmonically proportionate combination of sameness, difference and being (35a–b). The compound of the three constituents is divided in accordance with the interval of a musical scale (*harmonia*).[8] Being endowed with reason and harmony (36e–37a), the world soul is a formal ordering principle of the constituents and the interconnected elements of the universe. The *dēmiourgos* makes the immortal part of the individual souls from the remaining material of the world soul 'in somewhat the same way, but less pure'. The mortal parts of individual souls, made by the gods (created by the *dēmiourgos*) are prone to erratic and discordant motions (41d–42d). The conception of the *psyche* in the *Timaeus* as comprising the immortal part (reason) and the mortal parts (appetitive and spirited) consolidates the tripartite view of the soul in the *Phaedrus*, *Republic* and the *Laws*.[9]

The rational part of the individual soul must govern the two subordinate

6 Seaford (2004: 247–8) accentuates the self-sufficiency of the cosmos in 'needing no other' and being 'a sufficient acquaintance and friend for itself' (*Tim.* 33d).

7 Brisson and Meyerstein (1995: 23) point out that *anangkē* is usually translated as 'necessity' ('constraint regarded as law prevailing through the material universe'), but this is different from the way in which *anangkē* operates in the *Timaeus*.

8 See Cornford (1997: 60–7) on being, sameness and difference in the creation of the world soul.

9 Robinson (1990: 105) compares the three parts of the soul in the *Timaeus* to reason, spirit and appetite in the *Republic* (439a–441d).

parts of appetite and spirit and the body as the world soul governs the cosmos. But if the world soul and the individual soul are not isomorphic, how can the individual soul emulate the order-creating activity of the world soul? The congruence between the world soul and the individual soul is not structural since the world soul has pure reason whereas the individual soul is a tripartite composite of reason, spirit and appetite.[10] But there is a functional congruence: the order-sustaining functions are the same in the world soul and in the individual souls (90c–d). The world soul creates and sustains order within the cosmos, the individual soul, by studying the harmonious order of the world soul, strives to manifest order within itself.[11]

Cosmogony, *ātman* and *brahman* in the *Ṛgveda* and the *Upaniṣads*

> Then, in the beginning, from thought there evolved desire, which existed as the primal seed. (RV 10.129.4)[12]

The universe comes into being as an activity of desire. Among the various cosmogonic poems in the *Ṛgveda* and the *Upaniṣads* there is a common premise: all things have originated from one primal cause. In one cosmogonic poem the creation of the universe takes place through the sacrificial division of the body of a primeval progenitor (*puruṣa*): the sun from the eye, the moon from the mind, wind from the breath, sky from the head and earth from the feet (RV 10.90).

The coming to be of the universe in the *Ṛgveda* and the *Upaniṣads* could be characterised as 'spontaneous order' (self-organisation) in contrast to the mathematical order in the *Timaeus* where the cosmos as a living organism comes to be not as the result of matter's internal self-organisation but by rational order established from an external cause. However, similar to the conception of the universe as a work of a craftsman in the *Timaeus* the universe is compared to a work of a sculptor, a smith or a carpenter in the *Ṛgveda* (10.81). In the *Ṛgveda*

[10] Cornford argues that there is 'an irrational element in the World-Soul' (1997: 176, 209–10): The body of the world 'contains motions and active powers which are not instituted by the divine Reason and are perpetually producing undesirable results. Since all physical motion has its ultimate source in a living soul, these bodily motions and powers can be attributed to an irrational element in the World-Soul.' Notwithstanding Cornford's comprehensive and penetrating analysis of the *Timaeus*, the obduracy of necessity in disorderly motion does not entail imputing an irrational element in the world soul. As Cornford emphasises, since disorderly motion, chaos, has existed prior to the creation of the world soul and reason can mitigate 'discordant and unordered motion', by persuading necessity in 'the greatest part of things that become towards what is best', persistence of disorder does not provide the ground for the belief that the world soul is afflicted with an irrational component.

[11] Cornford 1997: 354.

[12] Translations of the *Ṛgveda* are adapted from Jamison and Brereton 2014.

(10.72) the gods are not at the very beginning but come into being subsequently as in the *Timaeus*. The genealogies and prodigious deeds of various gods (Agni, the fire god, Indra, the highest god, Varuna, the sky god, gods of the storm, and other major gods) are celebrated with elaboration of ritual and sacrifice throughout the *Ṛgveda* (1.26, 1.85, 1.92, 2.12, 4.18, 5.85). There is a closer interaction between the gods and the mortals than in the *Timaeus* as the gods are recipients of offerings and sacrifices, dispensers of alleviation of calamities, and averters of disasters who can be placated with entreaties.

In a notable later poem in the *Ṛgveda* all pervious perspectives on cosmogony are abruptly called into question, bringing the uncertainty of knowledge regarding the origin of the cosmos into the forefront:

> Who really knows? Who shall here proclaim it? – from where was it born, from where this creation?
> The gods are on this side of the creation of this (world). So then who does know from where it came to be?
> This creation – from where it came to be, if it was produced or if not –
> he who is the overseer of this (world) in the furthest heaven, he surely knows. Or if he does not know . . . ? (RV 10.129.6–7)

The uncertainty of the knowledge of the origin of the cosmos persists even with recourse to the higher authority of the gods, since what is sought is the primal cause before the gods came into existence. Inviting conjectures and disputations (perhaps not excluding the possibility of a plurality of universes), the correspondence with the emphasis in the *Timaeus* that all investigations in cosmology are provisional is significant: cosmogonic theses are speculative and incomplete as cosmology is not a closed system. With a direct reference to the poets (sages, *kavi*) who sought the connection between 'the existent' and the 'non-existent', enquiry into the beginning of the universe is an open-ended investigation in the realm of poetic insight. When regarded as a collection of cosmogonic verses, *Ṛgveda* is also in the realm of *muthos*. While Timaeus' discourse aims at alleviating the uncertainty in presenting itself as an approximation meriting confidence, the persistent questions, 'Who? When? Where?' in the *Ṛgveda* ignite a debate regarding the origin of the universe.

Continuing the enquiry into the origin of the universe, the *Upaniṣads* invoke Prajāpati, 'Lord of Creatures' (BU 3.9.6). Desiring expansion, Prajāpati begins to generate a variety of living beings from self-division. Again, desire is the cause of partition from the initial unity (*Prasna Upaniṣad* 1.4). This primeval desire as an impetus for the creation of the universe is distinct from the desire of the *dēmiourgos*, 'that all things should be good'. In the *Upaniṣads* it is not the desire for goodness which provides the motivation for the creation of the universe but a morally non-committal impulse for expansion. In the beginning *ātman* in the shape of *puruṣa* (person) desired a companion and divided himself into two (BU 1.4.1–3). Proceeding from this initial division the world and the deities arise out of *puruṣa* (*Aitareya Upaniṣad*, 1–2). The origin of the universe is not chaos but singularity. The universe comes into being from a process of separation and multiplication from simplicity to complexity and from division of one substance into the manifold of phenomena. Given this conception of the unity of the origin of all things in the universe, the central thesis of the *Upaniṣads* that the essential self (*ātman*) of each individual entity is identical with or incorporated within the totality of all that exists (*brahman*) can be regarded as a corollary (ChU 3.14.1–4; BU 2.5.19).

The earliest mention of *ātman* is in the *Ṛgveda* (1.115.1; 1.162.20; 10.16.3; 10.33.9).[13] Similar to the concept of *psyche* before Plato, *ātman* has a range of meanings.[14] *Ātman* is variously interpreted as breath, soul, essence, or the *true* self which underlies all change. 'Breath' in the wider sense includes breathing, thinking, speaking, seeing and hearing and is frequently equated with the life of the individual self (BU 1.5 21).[15] One pervasive meaning of *ātman* is 'the ultimate essence of a human being'.[16] *Ātman* is the common essence of all entities underlying the multitude of diverse manifestations.[17]

> As from the flames of fire, sparks fly out in every direction, so from this self (*ātman*) the vital functions (*prāṇa*) fly out to their separate places, and from the vital functions, the gods, and from the gods, the worlds. (KauU 4.19)[18]

Brahman also has a range of meanings as an epistemological and a metaphysical concept, including 'a formulation of truth' or 'ultimate and basic essence of the cosmos'.[19] In the *Upaniṣads*, two divergent perspectives on *ātman* and *brahman* are presented: some texts emphasise that *brahman* is identical with *ātman* while others consider that *ātman* is a part of *brahman*.[20] What is the identity or the constitutive relation which holds between *ātman* and *brahman*? Like rivers flowing in different directions which merge into the ocean and become one, individual souls are part of the ocean of one universal soul (ChU 6.10.1). *Brahman* is *ātman* when embodied within a particular individual entity.

13 Deussen 1906: 86.
14 For expositions of *psyche* prior to Plato see Snell (1946).
15 Olivelle 2008: l. The significance of *ātman* as breath can be compared to *psyche* in Homer as vital breath.
16 Olivelle 2008: lv.
17 Raju 1985: 26.
18 Translations of the *Upaniṣads* are adapted from Olivelle 2008.
19 Olivelle 2008: lvi.
20 Deussen 1966: 86–111, 182–212.

> That from which these beings are born; on which, once born, they live; and into which they pass upon death – seek to perceive that. That is *brahman*! (TU, 3.1)

When *ātman* (or *brahman* or *puruṣa*) enters into material bodies, the constituents of individual bodies are separated parts of universal elements within the individual embodiment.

> Tell me – when a man has died, his speech merges into fire, his breath into air, his sight into the sun, his mind into the moon . . . his material body into the earth, his self (*ātman*) into space, the hairs of his body into plants, the hair of his head into trees and his blood into water – what then happens to that person? (BU 3. 2.13)[21]

Both the identification and the incorporation of *ātman* within *brahman* aim at a comprehensive and fundamental principle underlying the multitude of phenomena.[22] When it is identified with *ātman*, *brahman* comprises the aggregate of all individual *ātman* and is coextensive with the totality of all that exists:

> *Ātman* is indeed *brahman*. It is also identified with the intellect, the mind and the vital breath, with the eyes and ears, with earth, water, air and sky, with fire and with what is other than fire, with desire and the absence of desire, with anger and the absence of anger, with the righteous and the unrighteous; this self that is made of everything. (BU 4.4.5)[23]

When the various applications of the concept of *ātman* are assembled, it can be understood as the synthetic unity of the functions of reason, intellect and sense perception.

There are significant differences between the world soul and individual soul on the one hand, and *ātman* and *brahman* on the other. *Ātman* and *brahman* are not *created*, as the world soul and the individual souls are in the *Timaeus*. To the extent that the individual souls in the *Timaeus* are neither identical with the totality of the constituents of the universe nor merge into the world soul, *brahman* is not analogous to the world soul. Even if the three parts of the soul in the *Timaeus* could be understood as forming a unity, this is distinct from *ātman* merging into

21 This is similar to the myth of creation of the primordial Titan, *Pan Gu*, in China, whose body is transformed to the sun, the moon, the earth and the ocean.

22 Olivelle 2008: lv. Brereton (1990: 118) observes that: 'Upanishadic teaching creates an integrative vision, a view of the whole which draws together the separate elements of the world and of human experience and compresses them into a single form. To one who has this larger vision of things, the world . . . forms a totality with a distinct shape and character.'

23 Yeats (1975: 9) encapsulates the main thought of the *Upaniṣads* as follows: to 'postulate an individual self possessed of such power and knowledge [and] to identify it with the Self without limitation and sorrow, containing and contained by all . . .'.

brahman.[24] However, *brahman* can be characterised as the soul of the universe, as that which animates the universe.

There are further differences between the *Timaeus* and the *Upaniṣads* regarding the goodness of the world. From readily observable phenomena questions arise concerning the goodness and the order in the universe emphasised in the *Timaeus*: What of the rampant and seemingly random evil in the world? More frequently not *nous* but 'the errant cause' seems to hold sway. One possible view of the problem of evil is developed in the *Upaniṣads*: the world is a battlefield of the demonic and the divine.[25]

> There were two kinds of descendants of *Prajāpati*, the *devas* (gods) and the *asuras* (demons). The *devas* were the younger, the *asuras* were the elder, and they contended for the world. (BU 1.3.1)

The divine, the demonic and the mortal all originate from one primordial being:

> The descendants of *Prajāpati* are of three kinds, the *devas*, men and the *asuras* who lived as disciples with their father, *Prajāpati*. (BU 5.2.1)

Prajāpati teaches the same to all:

> *Prajāpati* said 'We must seek and aspire to know the self which is free from evil, old age, death and sorrow, from hunger and thirst, and which desires and envisages what it ought to desire and envisage. One who has sought and understands the self attains all worlds and all desires.'
>
> The *devas* and *asuras* both heard these words and said, 'Well then, we will search for the self (*ātman*) by which one attains all worlds and all desires.' (ChU 8.7.1–2)

The life and death struggle between the divine and the demonic for the possession of the world and attainment of all desires ends with the victory of the gods.

> So long as Indra did not understand the self, the *asuras* (demons) conquered him. When he understood it he conquered the *asuras*, obtaining pre-eminence among all gods, supremacy and sovereignty over all beings. (KauU 4.20)

In the Vedas and the *Upaniṣads* there is no explicit argument for the continued existence of the created world as in the *Timaeus*, but from the eternity of *brahman* the same implication might be drawn. The identification or incorporation of *ātman* with *brahman* as the totality of all that exists would entail the existence of one universe as in the *Timaeus*. However, in the absence of the goodness of the

24 According to Guthrie, 'the three parts of the soul, when they reach the divine level, are not merely in harmony but merge into one, namely *nous*' (1962: 4:425).

25 In the *Mahābhārata* one hundred demonic sons are born from the beautiful Gandhari and resort to treachery to overthrow the Pandavas, the five sons of gods.

dēmiourgos which ensures the continuation of the universe (*Tim.* 41a–b), in the *Upaniṣads* the oceans, the heaven, the constellations and the abodes of the gods are ephemeral and immersed in the perennial cycle of destruction and creation:

> All this is perishable . . . The great oceans dry up; the mountains fall; the pole-star strays; the wind ropes (holding the stars) are cut; the earth is submerged; the gods depart from their place –
>
> In such a world of *samsara* (wandering back and forth) what good is it pursuing the enjoyment of pleasures . . . (MaiU 1.4)[26]

The answer to this question is self-knowledge.

Self-knowledge and the knowledge of the universe

The moral and epistemological significance of self-knowledge or self-realisation is pervasive in the *Upaniṣads*. The most fundamental thesis of the *Upaniṣads* is that the true self, *ātman* or *puruṣa* (person) is the same as the self of the universe, *brahman* (*Isa Upaniṣad*, 6–7; BU 2.5.19).[27] Self-knowledge consists in recognising that the true self, *ātman*, is identical with the totality of reality, *brahman*, and culminates in 'bliss'.[28]

> In the beginning this world was only *brahman*; therefore it knew even that the *ātman* is *brahman*, therefore it became all. It is the same with the sages, the same with men. Whoever knows the self as 'I am *brahman*', becomes this entire universe. Even the gods cannot prevail against him, for he becomes their *ātman*. Now, if a man worships another god, thinking: 'He is one and I am another', he does not know. (BU 1.4.10)

Cosmology is the prerequisite for self-knowledge and ethics in the *Timaeus* and the *Upaniṣads*. The knowledge of *psyche* and *ātman* is inseparable from the knowledge of the totality of existence and imbued with moral significance. The knowledge of the true self within the framework of cosmology is metaphysical in the *Timaeus* in so far as the *dēmiourgos*, the eternal model of the universe and the forms are concerned. But it is also empirical, since the activity of *psyche* takes place neither in solipsistic introspection nor is derived from *a priori* principles but in relation to the order and harmony of the planetary movements corresponding to the laws of musical harmony. The activity of *ātman* encompasses all that is encountered in existence.

The precedence of the soul over the body in Plato and the priority of the

26 Translations of the *Maitrāyaṇīya Upaniṣad* are adapted from Roebuck 2014. Olivelle 2008 does not include the *Maitrāyaṇīya*.

27 Olivelle 2011.

28 Raju 1985: 35–6.

spiritual over the transient material world in the Vedic tradition arise from the conception of what constitutes a moral life.[29] As in the *Timaeus* the real or true self is not the body, but the soul.[30] Socrates' exhortation in the *Timaeus* for all to attend to the divine part within, and his impassioned exhortation for tending to the good of the soul in the *Alcibiades* and in the *Gorgias*, are analogous with the admonition of the attachment to delusions of desire in the *Upaniṣads*.

> Carried along by the waves of the qualities, unsound, inconstant, disconnected, full of desires, wavering, he falls into believing, 'I am he, this is mine'; he binds himself with himself, as a bird with a net . . . (MaiU 3. 2)

Self-knowledge, the knowledge of the *ātman* as *brahman*, raises human beings to the level of the gods.

> Whoever knows 'I am *brahman*' becomes the self, *ātman*, of all, including the gods. (BU 1. 4.10)

In the *Upaniṣads* full equivalence between divine and human reality is affirmed by knowledge of the true self as *brahman*. In the *Timaeus* there is at most a parallelism between the divine and the human existence. Even when a soul attains goodness through reason and the result is *eudaimonia*, it is only an approximation to the divine.[31] As Pindar observed:

> Creature of a day – What is he?
> What is he not?
> Such is man – a shadow in a dream.
> The delight of mortals grows in a short time, and then it falls to the ground, shaken by an adverse thought.
> But when the brilliance given by Zeus comes, a shining light is on man, and a gentle lifetime. (Pindar *Pythian Ode* 8)

The chariot of the soul[32]

> Let us liken the soul to a pair of winged horses and a driver. The horses and drivers of the gods are noble and good but those of other beings are mixed . . . the charioteer

29 Plato emphasises the priority of the soul also at *Phaedo* 79dff., *Phaedrus* 245dff. and *Laws* 896c ('the soul is anterior to the body'). In the *Laws* the soul is the most divine and 'most his own self' (726a) which governs all things (896dff.). See also Bostock 1986.

30 For early developments of the view that the self is soul in Hesiod, Pindar, Pythagoras, Heraclitus and Empedocles, and that it may survive death, see Long 2015.

31 As reason is the divine element in man, in the activity of reason we can ascend to the level of the gods, 'becoming like a god (*homoiosis theoi*) insofar as it is possible' for a mortal (*Theatetus* 176a–b).

32 See also Magnone, Forte and Smith, and Schlieter in this volume.

> drives a pair: one of the horses is noble and good but the other is of opposite breed and character. So in our case the driving is of necessity troublesome and difficult . . . The soul looks after all that is inanimate . . . When it is perfect and fully winged it rises up and governs the whole world. But a soul which has lost its wing carries on only until it gets hold of something solid and then settles down taking on an earthly body . . . The whole now, soul and body fused, is called a living being with the epithet 'mortal'. (*Phdr.* 246a–c)[33]

In the chariot metaphor of the *Phaedrus* the soul is not a static substance but an activity, a dynamic process of its constituents. *Psyche* and *ātman* are likened to a chariot both in Plato and in the *Upaniṣads*, signifying the conflicting forces within the soul, which need to be harmonised. In the *Timaeus*, before the souls are placed in the bodies, the *dēmiourgos* placed each in a star, 'mounting them as it were in chariots' (41d–e).

The star-chariot of the soul in *Timaeus*, the chariot of the soul in the *Phaedrus* and the *Kaṭha Upaniṣad* illuminate the composite nature of *psyche* and *ātman* and the unity and harmony in the soul as the goals of moral autonomy and freedom.

> Know the self as riding in a chariot, and the body as the chariot. Know the intellect as the charioteer, and the mind as the reins. The senses, they call the horses, and the objects of the sense are the paths . . . [When] the self is unified with body, senses and mind, the wise call him the 'enjoyer'. (KaU 3.3–3.5)

The emphasis on the intellect and its function has some points of similarity to reason represented by the charioteer in the *Phaedrus*: only when the intellect is the driver can the soul attain true understanding of itself as *brahman* (KaU 3.6–9).

Immortality, divinity, *eudaimonia* and *dharma*

> There is one race of men, one race of gods; and from a single mother we both draw our breath.
> But all allotted power divides us: man is nothing, but for the gods the bronze sky endures as a secure home forever.
> Nevertheless, we bear some resemblance to the immortals, either in greatness of mind or in nature, although we do not know, by day or by night, towards what goal fortune has written that we should run. (Pindar *Nemean Ode* 6)

Pindar's view of man as having 'some resemblance to the immortals, either in greatness of mind or in nature', is further developed in the *Timaeus* as the gulf

33 The tripartite structure of the soul is further developed in the *Republic* (435c, 550b, 580d–581e): the 'rational' (*logistikon*), the 'irrational' or appetitive (*alogiston* or *epithumetikon*) and the 'spirited' (*thumoeides*).

between the gods and mortals is bridged, in so far as this is possible, by the activity of the soul.

> If a man perseveres in pursuing learning and wisdom he will certainly be led to immortal and divine thoughts reaching truth and will attain immortality to the full extent it is possible for human nature. (90b–c)

Plato concludes the *Timaeus* with a resounding affirmation of the possibility for achieving *eudaimonia* (happiness) for all those who strive to attend to the divine part of the soul.[34] Plato's conception of the divine is not that of the soothsayers or inspired poets but firmly grounded in the soul's activity towards beauty and goodness and the study of the natural phenomena, 'the thoughts and revolutions of the whole world'. The alignment of the activity of the *psyche* with the planetary movements revitalises its original state.

> The motions that have an affinity to the divine part in us are the thoughts and revolutions of the universe. These, therefore, are the ones that every one of us should follow. We should redirect the revolutions in our head that were thrown off course at the time of our birth by coming to learn the harmonies and the revolutions of the universe, and bring the intelligent part, in accordance with its original nature, into alignment with the objects of the intellect. We shall then attain the fulfillment of the best life set by the gods before mankind for the present and for the time to come. (90c–d)

The divine part in us is that which is conducive to the flourishing of the individual in unison with the order, goodness and beauty of the universe.[35]

The individual soul is urged to aspire towards goodness by studying the order and harmony of the cosmos.[36] The soul contemplates the harmony of the spheres, not turning inward but outward to the universe. In the contemplation of the beauty of the universe the soul reflects the goodness of the universe, linking the cosmological and the ethical. But it would seem that the goodness of the *dēmiourgos* and the universe is not moral but aesthetic goodness and beauty arising from the transformation of disorder (chaos or undifferentiated matter) to

[34] The soul is divine and immortal and ascends to abide with the gods when it is freed from bodily constraints (*Phd.* 80e–81a).

[35] Einstein reinvigorates Plato's insight on the interconnectedness of the individual and the universe: 'A human being is a part of the whole, called by us "the universe", a part limited in time and space. He experiences himself, his thoughts and feelings, as something separate from the rest – a kind of optical delusion of his consciousness. This delusion is a kind of prison for us restricting us to our personal decisions and to affection for a few persons nearest to us. Our task must be to free ourselves by widening our circle of compassion to embrace all living creatures and the whole of nature in its beauty' (Calaprice 2005: 206).

[36] As Robinson (1990: 105) has pointed out, the goodness of order is emphasised in the *Gorgias* (503–504d). Also in the *Republic* by creating order and harmony within, the soul attains virtue (431d–e, 442c–d, 443c–444a).

order. However, to the extent that moral goodness can be conceived as the order and harmony of the internal organisation of living beings which enables them to flourish together, it could be brought about by the contemplation of the order and harmony of planetary movements.

The goodness of the *dēmiourgos*, cosmos and the world soul are *a priori* and axiomatic. The *dēmiourgos* is good; the cosmos, being the work of a divine craftsman, is good; and the world soul and the divine part of individual souls, also the work of the *dēmiourgos*, are, therefore, good. The goodness of the individual soul is *a posteriori* and can only be achieved through continuous striving after the pattern of ordered harmony exemplified in the planetary movements.

By achieving immortality and attending to the divine element Plato means the continuous search for knowledge and truth. In the *Timaeus*, a just soul returns to its star, while an unjust soul is reincarnated (42a–d.). Being divine and immortal, the rational part of the soul ascends to its star. Only *nous* is free from the cycle of rebirth (42a–d); the appetitive and spirited parts are mortal.[37] The activity and the resulting condition of the soul determine the body it will occupy in rebirth: a well-ordered soul will be lodged in a higher form of life, the disordered in a lower form. The central place of the transmigration of the soul in Plato's ethics is elucidated by Luc Brisson in 'Myths in Plato's Ethics': Myths have 'a fundamental and permanent' importance in revealing 'the emergence of a tendency to orient ethics towards physics . . . by resituating man within his place on the scale of all living things'.[38]

The cosmogonic processes in *Ṛgveda* and the *Upaniṣads* seem morally and aesthetically neutral: the world is not described as good or beautiful. Unlike in the *Timaeus*, there is no motivation of the maker of the world to create a cosmos bestowing on it beauty and goodness; there is no eternal model, a paradigm of supreme goodness. However, an ethical conception of the cosmic order is emphasised in the *Ṛgveda*, the *Upaniṣads* and in subsequent Indian cosmologies.[39] While the anthropomorphic conceptions of the process of creation in the *Ṛgveda* and the *Upaniṣads* are distinct from the mathematical structures and the ordered harmony of the cosmology in the *Timaeus*, both regard the universe as a hierarchically organised and interrelated system in which order prevails. The concept of *ṛtá* (order, truth, cosmic order or course of nature) in the *Ṛgveda* can be compared to the concept of order in the *Timaeus*. Upheld by the gods, Varuna and Mitra (RV 1.2.8; 4.5.4–9), *ṛtá* is pervasive. Agni, the god of fire, is

[37] The customary view that only *nous* is free of the cycle of rebirth (for instance Guthrie 1971: 2:223–4) has been contested by Robinson 1990.

[38] Brisson 2004a: 63.

[39] Olivelle 2008: xlvii. 'The ethicization of cosmic order evident in the *Upaniṣads* remains a constant feature of later Indian cosmologies.'

'the guardian of *ṛtá*' (RV 1.1.8; 1.77.5). Usias, the Dawn, does not depart from *ṛtá* (RV 1.123.9). It might seem that *ṛtá* is similar to *anangkē*, necessity, in the *Timaeus* because of its inexorability. But unlike necessity, *ṛtá* has a moral function in sustaining world order. Cosmic and moral order are not inherent features of the universe in the Vedic and the Upaniṣadic texts as they are in the *Timaeus* but are maintained by gods.

> (Indra) lead us along the path of truth (*ṛtá*), across all difficult passages. (RV 10.133.6)

Ṛtá is the truth and cosmic principle which ensures the functioning of the universe. Conceived as the laws that sustain the continuity of the universe, *ṛtá* is aligned with the moral laws governing the realm of actions and develops into the concept of *dharma* (duty, justice, right action).[40] *Dharma* is both cosmological and ethical: it is that which sustains the world order and upholds justice, right action and duty.

Actions in accordance with *dharma* (in the sense of sacrifice, charity, study, asceticism) lead to 'the realm of the blessed', but only the knowledge of *brahman* leads to immortality.

> The one who abides in *brahman* achieves immortality. (ChU 2.23.1)

As in the *Timaeus*, immortality must be achieved by attending to the divine dimension. When the universe is divided into human beings, ancestors and gods, those who follow the world of the ancestors will return to be reborn in this world, while those who follow the world of gods will become immortal (BU 1.5.16; 6.2). This is partly analogous to the hierarchy of the gods and mortals in the *Timaeus* and the prospect of mortals becoming like gods, in so far as it is possible for mortals.

Paralleling the rebirth of discordant souls in the *Timaeus* (42b–c), the cycle of rebirth is also recurrent in the Vedic and the Upaniṣadic texts. The moral laws governing rebirth are the same for *psyche* and *ātman*: those who perform good actions are reborn in good circumstances and those who perform bad actions, into the opposite (ChU 5.10.7).

> As a man acts, as he behaves, so he becomes. A man of good actions will become good, a man of bad actions, bad. He becomes pure through pure actions, bad by bad actions. (BU 4.4.5)

'Thinking thoughts immortal and divine' and endeavouring 'to attain immortality in the fullest extent which human nature is capable of' (*Tim.* 90c), the soul moves upwards (ChU 8.6.6):

40 For the evolution of the concepts of *rita* and *dharma*, see Horsch 1967, Hacker 1965, and Jurewicz and Chaturvedi in this volume.

There is this verse:

'There are a hundred and one arteries of the heart.
One of them penetrates the summit of the head.
Moving upwards by it, a man reaches immortality.
The others lead to departing in different directions –
In different directions'

Epilogue: Convergent and divergent evolutions of ideas from the *Timaeus*, *Ṛgveda* and the *Upaniṣads* to the cosmology of the present

> We still do not know one thousandth of one percent of what nature has revealed to us.
> Whoever undertakes to set himself up as a judge of truth and knowledge is shipwrecked by the laughter of the gods.[41]

These remarks regarding the difficulty of knowing the nature of the universe have come down to us not from Greek or Indian philosophy but from Einstein. They echo the perspective of cosmology as an open-ended enquiry in the *Timaeus* and in the *Ṛgveda*. The metaphysical foundations as well as the mathematical and empirical aspects of Platonic, Vedic and Upaniṣadic cosmology have been compared to current research in cosmology.[42] The comparisons with science tend

[41] Einstein 1954: 28.

[42] In the later texts of *Purana*, the cycles of destruction and rebirth are attributed to the universe. This aspect of cosmology in Indian thought has been compared to the current views of cosmology by Carl Sagan (1980) and Firtjof Capra (1975). 'Hindu religion is the only one of the world's great faiths dedicated to the idea that the Cosmos itself undergoes an immense, indeed an infinite, number of deaths and rebirths. It is the only religion in which the time scales correspond, to those of modern scientific cosmology. Its cycles run from our ordinary day and night to a day and night of Brahmā, 8.64 billion years long. Longer than the age of the Earth or the Sun and about half the time since the Big Bang. And there are much longer time scales still' (Sagan 1980: 213–14). In 'Worlds on worlds are rolling ever', Shelley describes the cycle of creation and immortality:

Worlds on worlds are rolling ever
From creation to decay,
Like the bubbles on a river
Sparkling, bursting, borne away.
But they are still immortal
Who, through birth's orient portal
And death's dark chasm hurrying to and fro,
Clothe their unceasing flight
In the brief dust and light
Gathered around their chariots as they go;
New shapes they still may weave . . .

to emphasise either the *a priori* and metaphysical aspects of current cosmology or the mathematical and empirical aspects of Platonic, Vedic and Upaniṣadic cosmology. Beginning with Heisenberg, the parallels between particle physics, chemistry, cosmology and Plato's ideas regarding the origin of the universe continue to stimulate discussion.[43]

The philosophical impulse to seek unity among multiplicity permeating the account of the creation of the universe in the *Ṛgveda*, the *Upaniṣads* and the *Timaeus* continues to resonate in the present. Tracing the convergence and the divergence in the evolution of the concepts of cosmos, *psyche* and *ātman* aims at a reciprocal enhancement of our understanding of the continuing exploration of the nature of the cosmos and the soul which animate the universe. The conceptions of the universe and of the nature of soul in *Timaeus*, *Ṛgveda* and the *Upaniṣads* converge and overlap but do not coincide.

The ethics of *Timaeus* and the *Upaniṣads* have a thematic and discursive correspondence, laying the foundations for moral realism, the view that moral values, principles and actions have objective validity beyond individual preferences, cultural norms, conventions or social institutions. The knowledge of *ātman* and *psyche* prepares the ground for moral universalism and the autonomy and responsibility of the individual. Subjectivism and relativism are regarded as partial perspectives of the whole. Interpretive analyses of *ātman* and *psyche* as the constant and enduring self throughout persistent change can enhance our understanding of personal identity and continuity of consciousness.[44]

43 Heisenberg 1974. See also Brisson and Meyerstein 1995: 40–1. Machleidt (2005) explains that, as Heisenberg recognised, the ideas of modern particle physics which regard geometric symmetries as generating the particles from a few elementary components are close to Plato's views. Lloyd (2007) has emphasised the significance of *Timaeus* in symmetry analysis in inorganic and physical chemistry. Plato's questions in the *Timaeus* are still being asked in contemporary cosmology: whether the universe had a beginning and whether it has an external cause or is self-generated (Carroll 2010); whether the universe exists in time and why the universe exists (Leggett 2010).

44 'Whatever the date, those forest Sages began everything; no fundamental problem of philosophy, nothing that has disturbed the schools to controversy escaped their notice' (Yeats 1975: 11).

6

Plato and yoga

John Bussanich

Plato and South Asian yogic traditions espouse various soteriological goals – divinisation, *nirvāṇa*, the identity of *ātman* and *brahman*, and yogic aloneness (*kaivalya*) – but their prescribed methods for attaining them present striking similarities. In addition to right living and right beliefs, meditation and contemplation are valorised as essential means for the deconstruction of the empirical person. While the importance ascribed to such practices is widely recognised in South Asia, the prominent intellectualism of the Platonic dialogues and of Plato scholars has obscured the existential centrality of the practice of inwardness and tranquillity for philosophers who aspire to 'become as like god as possible' (*Theaet.* 176b1–2).[1] The goal of this chapter is to highlight this dimension of the Platonic way of life by demonstrating affinities with South Asian meditative praxis.

Platonists and Indian yogins embrace a way of life that integrates cognitive and affective aspects of human nature on a path that eliminates ignorance and suffering through the purification and simplification of consciousness. In Pierre Hadot's formulation, Greek thinkers practised the art of living as

> a concrete attitude and determinate life-style, which engages the whole of existence. The philosophical act is not situated merely on the cognitive level, but on that of the self and of being. It is a progress which causes us to *be* more fully, and makes us better. It is a conversion which turns our entire life upside down, changing the life of the person who goes through it. It raises the individual from an inauthentic condition of life, darkened by unconsciousness and harassed by worry, to an authentic state of life, in which he attains self-consciousness, an exact vision of the world, inner peace and freedom.[2]

[1] Annas (1999) and Sedley (2000) provide valuable accounts of divinisation, but ignore the practices that contribute to attaining godlikeness.

[2] Hadot 1995: 82–3.

I shall begin with the general principles that underlie Indian yogic practices.

- The highest knowledge cannot be conveyed via the written word, but rather must be transmitted orally, or even in silence, from teacher to pupil in conjunction with the practice of meditation.
- Psychology is equivalent to cosmology: the hierarchy of states of consciousness parallels precisely the basic structure of the cosmos.
- Attainment of progressively higher states of consciousness depends on two types of meditative practice: one that quietens the mind and calms the passions and one that inculcates wisdom through direct experiential knowledge of transcendent truths.
- Meditation helps to deconstruct the empirical personality, removing external accretions and attachments in order to reveal a pure underlying self or undifferentiated reality.
- Enlightenment entails liberation from the cycle of births and deaths.

Commitment to these principles grounds the theory and practice of meditation in the early and middle *Upaniṣads*, the early Buddhist canonical literature, in the *Mahābhārata*, and in the *Yoga Sūtra* (third–fourth centuries CE). The latter neatly schematises Brahminical thought in its well-known formulation of 'eight-limbed yoga' (*aṣṭāṅga*). 'The eight limbs are abstentions, observances, posture, breath control, disengagement of the senses, concentration, meditation, and absorption' (*yama-niyama-āsana-prāṇāyāma-pratyāhāra-dhāraṇā-dhyāna-samādhayo 'ṣṭāv aṅgāni*. YS 2.29).[3]

In both Hindu and Buddhist yogic traditions, aspirants begin with cultivation of the virtues, right living, and the acceptance of right views guided by faith in truths transmitted in scriptures or in authoritative traditions. Faith (Sanskrit *śraddhā*, Pali *saddhā*) in the Buddha's *dharma* and in the community (*saṇga*) and Vedantic reliance on 'great sayings' (*mahāvākyas*) like 'you are that' and '*ātman* is *brahman*' provide starting-points for reflection and forging a way of life. In Śāntideva's concise formulation: 'One who wishes to bring closure to pain, and to arrive at happiness' end, must plant firm faith as the root, and fasten the mind to enlightenment.'[4] *Śraddhā* is a multi-faceted virtue that comprises beliefs about the human condition as taught by the Buddha and confidence in the spiritual benefits to be achieved by practising the *dharma*.

Progress in right living through abstentions and observances is a precondition for mastering the subsequent limbs of yoga. Similarly, in the *Upaniṣads* one begins with ethical behaviour and quieting the mind. Vedic students are enjoined to practice asceticism (*tapas*), self-control (*dama*) and tranquillity

[3] Translations from the *Yoga Sūtras* are from Bryant 2009.
[4] Kapstein 2013: 107.

(*śama*), along with rightness (*ṛtá*), truth (*satya*) and Vedic study and recitation (TU 1.9). Indeed, all the virtues are considered forms of *tapas* (*Mahānār. Up.* 8). The *Upaniṣads* espouse inner asceticism in the form of yoking (*yoga*/*yukta*), i.e. controlling the senses, and concentration (*dhyāna*) as means to achieve direct experiential knowledge (*jñāna*) of the revealed truth that *ātman* is *brahman*, epitomised in the formula 'I am *brahman*' (*brahmāsmi*). Quieting the externally directed mind, or *manas*, which operates through the sense-organs (*indriya*), instils one-pointedness and tranquillity, the psycho-physical bases of *dhyāna*. Thus, the middle 'limbs' of *Yoga Sūtra* 2.29 – *pratyāhāra* (withdrawal of the mind from sense-objects and from the senses), *dhāraṇā* (concentration, fixing the mind on an object) and *dhyāna* (P. *jhāna* = meditation or concentration) – formalise practices that appear originally in the *Upaniṣads*.[5] Such cessative practices calm the mind and prepare the aspirant for entering the rarefied states of *samādhi* (absorption, trance, ecstasy), yogic *kaivalya* (aloneness), and the Buddhist *dhyānas* (concentrations or absorptions) leading to *nirvāṇa*. It can be argued that, because the more advanced spiritual exercises aim at transcending everyday life, their ethical implications are limited or that they are egoistic.[6] However, in order to discern the heart of ethical philosophies based on purification and inner concentration it is necessary to bracket the assumptions of our modern individualistic and activist ethics.

Perhaps the earliest passage on knowledge and concentration in the *Upaniṣads* states: 'He who knows this, therefore, becomes calm, composed, quiet, patient and concentrated (*samāhita*). He sees the self (*ātman*) in just himself and all things as the self' (BU 4.4.23). He who is freed from desire goes to *brahman* (BU 4.4.6). A later text adds:

> Not a man who does not abstain from bad acts, nor one who has not come to peace, not one who is not concentrated, nor one whose mind has not come to peace, shall reach this by means of knowledge. (KaU 2.24)[7]

In the *Upaniṣads* the first stage of concentration involves stilling the externally directed mind:

> When the five perceptions are stilled along with the mind (*manas*), and not even the higher mind (*buddhi*) stirs itself, they call that the highest state. This they consider yoga, the firm control in concentration (*dhāraṇā*) of the sense-organs. Then is one free from distractions, for yoga is the origin and the passing away. (KaU 6.10–11)[8]

5 *Pratyāhāra* is encouraged for the Vedic student's domestic life in ChU 8.15.

6 Steven Collins acknowledges that for Buddhists *nirvāṇa* is not a moral phenomenon, nevertheless it is the *summum bonum* (1998: 155). He notes that compassion for all sentient beings expresses the overarching ethical concern of meditation.

7 Trans. Hume 1921: 350.

8 Translations of the *Upaniṣads* are from Olivelle 2008 unless noted otherwise.

The *Kaṭha Upaniṣad* also employs the dynamic chariot image of the self, which is similar to the soul chariot in Plato's *Phaedrus* myth,[9] to represent how the higher part of mind stills the externally directed mind:

> 3. Know the self as a rider in a chariot,
> and the body, as simply the chariot.
> Know the intellect (*buddhi*) as the charioteer,
> and the mind (*manas*), as simply the reins.
>
> 4. The senses, they say, are the horses,
> and sense objects are the paths around them.
> . . .
> 5. When a man lacks understanding (*vijñāna*),
> and his mind (*manas*) is never controlled (*ayukta*);
> His senses do not obey him,
> as bad horses, a charioteer.
>
> 8. When a man has understanding,
> is mindful and always pure;
> He does reach that final step,
> from which he is not reborn again. (KaU 3.3–8)

The *Śvetāśvatara Upaniṣad* offers a similar account in a theistic key.[10] Yoking the yogin's mind carries thoughts to the heavens (2.1–3): 'When he keeps his body straight . . . and draws the senses together with the mind into his heart, a wise man shall cross all the frightful rivers with the boat consisting of the formulation (*brahman*)' (2.8); 'the man practising yogic restraint sees here the true nature of *brahman*, he is free from all fetters, because he has known God, unborn, unchanging and unsullied by all objects' (2.15).

The *Mahābhārata* clarifies the distinction between lower and higher mind: 'The mind (*manas*) travels far and moves in various directions; its essence is desire and doubt. But the person whose mind is well-controlled experiences bliss both in this world and the world beyond' (12.194.37).[11] The *Mahābhārata* also explicates the interdependence of ethical and contemplative virtues: 'Truth (*satya*), tending the sacred fire, living in isolated places, meditation (*dhyāna*), asceticism (*tapas*), restraint (*dama*), forbearance (*kṣanti*), freedom from spite,

[9] On the soul-as-chariot image in the two cultures see Forte and Smith, Magnone, and Schlieter in this volume.

[10] Besides *dhyāna* another term for meditation in the *Upaniṣads* is *upāsanā*. Bader (1990: 40) notes that *upāsanā* is more devotional than *dhyāna*. Typically, it specifies one-pointed meditation on a deity, in association with self-dedication and surrender, thereby awakening the heart.

[11] Wynne 2009: 179.

moderation in eating, withdrawal of the senses from their objects, controlled speech, and peace' (12.196.10–11).[12]

The Buddhist Pali Canon articulates the stages of meditative praxis more precisely than the earlier Brahminical texts. Meditation is an essential component of the Buddhist path, which comprises right conduct (*śīla*), concentration (*samādhi*) and wisdom (*prajñā*). The last two items in the eightfold noble path are mindfulness (S. *smṛti*, P. *sati*) and concentration (*samādhi*), respectively. (The scheme influenced Patañjali's eight-limbed yoga.) Moral intentionality and mindfulness, which are cornerstones of the Buddha's teaching, combine with concentration to produce 'emotional health, making the practitioner much less likely to want to violate the commitments of moral discipline'.[13] 'Because the Buddha argued that lack of wisdom and mental discipline results in behaviour that leads to suffering of both self and others, Buddhist traditions have understood *prajñā* – the wisdom and insight of understanding the nature of reality – and *samādhi* – the mental discipline and capacity for attention that enables equanimity – to be morally significant.'[14] The power and value ascribed to introspection and detachment is not a sign of egoism. Rather, the other-regarding virtues spring from self-abnegation.

Buddhist meditation (*bhāvanā*) is designed to remove cognitive delusion caused by dogmatism, doubt and ignorance, and emotional turbulence aroused by cravings. Reflecting its literal meaning, 'bringing into being', *bhāvanā* induces harmonious bodily and mental states. The Pali Canon features many types of meditation, some deriving from the Buddha's own experience, others from either Brahminical or non-Vedic sources. From the Buddha's encounters with two teachers before his awakening, Āḷāra Kālāma and Uddaka Rāmaputta, he learned two cessative meditations – on the 'sphere of nothingness' and on the 'sphere of neither perception nor non-perception'. He claimed that neither led to liberation. Wynne argues that these meditative practices derive from early Brahminism,

> the goal of which was thought to be a nondual state of meditation identical to the unmanifest state of *brahman*. In early Brahminical yoga, liberation was thought to be anticipated in a meditative trance which has passed beyond the possibility of cognition, a state in which the subject/object division has been dissolved . . . The adept, through his meditative trance, was thought to anticipate in life what he will realise at death – the nondual source of creation.[15]

Some pre-Buddhist yogic practices were probably accepted by the Buddha and reformulated into a new scheme, while others were rejected.

[12] Wynne 2009: 199.
[13] Goodman 2013: 555.
[14] Edelglass 2013: 476.
[15] Wynne 2007: 108.

Pali sources attribute to the Buddha the discovery and mastery of four states of concentration (S. *dhyānas*, P. *jhānas*), which led to the discovery of the four noble truths. In *Dīgha Nikāya* 16 the Buddha enters successively the *dhyānas* of the four form-spheres and then of the four formless spheres, thereafter resuming the four form-meditations in turn. After re-entering and then abandoning the fourth *dhyāna*, he entered *nirvāṇa*. Since the fourth *dhyāna* represents an advanced stage of cessation and is followed by entrance into *nirvāṇa*, for Buddhists the cessation of mental activity was not an absolute end in itself.[16]

We find here an articulated scheme of two types of meditation. The *dhyānas* form a progressive series of four calm meditations (S. *śamatha*, P. *samatha*), whose goal is *samādhi*. The second type is insight meditation (S. *vipaśyanā*, P. *vipasannā*), whose goal is wisdom or insight (S. *prajñā*, P. *paññā*). While *śamatha* calms and purifies emotions, *vipaśyanā* eradicates karmic impressions (*saṃskāras*) and the cankers (*āsrava*), leading to release.[17] As teachings were systematised, most authorities gave priority to the cultivation of insight over the practice of concentration. Nevertheless, influential authorities, like the great Tibetan saint Tsong Khapa, believed that the two practices are complementary.

> Not knowing this system, some even propound, 'If you are a scholar, you only do analytical meditation. If you are a spiritual seeker or adept you only do stabilizing meditation.' This is not the case, because each must do both . . . you must use discernment for both of these methods of meditation. If you lack or are deficient in such analytical meditation, then you will not develop stainless wisdom, the precious life of the path.[18]

Calm meditation gradually removes the defilements (*kleśas*) and the five hindrances of sensual desire, ill-will, lethargy, excitement/depression, and doubt.[19] These agitate the surface of the mind, obscuring its underlying purity, which is thought to be calm and tranquil. As Conze notes,

> Concentration results less from intellectual effort than from a rebirth of the whole personality, including the body, the emotions and the will . . . before spiritual concentration can even be approached, we must have stilled, or suppressed for the time being, five vices, which are known as the five hindrances and the observance of the moral rules must . . . have become nearly automatic.[20]

[16] See the distinction between enlightenment and final *nirvāṇa* in Collins 1998: 147ff.
[17] On the interaction of the *dhyānas* and insight-meditation see Collins 1998: 157–60, and Gombrich 1996: ch. 4.
[18] Tsong Kha-Pa 2000: 113.
[19] For the texts see Shaw 2006: 39–58.
[20] Conze 1956: 20.

Likewise, in the *Yoga Sūtras* (1.30–2) mental disturbances (*antarāya*) are removed through concentration and one-pointedness, preparing the mind for insight: 'Upon the destruction of impurities as a result of the practice of yoga, the lamp of knowledge arises. This culminates in discriminative discernment' (YS 2.28).

Buddhist calm meditation takes many forms. Some practices provide initial access to concentration, others lead to introvertive trance. Typically, one begins with recollection or mindfulness of the Buddha, Dharma, the Sangha, etc., or of death. The four *dhyānas* progressively concentrate on a wide variety of subjects such as breathing, the impermanence and foulness of the body, or the divine abidings (*brahmavihāra*): loving-kindness (*maitrī*), compassion (*karuṇā*), empathetic joy (*muditā*) and equanimity (*upekṣā*). The ethical effects of cultivating these four positive attitudes are evident in countering specific unwholesome states of mind like hostility, harmfulness, diṣsatisfaction, envy and honour-seeking, which lead to wrongdoing and the urge to distinguish oneself from others.

The four limbs of *dhyāna* detach the mind from the gross sense-sphere of desires and sense-objects (*kāmāvacara*), redirecting it first to the realm of pure forms or subtle materiality (*rūpāvacara*), and upon attainment of the fourth *dhyāna*, entrance into the formless realms (*arūpāvacara*). It is likely, says Gethin, that 'the four formless attainments . . . are presented as modifications and refinements of the fourth *dhyāna*', at which stage 'stilling and calming the mind is essentially complete'.[21] The four formless attainments involve cessation of thought, feeling and even breathing by concentrating on: infinite space (5), infinite consciousness (6), nothingness (7), and neither consciousness nor unconsciousness (8).

The *dhyānas* standardly possess these features:

> (a) first *dhyāna*: *vitarka* (applied thought), *vicāra* (sustained thinking, examination),[22] joy/physical rapture (*pīti*) and happiness/mental bliss (*sukha*), one-pointedness (*ekaggatā*)
> (b) second *dhyāna*: joy (*pīti*) and happiness (*sukha*), and one-pointedness (*ekaggatā*)
> (c) third *dhyāna*: equipoise (*upekṣā*), happiness (*sukha*), and one-pointedness (*ekaggatā*)
> (d) fourth *dhyāna*: equipoise (*upekṣā*), one-pointedness (*ekaggatā*), mindfulness (*sati*).[23]

21 Gethin 1998: 185. See Vetter (1988: xxi–xxiii) on whether the four formless attainments are part of the Buddha's original teaching. Wynne (2007: 43) cites Brahminic sources for these states.

22 *Vitarka* is the first alighting (of the mind on an object), while *vicāra* is the examination (*vicaraṇa*) of what has been recognised by *vitarka*. See Cousins 1992: 144.

23 The four *dhyānas* are also mentioned in the *Mokṣadharma* 12.188. See Bryant 2009: 70, Bronkhorst 1993: 68.

It is important to note that conceptual thought ceases in the second *dhyāna*; and tranquillity appears in the third and fourth *dhyāna*s with the absence of joy and happiness. Meditation thus begins with rational, discursive thought, but in the higher *dhyānas* the aspirant attains non-conceptual states as she enters the intermediary world of subtle forms.

In the fourth *dhyāna*, 'the meditator can focus fully on the development of insight and the wisdom that understands the four truths'[24] and that all things are impermanent, unsatisfactory and not-self. Insight also advances through levels, according to the scheme of the seven purifications. Proponents of the superiority of insight to calm meditation emphasise the importance of the insight that the four calm *dhyānas* are themselves impermanent and thus must be transcended.[25] Another factor, which cannot be examined here, is that various combinations of calm and insight are appropriate for individuals at different stages of the path. The essential points I wish to make in this brief survey of Buddhist meditative practice are that (a) the transcendent states of wisdom to which adepts aspire can only be attained through comprehensive purification of mind and heart, the attainment of tranquillity, and intense concentration; (b) wisdom far transcends beliefs or discursive intellectual knowledge; and (c) each attainment correlates with progressively higher cosmic levels.[26]

The meditative praxis of the *Yoga Sūtra* is similar to that of the *Upaniṣads* and the Buddhist suttas. The sense-withdrawal and concentration of awareness practised by Brahminic and Buddhist yogins retrace the cosmogony by ascending through the elements, the psychic faculties and mental states, ending in the cessation of thought and feeling.[27] The treatise begins by defining yoga as 'the cessation of the fluctuations of the mind' (*citta-vṛtti nirodaḥ*). The path leading to cessation (*nirodha*) comprises the eight-limbed yoga, as noted above (YS 2.29). Although rightly likened to the Buddhist eightfold path, Patañjalan yoga does not maintain the Buddhist distinction between calm and insight meditation.

- 'Concentration is the fixing of the mind in one place' (YS 3.1).
- 'Meditation is the one-pointedness of the mind on one idea' (YS 3.2).
- 'Absorption is when that same meditation shines forth as the object alone and [the mind] is devoid of its own nature' (YS 3.3).

[24] Gethin 1998: 187.

[25] Cf. Gethin 1998: 199.

[26] 'The visionary experience that was part of the Buddha's own Enlightenment process . . . produced a series of vivid images of the heavenly realms in which the meritorious deeds of men were rewarded and of the hells in which men received retribution for their sins. The meditative experience . . . led to the development of conceptions of cosmic worlds corresponding to the various levels of meditative consciousness' (Reynolds and Reynolds 1982: 15).

[27] Cf. Bryant 2009: 69, and Wynne 2007: 36ff.

- 'When these three are performed together, it is called discipline' (YS 3.4).
- 'From mastery of discipline comes the light of wisdom' (YS 3.5).

The apex of yogic practice is *samādhi*, which has two types: *saṃprajñātaḥ* and *asaṃprajñātaḥ*: '[The type of samādhi] supported by wisdom is accompanied by reasoning, reflection, bliss, and I-am-ness' (YS 1.17). This progression of *vitarka*, *vicāra*, bliss and *asmitā* parallels the mental states characteristic of the Buddhist *dhyānas*, with the exception of the fourth, which, as a purified form of self-awareness, does not fit precisely the Buddhist rejection of a persisting self. (It is closer to the illuminated awareness of *buddhi* in the *Kaṭha Upaniṣad* discussed above.) As in the Buddhist scheme, the initial stages of meditation include ratiocinative activity, marked here also by *vitarka* and *vicāra*. *Vitarka* is directed thought, a recognition that 'this is a dog', 'this is blue', etc. – the activity of bringing different objects into focus before the mind's eye.[28] On this sūtra, Vyasa defines *vitarka* as 'gross directing of the mind to an object'. Later sūtras add further points about these cognitive states:

> The attainment with reasoning (*vitarka*) is associated with concepts arising from knowledge of the meanings of words. (YS 1.42)
>
> When memory/mindfulness (*smṛti*) is pure the attainment without reasoning (*nir-vitarkā*) reveals only the object and mind as if empty of its own nature. (YS 1.43)

At this stage, as Bryant indicates, 'all knowledge of the object as conventionally understood has been suspended, and the mind has completely transformed itself into the object, free from a cognitive identification or self-awareness . . . the object stands out freed from the mental clutter of naming, identification, and recognition'.[29] *Vicārā*, the second stage of *samādhi*, which is more subtle than *vitarka*, is also divided into two sections: 'The states of samādhi with subtle awareness (*savicārā*) and without subtle awareness (*nirvicārā*), whose objects of focus are the subtle nature [of things], are explained in the same manner' (YS 1.44). These objects are the imperceptible, subtle elements (*tanmatras*) which are causes of the gross elements, the objects of *vitarka*. The attainment of *nirvicārā* brings 'lucidity of the inner self' (*adhyātmaprasādaḥ* YS 1.47), a state of wisdom (*prajñā*). The second type of *samādhi*, *asaṃprajñātaḥ*, like the formless Buddhist *dhyānas*, leads to cessation (*nirodha*) of impressions (*saṃskāras* YS 1.18, 50–1), a non-conceptual state.[30] Beyond this lies classical yoga's ultimate goal of aloneness or singularity (*kaivalya*, YS 2.25, 4.34), the luminosity of pure

28 Cf. Cousins 1992: 139.
29 Bryant 2009: 148.
30 Cf. Bryant 2009: 71.

consciousness (*puruṣa*) that lacks activity or object. 'Trance . . . approaches a condition of rapt attention to an objectless inwardness.'[31]

Plato

Plato scholars typically analyse arguments more than they explore the care of the self and philosophy as a way of life. This rationalist bias yields generalisations like Charles Kahn's that 'the fundamental conception of the Forms . . . is linguistic rather than visual in its orientation'.[32] Certainly, Socrates – as represented by Plato – seeks definitions and discursive knowledge, but this intellectual training is only a prelude to higher wisdom and ultimate liberation. Socrates observes 'There is likely to be something such as a path to guide us out of our confusion' (*Phd.* 66b2–3) about the true nature of the soul and its destiny. He exhibits deep confidence, hope and faith that after death good men will be welcomed by good gods and good men (63b5–c4), and that the mystery-teachings about the afterlife are true (63c1, 5, 67b7, 68a8). To conclude that these are merely corrigible beliefs, and hence inferior to discursive knowledge of forms as linguistic entities or propositions, fails to grasp the force of these existential commitments. Repetition of ἐλπίς (hope), and its verbal form ἐλπίζω, is one of many examples of the incantatory language Plato uses to complement dialectic. Socrates exhorts his interlocutors to be persuaded of the reality of the imaginal worlds depicted in the eschatological myths. Those who are not persuaded suffer, he says, from 'untrustworthiness and forgetfulness' (ἀπιστίαν τε καὶ λήθην, *Grg.* 493c3; cf. *Phd.* 69e3, *Phdr.* 240c). The Orphic-Pythagorean virtues of persuasion, trust, memory and truth condition the philosopher for transcendent perception of invisible realities.

Platonic recollection begins, as does yogic meditative praxis, with sense-perception, discursive thought, and belief in transcendent truths, but only gains access to unchanging Being by transcending these preparatory stages. Like Buddhist mindfulness towards the truths discovered by the Buddha, Platonic recollection is a type of meditation directed to the substantial reality of Forms, the experiences of the immortal soul in the imaginal realms of the afterlife, and the cosmic structures underlying the mechanisms of *karma* and rebirth. Of course, Socrates defends his metaphysical beliefs with arguments, but such 'true doctrines' are often introduced when the normal cognitive operation of his interlocutors has been suspended. For example, only when Meno's mind is numbed into perplexity does Socrates introduce immortality and recollection

[31] Conze 1956: 19.

[32] Kahn 1997: 354–5. Similarly, Cross 1965: 27–8, 'a Form, so far from being a "substantial entity" is much more like "a formula". It is the logical predicate in a logos.'

and say: 'I trust that this is true' (*Meno* 81a5–e2). There and in the *Gorgias* (493a) Socrates invokes as authorities certain priests and priestesses, Pindar and Orphic-Pythagoreans for the beliefs that the soul is immortal, that it must pay a penalty for wrongdoing, that it experiences post-mortem rewards and punishments, and that it is reborn many times. The *Seventh Letter* insists that 'we must always firmly believe the sacred and ancient words declaring to us that the soul is immortal, and when it has separated from the body will go before its judges and pay the utmost penalties' (335a2–5).[33]

The purpose of such 'true beliefs' and the spiritual virtues or attitudes that support them is to inspire seekers to tread the path of divinisation. It should be noted that Hadot's rich account of philosophy as a way of life, drawing as it does mostly on Hellenistic philosophy and on the Socrates of the early dialogues, largely ignores the otherworldly dimension of the later dialogues. Thus, his picture of Platonic spiritual exercises, which reflect the equivalence of psychology and cosmology, is incomplete.

The way in which the Socratic elenchus works on the minds of interlocutors in the early dialogues prepares for advanced forms of concentration described in the later dialogues. A passage in the *Sophist* summarises the cognitive, affective and ethical effects of Socratic refutation:

> The people who purify the soul . . . likewise think the soul, too, won't get any advantage from any learning that's offered to it until someone shames it by refuting it, removes the opinions that interfere with learning, and exhibits it purified, believing that it knows only those things that it does know, and nothing more. (230c5–d4)

The refutation of each false belief empties the mind of one thought after another, inducing successive non-conceptual states, ending in numbness and shame. Repeated refutations parallel the initial stages of yogic practice in breaking down the empirical ego. Final *aporia* indicates that no discursive account of virtue – even were it forthcoming – would be sufficient for being virtuous.

Deeper Platonic affinities with yogic meditation are evident in the middle and later dialogues. The *Phaedo*'s spiritual exercises intensify the purification begun with the elenchus. Here Plato is indebted to the Pythagorean way of life and in particular to its practice of stillness and silence. 'Among the Pythagoreans the practice of remaining silent for long periods – one of the most effective means for maintaining composure – is to some extent a continuation of the practice of shamans and yogis.'[34] Pythagorean silence does not mean total muteness; it also involves reticence to speak about esoteric practices and 'deep attentive listening

33 See the 'true accounts' of the mechanisms of *karma* and karmic ethics in *Laws* 870d5–e3, 872e–873a, 903d3–904e3, 959b3–c2, and Bussanich 2013a.

34 Burkert 1972: 179.

to the word of the Master and to the divine within and outside individuals'.[35] Parmenides' practice of stillness, a widespread Pythagorean mental discipline (DL ix.21), can be taken as meditative preparation for making the mind changeless and timeless like being.[36] Similarly, the practice of purification Socrates presents in the *Phaedo* withdraws consciousness from sense-objects through introspective concentration (64e5–6, 65c7–9, 66a, e2–4, 67d1, 79d, 81bc).[37] 'Purification . . . [is to] separate the soul as far as possible from the body and accustom it to gather itself and collect itself out of every part of the body and to dwell by itself as far as it can both now and in the future, freed, as it were, from the bonds of the body' (67c6–d1).[38] Inasmuch as philosophy is 'practice for dying and death' (64a3, 67d12–e6, 81a1–2), meditation on the separation of the soul from the body initiates the inward journey. By withdrawal from the sensible world, 'The soul of the philosopher achieves calm (γαλήνην) from such emotions; it follows reason and ever stays with it contemplating the true, the divine' (84a6–8). The meditative practice of stillness is what enables the mind to attain direct perception of the Forms: 'When the soul investigates by itself it passes into the realm of what is pure, ever existing, immortal and unchanging, and . . . its experience (τὸ πάθημα) then is what is called wisdom' (79d1–7). The striking description of wisdom as experience suggests that this is a non-conceptual state of awareness. Received scholarly opinion that the procedure described here is simply abstraction in search of discursive definitions and propositions is a woefully inadequate account of Plato's views.

Direct knowledge (ἐπιστήμη) of the Forms is also infallible, non-representational and non-propositional.[39] The *Republic* adds the crucial point that knowing the Forms requires 'grasping' the Good as the first principle of all (*Rep.* 511b). The highest knowledge is a state as compared to dialectic, which is a method. In its movement among Forms (511b7–c2) dialectic is likened to gymnastics (539d8–10).[40] At best it yields *dianoia*, the discursive, representational kind of knowledge that leads to but is transcended by vision of the Forms

[35] Gemelli Marciano 2014: 144.

[36] Cf. Burkert 1969: 28, Kingsley 1999: 173–83, 250–1, and Gocer 2000: 18.

[37] The *Phaedo*'s introspective concentration is like *Bhagavad Gītā* viii.12: 'Having restrained all the doors of one's body, and arresting the mind in one's heart, one practices the Yoga of steadfast concentration by gathering the entire vital force on the top of the cranium.'

[38] Cf. Gernet 1981: 360. Vernant 2006: 126–32, 144–8, and Detienne 1963: 71–3; see in these passages the concentration of the vital energies of a person into her essence and implicit reference to breathing exercises. Detienne cites parallels with the Hippocratic Περὶ διαίτης (*Peri diaites*) on detachment from bodily awareness in sleep (73–6), and with the Pythagorean practice of incubation, shamanism and ecstasy (76–81).

[39] See Gerson 2003: 158–64.

[40] See Gerson 2003: 186–90.

(532c), an experience that is happy (516c), intensely blissful (like living in the Isles of the Blessed, 519c) and 'a rest from the road . . . and an end of journeying for the one who reaches it' (532e). Only after practising dialectic for five years and bearing political responsibilities for many years (539d–540a), can philosophers experience the complete cognitive and psychic transformation necessary to achieve the vision of the Form of the Good.[41] Another striking metaphor for a non-conceptual unified state of being that transcends the distinction between subject and object appears earlier in the dialogue:

> It is the nature of the real lover of learning to strive for what is, not remaining with any of the things that are believed to be, but as he moves on, he never loses the edge of his eros, never falls back from it, until he grasps the being of each nature itself with the part of his soul that is fitted to grasp it, because of its kinship with it, and that, once getting near what really is and having intercourse with it (μιγεὶς τῷ ὄντι ὄντως) and having given birth to understanding and truth, he knows, truly lives, and is nourished. (*Rep.* 490a–b)

This movement from discursive to intuitive knowledge of the Forms, which are unified in grasping the Good, and finally to a non-conceptual, ecstatic union is analogous to the progression in the yogic traditions through ever more concentrated forms of blissful absorption. A key difference is that Plato employs the language of religious vision to characterise the supra-rational mind and light imagery to convey the luminosity of Being.[42] The classical yogic texts eschew visual metaphors, but nevertheless speak of the light of wisdom and bliss.[43]

In Platonic care for the self, training to achieve internal repose looms large. At the end of the *Phaedo* Socrates admonishes his pupils to 'keep quiet and persevere' (107e2) as they witness his death. In the *Republic* (604b–e) Socrates counsels stillness when overcome with grief and suffering. After drinking the hemlock Socrates remarks: 'I am told one should die in good-omened silence. So keep quiet and control yourselves' (*Phd.* 117e2). The stillness Socrates praises in the *Phaedo* is necessary for progress in dialectic. As this remarkable passage from the *Republic* shows, the 'reason' active in the highest sense is not discursive or inferential or instrumental:

> I suppose that someone who is healthy and moderate with himself goes to sleep only after having roused his rational part (λογιστικὸν) and feasted it on fine arguments and speculations (λόγων καλῶν καὶ σκέψεων), and having attained clear

41 See the brilliant discussion of the visionary and affective dimension of Platonic contemplation in Nightingale 2004: 110–14.

42 See Nightingale 2004 *passim* on how Platonic and Aristotelian *theōria* borrowed from religious pilgrimage and viewing sacred sites.

43 Popular Buddhist literature like the *Jātaka* tales features visionary tours of the *deva*-worlds, corresponding to the *dhyānic* states. See Collins 1998: 297–319.

> self-consciousness (σύννοιαν αὐτὸς αὑτῷ); second, he neither starves nor feasts his appetites, so that they will slumber and not disturb his best part with either their pleasure or their pain, but they'll leave it alone, pure and by itself, to get on with its investigations, to yearn after and perceive something in the past or present or future that it doesn't know. He's also calmed down his passionate part and doesn't go to bed in an emotionally disturbed state because he's been angry with someone. And when he has quieted these two parts and aroused the third, in which reason (τὸ φρονεῖν) resides, and so takes his rest, you know that it is then that he best grasps the truth and that the visions that appear in his dreams are least lawless. (*Rep.* 571d6–572b1)

The Platonic practice of ἡσυχία, like yogic *śamatha*, purifies and simplifies the mind, bringing it to higher states of consciousness. Here, detaching the higher mind from bodily sensations and emotions activates a meditative state in which the soul transcends time and apprehends the truth. The reference to 'past, present, and future' echoes Homer's (*Il.* i 70) description of the μάντις Calchas, ὃ ᾔδη τά τ'ἐόντα τά τ' ἐσσόμενα πρό τ'ἐόντα. It is not in fact a simple regimen in preparation for sleep.[44]

A fascinating passage in Aelian suggests connections between this spiritual exercise in the *Republic* and passages in the *Timaeus* and *Laws*: 'The Peripatetics say that during the day the soul is enveloped by the body and is a slave to it, unable to see the truth clearly; but at night it is freed from this servitude and, taking the form of a sphere in the parts around the chest, it becomes more prophetic' (Aelian *Varia Historia* iii.11). Some texts express homologies between cosmos and psyche. Inasmuch as axial rotation is most appropriate to intelligence (νοῦς), the Demiurge caused the universe 'to turn about uniformly in the same place and within its own limits and made it revolve round and round' (*Tim.* 34a4). Divine thinking is a kind of meditative state depicted as 'rotation, an unvarying movement in the same place, by which the god would always think the same thoughts about the same things' (*Tim.* 40a). *Laws* 897d–898b expands on the image and stresses the ineffability of this 'motion':

> ATHENIAN: 'So what is the nature of rational motion (νοῦ κίνησις)?' (897d3) 'It is impossible to look directly at νοῦς – it's like looking at the sun . . . that [motion] taking place in a single location necessarily implies continuous revolution round a central point, just like wheels being turned on a lathe; and this kind of motion bears the closest possible affinity and likeness to the cyclical movement of reason (νοῦς).' (898a)

44 Detienne 1963: 77–9 cites several texts on the soul apprehending the truth in sleep. Cicero *De divinatione* i.30: 'When, therefore, the soul has been withdrawn by sleep from contact with sensual ties, then does it recall the past, comprehend the present, and foresee the future. For though the sleeping body then lies as if it were dead, yet the soul is alive and strong, and will be much more so after death when it is wholly free of the body.'

E. N. Lee explores the phenomenology: 'this sort of "circling" is a motion that does not move toward any goal – not even itself . . . it is complete at every moment of its course'.[45] 'It is a dynamic wholeness . . . [showing] involvement or co-ordination of all its parts in that motion, its total absorption in the motion'; 'the image conveys a compelling sense of a fully focussed . . . non-localized consciousness . . . elimination of perspective. There is thus a kind of cancelling of perspectivity effect'.[46] I see here a Platonic adaptation of Parmenides' image of unchanging, eternal Being as a sphere in order to represent symbolically, through the figure of axial rotation, a divine, non-intentional meditative state that can be compared with yogic *samādhi*.

The Platonic practice of stillness and concentration, in conjunction with the cultivation of intellectual virtue, leads to the transformation of a person's substance by the removal of hindrances and defilements, as in the yogic traditions. The effects of pains, pleasures and unjust actions on the soul are likened to scars and stamps (*Grg*. 525a), rivets (*Phd*. 83d)[47] and incrustations (*Rep*. 611d–612a) attached to the soul, which, like karmic impressions (*saṃskāras* and *vasanas*) in yogic traditions, determine future births and one's experiences in heaven and hell states. Without eradication of such impressions, the soul cannot be free, unified and wise. The *Republic* passage presents the image of the sea-god Glaucus. Once incrustations accumulated through repeated embodiments have been removed from his body, one can 'see the soul as it is in truth . . . as it is in its pure state'. For Plato the soul's ultimate goal is to be freed from the cycle of births and deaths in order to achieve blissful immortality. Certainly, Plato is not as explicit on this point as are the South Asian traditions, but I believe that the preponderance of evidence supports this reading.[48]

45 Lee 1976: 78.

46 Lee 1976: 80, 81.

47 In *Phd*. 81cd disembodied souls that are bound to the senses and the physical world wander as ghosts around graves 'paying the penalty for their previous bad upbringing'.

48 (a) Socrates claims that 'those who have purified themselves sufficiently by philosophy live in the future altogether without a body; they make their way to even more beautiful dwelling places which it is hard to describe clearly' (*Phd*. 114c). (b) Philosophers who have served the kallipolis 'will depart for the Isles of the Blessed and dwell there' (*Rep*. 540b5–7). (c) 'When the mind conforms to the universe's harmonies and with the forms, it returns to its original condition. And when this conformity is complete, we shall have achieved our goal: that most excellent life offered to humankind by the gods, both now and forevermore' (*Tim*. 90d). (d) 'The law of Destiny is this: If any soul becomes a companion to a god and catches sight of any true thing, it will be unharmed until the next circuit; and *if it is able to do this every time, it will always be safe*' (*Phdr*. 248c2–5, emphasis added). (e) Upon completion of a cycle souls return to their celestial starting point, except for philosophical lovers who, 'with the third circuit of a thousand years, *if they choose this life three times in succession, on that condition become winged and depart, in the three thousandth*

The Platonic dialogues do not describe meditative techniques as extensively as South Asian texts do. However, Plato does not represent Socrates solely as a master of dialectic; he is also much like a yogic figure, who is regularly subject to daimonic, ecstatic experiences. At the beginning of the *Symposium*, Aristodemus reports that Socrates fell behind on the way to the drinking party and stood in a porch. 'It's one of his habits, you know; every now and then he just goes off like that and stands motionless, wherever he happens to be. I'm sure he'll come in very soon, so don't disturb him; let him be' (*Symp.* 175b2–5). In the final section of the dialogue, Alcibiades reports that at Potidaia Socrates astonished his fellow soldiers by standing in the same spot 'lost in thought' from sunrise to sunrise. On the second morning 'he said his prayers to the sun and went away' (220d4–5).[49] Scholars claim that these episodes simply involved intense thinking, a view that strains credulity and which is belied by the physical circumstances.[50] The fact that Socrates stood motionless for twentyfour hours, without ill effects, is strong evidence that Socrates' mind and his body were in an altered state. In light of his spiritual experiences – his dreams[51] and daimonic interventions – it is more likely that Socrates was absorbed in a meditative trance of complete detachment from normal sensory awareness and his normal conscious, interactive self.[52] I believe that Socrates' own perplexity, his unknowing, is the mental residue of these non-conceptual, absorptive states. That they may persist in the midst of external action is suggested by Alcibiades' report about Socrates' preternatural calmness on the battlefield at Delium (*Symp.* 221b; cf. Aristophanes *Clouds* 362–3) and his detachment from temperature extremes (219b–220b), even to the extent of walking barefoot through ice and snow. Xenophon admired his self-sufficiency and freedom from desire (*Memorabilia* 1.2, 5–6, 2.1.1), asserting that self-control (*enkrateia*) was the foundation of virtue (1.5.5) and necessary for achieving wisdom (4.5.6, 7, 9).

The detachment of the yogic kind (*vairagya*) that Plato attributes to Socrates, which he also valorises in his portrait of the philosopher in the *Republic*, cannot be achieved by discursive intellectual activity. As we have seen, concentration and the practice of stillness are essential components of the care of the self and the pursuit of wisdom. These Pythagorean practices lived on in the Academy. Diogenes says of Xenocrates, Plato's second successor as head of the Academy: 'Being most free of pride, he often during the day would retire

year' (*Phdr.* 249a3–5, emphasis added). In Bussanich 2013a I argue that these and other passages express Plato's commitment to the philosopher's liberation from the rebirth cycle.

49 On Pythagorean identifications of the sun/Helios with Apollo see Burkert 1972: 149–50.

50 See Vlastos 1991: 97 n51, and Dover 1980: 173.

51 For Socrates' dreams see the opening frames of the *Crito*, *Phaedo*, and even the *Protagoras*.

52 On the remarkable variety of scholarly opinion on Socrates' religious experiences see Bussanich 2013b.

into himself, and he devoted, it is said, a whole hour to silence' (DL 4.11). In late antiquity, such spiritual exercises were the animating heart of Neoplatonic philosophy.[53]

[53] See Plotinus *Enneads* V.1.2.14ff., VI.9.11.8–16.

7

Technologies of self-immortalisation in ancient Greece and early India

Paolo Visigalli

Nowadays, the mention of 'technologies' and 'immortality' in the same breath brings to mind futuristic biochemical methods to stop bodily decay, restore youth, and transfer a mind's contents and processes to an artificial, unalterable substratum. And yet of course a wide variety of past cultures have also been concerned with attaining some sort of immortality. This essay explores the idea, present in both ancient Greece and early India, that immortality can be achieved through some structured methods, what I call 'technologies of self-immortalisation'. At the outset, three key terms require qualification: 'immortality', 'self' and 'technologies'.

What, then, is immortality? Despite the variety of beliefs about immortality, we may envision two main models: as a never-ending bodily existence, and as the indefinite continuation of one's 'self' in an afterlife.[1] The former model, for example, is the one advanced by Daoist and Western alchemists. In their mountain dwellings and hidden laboratories, they sought to make their body eternal through a regimented lifestyle, sexual techniques, the manipulation of substances and the ingestion of elixirs.[2] The latter model, common to many religious traditions, is the one relevant to this essay.

The notion of 'self' is a complex one. This term, it would appear, sits together with a number of other concepts, most notably the 'soul'. And, as emphasised by

[1] A third model of immortality as an eternal bodily afterlife is also worth mentioning. Most notably, such a model is adopted in (early) Christianity and Islam. A useful treatment of different kinds of immortality is Andrade 2015.

[2] Pregadio (2014) offers an informative introduction to Daoist alchemy. For an influential yet controversial attempt to interpret the nature and function of alchemical practices from a phenomenological perspective, see Eliade 1978. For a recent and comprehensive treatment of Western alchemy, see Principe 2012.

philosophers, classical scholars and anthropologists,[3] it is inherently linked with a set of yet other themes, such as 'self-awareness', 'introspection', 'personhood' and 'identity'. For the purposes of this chapter, I look below not at unanalysed assumptions about the self, however this latter may be understood, but at consciously formulated ideas about how to produce an immortal self through the application of certain methods.

I call such methods 'technologies', borrowing the term from Michel Foucault's influential 'Technologies of the Self'.[4] In that essay, Foucault defines 'technology' as a set of practices, literary genres, and attention to certain ways of thinking, all of which contribute to producing a particular kind of self-understanding. I take from Foucault the notion of 'technology' as a hybrid network of both practice (e.g. letter writing) and mental habit that is nourished by psychophysical exercises (e.g. meditation). There is a difference, however. While Foucault is concerned mainly with the exploration of how these technologies of self-caring and self-knowledge produce a certain self-understanding, I will emphasise below how composite psychophysical practices are aimed at producing a post-mortem immortal self.

I focus on two case studies. For India I explore the ritual creation of an immortal self (*ātman*) in the ritual of the construction of the fire altar (*agnicayana*). For Greece I examine the theme of self-immortalisation through the practice of philosophy in Plato's *Timaeus*. I begin with the latter.

Ancient Greece: immortality as a rational choice

Recent scholarship has shown that there was an intense preoccupation among Greek and Latin philosophers with the idea of what makes one an individual 'self'.[5] Although the related notion of an immortal self or soul has also been subject to scrutiny, there is no consensus among researchers on some significant respects. Specifically, scholars disagree on when and how the idea of an immortal soul emerged in Greece. Thus, to select two authoritative voices, Jan Bremmer emphasises that the rise of this idea is the result of a process internal to Greece, which took place among the Pythagoreans and in the Orphic cults. It is in these diversified yet loosely connected cultural milieus, Bremmer argues, that there was an 'enormous re-evaluation of the soul', an 'upgrading' of the

3 See, inter alia, Frede and Reis 2009; Gill 2006 and 2001; Remes and Sihvola 2008; Sorabji 2006; Taylor 1989; Carrithers, Collins and Lukes 1985.

4 Foucault 1988.

5 Thus, for example, the varieties of self in Greece and Rome have been ably examined by Richard Sorabji and Christopher Gill in several contributions, some of which are referred to in note 3 above.

soul, which from its shadowy presence in Homer came to be seen as divine and immortal.[6] By contrast, Walter Burkert contends that the notion of an immortal soul, a *psyche* or *pneuma* that reaches a heavenly abode, is not the result of an internal development, but rather comes from outside Greece. He proposes identifying the sources of such an idea in the 'melting pot of influences'[7] which constitute the background of the origins of Greek thought in the wider context. Thus, Burkert suggests that the idea of the ascent of the soul to heaven, where it attains 'celestial immortality', represents the influence of Iranian sources, in particular, the Zoroastrian Avestan, whereas the notion of '[t]ransmigration, connected with Pythagoras and "Orpheus" and wrongly credited to the Egyptians by Herodotus, must ultimately derive from India'.[8]

This striking difference of opinion evinces the difficulties faced by scholars grappling with early Greece's lacunose and fragmentary evidence. Analogous difficulties inherent in the oldest Greek sources persuaded me to focus on Plato, rather than to venture into some supposedly older material. In particular, I initially considered exploring the interplay of ritual and immortality in early Greece as a way to think comparatively about the Indian ritual I focus on below. It seemed especially promising to explore the role of ritual in mystery religions' 'transformative experience',[9] or to look at the ritual prescriptions among the Pythagoreans.[10] But this initial project foundered because of the dearth of evidence concerning mystery cults' rituals, and the discrepancy in time between the available sources and the earlier period I wanted to investigate.[11]

It appears that in early Greece, however, there was perhaps another 'technology of immortality', which from early on ran parallel to the mysteries' mystical path: the path of philosophy. Immortality was within the philosopher's purview; it could be attained by deliberately *choosing* to lead the theoretical life. Here two points are worth recalling. First, as Pierre Hadot has taught us,[12] we should not forget that philosophy was for many Greek thinkers not a disembodied intellectual practice, but a holistic way of life. And it is within such a wide notion of

6 Bremmer 2001: 23.

7 Burkert 2008: 74.

8 Burkert 2008: 74.

9 'Verwandelnde Erfahrung' is the title of the fourth chapter of Burkert's (1991) German edition of his 1987 *Ancient Mystery Cults*. In the English version, the title reads 'The extraordinary experience'.

10 On the ritual rules and the 'countless prohibitions and obligations' among Pythagoreans, see Riedweg 2005 (= 2002): 63–7.

11 As Albinus (2000: 101) notes, although the Orphic tradition might even stretch back to the seventh century BCE, 'most of the surviving fragments and references stem from informants of Hellenistic or Roman times'.

12 However, for a criticism of Hadot's understanding of ancient philosophy, see Cooper 2007: 20–3; 2012: 17–21.

philosophy that we need to place the search for immortality. Second, the theme of self-immortalisation which I am investigating here is closely tied to, and must be considered in relation with, the theme of self-divinisation. This latter is already found in Pre-Socratic philosophy. Most notably, the theme is developed in some of Empedocles' fragments portraying the practitioner of the theoretical life, the philosopher, as someone that rises above the human and becomes, at least in part, divine. For Empedocles, because understanding is a divine practice, to do philosophy is not only a method for self-cultivation, but also for self-divinisation.[13]

The idea that thought is divine, and that its cultivation enables one to overcome the gap between human and divine, filtered down to later traditions. It was appropriated and redrawn most notably by Plato as part of his 'project of making ourselves as godlike as possible'.[14] It is in this connection that Plato elaborates on the theme of the soul's immortality.

Plato discusses this theme in several passages, developing not one notion of immortality, but several. Three main Platonic kinds of immortality have been identified recently by David Sedley: 1) immortality is part of the soul's essential nature; 2) immortality is conferred on the soul by an agent or cause, such as the demiurge; 3) immortality is won by each individual. Sedley calls these three kinds 'essential', 'conferred' and 'earned' immortality.[15] According to him, furthermore, Plato is less an innovator than an interpreter and defender of tradition, because his threefold treatment of immortality 'seek[s] to incorporate, interpret and build on existing religious traditions'.[16]

In what follows, I attend to 'earned immortality' only.[17] Focusing on the *Timaeus*, which Sedley identifies as the locus wherein earned immortality is treated most fully, I intend to consider some aspects of Plato's argument more closely.

At a first level of analysis, we see that in the *Timaeus* immortality marks the divide between the demiurge and its creatures. While the former is intrinsically immortal, the latter, the gods and the universe, are not. Unlike their creator, the gods are not 'altogether immortal and indestructible' (41b).[18] Nonetheless,

13 Consider Michael Puett's (2002: 57–62) suggestive interpretation of fragments 6, 17, 21, 27, 111, 115, 117, 128, 132, 133, 136.

14 Sedley 2009: 145.

15 As Sedley emphasises, these three are not the only kinds of immortality touched upon by Plato; thus, for instance, Plato also discusses immortality in a weaker sense, by vicarious prolongation through one's progeny or one's glorious deeds (e.g. literary or intellectual heritage).

16 Sedley 2009: 145.

17 Sedley considers it as 'reflecting the religious idea of apotheosis as a reward for high-achieving mortals' (2009: 157).

18 Citations form *Timaeus* are from Robin Waterfield's (2009) recent translation, with some minor modifications in a couple of passages.

they do partake of immortality because the demiurge wants them to be immortal (a situation that readily fits under the heading 'conferred immortality' in Sedley's classification). Man, on the other hand, is portrayed as a hybrid being, an admixture of mortal and immortal components. The human body and all the organs that are created by the gods at the behest of the demiurge are mortal; immortality belongs only to the highest, rational part of the human soul that is generated directly by the demiurge. Accordingly, we would expect the highest soul to enjoy the same kind of conferred immortality as the gods. But the text intriguingly adds that, although they undergo the same creational process, the soul-stuff with which the demiurge first created the gods and the soul-stuff with which he made the human soul present different grades of purity. This difference is nowhere elaborated further, however.

The human soul is not uniform, but composite. It consists of three parts that are given 'separate residences' (72a) in the body. The head is the location of the immortal, rational soul, which is also called δαίμων (90a;c); the chest harbours the passionate soul, and the abdomen the appetitive soul. Thus, although man's soul is immortal, it is associated with the body and all its passionate and appetitive drives. Nevertheless, however grim the soul's condition may at first appear, the text repeatedly emphasises that the human constitution is the best possible one. By closely following the demiurge's instructions, the gods made humans in such a way as to ensure that they could best avoid coming 'to an end straight away, without having attained its proper end (ἀτελὲς)' (73a).

But what, then, is the proper end (τέλος; 90d) of human existence in positive terms? And what is immortality's role in all of this? The text is fairly clear: man is placed in the best condition 'to give himself the best chance of living the life of reason (κατὰ λόγον ζῴη)' (89d). That is, the end of man's existence is to attend 'to the most divine part (τοῦ θειοτάτου) of us' (73a). While the cultivation of one's rational soul demands strenuous exercise, the 'desire of the most divine part of us for wisdom (τὸ θειότατον τῶν ἐν ἡμῖν φρονήσεως)' is in-built in man's constitution as one of 'the two fundamental desires that human beings possess', the other being 'the bodily desire for food' (88b).

It is especially revealing that for Plato attending to the rational soul is part and parcel of a composite method of self-care involving taking care of one's body. One must tend to the 'bodies and the minds' (87c); one 'creates' a 'sound constitution' (88e) in the same way as one perfects one's soul. Both intellectual and physical 'exercises'[19] are two interlinked aspects of one and the same training aimed at attaining the good life.

To conclude, even though the rational part of the soul is essentially immor-

[19] Note the several occurrences of derivatives of γυμνάζω in the *Timaeus*' concluding section; e.g. γύμνασις (89a), γυμνάσιον (89e).

tal, because, like the gods, it is the product of the demiurge, it remains up to us to enhance, and perhaps even to rediscover, its immortality. The way to do so is through the technology of philosophising, a composite psychophysical training. Because we deliberately choose whether or not to pursue the theoretical path, it seems proper to borrow David Sedley's words and speak of an 'immortality by self-definition'.[20]

Early India: ritual construction of immortality

Several recent contributions have investigated the notion of the 'self' in classic, medieval and pre-modern India.[21] Although many of these contributions explore perceptively a wide variety of Hindu and Buddhist notions of the self, they do not take into account the Vedic evidence; pre-*Upaniṣad* texts are only briefly mentioned, if at all. While it is of course reasonable to focus on the *Upaniṣads* and the later traditions, it should not be forgotten that sophisticated reflections about man's constitution, his place in the universe, and his 'self' are also evident in earlier Vedic literature.[22]

In this respect, other scholars have persuasively argued that there is a close connection between the speculations on the self in the *Upaniṣads* and the earlier ritual speculations in the *Brāhmaṇas*. In particular, it has often been suggested, though perhaps never fully explored, that the speculations on the *agnicayana* ritual, 'the piling of the fire [altar]', play a central role in the formation of the Upaniṣadic notion of an immortal self (*ātman*). The locus classicus here is the tenth book of the *Śatapatha Brāhmaṇa*, a large text of ritual hermeneutics composed around the eighth century BCE and traditionally attributed to Yājñavalkya.[23] In what follows, I will reconsider some key aspects of this text to gain clarity on the question 'How does one construct ritually an immortal self?' Before I do so, it will be necessary to provide a brief description of the *agnicayana* ritual ceremony.

The *agnicayana* is one of the most elaborate Vedic rituals. Its defining feature is the construction of an offering altar, which is piled from a thousand kiln-bricks. The altar is built on the eastern end of a delimited ritual enclosure that is provided with a roof. Made of five layers of bricks, the altar can assume various shapes. In its most recognised form it takes the shape of a bird of prey.

20 Sedley 2009: 159.

21 An incomplete reference list would include Dasti and Bryant 2014, Ganeri 2012a, 2012b, 2007, Kuznetsova, Ganeri and Ram-Prasad 2012, Siderits, Thompson and Zahavi 2010.

22 For a brief presentation of the Vedic notions of the soul and personhood, see Oberlies 1998: 497–506, with references. On the key term *ātman* and its complex semantics, see Renou 1952, Jurewicz 2007, and Kulikov 2007; cf. also Pinault 2001.

23 See Eggeling 1882: 30ff.

To study this ancient Vedic ritual, we not only have texts, but can also take into account the living tradition. From the late 1960s, scholars became aware that the *agnicayana* was still being performed, if only occasionally, in some relatively secluded areas of India. In particular, attention was drawn to the community of the Nambudiri Brahmins in Kerala, in the southwest corner of India. There a few families of Brahmins had preserved the Vedic ritual tradition alive. The merit for drawing attention to this largely self-contained community goes to the Indologist and philosopher Frits Staal (1930–2012). On his solicitation, some Nambudiri ritual experts agreed to perform the ceremony of the twelve-day *agnicayana*, from 12 to 25 April 1975. It was meticulously documented by a troop of experts led by Staal, and the outcome of this work was published in 1983, in two mammoth volumes including a fifty-minute recording documenting the salient aspects of the ritual performance.[24]

The following description takes the twelve-day *agnicayana* as a model and covers only some notable aspects of the ritual performance, barely enough to give an impression of the ritualists' extraordinary attention to detail.[25]

After the proper time and place have been established, it is necessary to take the measurement of the patron of the sacrifice (*yajamāna*), the man on whose behalf the ritual is performed. The sizes of the ritual enclosures and of the fire altars are functions of his physical size. As I will elaborate below, this is an important point as the fact that the ritual is tailored to the patron of the sacrifice will enable him to obtain the sacrifice's result, immortality. Then the patron and his priests enter the ritual enclosure together, carrying in pots the three sacred fires belonging to the patron. Ritual objects made of clay are prepared, such as the head of a horse, a man, a bull, a ram and a he-goat, which are then built into the altar. In ancient times, these heads may have been those of sacrificed victims. Afterwards, the five main priests who will play the most important role in the ritual performance are selected. Then there is the consecration of the patron. He is made to sit on an antelope skin, a turban is wrapped around his head and he is given a staff. For the next twelve days, until the end of the ritual, the patron will have to carry around the staff and sit on the antelope skin. He will also have to abstain from washing himself, from sexual intercourse and from speaking, except for the recitation of the sacred verses.

On the fourth day of the performance, stalks of the sacred Soma plant are ritually purchased, outside the ritual enclosure. They are placed on a bullock skin and carried on the Soma cart into the ritual arena. The Soma is treated as

[24] Staal 1986.

[25] For a more detailed description of this complex ritual, see Eggeling 1897: xiii–xxvii, Kane 1941: 1246–55, and Staal 1986: 55–8. See also Glucklich's (2008: 36–42) brief, yet perceptive, discussion. Cf. also Dumont 1951.

if it were a royal guest – it is installed on a throne, and homage is paid to it. After that, the ground for constructing the fire altar is prepared. The preparation requires the burial of the clay object made on the first day of the ritual as well as of a live tortoise and a golden image of a man. Then, the first layer of brick is laid. Over the course of the next four days, one further layer of the fire altar is laid each day. Each of the five layers consists of 200 bricks. The odd layers point in one direction, the even layers in another. In the first, third and fifth layers a 'naturally perforated stone' (*svayamātṛṇṇa*) is put in the middle of the fire altar. These stones are not artefacts, but perforated pebbles found in nature. If fully perforated pebbles cannot be found, pebbles with dents or small depressions are also acceptable. Once the altar is completed, Agni, fire, is installed in the centre of the last layer of the brick altar. A long offering of clarified butter is poured into it, followed by several other offerings.

From the tenth day, the ceremony will continue throughout the next two days including the nights. At daybreak the morning pressing of Soma is carried out. After a complex series of minor rituals, the priests crawl all together towards the fire altar and make an oblation. Then they drink the Soma. During the midday Soma pressing the priests are offered the compensation for the ritual performance and the patron of the sacrifice is anointed as in a royal consecration. After the evening Soma pressing a series of chants, recitations, oblations to Soma and Soma drinking are performed. This is completed at dawn on the twelfth day. After the performance of an expiation rite, whose aim is to remove potential ritual mistakes made during the performance, the patron and his wife, together with the priests, take the ritual bath which concludes the ritual. Then the patron carries home the three sacred fires to which he will offer an oblation of clarified butter in the morning and the evening, for the rest of his life. Finally, the ritual enclosure is set on fire.

What is this extremely elaborate ritual all about? According to the Nambudiri ritual experts interviewed by Staal, they perform the *agnicayana* in order to obtain immortality. This belief is in line with the traditional interpretations found in Vedic literature.[26] Specifically, the *agnicayana* is supposed to bring about a twofold result: to provide the patron of the sacrifice with 1) wealth, prosperity and a 'whole life' (*sarvam āyus*), that is, a life extended to its full span, traditionally fixed at 100 years; and 2) post-mortem immortality.[27]

The most detailed interpretation of the *agnicayana* is found in the tenth chapter of the *Śatapatha Brāhmaṇa*. Traditionally known as the *agnirahasya*,

[26] See, for instance, *Taittirīya Saṃhitā* 5.4.11: 'He who desires heaven should build a falcon-shaped altar because the falcon is the fastest among all birds. Having become a falcon himself, the sacrifice flies up to the heavenly world' (trans. Glucklich 2008: 40).

[27] See Eggeling 1897: xxiii.

'the secret of the fire', this chapter provides a wide variety of interpretations. In reconsidering this text, my concern is to gain clarity on the question 'How does the patron of the sacrifice obtain immortality?' Or, more precisely, 'How does he ritually construct for himself a "divine self/body" (*daiva ātman*)?'

For the ritual to be effective, two interrelated requirements must be fulfilled: the flawless performance of all ritual acts, and the concomitant awareness on the part of the ritual participants of the acts' symbolic, hidden import. Rather than adopting an evolutionary reading of the history of Brāhmaṇa thought, and subjectively considering ritual speculations as a later accretion, a more adequate description of the ancient ritualists' intention would regard both ritual performance and the attendant speculations as two sides of the same coin. This interpretation seems to be in line with what is stated at *Śatapatha Brāhmaṇa* 10.4.3.9: 'one becomes immortal . . . by means of knowledge (*vidyā*) or ritual action (*karman*)'.[28] This statement does not mark an either/or alternative, but identifies ritual action-cum-knowledge as the necessary instrument for attaining immortality: there follow the words 'it is this fire altar that is knowledge, and this fire altar that is ritual action'. Speculations play an important part, yet, unlike in some Upaniṣadic passages, they do not involve a depreciation of the ritual acts. Both ritual practice and speculations are equally essential components of the ritualists' technology of immortality.[29]

It is difficult to provide a lucid description of the *Śatapatha Brāhmaṇa* speculations. Intertwined with fragmentary references to cosmogonies and myths, speculations about specific ritual episodes and about the names of particular ritual stages and implements follow each other without interruption. To try to bring order to this dizzying speculative vortex would be to force it into a straitjacket. In spite of their variety, however, these speculations tend to converge on a central point: the *identification* of the patron of the sacrifice with a set of other entities.

Because the notion of identification plays a central role in the ritualists' speculations, a few more words are in order here. It has often been observed that the Vedic thinkers conceived of the universe as a complex web of connections underlying the seemingly disparate elements of reality.[30] Their central concern was to identify these hidden connections, which are most typically designated by the technical term *bandhu*, 'bond, connection',[31] whereby they presumed to

28 A similar formula occurs in ŚB 10.4.4.4.

29 The close connection between action and knowledge seems to be reinforced by the etymological elucidation in ŚB 6.2.3.1, which links *ci*, 'to pile up [the fire altar]' and *cit*, 'to think hard on something'; cf. Silburn's (1989: 66) remarks on this passage.

30 For a clear and informative description of this central feature of the Vedic worldview, see, e.g., Jamison and Brereton 2014: 23–4, and Olivelle 1998: 24–7.

31 This term has been studied by Renou 1946, Gonda 1965, Oguibenine 1983, and Smith 1989. Among the other terms designating the Vedic connections, *ādeśa* (for which see,

obtain powerful knowledge about the way things *really are*. Modern commentators refer to these connections with a variety of terms (e.g. 'identifications', 'homologies', 'connections', 'interlinkages'), which reflect more or less diverging interpretations of their nature and function. For our purposes, suffice it to say that the Vedic system of connections is the 'episteme'[32] informing some of the ways in which Vedic thinkers thought, and that the identifications of the patron of the sacrifice in the *agnicayana* must be understood within this wider thought-world.

Among the multiple and ever-shifting identifications obtaining in the *Śatapatha Brāhmaṇa*, the fundamental one links Prajāpati, the year, the fire altar (commonly simply referred to as *agni*, 'fire'), and the patron of the sacrifice. This veritable identification chain provides the basis for the 'sacrificial metaphysics'[33] of the *agnicayana* performance, in which different frameworks of reference and attendant symbolic meanings are integrated in one polyvalent discourse. Thus, to explain, the text often relates the cosmogonic myth of Prajāpati, 'the lord of creatures', the main divine figure in the *Brāhmaṇas*. Prajāpati was the first being and generated all creatures out of his own body. Because this act left him exhausted and disunited, a *ritual* reintegration of all creatures into his body was then necessary to assure his wholeness. The performance of the *agnicayana* is seen as the re-enactment of this primordial reintegration. Prajāpati is, furthermore, identified with the year, which in turn symbolises time both in its entirety as unlimited extent and in its destructive aspect as death, 'the one that puts an end' (*antaka*) to one's lifespan. The fire altar is another element in the identification chain; it stands for the spatial dimension and symbolises the whole universe. Lastly, the identification between the fire altar and the patron (and consequently between the latter and all the other entities above) introduces yet another dimension, that is, the individual 'self' (*ātman*).

The interrelatedness of the identification chain's multiple dimensions is enacted and reinforced through the ritual performance. Thus, the ritual placing of the fire altar's bricks in the right order does not only symbolise the creation of space through the reconstruction of a miniature representation of the visible universe; it also operates on the other levels of the identification. Accordingly, by doing so it reintegrates Prajāpati's scattered limbs into a whole body, and organises the disunited time's portions into a temporal structure. Also, and more germane to our concerns here, such a performance produces a cohesive, immortal 'self' (*ātman*).

Thieme 1968, Kahrs 1998: 178–83, and Pontillo 2003) and *upaniṣad* (see, e.g., Falk 1986 and Olivelle 1998: 24) have attracted particular attention.

32 See Smith 1989: 47–8; Smith references Michael Foucault's work.

33 Eggeling 1897: xvii.

But how exactly is the *agnicayana* supposed to make the patron immortal? It is useful to attend briefly to the vocabulary qualifying the ways in which immortality is attained. Most fundamentally, the immortal self is won through an act of (re-) construction, which is commonly expressed in Sanskrit with forms of *saṃ-skṛ*, 'to put together', from the same root as 'Sanskrit'.[34] This finding is in line with B. K. Smith's thesis that ritual has a predominantly constructive function in Vedic India. As Smith has convincingly argued,[35] ritual is the means by which Vedic ritualists constructed their world; most notably, with ritual they constructed existence on the level of cosmogony (reintegration of Prajāpati's dismembered body), on the level of human beings (the *saṃskāra* 'rite of passage' marking the important stages in the highborn's life), and on the level of life after death. Thus, the *agnicayana* can be regarded as a complex ritual of reintegration enabling the patron to gradually and painstakingly *construct* his immortal self.

In addition to the central notion of 'constructing', yet other terms are used; immortality can also be 'reached' (*naś*), 'obtained' (*āp*) and 'enclosed' (*ava-rudh*).The idea would seem to be this: by ritually reconstructing the universe one encompasses space and time within the ritually constructed fire altar, becomes lord over the universe, and thereby reaches immortality.

How can we envision the patron's transition from the mortal to the immortal sphere? Paul Mus has long since offered a fascinating answer to this question.[36] In his view, the *agnicayana* is premised on the recognition of a radical discontinuity between the contingent and finite world of men and the permanent world of immortality. In sharp contrast to the *Upaniṣads*, in which the identification of the individual *ātman* and the immortal *brahman* is based on the recognition of a deeper, ontological continuity between the two, the *Brāhmaṇas* manifest a fragmented universe. Immortality is accessible to the patron of the sacrifice only by means of the fire altar, which becomes his ritually constituted self. Recall that the sizes of the ritual enclosures and of the fire altar are functions of the patron's physical size. A 'rupture of plane' takes place whereby the patron's 'substitute body',[37] the fire altar, is transposed into a cosmic, enduring reality. Francis Clooney gives a lucid summary of Mus' main ideas:

> In building the sacrificial altar in the carefully prescribed manner, the sacrificer is constructing his own self out of temporal, discontinuous, and finite elements such as bricks. This construction identifies the sacrifice with Prajāpati and the cosmos, not

[34] See Smith 1989: 101 and Thieme 1982.

[35] Smith 1989.

[36] Mus 1935. I regret that Mus' book was not available to me at the moment of writing; I therefore rely on the summary of Mus' main themes given in Reynolds 1981 and further developed by Clooney 1990: 196–205.

[37] See Reynolds 1981: 231.

> by some direct imitative (iconic) resemblance, but by an imitation of Prajāpati's primordial self-construction in the original act of the sacrifice. Acknowledgment of the contingency of human effort and human materials leads not to a cessation of action, but to a particular arrangement of actions in order to transcend their limitations; for through the finite the finite can be transposed into the unlimited.[38]

To conclude, the *agnicayana* is a complex ritual technology whereby the patron constructs an immortal, extracorporeal self for himself. This immortal self is 'projected into another ontological sphere, into a *loka* ["world"] other than the earthly one',[39] and will be accessible only after death.

Some comparative considerations

The comparison of the Greek and Indian evidence allows us to ask some intriguing cross-cultural questions about immortality. What is the relation between the immortal being and the person that once lived? Is there any continuation of a personal identity? In other words, what does one retain of 'oneself' in immortality? A little thought experiment might be helpful here. If someone were to visit Plato or Yājñavalkya in their respective states of immortality, would it still make sense to speak of a 'Plato' and a 'Yājñavalkya'? Would they respond to such appellations – 'I am Plato', 'I am Yājñavalkya'? The latter would perhaps answer with a faint nod; the former would surely be silent.

In ancient India, there is not *one* immortal self, but there are as many selves as ritual actors. The ritual performance through which immortality is attained is not regarded as the operation of a particular subject, but derives its efficacy from nothing other than itself.[40] The ritual event is thus foregrounded, whereas the human element is 'decentred'.[41] Nonetheless, each such performance contributes to constructing an individual, immortal self. That is, because the divine self (*daiva ātman*) is the result of one's ritual, such a self is individually specific in that it correlates with one's ritual performances in this world. In this respect, it is helpful to cite B. K. Smith again: 'The collective oblation one offers over the course of the years – that is, the quantity and quality of his sacrificial history – determines the *daiva ātman* as it is transformed from offering to transcendent identity.'[42] There are, therefore, different grades of immortality.

In *Timaeus*, immortality is in essence a process of depersonalisation. It is a return to the primordial moment when all individual souls created by the

38 Clooney 1990: 196–7; see also Silburn 1989: 90ff.
39 Smith 1989: 103.
40 See Silburn 1989: 57.
41 This notion is developed in Clooney 1990: 163ff.
42 Smith 1989: 117.

demiurge were exactly identical to one another (41e). The soul's diversification into distinct human beings, man and women, animals and lower living creatures results from the individual souls' behaviour in their successive reincarnations. The individual's pursuit of immortality, the training for becoming immortal, can thus be seen as the attempt to reabsorb one's individual chain of reincarnation in a way that corresponds to the reverse order of the development and history of this universe. After death, the individual who has perfected himself by following his immortal soul and living a philosophical life will return to the star with which it was originally associated (42b).

Immortality is represented differently in the two texts under scrutiny. In stark contrast to some *Upaniṣad* passages portraying the self as inhabiting the innermost core of ourselves and lying beyond life's changes and experience – beyond the grip of death[43] – the *Śatapatha Brāhmaṇa* describes an external, disembodied self, the immortality of which is precarious. The ritual construction of one's divine self correlates with the quality and quantity of the ritual performed, which determines the kind and duration of the ritually constructed divine life. Immortality is not won once and for all, but is provisional and reversible; once the patron dies, his ritually constructed divine self needs his progeny's ritual acts to continue to exist.

Conversely, in Plato's *Timaeus* man's immortality is a given. The 'immortal principle of soul (ἀρχὴν ψυχῆς ἀθάνατον)' (69c) is planted in one's own constitution. It is true that immortality needs to be regained, as it were, by strenuous bodily and intellectual exercise. Nonetheless, it can be attained precisely because it is already there. In ancient India, on the other hand, there appears to be an ontological rupture between man's predicament and immortality. Being mortal by definition, man can obtain immortality not by centralising all his efforts on his immortal core – such a thing is in fact absent – but through ritually fashioning a substitute body. For Plato, the path to immortality consists in cultivating something which is already in ourselves; for Yājñavalkya, immortality is a ritually constructed extracorporeal residence.

Even though both kinds of immortality can be fully realised only post-mortem, they differ as to the degree to which they inform the present life. In order to attain their final, sidereal immortality, Plato's disciples must cultivate their rational soul in this life. A more rational and therefore ethically just behaviour seems to be this training's necessary outcome. For the ancient Indian practitioners, the pursuit of immortality happens entirely through and within the highly technical domain of ritual. Once he has built a divine body for himself, nothing would seem to change in the sacrificial patron's daily life. In short, while

[43] See BU 1.3.12; 3.1.3.

Plato's search for immortality emphasises *this* life, Yājñavalkya's ritual technology is centred on *this* ritual.

We must however avoid reading the above observations through the conventional lens magnifying a reified view of the Greek and the Indian traditions. It would be especially misleading, I believe, to read the correlation between immortality and ethics in Plato and the apparent absence of ethical implications in the *Śatapatha Brāhmaṇa*, as well as the former's emphasis on self-definition and the Indian centrality of a ritual-cum-knowledge, as reinforcing the die-hard stereotypes about rational Greece and mystical India. While the differences identified above are, in my opinion, real, they do not readily fit that old-fashioned yet still partly dominant model. In this respect, note that Plato's fundamentally positive belief in the teleology of the cosmos and the highest soul's immortality appears as more mystically oriented, and perhaps farther removed from our modern sensibility, than the *Brāhmaṇas*' vision of a precarious immortality, always in need of reinstatement.

Acknowledgements

I wish to thank Gastón Basile, Olivier Dufault and Luke Parker for reading an earlier draft of this paper and providing several useful comments. Special thanks go to Susanne Gödde and Kenneth Yu for their critical remarks, and to Martin Hose for lending me some books from his personal library.

8

Does the concept of *theōria* fit the beginning of Indian thought?

Alexis Pinchard

Is early Indian thought more interested in salvation than in truth?

In 'Philosophy and the Crisis of the European Man',[1] while aiming at characterising the intellectual attitude of the primeval European thinkers in contradistinction with other wise men of the same time in India and China, Edmund Husserl attributes the concept of 'philosophy', understood as the quest for the firm basement of any future science, only to the Greek Pre-Socratics. Of course both Indian and Greek thinkers consider the universe as a whole and they try to explain it from a single principle inasmuch as it constitutes a whole. They both care about what is universal, and might have expressed true assertions about it. But, according to Husserl, the purpose of such global explanations is different on each side, and therefore Indian thinkers still belong to the so-called 'mythical-religious' mentality whereas only Greece reaches the pure philosophy that implies the autonomy of rational thought. With the word 'autonomy' Husserl does not only mean that the individual mind thinks by itself, without considering tradition or sacred revelation,[2] but also and mainly that rational thought has rational goals. In Husserl's view rationality did exist in the mythical-religious mentality of India and China, but not in a sovereign way. Only the early Greek thinkers would be concerned with the research for truth for the sake of truth. This love of truth would be independent from the benefits that the possession of truth may bring to the lover, for example immortality. Thus, thanks to the Greek starting point, the

[1] Husserl 1965: 164–6.

[2] Bernabé-Mendoza (2013: 32–3) has shown that the Vedic cosmogony of RV 10.129 already claimed to be independent from any previous tradition. This relatively autonomous thinking reminds us of the Pythagorean appearance of rationality in the same realm of cosmogony. But real autonomy does not only consist in independence from tradition, as Husserl rightly noticed. The question of what purpose rationality is used to remains crucial.

discovery of truth can appear as the main task of all mankind, progressing generation by generation, step by step *in infinitum*. Europe would be responsible for this spiritual inheritance of a continuous progress in pure knowledge. By contrast Indian thinkers would be mainly interested in personal salvation. In India knowledge could be useful, and even necessary to escape death and every evil, but it is not the highest goal by itself and in itself. It is just a means to release the soul from the bounds of body, disease, fear and death. The evidence for such a thesis would be the fact that real philosophy, i.e. the Greek quest for the knowledge of the first principles of the universe and of thought, is born from wonder (*thaumazein*), as Aristotle states in the *Metaphysics* A2, because to wonder implies acknowledging one's own ignorance:

> That it is not a productive science is clear from a consideration of the first philosophers. It is through wonder that men now begin and originally began to philosophise; wondering in the first place at obvious perplexities, and then by gradual progression raising questions about the greater matters too, e.g. about the changes of the moon and of the sun, about the stars and about the origin of the universe. Now he who wonders and is perplexed feels that he is ignorant (thus the myth-lover is in a sense a philosopher, since myths are composed of wonders); therefore if it was to escape ignorance that men studied philosophy, it is obvious that they pursued science for the sake of knowledge, and not for any practical utility. (Aristotle *Metaphysics* A2, 982b)

According to Aristotle, the common rooting in wonder makes the link between the Pre-Socratics, Plato and Aristotle, even if the doctrines about the first principle are not the same since several Pre-Socratics were materialist, as for example Thales. It brings out philosophy as a spiritual phenomenon endowed with an intrinsic unity. According to Husserl, the concept of *theōria*, as elaborated by Aristotle in his *Nicomachean Ethics* and *Metaphysics*, would not fit the beginning of Indian thought, although it does fit the Pre-Socratic beginning of philosophy. In Greece too, the knowledge of the highest principle produces some benefit for the knower, especially pleasure, but it is only in Greece that this external benefit is not the main motive for undertaking metaphysical researches. Moreover, pleasure supervenes on Greek theoretical activity only if pleasure is not consciously intended therein. It is only in Greece that reflection about the universe as a whole ruled by a unique principle constitutes the expression of a spiritual freedom.

Of course this thesis of Husserl is quite simplistic and in this chapter I aim at refuting it, but it is not very easy to do so because it implies a change in our views both of Greek and of Indian early philosophy. In this chapter I do not directly address the cause of the famous striking similarities between Greek and Indian early thoughts, but rather the question of the extent of these similarities. The question of their possible origin will come later.

First, let us see what seems to sustain Husserl's view.

In the *Upaniṣads* the knower globally identifies with the object of his knowledge, or rather he realises that since the very beginning of his conscious existence he already was secretly the same thing as what he knows. Therefore he becomes himself the highest principle which constitutes the universe as a whole when he gets an intuition thereof. Such a process of identification seems to concern not only the intellect but every aspect of the person, including its body, because the highest principle may be related to the body, when it is for example breath or fire. The highest knowledge does not necessarily have a *meta*-physical object, although the highest principle is always invisible and concealed inside the human being. Therefore the presentation of the highest knowledge cohabits in the *Upaniṣads* with magic tricks and aggressive spells (see for example the *parimara* ritual, 'death around', of KauU 2.12) in order to get power, wealth and glory in society:

> Verily, he who knows the chiefest (*jyeṣṭham*) and best (*śreṣṭham*), becomes the chiefest and best of his own [people]. Breath (*prāṇa*), verily, is chiefest and best. He who knows this becomes the chiefest and best of his own [people] and even of those of whom he wishes so to become. (BU 6.1.1)

Even the gods obtain some benefit from their knowledge of the highest principle. Indeed they are gods, endowed with immortality and universal power, just because they unite with it:

> Verily, those gods who are in the brahman-world meditate upon that Self (*ātman*). Therefore all worlds and all desires have been appropriated by them. He obtains all worlds and all desires who has found out and who understands that Self. (ChU 8.12.6)

Because of its supposed power in the realm of everyday life, the highest knowledge is a useful treasure jealously kept in the circle of family and initiates, just like the family-*maṇḍalas* of the *Ṛgveda*, which were composed and transmitted in the same real or symbolic male lineage.[3] Sacred knowledge is not exhibited on the *agora* in order to be tested through a free dialogue with anybody. The process of transmission occurs generation by generation along an initiatory thread and is organised by fixed rules. It is not spread out among citizens so that each one could contribute to its indefinite development. Such a selective teaching creates both power and obligations for the recipients. These obligations consist in ritual, pedagogical and spiritual duties.

But there is a crucial difference between the knowledge of a mere magic for-

[3] *maṇḍala* II to VII. For the same restriction of transmission concerning the Avesta, see Panaino 2003.

mula and the Upaniṣadic highest knowledge, which is always a self-knowledge: whereas the magic formula destroys a certain evil or a certain enemy in certain circumstances, the self-knowledge releases man from every aspect of his finiteness because the self he identifies with is infinite. Such a knowledge really brings salvation. Moreover it is said that every aspect of his person is completely saved because only the part of him that identifies with his true secret self, be it intellectual or not, constitutes his real person. There is no real division between a spiritual part and a social part because one of them is unreal. The assertions concerning the glory and the power of the one 'who knows thus' (*ya evaṃ veda*) have to be interpreted: who is this one? Of course the visible body remains mortal but the wise man, with all its real parts, reaches immortality:

> *akāmó dhī́ro amŕ̥taḥ svayaṃbhū́ rásena tr̥ptó ná kútaś canónaḥ /*
> *tám evá vidvā́n ná bibhāya mr̥tyór ātmā́naṃ dhī́ram ajáraṃ yúvānam* //44//

> Free from desire, wise, self-existent, satisfied with sap [ritual drink], not deficient in any respect, one is not afraid of death if one knows this wise, immortal and unaging One as oneself. (AV 10.8.44, hymn devoted to Skambha, the cosmic pillar)

The self-knowledge provides victory, but such a victory does not follow a fight against a particular enemy. It deals with a victory against everything that has a form and a name in the world. Victory here means access to an absolute transcendence:

> He obtains the victory of the sun, indeed, a victory higher than the victory of the sun is his, who, knowing this thus, reverences the sevenfold Sāman, measured in itself, as leading beyond death – yea, who reverences the Sāman! (ChU 2.10.6)

This salvific function of self-knowledge in the *Upaniṣads* constitutes their real unity beyond the multiplicity of the doctrines concerning the nature of the Self. It implies that this Self is impassive even though it works as the subject of every experience, including the experience of pain. It is the light which illuminates pain, but not pain itself, and it is the same for pleasure.

> *sūryo yathā sarvalokasya cakṣuḥ na lipyate cākṣuṣair bāhyadoṣaiḥ /*
> *ekas tathā sarvabhūtāntar ātma na lipyate lokaduḥkhena bāhyaḥ* //11//

> As the sun, the eye of the whole world, is not sullied by the external faults of the eyes, so the one Inner Self of all things is not sullied by the evil in the world, being external to it. (KaU 5.11–12)

Therefore the specific immortality of the Self is not a merely temporal continuation of our everyday life, with its various pains and pleasures, but a sudden getting in touch with eternity. Therefore the *ātman* is not the *bhokr̥*, the agent of enjoyment, which has preferences and aversions. For example, while Prajāpati teaches Indra about the true nature of the self, Indra wants to obtain something enjoyable (*bhogyam*) and, at the beginning, he does not understand that the pure consciousness – unlike the relationship consisting in enjoying[4] something – is not an object relationship:

> 'Now, when one is sound asleep, composed, serene, and knows no dream – that is the Self (*ātman*)', said he [Prajāpati]. 'That is the immortal, the fearless. That is the brahman.'
> Then with tranquil heart he [Indra] went forth.
> Then, even before reaching the gods, he saw this danger: 'Assuredly, indeed, this one does not exactly know his Self (*ātmānam*) with the thought "I am he", nor indeed the things here. He becomes one who has gone to destruction. I see nothing enjoyable (*bhogyam*) in this.' (ChU 8.11.1)

Thus the kind of benefits the Upaniṣadic mystic knowledge can bring are at the same time greater than any benefit that a mundane power may bring, and more abstract. Moreover these benefits are not external to knowledge since they result from the features of the very object of knowledge, that is, the Self. Here knowledge is not a mere means that one could leave once it has worked. Self-knowledge is so important that it changes life: it does not mean that it is a mere tool. The power of the old Indian self-knowledge is perhaps not as remote from the purity of the Greek *theōria* as Husserl thought.

Back to Greece: searching for immortality through philosophy

Second, Husserl's view about the Pre-Socratics is quite idealistic. Indeed he confuses their passionate interest in knowledge with Immanuel Kant's ethics. In the Pre-Socratics we can also find rivalry, challenge, the quest for dominion. The well-known imitation of god that we find in Plato (*homoiōsis tōi theōi*) worked earlier as an imitation of divine power on earth. For example Empedocles praised his own wisdom inasmuch as it made him 'immortal god instead of mortal' (θεὸς ἄμβροτος, οὐκέτι θνητός), bringing him also glory and political success (31 DK B112). The imperishable fame provided to heroes by poets like Homer (*kleos aphthiton*)[5] has echoes in such a self-narrative. Moreover Parmenides' deity is supposed to deliver knowledge which makes the philosopher able to master the world of appearances in which he lives. Through the cosmological knowledge the philosopher can anticipate the phenomena better than other mortals and thus better survive and succeed on the political level:

> τόν σοι ἐγὼ διάκοσμον ἐοικότα πάντα φατίζω,
> ὡς οὐ μή ποτέ τίς σε βροτῶν γνώμη παρελάσσηι.

4 See the Sanskrit root *BHUJ*-, 'to enjoy', 'to make use of'.
5 See Homer *Iliad* 3.276 = 320; 7.202; 24.308.

> This order of things I declare to you to be likely in its entirety, in such a way that never shall any mortal outstrip you in practical judgment. (28 DK B8.60–1)

But concerning the knowledge of 'the unmoved heart of truth' itself, Eleaticism does not neglect its internal benefit for the soul. Being, which has to be seized by an intellectual intuition after the sensuous cognition has been refuted, stands beyond every pair of contraries including pain and pleasure, disease and health:

> So then the all is eternal and infinite and homogeneous; and it could neither perish nor become greater nor change its arrangement *nor suffer pain or distress*. If it experienced any of these things it would no longer be one; for if it becomes different, it is necessary that being should not be homogeneous, but that which was before must perish, and that which was not must come into existence. If then the all should become different by a single hair in ten thousand years, it would perish in the whole of time. And it is impossible for its order to change, for the order existing before does not perish, nor does another which did not exist come into being; and since nothing is added to it or subtracted from it or made different, how could any of the things that are change their order? But if anything became different, its order would already have been changed. *Nor does it suffer pain, for the all could not be pained since it would be impossible for anything suffering pain always to be; nor does it have power equal to the power of what is healthy. It would not be homogeneous if it suffered pain; it would suffer pain whenever anything was added or taken away, and it would no longer be homogeneous. Nor could what is healthy suffer a pang of pain, for both the healthy and being would perish, and not-being would come into existence. The same reasoning that applies to pain applies also to distress.* Nor is there any void, for the void is nothing, and that which is nothing could not be. Nor does it move, for it has nowhere to go to, since it is full; for if there were a void it could go into the void, but since there is no void it has nowhere to go to. It could not be rare and dense, for it is not possible for the rare to be as full as the dense, but the rare is already more empty than the dense. (Melissus, 30 DK B7, emphasis added)

Of course, if the One is the only reality, what knows it on the one hand and, on the other hand, the One itself, cannot be different. Therefore what applies to it applies also to the soul of the perfect philosopher. This emancipation from becoming and from the various psychological affects that becoming implies clearly reminds us of Upaniṣadic salvation. The Upaniṣadic Self too stands beyond the alternation of night and day, of good and evil:

> Then, just as one driving a chariot looks down upon the two chariot-wheels, thus he looks down upon day and night, thus upon good deeds and evil deeds, and upon all the pairs of opposites. This one, devoid of good deeds, devoid of evil deeds, a knower of brahman, unto very brahman goes on. (KauU 1.4)

Furthermore Husserl defines the emergence of Pre-Socratic thought as the emergence of the common project to develop knowledge of the universe *in infinitum*. But how could Eleatic being, which is absolutely one, give place to a progressive and possibly infinite inquiry? Being, because of its simplicity, can only be entirely known or ignored. It is seized by an instantaneous intuition which, so to speak, immediately brings the intellect to the very middle of absolute being itself: τὸ γὰρ αὐτὸ νοεῖν ἐστίν τε καὶ εἶναι, 'the same is to think and to be' (Parmenides, B3). *Noeîn* implies a jump to a new level of experience, but it does not deal with the progressive analysis of normal empirical data. This is why such knowledge, in Greece too, can have a soteriological dimension. Our finiteness is not a fatality. Such knowledge is not the *result* of a previous break with the sensuous cognitions through which we act in order to save our life with its intrinsic vulnerability, but the break itself. The various metaphysical arguments about Being prove only that there is no other real object of knowledge, but they do not result in an increasingly precise knowledge of Being. Therefore Husserl's view about progress in philosophy would better apply to the Ionian school, which addresses *phusis*, or to Eleatic cosmology as a mere arrangement of phenomena, but does not fit the whole Pre-Socratic movement. For example it works with just a part of Xenophanes' thought: 'In the beginning the gods did not at all reveal all things clearly to mortals, but by searching men in the course of time find them out better' (21 DK B18).

The Eleatic stress on immediate intuition as the only way to know the highest principle offers another great similarity with the *Upaniṣads*:

> *pratibodhaviditaṃ matam amṛtatvaṃ hi vindate* /
>
> When it is found by intuition, it is thought: so one finds immortality. (KU 2.4a)

Of course, in Greece, the idea that this intuition of absolute reality immediately produces immortality for the soul of the wise man is not clearly expressed before Plato and Aristotle. When the soul is the subject of a certain knowledge, this knowledge can change the knowledge of which the soul is the object, because to be the subject of this very knowledge changes the soul itself: this fact is only alluded to in the Pre-Socratics. Nevertheless, we can find in the Pre-Socratics some traces of this salvific power of knowledge inasmuch as philosophy and mystery cults echo each other.

Against Husserl's rejection of the question of salvation from the earliest Greek philosophy, let us first note that the philosophers who have elaborated the concept of pure *theōria* – I mean Plato in his *Theaetetus* and Aristotle in his *Metaphysics* – are exactly the same as those who claimed that this very *theōria*, while applying to the highest principle of reality, lets the thinking part of the soul (*nous*) reach a special degree of immortality, beyond space and time, whether the common soul of human beings possesses a finite or an infinite duration:[6]

[6] Adluri-Bagchee (2012) has shown that these two levels of immortality occur in ancient Brahmanic culture. It is one more Indo-Greek parallel.

> If then the intellect is something divine in comparison with man, so is the life of the intellect divine in comparison with human life. Nor ought we to obey those who enjoin that a man should have man's thoughts and a mortal the thoughts of mortality, but we ought so far as possible to achieve immortality, and do all that man may to live in accordance with the highest thing in him; for though this be small in bulk, in power and value it far surpasses all the rest.
>
> It may even be held that this is the true self of each,[7] inasmuch as it is the dominant and better part; and therefore it would be a strange thing if a man should choose to live not his own life but the life of some other than himself.
>
> Moreover what was said before will apply here also: that which is best and most pleasant for each creature is that which is proper to the nature of each; accordingly the life of the intellect is the best and the pleasantest life for man, inasmuch as the intellect more than anything else is man; therefore this life will be the happiest. (Aristotle *Nicomachean Ethics* X, 7)

Already in Diotima's speech Plato has established such a connection between the contemplation of the highest reality, i.e., the intelligible Form of Beauty, and the access to a peculiar immortality, not exceeding the brief moment of the intellection, different from the temporal immortality of the soul as a principle of life demonstrated in the *Phaedo* and in book X of the *Republic*:[8]

> ἢ οὐκ ἐνθυμῇ, ἔφη, ὅτι ἐνταῦθα αὐτῷ μοναχοῦ γενήσεται, ὁρῶντι ᾧ ὁρατὸν τὸ καλόν, τίκτειν οὐκ εἴδωλα ἀρετῆς, ἅτε οὐκ εἰδώλου ἐφαπτομένῳ, ἀλλὰ ἀληθῆ, ἅτε τοῦ ἀληθοῦς ἐφαπτομένῳ· τεκόντι δὲ ἀρετὴν ἀληθῆ καὶ θρεψαμένῳ ὑπάρχει θεοφιλεῖ γενέσθαι, καὶ εἴπέρ τῳ ἄλλῳ ἀνθρώπων ἀθανάτῳ καὶ ἐκείνῳ;

> 'Do but consider', she said, 'that there only will it befall him, as he sees the beautiful through that which makes it visible, to breed not illusions but true examples of virtue, since his contact is not with illusion but with truth. So when he has begotten a true virtue and has reared it up he is destined to win the friendship of the divinity and, above all men, to become immortal.' (*Symp.* 212a)

Therefore it would be strange if the salvific power of the *prōtē philosophia* (the 'primary philosophy', later called 'Metaphysics': Aristotle *Metaphysics* E, 1026a 24) were incompatible with the freedom and the disinterestedness which define it. Furthermore, the *prōtē philosophia* is free from any mundane interest

7 Unlike Sorabji (2006: 118), I do not think that the verb *doxeiē* means that Aristotle wanted to express some distance from the view that intellect is the true self of the man. For the view that intellectual life brings pleasure, which is typically Aristotelian, cannot be separated from the selfhood of the intellect.

8 For the immortality of the unfair and anti-philosophical soul, see Plato, *Republic* X, 610e. It is consistent with *Leges* X, where every soul is defined as a self-moving movement, and thus as a permanent movement, whatever kind of movement it gives to itself. The circular movement of intellection is only one kind among the various kinds of movement a soul can produce for itself.

just because it is a 'twice divine' science which implies a kind of salvation by itself: it has the autonomous divinity as its object but also as its subject (Aristotle *Metaphysics* A2), so that he who has got this science merges into divinity and so into its essential self-sufficiency and immortality inasmuch as he knows. Deity is not a slave, even of its own needs, because it has no need. Therefore spiritual divinisation is the condition of disinterestedness. Subsequently the intellective knowledge of the first principles is not a mere means to gain immortality, a means that one could leave once the goal is reached. This knowledge produces immortality when it is desired for itself, just like it produces pleasure, I mean like youth produces the flower according to Aristotle's very words. Indeed immortality is not an effect of the intellective knowledge, standing outside this knowledge, but just a way to express the fact that such a knowledge gets in touch with what is universal and necessary. Theoretical immortality is not something more which would be added to the normal existence. It is not a 'plus'. It concerns the level of being, but not the level of having. This is why Greek immortalisation through and in philosophy consists in focusing on oneself, if the self is correctly understood: the intellect is the very self of man, the man of the man so to speak, as Plato shows in the theriomorphic allegory of the soul which is to be found at the end of the *Republic*.[9]

Second, in the Pre-Socratics knowledge appears as endowed with a salvific dimension only when its transmission takes on the form of an initiatory revelation reflecting mystery cults. For example, Empedocles seems to use the vocabulary of the mysteries[10] in order to describe the destiny of wise men. Their intellectual virtue is supposed make them equal to the gods. They will share the table of the gods,

> εἰς δὲ τέλος μάντεις τε καὶ ὑμνοπόλοι καὶ ἰητροί
> καὶ πρόμοι ἀνθρώποισιν ἐπιχθονίοισι πέλονται,
> ἔνθεν ἀναβλαστοῦσι θεοὶ τιμῇσι φέριστοι.
> ἀθανάτοις ἄλλοισιν ὁμέστιοι, αὐτοτράπεζοι
> ἐόντες, ἀνδρείων ἀχέων ἀπόκληροι, ἀτειρεῖς.

9 See Plato *Republic* IX, 588d. Sorabji (2006: 116–17) correctly underlines Plato's view that the intellect is the true self of the man, but he does not clearly distinguish the two kinds of immortality that Plato considers. Of course the relation between these two ways to escape our bodily finiteness is very problematic, but an afterlife of pure thinking (see Sorabji 2006: 314) is not the only Platonic afterlife. Indeed the immortality of pure thinking can begin right now and has not to wait for any afterlife, even if it can develop better in the afterlife. The intellect is the true self of the man, so that any kind of human immortality must concern the intellect, but the problem is that some intellects are not faithful to their true nature and give up thinking.

10 For a compelling demonstration of the narrative and stylistic parallels between Empedocles and the Orphic gold tablets, see Herrero de Jáuregui 2013: 31–55.

> Finally they come among earthborn humans as soothsayers, poets, physicians and war chiefs. Hence they rise up as gods full of honours, sharing the hearth and the table of the other immortals, taking part neither in the sorrows of men nor in tiredness. (B146–7)

This privilege looks like the privilege of 'the ritually pure men' according to some writings attributed to Musaeus and his son Eumolpus by the itinerant Orphic priests.[11] Such an elevation put an end to the exile of the *daimon* from its original divine condition. Since the similar knows the similar, philosophical knowledge is a way to restore the primeval unity of the *sphairos* (the divine and homogeneous mass of being constituting the first step in Empedocles' cosmogony [B29]), which has been disturbed, at the individual level, by a voluntary ritual fault (to sacrifice animals, see B115). Universal knowledge reintroduced Love into the microcosm. Therefore to understand Empedocles' lesson guarantees salvation, even if the macrocosm remains under the common influence of Love and Strife.

Other allusions could be found in Parmenides, Heraclitus and in the Derveni Papyrus.[12] But they are only allusions. The *Hinterwelt*, in the sense of Nietzsche, relies on a *Hintertext*: the modern reader has to insert the fragments into a web of symbols and similes that are not directly included in the text in order to show the immortalising dimension of the personal practice of philosophy.

Nevertheless, in Greece as well as in India, there is an analogy between ritual knowledge and knowledge of the highest principle of the universe inasmuch as both aim at immortalising men and both are reserved for the happy few; in both cases the analogy reveals a concealed but essential aspect of what is compared. But the dynamic of the comparison is inverted between these cultures. What is obvious and superficial on one side is obscure and essential on the other side and reciprocally. In the Veda immortalising knowledge first appears as ritual knowledge, but then it must disclose itself as knowledge of the highest principle of the universe in order to reach its actual goal, which is the immortalisation of the individual. This transformation is possible only inasmuch as the elements of rites – thoughts, words, actions – are viewed as real things, existing by themselves forever, but not as peculiar cultural manifestations. Progressively the ritual injunctions appear as the true laws of nature and the inquiry about the real meaning of ritual acts, while obtaining the immortalising value of the external practice of the ritual itself, becomes a global attempt to give sense to the whole cosmos. The immortalising activity becomes an intellectual one. Between the

11 About the συμπόσιον τῶν ὁσίων in Hades according to the Orphic tradition, see Plato, *Republic* II, 363c.

12 For the Pre-Socratics in general see Bernabé 2002. For Parmenides see Feyerabend 1984 and Pinchard 2009: 563–73. For the Derveni Papyrus see Betegh 2004: 360–4.

beginning and the end of this process the form of transmission remains the same: oral, esoteric and finally intuitive.

Now in Greece the knowledge of the first principle is initially positive and public. But it must disclose itself as bearing the same form as certain ritual knowledge – that is, the secret knowledge imparted in mystery cults – in order to take over its immortalising power. The *prōtē philosophia* can evolve thus inasmuch as, on the one hand, mystery cults, by consisting of the re-enactment of an archetypical gesture, are for the soul a way to reintegrate its divine origin, and, on the other hand, the intuitive knowledge of the first principle implies a merging of the *ego* with the principle itself. This slow transformation is not necessarily and mainly chronological: rather it deals with an exegetical dialectic going deeper and deeper.

Wonder and love of truth in the *Upaniṣads*

Just like the Pre-Socratics, the *Upaniṣads* claim that the mystic knowledge, inasmuch as it brings out immortality, has to be understood in the perspective of a dialogue with the ritual tradition because the ritual tradition also faces our finiteness. There is a rivalry between two kinds of immortalising knowledge. In the older stratum of the Vedas, the *Brāhmaṇas* intended to let the 'sacrificer' (*yajamāna*) reach 'immortality by means of what is mortal', that is by sacrificial victims correctly laid out in space and time (*martyenāmṛtaṃ īpsaty*, AiĀ II, 3, 2). The knowledge presented in the *Brāhmaṇas* is supposed to point out the correct actions to be done in order to become immortal. Such a knowledge has a practical value but it is not immediately immortalising by itself. It just supplies a pattern for the crucial deed. By contrast Upaniṣadic wisdom has to be immediately immortalising by itself, and so cannot work as a mere means.

Finally the desire for truth for the sake of truth and the wonder really play a crucial part also in the *Upaniṣads*, maybe even more so than in Greece.

First, there is a real worrying about the essence and the definition of the Self (*ātman*), not only about its power. The Greek *tí esti* question ('what is it?'), so simportant in Plato[13] and Aristotle,[14] has echoes in this ChU passage:

> Prācīnaśāla Aupamanyava, Satyayajña Paulushi, Indradyumna Bhāllaveya, Jana Śārkarākshya and Buḍila Āśvatarāśvi – these great householders, greatly learned in sacred lore (*śrotriya*), having come together, pondered: 'What is our Self? What is the brahman (*ko na ātmā kim brahma*)?' (ChU 5.11.1)

[13] For the connection between this question and the intelligible Forms, see Plato, *Timaeus*, 50b 1: the sensible qualities inscribed in the *chōra* cannot work as a satisfying answer to the question 'what is it?' This question fits only intelligible Forms if some specification is expected.

[14] See for example Aristotle, *Metaphysics* 1026a 4.

But in India this question does not receive any definitive answer because the *ātman* is even stranger than what it is supposed to explain. In the Vedas there is a real wonder about natural phenomena, but the most wonderful thing is the paradoxical nature of the Self which offends the law of non-contradiction:

> *katháṃ vā́to nélayati katháṃ ná ramate mánaḥ /*
> *kím ā́paḥ satyáṃ prépsantīr nélayanti kadā́ caná //37//*
> *mahád yakṣáṃ bhúvanasya mádhye tápasi krāntáṃ salilásya pṛṣṭhé /*
> *tásmin chrayante yá u ké ca devā́ vṛkṣásya skándhaḥ parita iva śā́kʰāḥ //38//*
>
> How is it possible that the wind does not cease? How is it possible that the mind does not rest? Why do the Waters, seeking to attain truth, at no time so ever cease? *The great marvel in the midst of nature* (*mahád yakṣáṃ bhúvanasya mádhye*) strode in penance on the back of the Ocean – in it are set whatever gods there are, like branches of a tree roundabout the trunk. (AV 10.7.37–8, to Skambha, the cosmic pillar, emphasis added)

The syntagma *mahád yakṣáṃ bhúvanasya mádhye* occurs elsewhere in a similar context, while alluding again to the chief principle of all the world :

> *dūré pūrṇéna vasati dūrá ūnéna hīyate /*
> *mahád yakṣáṃ bʰúvanasya mádʰye tásmai balíṃ rāṣṭrabʰṛ́to bʰaranti //15//*
>
> In the distance it dwells with the fullness, in the distance it is devoid of deficiency – *the great marvel in the midst of nature*: to it the kingdom-bearers bear tribute. (AV 10.8.15, to Skambha, the cosmic pillar, emphasis added)

The word *yakṣa* itself ('marvel') is connected with the *brahman* in the *Upaniṣads*. The *brahman* is superior even to the gods to whom it grants immortality, so that it goes beyond their understanding. When the *brahman* directly appears the gods must acknowledge their inferiority:

> *brahma ha devebhyo vijigye / tasya ha brahmaṇo vijaye devā amahīyanta / ta aikṣantāsmākam evāyaṃ vijayo 'smākam evāyaṃ mahimeti /*
> *tad dhaiṣāṃ vijajñau / tebhyo ha prādur babhūva / tan na vyajānata <u>kim idam yakṣam</u> iti . . .*
>
> Now, the brahman won a victory for the gods. Now, in the victory of this brahman the gods were exulting. They bethought themselves: 'Ours indeed is this victory! Ours indeed is this greatness!'
> Now, It understood this of them. It appeared to them. They did not understand It. 'What wonderful being (*yakṣa*) is this?' they said. They said to Agni (Fire): 'Jātavedas, find out this – what this wonderful being is.' 'So be it.' (KU 3.1–2)

The chief principle of all the world is a 'marvel' because, like a riddle, it offends the law of non-contradiction. It can contain contraries because it stands beyond:

pūrṇā́t pūrṇám úd acati pūrṇā́m pūrṇéna sicyate /
utó tád adyá vidyāma yátas tát pariṣicyáte //29//

The full from the full he bends up; the full is poured with the full; also that may we know today, whence that is poured out. (AV 8.29, to Skambha, the cosmic pillar)

yád éjati pátati yác ca tíṣṭʰati prāṇád áprāṇan nimiṣác ca yád bhúvat /
tád dādhāra pṛthivī́ṃ viśvárūpaṃ tát saṃbhū́ya bhavaty ékam evá //11//

What stirs, flies, and what stands, and what is breathing, not breathing, winking – that, all-formed, sustains the earth; that, combining, becomes the One. (AV 10.8.11, to Skambha, the cosmic pillar)

Since contradiction belongs to the very nature of the chief principle, human wonder is not destined to disappear with the reaching of ultimate knowledge, but to become more and more intensive. The search is to be continued. Therefore Prajāpati as cosmic god is sometimes called 'Who' by name (Ka), when he [?] has his *anirukta* ('unarticulated') form, which is the primeval one.[15] His very essence is a perpetual question, asked by himself. This permanent wondering is just the contrary of what Aristotle attributes to the course of metaphysical research:

> The acquisition of this knowledge, however, must in a sense result in something which is the reverse of the outlook with which we first approached the inquiry. All begin, as we have said, by wondering that things should be as they are, e.g. with regard to marionettes, or the solstices, or the incommensurability of the diagonal of a square; because it seems wonderful to everyone who has not yet perceived the cause that a thing should not be measurable by the smallest unit. But we must end with the contrary and (according to the proverb) the better view, as men do even in these cases when they understand them; [20] for a geometrician would wonder at nothing so much as if the diagonal were to become measurable. (Aristotle *Metaphysica* A2, 983a 11–20)

Therefore the desire for mystical knowledge does not cease when the knowledge is obtained. The desire for truth and the possession of truth cannot be contrasted, whereas Aristotle said that the stable possession of the truth was better than researching the truth.[16] Vedic contemplation is active, although it does not deal with the consumption relationship expressed by the Sanskrit root *BHUJ-*. Thus the Self himself is said to love truth just like the mystical ascetic.

[15] See TB II, 2, 10.60–1. See also AiB XII, 10, 1: *aham etad asāni yat tvam aham mahān asānīti / sa prajāpatir abravīd atha ko 'ham iti yad eva etad avoca ity abravīt / tato vai ko nāma prajāpatir abhavat* ('[Indra:] "I want *to be what you are*, I want to be great!" Then Prajāpati answered: "Who [shall] I [be]?" [Indra] said: "Just what you uttered!" Therefore Prajāpati truly became Who by name.') Commented by Gonda 1985.

[16] See Aristotle, *Nicomachean Ethics* 10.7, 1177a 26–7.

Satyakāma is both a name of the ultimate *ātman* and the name of a wisdom hero, beyond all the social proprieties and all *varṇa*-laws:

> Once upon a time Satyakāma Jābāla addressed his mother Jabālā: 'Madam! I desire to live the life of a student of sacred knowledge. Of what family, pray, am I?' Then she said to him: 'I do not know this, my dear – of what family you are. In my youth, when I went about a great deal serving as a maid, I got you. So I do not know of what family you are. However, I am Jabālā by name; you are *Satyakāma* by name. So you may speak of yourself as Satyakāma Jābāla.' Then he went to Hāridrumata Gautama, and said: 'I will live the life of a student of sacred knowledge. I will become a pupil of yours, Sir.' To him he then said: 'Of what family, pray, are you, my dear?' Then he said: 'I do not know this, Sir, of what family I am. I asked my mother. She answered me: "In my youth, when I went about a great deal serving as a maid, I got you. So I do not know this, of what family you are. However, I am Jabālā by name; you are Satyakāma by name." So I am *Satyakāma* Jābāla, Sir.' To him he then said: 'A non-brahman (*a-brāhmaṇa*) would not be able to explain thus. Bring the fuel, my dear. I will receive you as a pupil. You have not deviated from the truth (*satya*).' (ChU 4.4.1–5, emphasis added)

And now *satyakāma* as an epitheton:

> *ya ātmā apahatapāpmā vijaro vimṛtyur viśoko vijig^hatso 'pipāsaḥ satyakāmaḥ satyasaṃkalpaḥ so 'nveṣṭavyaḥ sa vijijñāsitavyaḥ /*
>
> 'The Self (*ātman*), which is free from evil, ageless, deathless, sorrowless, hungerless, thirstless, whose *[object of] desire is the truth* (*satyakāma*), whose conception is the truth – He should be searched out, Him one should desire to understand. He obtains all worlds and all desires who has found out and who understands that Self.' Thus spake Prajāpati. (ChU 8.7.1, emphasis added)

Of course, if the mystic knowledge is an identification process, the *ātman* as highest object of knowledge must bear in itself the desire of the knower for truth. Furthermore the *ātman* is *satya* (KauU 5). Therefore the absolute reality has to be defined as dynamic self-love. The self is what it is just because it is determined by this reflective process. The Self is not a dead thing:

> *tad dha tadvanaṃ nāma / tadvanam ity upāsitavyaṃ / sa ya etad evaṃ vedābhi hainaṃ sarvāṇi bhūtāni saṁvāñchanti*
>
> It (the *brahman*) is Desire-of-it by name (*tadvana*).[17] As 'Desire-of-it' it should be worshiped. For him who knows it thus, all beings together yearn. (KU 4.6)

17 The compound *tadvana* is difficult for several reasons. How should we understand the relationship between its two parts? Here I do not follow Hume's translation ('It-is-the-Desire') and I take the proper name *tadvana* as a *tatpuruṣa* because elsewhere the *ātman* is qualified with the bahuvrīhi *satyakāma* (ChU 8.7.1) which obviously means 'who has the truth as an object of desire'. The second difficulty is the word *vana-*. It seems to rely on the Ṛgvedic

Thus ultimate knowledge, inasmuch as it is knowledge of the Self by the Self, consists in a certain internal behaviour defined by its intrinsic quality, but not in the specification of an object distinguished from other possible objects. It is expressed by the negation of the principle of excluded middle: 'It is other than the known, and other than the unknown' (KU 1.3). The Self is desire of desire, *in infinitum*: the desire of desire is desire for its own self, but the self is desire, so the circle is closed. Such a circle is more important than the starting point and the arrival point.

Now we can distinguish the authentic disinterestedness of the theoretical attitude which belongs to philosophy and the negation of selfhood. There is no real negation of selfhood in philosophy:

> Then spake Maitreyī: 'What should I do with that through which I may not be immortal? What you know, Sir – that, indeed, explain to me.' Then spake Yājñavalkya: 'Though, verily, you, my lady, were dear to us, you have increased your dearness. Behold, then, lady, I will explain it to you. But, while I am expounding, do you seek to ponder thereon.' Then spake he: 'Lo, verily, not for love of the husband is a husband dear, but for love of the Self (*ātman*) a husband is dear. Lo, verily, not for love of the wife is a wife dear, but for love of the Self a wife is dear. Lo, verily, not for love of the sons are sons dear, but for love of the Self sons are dear. Lo, verily, not for love of the wealth is wealth dear, but for love of the Self wealth is dear. Lo, verily, not for love of the cattle are cattle dear, but for love of the Self cattle are dear. Lo, verily, not for love of Brahmanhood is Brahmanhood dear, but for love of the Self Brahmanhood is dear. Lo, verily, not for love of Kṣatrahood is Kṣatrahood dear, but for love of the Self Kṣatrahood is dear. Lo, verily, not for love of the worlds are the worlds dear, but for love of the Self the worlds are dear. Lo, verily, not for love of the gods are the gods dear, but for love of the Self the gods are dear. Lo, verily, not for love of the Vedas are the Vedas dear, but for love of the Self the Vedas are dear. Lo, verily, not for love of the beings (*bhūta*) are beings dear, but for love of the Self beings are dear. Lo, verily, not for love of all is all dear, but for love of the Self all is dear. Lo, verily, it is the Self (*ātman*) that should be seen, that should be hearkened to, that should be thought on, that should be pondered on, O Maitreyī. Lo, verily, in the Self's being seen, hearkened to, thought on, understood, this worldall is known. (BU 6.4.4–6)

This text does not prove the impossibility of disinterestedness in human activities. But if the theoretical attitude brings us in touch with the absolute reality, and if this absolute reality is self-desire, the theoretical attitude implies the love of oneself inasmuch as the core of the person is nothing individual but the

noun *vánas-*, 'desire', but it is a hapax. But the whole compound might imply a pun on *tattva-* ('reality'), which is well attested concerning the brahman (see for example KaU 6.12–13).

most universal power. Therefore the cult of selfhood typical for Indian philosophy is very different from a restricted selfishness, and the disinterestedness of the theoretical attitude cannot be restricted only to Greek thought. Husserl was wrong to do so.

9

Self or *being* without boundaries: on Śaṅkara and Parmenides

Chiara Robbiano

> There can be no difference anywhere that doesn't make a difference elsewhere . . . The whole function of philosophy ought to be to find out what definite difference it will make to you and me, at definite instants of our life, if this world-formula or that world-formula be the true one.
>
> William James, 'What Pragmatism Means'[1]

This chapter focuses on a similar argument made by Parmenides[2] and Śaṅkara[3] involving the claim that *boundaries* between everyday entities are superimposed and not real. I hereby continue my exploration of the similarity of the *arguments* of the two philosophers, who, so far, have been compared only either as adherents of monism, or in order to show historical dependence, mostly of Greek thought on the Veda.[4] I will show how Parmenides and Śaṅkara argue that any boundary that we believe to be real and capable of separating the many individuals and things can be proven to be superimposed by humans on *being* rather than being real.

As a foil, I will mention an alternative metaphysical framework – which has

1 McDermott 1978: 379.

2 Parmenides was a Greek philosopher of the early fifth century BCE, i.e. before Socrates and Plato. He wrote a poem in which he describes a journey that takes him first beyond the Gates of Night and Day and then beyond what can be seen as all opposites and dualities, the duality of knowing and *being* or subject and object included. Of this poem only quotations by other authors survive.

3 Śaṅkara was an Indian philosopher of the eighth century CE; his school was called Vedānta, meaning the last part of the Veda. He wrote commentaries on the Vedānta or *Upaniṣads* and on other important texts like the *Brahmā Sūtra*. He is an exponent of *Advaita* Vedānta, i.e. *non-dual* Vedānta, which signals that he interprets literally the Upaniṣadic claim that *ātman*, or our Self, is the same as *brahman*, i.e. the essence of reality.

4 For a comparison between Śaṅkara's and Parmenides' arguments based on separation or discrimination, see Robbiano (2016). In this paper I also offer an extensive review of the existing comparisons between these two philosophers.

been adopted for instance by Descartes, and which might be regarded as part of the default everyday Western metaphysical framework – according to which reality is fundamentally fragmented in separate things and individuals.[5]

Parmenides and Śaṅkara acknowledge the existence of a fundamental reality: undivided *being* or Self. The other side of the coin of an undivided *being* is the lack of reality of the boundaries superimposed on *being*.[6] The question is: what makes them regard anything that differentiates one thing from the next as a superimposition, which is less real than undivided *being*? I will show that the argument involves the 'epistemological weakness' of what is superimposed on undivided *being*. This argument points at the impossibility of 'knowing' – in a special sense that is radically different from having opinions – anything other than *being*, which involves the impossibility of knowing any boundary. The step from the impossibility of knowing anything other than *being* to the lack of reality of any second *being* might sound like a fallacy, since it takes an unwarranted step from epistemology to ontology. However, for a certain conception of knowing and *being* that entails their identity, there is no fallacy. I argue that this identity makes sense on both Parmenides' and Śaṅkara's terms. I will show this by suggesting how to interpret what they refer to as 'knowing' or 'higher knowledge', and by trying to shed light on the assumption on which the undividedness of being is based.

Finally I will look at hints in their writings which suggest that understanding the identity of knowing and undivided *being* might facilitate *experiencing* the lack of boundaries, which in turn might result in experiencing invulnerability, 'unshakenness', liberation and compassion.

The common starting point – the certainty

Both Śaṅkara and Parmenides, like many other philosophers, were prepared to submit any accepted opinion to a rational test. In different traditions there have

5 In Robbiano (forthcoming) I sketch this contrast between Śaṅkara, on the one hand, and Avicenna and Descartes, on the other, in order to show that many interpreters of Parmenides who look for the implicit subject of the subjectless 'is' in DK B2 embrace the Aristotelian assumption that predicates and attributes must be owned by a substance, as Avicenna and Descartes had done. In that paper I argue that scholars, rather than taking an assumption for granted, should argue to support it. I try to make scholars aware of the assumption they perhaps unconsciously superimpose on Parmenides' fragment, by making them aware of an alternative assumption, which has been chosen by Śaṅkara (a thinker similar to Parmenides) and which leads him to regard any substance as an illusory superimposition on trustworthy *being*.

6 I write '*being*' for the trustworthy reality in Parmenides' philosophy and 'being' for any other less marked occurrence of this word.

been philosophers who were prepared to regard everything they had believed so far as mere opinion and illusion; they wanted to doubt everything and to start from scratch. Think, for instance, of the process of Cartesian doubt, which stops only at the realisation that the activity of thinking, notwithstanding any incorrectness of the thoughts, cannot be doubted. At this point, Descartes' assumption kicks in: if the attribute of thinking is indubitably there, there must be a substance supporting it, more specifically a thinking substance: a mind or a soul.

Śaṅkara and others asked themselves a similar question in their quest for the foundation of the knowledge of reality: does anything exist beyond doubt? The first step in answering this is similar both in Descartes and Śaṅkara: they called it either 'being self-aware', or 'thinking', or '*being*' or 'am' or 'is'. I appreciate the difference between 'being self-aware', 'thinking' and '*being*'; however, at this point of their argument, which I am calling the first step, they seem to play the same role: they are used by different philosophers to refer to their recognition of an immediate certainty whose content or description they offer in what I call the second step. None of them doubted that there is a fundamental certainty. In *Meditation* 2 Descartes writes:

> in that case I too undoubtedly exist, if he is deceiving me; and let him deceive me as much as he can, he will never bring it about that I am nothing so long as I think that I am something. So after considering everything very thoroughly, I must finally conclude that this proposition, *I am, I exist*, is necessarily true whenever it is put forward by me or conceived in my mind.[7]

Likewise, Śaṅkara says: 'everyone is conscious of the existence of (his) Self and never thinks "I am not"' (BSB I.1.1: 200). Both Descartes and Śaṅkara take a similar first step in the common journey or quest for what is real and what we really are: nobody would or could deny being self-aware or thinking. I submit that the following lines from Parmenides' poem refer to this same first step:

> Come now, I will tell you, and once you have heard my story take it with you, what routes of the quest are the only ones to know:
> the one that 'is' and that it is not possible not to be
> – it is the course of trust, for reality follows – (28 DK B2.1–4)[8]

I interpret these lines of Parmenides' poem as communicating that the indubitable starting point about which nobody can have doubts is 'is'. Parmenides expresses the trustworthiness of the subjectless 'is' and that it is impossible that 'is not'. Many different interpretations have been given of these lines and

[7] Adam and Tannery 1964–76: VII, 25, translation in Cottingham 1985: II, 16–17.

[8] Unless otherwise specified, all translations from Parmenides are mine. I have attempted to stay as close as possible to Parmenides' Greek.

of the lack of a subject of the phrase 'that is' – and the vast majority of them concentrated on supplying a subject.[9] On the contrary, I maintain that the lack of a subject is crucial to Parmenides' message that contrasts the trustworthiness of the mere fact of being with the opinions that we might have about what subject(s) might be said to display the property of being.

Descartes, Parmenides and Śaṅkara and their different second step

It seems that philosophers who agree that there is a certainty, which might be referred to as 'being self-aware' (or 'thinking', 'knowing', 'being') to start with, can take two different steps. The disagreement seems to be between those who, like Descartes – after agreeing on the trustworthiness of being self-aware – regard the addition of a subject to this being self-aware as a *necessary* and *equally trustworthy* step as the initial certainty, and those who, like Parmenides and Śaṅkara, regard the addition of a subject as an untrustworthy next step.

For Descartes, when the need for characterising this indubitable starting point emerges, the characterisation is not presented as a second step, but as obvious, natural and necessary. In Descartes' metaphysics the certainty is characterised as belonging to the thinking-thing that is doing and owning the thinking. Descartes takes for granted the Aristotelian assumption that predicates must be owned by substances and adapts it to his new kind of dualism.[10] He regards this assumption, not as something one might choose or not, but as 'something very well known by the natural light': 'we should notice something very well known by the natural light . . . wherever we find some attributes or qualities there is necessarily some thing or substance to be found for them to belong to'.[11] Descartes adapts Aristotle's assumption that predicates must be owned by substances, and does not ascribe the attribute of thinking to the Aristotelian individual, consisting of matter and form, but to a disembodied individual thinking substance, to start with.

However, the inference from 'there is some thinking' to 'there is a "me"' – be it an embodied individual or a disembodied mind (thinking thing) – who owns the thinking does not go without saying. This is just one of the possible assumptions that have been chosen by those who wanted to articulate this certainty. A different assumption has led other philosophers to a different metaphysics, with possibly different existential and ethical implications.

9 See Robbiano (forthcoming) for a detailed analysis of the problems involved in regarding 'estin' as having an implied subject.

10 This innovation costs him some quite precarious steps before he can rescue the existence of the body from the flames, but this is another story and a quite well-known one.

11 Descartes, *Principles of Philosophy*, Part 1.11, in Adam and Tannery 1964–76: VIII, A 8, translation in Cottingham 1985: I, 196.

Śaṅkara – just like Descartes – observes himself thinking and, reflecting on what must be real and trustworthy, finds that one cannot doubt being self-aware. But, differently from Descartes, he claims that if he is certain of being self-aware, then his certainty is of undivided existence, which he expresses as certainty of the existence of *brahman*, which is the same as *ātman*, the Self:

> the existence of brahman is known on the ground of its being the Self of every one. For every one is conscious of the existence of (his) Self, and never thinks 'I am not'. (BSB I.1.1: 200)

The superimposition of our psychophysical make up on the undivided *being* or Self – which might be described as a witness[12] – which we recognise immediately by being self-aware, is a mistake made by ignorant people, according to Śaṅkara.[13] Śaṅkara would accuse Descartes of exactly this mistake: the one of ascribing existence or self-awareness (regarding it as a predicate in need of a subject) to a separate substance, e.g. an individual, a body or a soul.[14] Their mistake is a fruit of the human mind superimposing what is not Self, e.g. separated individuals, on the Self.[15] The question is: do they have an argument for concluding that Self or *being* is undivided? If they do, on what assumption is their argument based?

The argument of epistemological weakness of boundaries

In order to find out how Parmenides and Śaṅkara come to conclude that being is undivided, we will have to look at why there is nothing that they recognise to

12 Śaṅkara: 'Attributes of the body are superimposed on the Self, if the man thinks of himself (his Self) as stout, lean, fair, as standing, walking, or jumping. Attributes of the sense-organs, if he thinks "I am mute, or deaf, or one-eyed, or blind." Attributes of the internal organ when he considers himself subject to desire, intention, doubt, determination, and so on. Thus the producer of the notion of the Ego (i.e. the internal organ) is superimposed on the interior Self which, in reality . . . is the witness of everything' (BSB I.1.1: 198).

13 Śaṅkara: 'That the Self, although in reality the only existence, imparts the quality of Selfhood to bodies and the like which are Not-Self is a matter of observation, and is due to mere wrong conception' (BSB I.1.5: 205).

14 In Siderits, Thompson and Zahavi's words, Descartes is a substantialist, i.e. someone who 'thinks of the self as a substance, with consciousness as its essential nature – hence belonging to a distinct ontological category from that of consciousness'. Śaṅkara and – I suggest – Parmenides belong to what they call non-substantialist self theorists: those who 'hold that the self is not a substance or property-bearer standing in relation to consciousness that is in some sense distinct from it'. They see 'the self as just consciousness itself' (2010: 4).

15 Śaṅkara: 'As the passages "I am Brahman", "That art thou", and others, prove, there is in reality no such thing as an individual soul absolutely different from Brahman, but Brahman, in so far as it differentiates itself though the mind (*buddhi*) and other limiting conditions, is called individual soul, agent, enjoyer' (BSB I.1.31: 209).

be as trustworthy as the initial, indubitable certainty – referred to as 'is', *being*, *brahman*, Self.

The first certainty has a phenomenological hue. It is the reflection on an indubitable experience: there is *being* or thinking; self-awareness guarantees the trustworthiness and reality of this first given. A second certainty – a certainty of something different – would be the only way to secure the trustworthy existence of something else next to the first certainty. A second certainty would also be the only way to secure the existence of the first boundary between two equally certain existents. However there is no such 'second certainty'. There is no 'knowledge' of a second *being*, no 'knowledge' of a boundary.

The scare quotes around knowledge signal that both Parmenides and Śaṅkara agree on there being two kinds of knowledge available to human beings: one that consists of untrustworthy opinions that focus on individuals and on change; the other, trustworthy, that realises undivided *being*, which is at the same time the only reality and the only real 'knowing'.[16] *Being* is therefore regarded as undivided and more fundamental than its alleged fragmentation along the boundaries that separate things and individuals, by appealing to the impossibility of 'knowing' anything other than *being*.

In more detail, Parmenides' argument of epistemological weakness goes along these lines: 'is' is the indubitable starting point, since we are certain that 'is' is the case ('it is the course of trust' [B2.4]). Whereas 'is' is an immediate certainty, there can never be a second certainty as strong as this one. The alleged second certainty would be certainty of something next to *being*, and different from *being*. B2 explains that one cannot trust both 'is' and anything next to it. In fact, there is no knowing of anything else next to 'is', i.e. of what is not 'is', of what is other than 'is'.

> the other that 'is not' and that should not be
> I point out to you that this route is a journey we have no experience of,[17]
> for not-being can you neither recognise, since it is impossible to accomplish [such a journey] nor can you ever point out [not-being]. (B2.5–8)

Knowing something different from 'is' would postulate the possibility of being aware of two 'beings': one which we might call '*being*', the other which we

16 Parmenides: 'And you are required to find out everything, / on the one hand, the unshaken heart of the trustworthy reality, / on the other hand, the opinions of mortals, where there is no true trust . . .' (28 DK B1.28–30). Śaṅkara: 'Brahman is apprehended under two forms; in the first place as qualified by limiting conditions owing to the multiformity of the evolutions of name and form (i.e. the multiformity of the created world); in the second place as being the opposite of this, i.e. free from all limiting conditions whatever' (BSB I.1.1: 206).

17 Or 'that cannot be inquired into'. But see Robbiano (forthcoming) for the justification of this translation.

might call not-being, since it is not the same as what we called '*being*'. An example of the alleged second certainty would be the alleged certainty that there is an owner of this certainty, which is different from this certainty. Śaṅkara makes this point very clearly: one cannot have two selves.

> the Self within is one only; two internal Selfs are not possible. But owing to its limiting adjunct the one Self is practically treated as if it were two; just as we make distinction between the ether of the jar and the universal ether . . . (BSB I.2.20: 210)

In parallel with the distinction between Parmenides' 'is', which is trustworthy and cannot not be, and the 'is not' of which we have no knowledge, Śaṅkara stipulates the importance of the distinction between what is real and eternal (*brahman*) and what is not eternal (any superimposition). A justification of this discrimination is epistemological: it impossible to have any proof of the existence of what is not eternal, next to what is eternal:

> there can exist nothing different from brahman, since we are unable to observe a proof for such existence . . . 'Being only this was in the beginning, one, without a second.' (BSB III.2.32: 253)

The epistemological weakness of the assumption of plurality consists of showing that we are never acquainted with anything with the same – complete – degree of certainty that accompanies our knowing the first fundamental fact.

Therefore *being* is undivided and more fundamental than its alleged fragmentation along the boundaries that separate things and individuals. Is this a fallacy since it jumps from not knowing to not being? To find out if this is a fallacy we must look at what kind of knowing is assumed to count as real, trustworthy knowledge.

The assumption is that 'knowing' is self-awareness. The fundamental certainty is phenomenological: it is the only indubitable experience, referred to as 'is', 'being', 'thinking', 'knowing', 'being conscious'. If *being* is the same as knowing, there is no fallacy.

One way to make sense of this undivided 'Self', '*being*' or 'is' is that it is what is fundamentally there in each of our experiences; different experiences might be distinguished by means of words, but what can be said with certainty of all of them is just 'is'. In other words, there cannot be any experience of anything separated from this 'is'; that is, we have different words and descriptions for our different experiences, but they are all experience of 'is', they are never experience of 'is not'. There is no experiencing of not experiencing: no awareness of not being aware. Whatever we are doing we could never qualify it as 'not-being': always as '*being*'. There are not two separate domains in our experience, which we can access in the same way as we access the immediate certainty of being (or being self-aware).

In conclusion, according to our philosophers, we need to epistemologically discriminate between what is real and trustworthily accessible, and what is superimposition, which is not trustworthy: what we superimpose is not a second being, but some kind of illusion or opinion 'projected' onto the only real *being*.[18]

As a consequence of the impossibility of knowing anything other than *being*, we cannot know any boundary with certainty. We cannot claim trustworthy knowledge of any boundary, since there is no not-being – the alleged second being might be called not-being – which would imply the existence of the boundary between *being* and not-being. With no first trustworthy boundary, no other boundary can be regarded as trustworthy, thus no knowledge can be claimed of the many things, separated by unreliable boundaries.

Parmenides' and Śaṅkara's reasoning contrasted to Descartes'

Both Parmenides and Śaṅkara argue along these lines: everybody agrees that 'is' is the case, rather than 'is not'. They both shared this step with Descartes: there is something indubitable, which I have paraphrased above as 'there is self-awareness'.

At this point Descartes went for the following assumption: thinking and being must belong to a substance, i.e. an independent portion of reality. This assumption led him to the next step: When I say 'there is thinking', then thinking and being must belong to a substance; this substance is 'me': therefore *I* am.

Descartes concluded: 'I' is an independent substance: an individual mind. In other words: 'thinking' or 'is' or 'am' belong to me: a mind separate from the rest of reality. I will not go into the well-known arguments by means of which Descartes 'proved' the existence of bodies; at the end of the story, according to him, reality is full of separate individuals and separate things, some of which are endowed with a mind.

Parmenides and Śaṅkara went for a completely different assumption: 'is' or *being* is the only trustworthy reality: nothing other than 'is' is knowable in

18 Śaṅkara: 'This superimposition thus defined [of the Non-Self superimposed on the interior Self] learned men consider to be Nescience (*avidyā*), and the ascertainment of the true nature of that which is (the Self) by means of the discrimination of that (which is superimposed on the Self), they call knowledge (*vidyā*) . . . The mutual superimposition of the Self and the Non-Self, which is termed Nescience, is the presupposition on which they base all the practical distinctions . . .' (BSB Introduction: 197). Discrimination or division (*krisis*, *viveka*) is a crucial methodological tool, which does not separate two domains of being, but two aspects: it draws a distinction, an epistemological division, i.e. a discrimination between lower and higher knowledge, or two ways of 'looking' at the same. About the method of discrimination for these two philosophers, and other similarities in their methods, see Robbiano (2016).

a reliable way. In other words: I cannot know 'is not' or not-being. Part of this assumption is their conception of knowing, which is the same as *being* (B3), and which can be made sense of by dubbing both knowing and *being* as being self-aware. Our experience, which is all we have or are, can be described in terms of being, but also in terms of knowing. They are *not* two separate items. It is a kind of 'knowing' in which there is no fundamental division between the subject that knows and the object that is known, since there are not two fundamentally separated realities that we can experience next to each other. Therefore knowing, or being-aware, is *being*.

Parmenides and Śaṅkara concluded: *being* – that is the same as 'knowing', or *brahman* that is the same as the Self (*ātman*) – is fundamentally undivided. In fact, the first alleged boundary is not knowable, not possible to experience; it is not part of the indubitable 'is'. Therefore the boundary between knower and known and any other boundary or distinction we superimpose on *being*, in order to make sense of it, are the fruit of our custom, our language or our theories.

Existential consequences of boundaries are superimposed and not real

The choice of the assumption that knowing is being self-aware – which leads to the conclusion that the fundamental reality is undivided, that is, not admitting of any division, not even the subject-object division – is quite a strong choice.

On the one hand, the exclusive trust accorded to undivided *being*, leads our philosophers to dismiss any specific knowledge. In fact, both scientific knowledge (cf. Parmenides' opinions about astronomy [B10, 11, 12, 14, 15] or embryology [B17]) and moral knowledge (e.g. on what rituals and actions to perform) are regarded as untrustworthy: as non-reliable opinions or Nescience.[19] Śaṅkara tells us that all practical distinctions are based on ignorant superimposition. Parmenides claims that postulation of *two* entities, which is needed for any scientific inquiry, creates a deceitful cosmos or order.[20]

Does the tenet that boundaries, being epistemologically untrustworthy, are therefore superimposed rather than real have any *existential* relevance? What difference might it make to take a step in the direction of such a metaphysics,

[19] Śaṅkara: 'The mutual superimposition of the Self and the Non-self, which is termed Nescience, is the presupposition on which they base all practical distinctions – those made in ordinary life as well as those laid down by the Veda – between means of knowledge, objects of knowledge (and knowing persons), and all scriptural texts . . . For such texts as the following, "A Brāhmaṇa is to sacrifice", are operative only on the supposition that on the Self are superimposed particular conditions such as caste, state of life, age, outward circumstances, and so on' (BSB, Introduction, 197–8).

[20] 28 DK B8.51–3: 'And after this, learn the opinions of the mortals / listening to the deceitful order of my words. / For they decided to name two forms . . .'

which rejects the reality of individuals and, by doing so, might sound much less palatable than the step taken by Descartes, who assumed that the immediate certainty of existing (or of being conscious or of thinking) must be owned by an individual? After all, it might seem more 'natural' to identify with and be sure of this individual that carries our name, rather than being certain of and identifying with undivided *being*.

I hereby enter the terrain of the 'pragmatic consequences' of Parmenides' and Śaṅkara's metaphysics. In the last part of this chapter I will follow James' advice about the function of philosophy quoted as my epigraph. I would like to suggest that a metaphysics like that embraced by Śaṅkara and Parmenides might have an existential relevance that can be expressed in terms of invulnerability and unshakenness (Parmenides), and freedom and compassion (Śaṅkara).

The existential relevance for Parmenides: undivided *being*, on which boundaries are superimposed, is invulnerable and unshaken

According to Parmenides, *being* is undivided and homogeneous. There cannot be divisions or discontinuities in 'is', since only not-being could have drawn division into *being*. But not-being is not knowable (B2.5–8) and knowing is *being* (B3), therefore there is no not-being: not-being is just an opinion and not real.

> neither should it be bigger at all
> nor smaller at all whether on one side or another.
> In fact, there is neither not-being which would stop it from coming
> towards the same, nor is *being* in such a way as to be
> more than *being* on one side or less on another, since it is all inviolable . . .
> (B8.44–8)

The absence of not-being, which has been ruled out since it is unknowable, is what allows 'is' to be safe, and homogeneous, with no interruption, discontinuity, separation:

> Neither is it divisible, since it is all the same:
> nor more anywhere in any respect, which would prevent it from being united, nor in any respect inferior, but all is full of *being*,
> thus [it] is all continuous . . . (B8.22–5)

Reality 'is': after an 'is' there is another 'is' and then another 'is' with no discontinuity between them: 'for *being* draws near *being*' (B8.25).

As soon as we talk about an edge, a boundary, or about two different kinds of beings, or two beings, or being and not-being, we enter the territory of the opinions. The only limit or boundary that applies to *being* is the oxymoronic 'ultimate boundary' made invincible by *anangkē*: it is not a boundary that separates two domains but a very unique one that has no outside. Such an 'ultimate boundary' suggests that *being* is protected, inviolable,[21] since there is nothing on the outside that might endanger it. *Being* is invulnerable and can be trusted to always be there.

> Remaining the same and in the same it lies by itself
> And thus it remains where it is firmly; for mighty *anangkē*
> holds [it] in the bonds of the limit, which bars its way all around . . . (B8.29–31)

> But since the limit is ultimate, [*being*] is perfect
> from every point of view . . . (B8.42–3)

The absence of not-being, i.e. anything trustworthy next to *being*, ensures that *being* is not only undivided but also undisturbed by any incursion: there can be no diminishing, dying, changing: it is safe and invulnerable. *Being* is called perfect or complete[22] and full.[23]

Might these characterisations of perfection and invulnerability hint at the quality of the *experience* of non-dually knowing *being*? Might Parmenides' *being* refer to the undivided inner self,[24] which, unthreatened by anything outside of it, is not only invulnerable but also unshaken? When the quest for *being* is announced, the goal of the search is pointed to as the unshaken heart of the trustworthy reality:

> And you are required to find out everything,
> on the one hand, unshaken heart (*atremes ētor*) of the trustworthy reality.
> (B1.28–9)

Unshaken refers in Homer to the untroubled state of mind, e.g. of gods or heroes peacefully sleeping[25] or standing calm and untroubled on the battlefield.[26] Coxon observes that '*ētor* [heart] is never used in Greek except of a human or divine person, of whom it refers to the heart or inner self as the seat of emotion, virtue

21 28 DK B8.48: 'all is inviolable' (πᾶν ἐστιν ἄσυλον).

22 28 DK B8.42–3: 'But since the limit is ultimate, [*being*] is complete / from every point' (Αὐτὰρ ἐπεὶ πεῖρας πύματον, τετελεσμένον ἐστί / πάντοθεν).

23 28 DK B8.24: 'but all is full of *being*' (πᾶν δ' ἔμπλεόν ἐστιν ἐόντος).

24 Coxon 1986: 168.

25 In Homer we do not find the adjective *atremēs*, but the adverb *atremas*. There are passages where Zeus (*Il.* 14, 352: *Thus in quiet slept the Father on topmost Gargarus*) and Odysseus (*Od.* 13, 92: *but now he slept in peace, forgetful of all that he had suffered*) sleep *atremas* (peacefully). Cf. Śaṅkara, BSB I.1.19 (*Essential Vedanta*: 206–7): 'But when he, by means of the cognition of absolute identity finds absolute rest in the Self consisting of bliss, then he is freed from fear of transmigratory existence.'

26 Cf. the passage at *Il.* 13, 278–87 with the comparison between the two kinds of warriors: the one who is afraid, changes colour and does not stand *atremas*, and the one who does.

and life'.[27] This might suggest that one who realises and holds on to the trustworthy 'is' has nothing to fear:

> But *akinēton* (unmoving or unshaken) in the limits of huge bonds
> [it] is without start and without stop, since birth and death have strayed very far away, pushed away by true trust. (B8.26–8)

Coxon puts *akinēton* here in relation with the *atremes ētor* of B1, suggesting that it could refer to 'other than local stillness', and quoting a passage where *akinēton* means 'steadfast'.[28]

Being is safe, and invulnerable, protected from any intrusion, since the existence of any intruder, i.e. anything next to *being*, has been ruled out as a consequence of the untrustworthiness of our knowledge about it. The suggestion might be that, if *being* is self-awareness, if undivided self-awareness is what we trustworthily are, then there is nothing we should fear.

The existential relevance for Śaṅkara: freedom and compassion

For Śaṅkara, the choice of the assumption that makes him interpret the first certainty as the undividedness prior to any form or division (rather than something belonging to an individual) is not only metaphysically and epistemologically significant, but also existentially relevant. Regarding separate individuals as superimpositions might pave the way towards *experiencing* the lack of divisions or boundaries, i.e. towards the non-dual experience of *brahman*.

When one identifies with the only existent, one can also experience fullness in the sense of perfection.[29] If nothing can get in one's way and limit one, not only perfection and lack of fear might result, but also freedom. Śaṅkara describes the experience of *brahman* in terms of liberation. This freedom can also be seen as freedom from identification with something changeable and vulnerable such

27 Coxon 1986: 168. Cf. Seaford's chapter in this volume, who, from a different perspective, points to Parmenides' appeal to introspection in his search for *being*, to the subjective dimension suggested by the words *atremes and ētor*, and to the 'positive psychological effects of the merging of subject with object'.

28 Coxon 1986: 206. 'The adjective *akinēton* is older than Parmenides (Hes. *Op*. 750), and is used in the fifth century by Pindar, Sophocles, Aristophanes and the historians. That it alludes in Parmenides, as often elsewhere, to other than merely local stillness is shown by the phrase *atremes êtor* (fr. 1,29) which foreshadows the argument of fr.8; cf. Soph. *Ant*. 1027, *akinētos pelei* ("is steadfast"); 1060, *takinēta* ("secrets").'

29 In the words of one of the most authoritative scholars of Advaita (Deutsch 1973: 9), realising *brahman* leads to the experience of the timeless plenitude of being: 'Brahman, the One, is a state of being. It is not a "He", a personal being; nor is it an "It", an impersonal concept. Brahman is that state which *is* when all subject/object distinctions are obliterated. Brahman is ultimately a name for the experience of the timeless plenitude of being.'

as an individual. Śaṅkara explicitly identifies the non-dual reality of *brahman* with liberation:

> this [*mokṣa* / liberation] is eternal ... without undergoing any changes ... omnipresent as ether, free from all modifications, absolutely self-sufficient, not composed of parts, of self-luminous nature ... It [i.e. *mokṣa*] is, therefore, the same as brahman ... (BSB I.1.4: 202–3)

Moreover, the experience of the lack of divisions might well be an experience of continuity, of a shared common ground, of connection to others, seen as non-different from or continuous with us. A compassionate attitude might well result from seeing others as part of us, which might manifest itself as sharing suffering and joy, i.e. spontaneously attempting to remove their suffering and rejoicing at their happiness:

> a Master ... continually established in the Absolute, calm like the flame when its fuel is consumed; a boundless ocean of spontaneous compassion for which there is no reason, a friend to all good people who surrender to him.[30]

Śaṅkara's enlightened or liberated person – i.e. the one who has not only understood but also experienced his or her own identity with *brahman* (undivided *being* or absolute reality) – will be a boundless ocean of spontaneous compassion. Deutsch comments:

> The quality then that ought to inform human action is non-egoism, which, positively expressed, is what the Advaitin understands to be 'love'. One must interrelate with 'others', one must conduct oneself, with the knowledge that the other is non-different from oneself. Love, the meeting of another in the depth of being, must be grounded in knowledge, and when it is so grounded, it expresses itself in every action that one performs.[31]

Compassion springs from the assumption that the *connection* between what I call 'me' and what I call 'the other' is stronger than our apparent separation. Our separation is secondary since it is result of superimpositions, for instance, of this body and these thoughts, on what I more fundamentally am, which is non-different from what the other is.

Conclusion

Both Parmenides and Śaṅkara agree with Descartes and others that there is a trustworthy, indubitable phenomenological starting point, which is both episte-

[30] Śaṅkara, *Vivekacūḍāmaṇi* 34–5, in Grimes 2004: 76.

[31] Deutsch 1973: 102.

mological and metaphysical, and which might be hinted at as 'being', or 'being self-aware'.

Neither Parmenides nor Śaṅkara have Aristotle in their tradition to suggest that an activity must always be a characteristic, predicate or accident of a substance. They can both conceive of a predicate without a subject. They can both conceive of unowned being.

Both Parmenides and Śaṅkara show that the existence of anything singled out from *being* is a matter of opinion, since we cannot trust any of the boundaries we project on *being*. I have argued that the fundamental argument for drawing conclusions on the status of boundaries is the one based on their 'epistemological weakness'. It is the distinction between two kinds of knowledge, the one untrustworthy and the other trustworthy, that allows Parmenides and Śaṅkara to label the reality of boundaries and separate individuals and things as less fundamental than the reality of undivided *being*. Our knowledge of boundaries and separate entities is of a radically different kind than the higher, trustworthy 'knowing', which is *being* and which is assumed to be phenomenological knowledge or self-awareness.

We can trustworthily know undivided *being*, which is what we are: *being*, which is the same as knowing, interpreted as self-awareness. On the contrary, we cannot trustworthily know anything other than that; therefore we cannot trust any of the boundaries we project on *being*. The existence of any individual substance, like a mind or a body, is not something we can have trustworthy knowledge of: any second 'item' next to *being* is the fruit of untrustworthy opinions.

One who holds a metaphysics of the undividedness of reality and who sees boundaries between separate things and individuals as superimpositions might enjoy the *experience* of the lack of divisions: an experience of inviolability, freedom and connection to others. Parmenides' and Śaṅkara's arguments seem, in fact, to point to their existential consequences, which lead one from the impossibility of knowing not-being to the unreality of any boundary, and, possibly, to the experience of invulnerability, unshakenness, liberation and compassion.

Acknowledgements

I am very grateful to Richard Seaford for inspiring me to think about the Self in Greek philosophy; to my students of the Senior Seminar in philosophy 'East and West: the arbitrariness of divisions' (Fall 2013), especially Matthew Quinn, who made a fundamental remark on the relation between epistemology and ontology in Parmenides, and Ilona de Jong, who later wrote a thesis on Śaṅkara under my supervision and brought the issue of compassion to my attention; to all participants in the Philosophy Discussion Group (2013–15) at University College Utrecht, especially Jori Jansen, Ben Kiderman, Timothy Merkel and Jan van

Ophuijsen, for their generous and insightful comments on the topics dealt with in this chapter; to Mariette Willemsen for inviting me to speak about compassion at Amsterdam University College; to Joanna Jurewicz, Frank Köhler, Paolo Magnone and Richard Seaford, my co-participants on the panel 'Images for Consciousness in Indian and Greek thought', at the International Conference on Consciousness, Value and Reality: East and West (Kolkata 2015); and to all participants in the conference Ātman and Psychē: Universe and inner self in early Indian and early Greek thought (Exeter 2015) for our inspiring conversations.

10

Soul chariots in Indian and Greek thought: polygenesis or diffusion?

Paolo Magnone

Not only the classicist, but even the layman with a casual interest in Greek philosophy is familiar with the allegory which Plato employs in the *Phaedrus* to describe the nature of the soul in terms, as he says, that are 'within human power':

> Let [the soul] be likened to the composite inborn power of a pair of winged horses and of a charioteer . . . (246a)

Both classical scholars and cultivated laymen alike, on the other hand, have seldom been aware of a strikingly similar allegory occurring in one of the most celebrated works of the final period of Vedic literature, the *Kaṭha Upaniṣad*:

> Know that the Self is the rider in a chariot, and the body is the chariot; and know that the intelligence is the charioteer, and the mind is the bridle. They say that the senses are the horses, and the sense objects are their lanes . . . (KaU 1.3.3)

For their part, indologists have taken due notice of the puzzling similarity from early on, albeit with differing assessments. Already a century ago, in connection with the *Kaṭha* passage, Keith observed that 'the contrast with the Platonic metaphor of the *Phaidros* is as obvious as the parallel', further on passing his judgement that in spite of the interesting parallelism 'the details of the two [metaphors] are perfectly distinct, for Plato uses the conception to illustrate the struggle between the rational and the irrational elements in the soul, and his distinction of θύμος and ἐπιθυμία has no real parallel in the *Upaniṣads*'.[1] On the other hand, Belvalkar and Ranade evidently did not share his caution, as they enthusiastically aver that 'the extraordinary resemblance of the two descriptions down to the smallest details staggers us, and we must confess we do not know how to account for it'.[2] Almost

[1] Keith 1989: 555, 613.

[2] Belvalkar and Ranade 1974: 263.

in between there is Radhakrishnan's opinion that 'in spite of difference in details, the *Kaṭha* and Plato agree in looking upon intelligence as the ruling power of the soul . . . and aiming at the integration of the different elements of human nature'.[3] More recently McEvilley, who must be credited with the first serious attempt to posit with amplitude and lucidity the question of possible reciprocal influences between early Greek and Indian thought in his path-breaking essay on *The Shape of Ancient Thought*, confines himself to observing that 'the similarity in imagery is intriguing' but answers Friedländer's[4] wondering whether the figure might have travelled from the Far East to Plato with the milder suggestion of a possible common Indo-European heritage.[5]

This last remark introduces us to our subject: are the two metaphors linked by a process of westward diffusion, or did they originate independently,[6] possibly as independent developments of a common Indo-European stock? This paper purports to show that the former hypothesis (i.e. the hypothesis of westward diffusion) appears to be the more plausible one. However, because assessments of this sort, in the lack of direct proof, are to such a great extent influenced by theoretical assumptions, I will premise some considerations of a general methodological nature.

Methodological considerations

A major stumbling block for any comparative enterprise investigating possible influences between ancient Greek and Indian thought has always been the his-

3 Radhakrishnan 1994: 623.

4 Friedländer 1964: 205.

5 McEvilley 2002: 185. He goes so far as to suggest that 'the allegory of the Self [may be] a development of the Homeric chariot hero on the one hand and of the hero of the Bhārata war on the other', which is scarcely tenable, as the *Mahābhārata* epic is generally believed to be later than the *Upaniṣads*.

6 Both Schlieter and Forte-Smith, in their contributions on the same subject to the present volume, subscribe to the hypothesis of independent origination, albeit on different grounds. While our respective appraisal of the many aspects involved may be different, I appreciate Schlieter's perspective – stressing the primacy of cognitive metaphors in shaping conceptual thought and positing a shared metaphorical ground as a precondition for the independent (in his view) origination of the philosophical chariot metaphors (or rather allegories) in the *Phaedrus* and the *Kaṭha Upaniṣad* – as capable of throwing complementary light on my own. On the other hand, while I also appreciate Forte and Smith's stress on intertextuality as a useful, nay, indispensable key to a proper understanding of texts – of which they offer many apt examples (if at places a bit far-fetched, in my opinion) – I think they rely too one-sidedly on it to make sense of any given text. I believe there is more to Parmenides' proem or the *Kaṭha Upaniṣad* than can be made out by falling back on their Homeric and Vedic intertexts – but of course here we border on the domain of fundamental philosophical options: I do not defer to Derrida's *différance*, but rather side with Vedantic (and Parmenidean) *astikatva*.

torian's unwillingness to concede anything in the absence of sound historical documentation. To me this is just a particular instance of the scholars' partiality for their own favourite method of going about a subject of research – a partiality which is understandable, but nevertheless a bane to the progress of science. If historical documentation were always indispensable, whole disciplines like folklore would *ipso facto* simply dissolve into thin air. Folklorists are hardly ever able to document the historical vicissitudes of transmission of folk tales, customs, rituals, etc., which has not prevented them from developing significant and fruitful discourse about their subject matter.[7]

What is needed to satisfy the historian, in my view, is merely to establish that the historical conditions were actually there which could have made cross-cultural contacts possible. Being myself no fully-fledged historian, I will just refer to the opinion of one such, who, writing a booklet with the explicit intent of debunking what he regarded as (in his own words) the 'inflated, doubtful, simplistic and misleading' claims of the proponents of the 'Indian hypothesis', had nevertheless to concede:

> Historical circumstances appear to favor lasting exchanges between India and the East in the ancient world. Phoenician traders were carriers of Indian commodities for centuries. Persia imposed a long rule on north-western India, *bridging east and west* [emphasis added]. Alexander the Great's hellenising crusade . . . brought in his wake artists, philosophers, historians and naturalists, thus preparing ground for the remarkable Greco-Bactrian kingdoms of the following century. The powerful empire of the Kushans was in touch with the masters of Rome, and the Roman eagle adorned trading posts on the coast of Coromandel . . . Persian, Greek and Roman officials, civilians and military, had direct experience with India for about seven hundred years.[8]

So much for the viability of the hypothesis of influences between early Greek and Indian thought.[9] Since, however, we cannot progress further on this ground

7 For a detailed examination of the various flavours of the comparative method as employed in anthropology and folklore see, e.g., Dundes 1986.

8 Stunkel 1979: 1.

9 Forte and Smith object that cross-cultural contacts concerning the secret lore of the *Upaniṣads* would be virtually impossible, because the persons involved 'would have had to be Vedic initiates and committed to memory the corpus of *Kaṭha* texts before instruction in an *Upaniṣad* would be permitted'. Of course, this is true, in principle. But the very fact that the *Upaniṣads* repeatedly inculcate the prohibition to divulge certain doctrines to unfit persons (examples quoted in Deussen 1906: 11) speaks for the actual, if sporadic, occurrence of such divulgations, which could involve just those particular *rahasyas*, detached from the embedding corpus. After all, the same strict requirements for Vedic transmission had been in force at least up to the inception of Western Indology, which did not prevent Anquetil Duperron from coming by the *mysterium tegendum* of the *Oupnek'hat* (on its own account

by way of direct historical verification of actual contacts and transmissions, we are left with the only option of arguing from similarities that could bespeak a common origin or a filiation. I submit that there is nothing inherently unsound in this endeavour. On the contrary, it is part and parcel of the method of other disciplines, such as, again, folklore, or, to add a fresh example, philology. Philologists are usually unable to reconstruct the historical vicissitudes of the copying of manuscripts, but are guided in postulating stemmatic relationships by coincidences of details (*errores coniunctivi*). Of course, care must be exercised: all coincidences of scribal errors are not suitable to postulate dependencies, for trivial mistakes related to common scribal propensities could have arisen independently.

In much the same way, all similarities between cultural constructs are not apt to establish connections. Stunkel summarises the argument from similarities as 'the postulation of a mechanism of intellectual and spiritual transmission beyond historical verification, but which one must adopt and respect if parallels [allegedly] "not easy to ascribe to chance" are to be explained', lamenting that 'the diffusion of religious attitudes and ideas is construed as tenuous, piecemeal, unconscious, fragmented in time and unspectacular in the act of transmission and reception'.[10] This is not the place to examine the import of each of these charges in detail: suffice it to say that in my view, some are correct, some are not, indeed, they find fault with what I actually regard as conditions of effectual comparisons.

As to the charge of tenuity, I agree that parallels of a very general nature, not substantiated by similarities of details, are inconclusive, for similar general ideas could very well have cropped up independently from shared psychological and cultural grounds. This is akin to the aforesaid scribal proneness to mistakes due to homoioteleuton, haplography, dittography and the like. On the other hand, as to the charge of fragmentariness, I actually regard it rather as a requisite of fruitful comparison, in the same way as the more haphazard scribal errors are, the more telling they are and the more apt to function as *errores coniunctivi* to establish stemmatic dependencies.

Let me clarify with a well-known example taken from the more congenial field of comparative mythology and folklore. As is well known, the deluge myth has enjoyed a wide diffusion all over the Eurasian continent and beyond,[11] prompting the inevitable question of polygenesis versus monogenesis and diffusion. All versions agree on but few fundamental points: mankind is swept away by a deluge, except for one or more people surviving in a vessel, who are entrusted with the task of the renewal. However, we should hardly be justified

already the fruit of a disclosure to a Muslim prince – hardly a worthy recipient of the sacred Vedic lore!).

10 Stunkel 1979: 4.

11 For an ample survey see Dundes (ed.) 1988.

in grounding any presumption of a common origin on the strength of such similarities: after all, flood is one of the few fitting ways to end the world which experience suggests to primitive folks; to survive a flood you need a vessel of sorts; and in the aftermath survivors must find a way to repeople the empty world. On the other hand, more particular coincidences of casual details not integral to the overall structure of the myths make a strong case for diffusion. For instance, within the fold of the biblical and near-eastern versions of the deluge myth, the correspondences in the episode of the birds sent out as scouts are too precise to admit of an independent origin. When the existence of a Chaldean account of the deluge myth was first brought to the attention of the world by George Smith's famous lecture in 1872, the sheer force of such coincidences was enough to unsettle the cherished certitudes of confessional biblists about the absolute originality of the Bible, whose dependence on Sumero-Accadian archetypes was established even in the utter lack of historical documentation and has never been called to question ever since.[12]

In much the same way, I contend that there may not be much to be gained for the comparatist interested in investigating possible cognations by taking stock of wide-ranging similarities between ancient Greek and Indian doctrines, like, say, the Parmenidean, or rather Melissian, principle: οὐδὲν ἐκ μηδενός (Melissus, fr. 1), and its intriguing counterpart (although lacking all the speculative elaboration) in the Upaniṣadic master Uddālaka's rhetorical question: *katham asataḥ saj jāyeta*, 'how could being be born from non-being?' (BU 6.1.2). After all, it is only reasonable that overarching conceptions like the metaphysics of Being may have developed independently in different cultures, possibly (in this case) against the common Indo-European backdrop of shared linguistic categories. On the other hand, the concurrence in details of lesser import, such as are not required either by logical necessity or psychological inclination does require an explanation, to the extent that the concurrence is too specific to be ascribed to mere chance.

One such instance is, in my opinion, the parallel occurrence of the allegory of the soul chariot in Plato's *Phaedrus* and in the *Kaṭha Upaniṣad*. Let us briefly review the passages in question.

The chariot allegory in Plato's *Phaedrus*

The *Phaedrus* is a very complex dialogue, whose chief aim is to establish the superiority of philosophical discourse, caring for truth, over rhetorico-sophistic

[12] On the other hand, the utter lack of any such correspondences, together with other considerations, in my view provides a good reason for establishing the originality of the Indian flood myth vs. the Classical and Near-Eastern versions. See Magnone 2000, 2004.

discourse, geared only to success. Socrates runs into Phaidros on his way back from listening to a lecture by Lysias, in which the celebrated rhetor claimed to demonstrate the extravagant assumption that it be better for the beloved to please the unloving rather than the loving one. In order to defuse the young man's enthusiasm and win his admiration, Socrates undertakes to improvise a lecture in the same strain, but soon professes to repent the 'sacrilege' against the god Eros, and feels obliged to pronounce in atonement a second discourse of retraction, after the manner of Stesichoros' famous Παλινῳδία. In this second discourse Socrates impugns Lysias' thesis according to which the unloving one should be preferred on account of being more reasonable: the lover's presumed folly is no human foolishness, but divine μανία: a superhuman possession aroused when the sight of human beauty awakens the dim memory of divine beauty, which the immortal soul once beheld in the region 'above the heaven' before incarnating in a mortal body.

Against this backdrop, the chariot allegory is immediately preceded by a proof of the immortality of the soul (*Phdr*. 246ff.), after which Socrates introduces the theme of its 'aspect'[13] (ἰδέα). To define its essence, namely what the soul really is (οἷον μὲν ἐστι), is beyond the reach of human capabilities, says Socrates, but it is indeed possible to say what it is like (ἔοικε). Let us read Plato's words:

> Let [the soul] be likened to the composite inborn power of a pair (ζεῦγος) of winged horses and of a charioteer. However, both the horses and the charioteers of the gods are all good, and of good descent; but as for those of the others, it is a mixed affair; and first of all our driver leads an ill-assorted pair (συνωρίς), and secondly one of the horses is himself noble and of like descent, but the other is quite the opposite, and of opposite descent: so that difficult indeed and troublesome is of necessity the driving for us [mortals]. (*Phdr*. 246a–b)[14]

It is worth noticing, with Robin,[15] that although ζεῦγος is the word usually employed for a pair of horses, in applying the metaphor to the human soul Plato makes use of the word συνωρίς instead (which I have accordingly translated as 'ill-assorted pair') to signify that the human horses are not really paired, or 'on the same par', so to speak, but they are extrinsically conjoined (συν-ωρίζω) in spite of their different natures.

[13] Thus translates Velardi (2002: 185), on account of the fact that here, as Plato himself says, we are dealing with a metaphoric image of the soul.

[14] ἐοικέτω δὴ συμφύτῳ δυνάμει ὑποπτέρου ζεύγους τε καὶ ἡνιόχου. θεῶν μὲν οὖν ἵπποι τε καὶ ἡνίοχοι πάντες αὐτοί τε ἀγαθοὶ καὶ ἐξ ἀγαθῶν, τὸ δὲ τῶν ἄλλων μέμεικται. καὶ πρῶτον μὲν ἡμῶν ὁ ἄρχων συνωρίδος ἡνιοχεῖ, εἶτα τῶν ἵππων ὁ μὲν αὐτῷ καλός τε καὶ ἀγαθὸς καὶ ἐκ τοιούτων, ὁ δ' ἐξ ἐναντίων τε καὶ ἐναντίος: χαλεπὴ δὴ καὶ δύσκολος ἐξ ἀνάγκης ἡ περὶ ἡμᾶς ἡνιόχησις. (All translations are mine).

[15] Robin 1970: lxxx n. 1.

Plato does not specify the other constituents of the chariot; since, however, he says further on, while distinguishing between the mortal and immortal living beings, that the whole soul is the one who 'takes care' (ἐπιμελεῖται) of the soulless, viz. the body, the supposition lies near at hand that the chariot represents the latter. Although the tenor of the Platonic text is not quite clear at places, it seems that both the souls of the gods and those of men are joined to motionless bodies which acquire the appearance of self-mobility in the union, thanks to the inherent moving power of the soul. Nevertheless, there are differences in either case, namely: in the first place, the souls of the gods never lose their wings; and secondly, they are forever joined to their respective bodies. So much for the souls of the immortals, as Plato himself does not wish to belabour the matter, relinquishing it to godly *placet*.

As for ourselves, beings called 'mortals' were originated in consequence of the loss of the wings and the ensuing fall of the soul from heaven to earth, where it clung to a solid body in which it established its dwelling. But how did the loss of the wings come about? It pertains to the nature of the wings to lift what is bound downwards, and for that reason they are the most godlike among corporeal things. Therefore, as the divine is beautiful, wise and good, the wings are nourished and grown by similar things, but they are consumed and destroyed by the opposite. Now the gods led by Zeus revolve in the heaven in their winged chariots governing the universe in good harmony, followed by whoever so wishes and is able, for gods know no jealousy (φθόνος). But when they convene to a banquet, they proceed towards the culmination of the interior cusp of heaven (ὑπουράνιος ἁψίς) and they pass to the other side, where the plain of truth (ἀληθείας πεδίον) stretches out in the region above the heaven (ὑπερουράνιον τόπον). There the charioteers sate themselves on the sight of the substances that really *are* and feed on the pure science which is not affected by becoming and variability, but only pertains to true being. And once they are sated, they revert to their seats under the vault of heaven, unharness their horses and feed them on nectar and ambrosia. But mortals have a hard time trying to follow the gods, because the horses are difficult to control, so that the charioteers can only take a glimpse of some of the true substances, or of none at all; and in the ensuing flurry and in the collision of chariots vying for the precedence some horses are maimed and lose their wings. And the charioteers who do not get a view of the pure science of reality have to feed on opinion, which in turn entails the loss of the wings.

The chariot allegory in the *Kaṭha Upaniṣad*

The *Kaṭha Upaniṣad* in its present form consists of six chapters termed *vallīs* ('creepers') in two sections of three chapters each, but the original core may have comprised only the first two (or three) *vallīs*,[16] dealing with the teachings imparted by the death god Yama to the boy Naciketas, who had reached while still living the abode of the dead through his father's curse. To acquit himself of faulty hospitality Yama grants the boy three wishes, and Naciketas chooses as third the solution of his doubts about the continuation of existence beyond death. After a few vain attempts to elude the question by offering various boons in exchange, finally Yama praises the boy's steadfastness and reveals to him the doctrine of the knowledge of the Self (*ātman*) which rescues the wise from the wheel of rebirths and of reiterated death.[17] The high-flown celebration of *ātman* which concludes the second *vallī* links up with the third, which purposes to show the path to reach the supreme abode of the *ātman* through the practice of *yoga*, introduced precisely by the chariot allegory:

> Knowers of *brahman* . . . call Shadow and Light the two, drinkers of Truth (*ṛta*) in the world of their deeds,[18] [the one] installed in the cave of the heart, [the other] in the supreme region beyond. . . . Know that the Self (*ātman*) is the rider in a chariot, and the body is the chariot (*śarīra*); and know that the intelligence (*buddhi*) is the charioteer, and the mind (*manas*) is the bridle. They say that the senses (*indriya*) are the horses, and the sense objects (*viṣaya*) are their lanes (*gocara*). The wise call Enjoyer (*bhoktṛ*) the yoke (*yukta*) of Self, senses and objects. But as for him who has no understanding (*vijñāna*) and whose mind is ever unyoked (*ayukta*), his senses are unrestrained, like bad horses for a charioteer; on the other hand, for him who has understanding and whose mind is ever yoked (*yukta*), his senses are

16 The first three, according to Deussen (1897: 264); or just the first two, according to Olivelle (1998: 372). However, as Deussen (1897: 278) remarks, the last two strophes of the third *vallī* look like the epilogue of the original *Upaniṣad*.

17 According to Forte and Smith there is 'no self-realization or arcane knowledge about *brahman*' taught in this *Upaniṣad*, nor any philosophical doctrine of monism or of whatever other description; indeed, their paper purports to be 'an attempt to demonstrate that the chariot in the *Kaṭha Upaniṣad* still refers to the sacrifice and constitutes a metaphysical theorisation of the operations of the fire altar'. This is indeed an astounding proposition, which runs counter to all the commonly held lines of interpretation of the *Upaniṣad* both Western and Indian. Of course, it is impossible to go into its merits in the space of a footnote; I shall be content with pointing out what I regard as the fundamental flaw in Forte and Smith's analysis, namely that it begs the question, in that it only deals with such passages as are amenable to be read in connection with the ritualistic brahmanical background (the first *vallī* up to the grant of the second boon; and the beginning of the third *vallī*, up to [and obviously including] the chariot metaphor), whereas it omits to take stock of those very passages (the concluding part of first *vallī* with the request of the third boon, of paramount importance; and the whole of the second *vallī*, devoted to the praise of the path of knowledge, culminating in the realisation of the *ātman*, as Yama's fulfilment of the request) where the *Upaniṣad* really comes into its own, pouring, as it were, the new wine of the metaphysics of *brahman-ātman* into the old wineskins of ritualistic thought.

18 Reading with Śaṅkara *svakṛtasya*; otherwise *sukṛtasya* 'of good deeds'.

> indeed restrained, like good horses for a charioteer. He who has no understanding, is mindless and ever impure, does not reach that region, and incurs rebirth in the flux of existence (*saṁsāra*); but as for him who has understanding, is mindful and ever pure, he does indeed reach that region whence he is not born again. A man whose understanding is his charioteer and whose mind his bridle reaches the end of the road, that supreme region (*parama pada*) of Viṣṇu. (KaU 1.3.1; 1.3.3–6)[19]

In this short passage there occurs three times the word *yukta*, from root *yuj*, 'yoke, join', which, beside its literal meaning referring to the action of yoking or harnessing draught animals, is also employed in the figurative meaning of 'subjugating' passions and the like. The latter meaning lies at the foundation of the name of Yoga, one of the six classical schools of Indian philosophy, in so far as the proper object of Yoga is precisely the subjugation of psychical functions.[20] As a matter of fact, the passage quoted above is immediately followed by a rudimentary sketch of the way of introversion advocated by Yoga, which (sketch) is considered one of the most ancient documents of the proto-history of that school of thought.[21] According to the retroversion procedure elsewhere imaginatively styled as *pratiloma*[22] (i.e. literally 'against the hair'), which lies at the core of Yoga, each of the psychical faculties, which normally act outwardly, must be made to flow back inwardly to its source, or, as our *Upaniṣad* says, it must be 'curbed' by the faculty which stands higher in a hierarchy comprising, from low to high, senses and their objects, mind, intellect, the 'great Self' (*ātmā mahān*) and the unmanifest

19 *ṛtaṃ pibantau svakṛtasya loke guhāṃ praviṣṭau parame parārdhe | chāyātapau brahmavido vadanti . . . || . . . || ātmānaṃ rathinaṃ viddhi śarīraṃ ratham eva tu | buddhiṃ tu sārathiṃ viddhi manaḥ pragraham eva ca || indriyāṇi hayān āhur viṣayāṁs teṣu gocarān | ātmendriyamanoyuktaṃ bhoktety āhur manīṣiṇaḥ || yas tv avijñānavān bhavaty ayuktena manasā sadā | tasyendriyāṇy avaśyāni duṣṭāśvā iva sāratheḥ || yas tu vijñānavān bhavati yuktena manasā sadā | tasyendriyāṇi vaśyāni sadaśvā iva sāratheḥ || yas tv avijñānavān bhavaty amanaskaḥ sadāśuciḥ | na sa tat padam āpnoti saṁsāraṃ cādhigacchati || yas tu vijñānavān bhavati samanaskaḥ sadā śuciḥ | sa tu tat padam āpnoti yasmād bhūyo na jāyate || vijñānasārathir yas tu manaḥpragrahavān naraḥ | so 'dhvānaḥ pāram āpnoti tad viṣṇoḥ paramaṃ padam.*

20 Cf. *Yoga Sūtra* 1.2: *yogaś cittavṛttinirodhaḥ.*

21 Under their presumption that the *Kaṭha Upaniṣad* be nothing more than a 'poetic recreation' of its 'source [*Brāhmaṇa*] text', Forte and Smith quickly dispose of this passage in a couple of sentences as 'definitions of *ātman* and *puruṣa* contoured by Vedic ritual reveal[ing] that the text describes the [ritual] transmission of the terrestrial self to the heavenly self'. It might be so – but here again, one would expect a bit more of careful reasoning when calling into question the unanimous interpretative tradition both Western and Indian, which envisages this very text as the foundation stone of the classical Yoga *darśana*.

22 As explained in the *Rājamārtaṇḍa* commentary at *Yoga Sūtra* 1.2: 'The mental organ is an evolute of pure *sattva* and the psychic functions are its secondary modes. Yoga consists in their inhibition, namely in their dissolution in their source by stopping their extroversion by means of a process "against the hair" of introversion' (cf. Magnone 1999: 25).

(*avyakta*), to finally end up in the awareness principle (*puruṣa*) which is the final goal (*parā gatiḥ*) of the process. It is worth observing that the term that I have translated as 'curb' is a form of root YAM, 'restrain', which once again is frequently employed in connection with riding and draught animals.

These details of lexical usage manifest the close relationship between the chariot imagery and the beginnings of Yoga in the *Kaṭha Upaniṣad*. We must not overlook that what we have here is something more than just an allegory of the soul and the physio-psychic complex. The reining of the horses by the charioteer through the reverberations of the lexical choices distinctively hints at the process of Yoga, and the final goal of the journey, the supreme region of Viṣṇu, represents the final resolution in the awareness principle termed *puruṣa* which is the goal of the yogic process.

Actually, the technical term *puruṣa* (literally 'man' in the sense of ἀνήρ), which designates the awareness principle in the Sāṃkhya-Yoga philosophy, has evolved from very ancient roots in the cosmogonic hymn *Ṛgveda* 10.90 (end of II millennium BCE?), and on the religious side has acquired strong connections within the fold of Hinduism with the aspect of supreme Godhead named Viṣṇu. This explains why the resolution into the *puruṣa* is intimated within the allegory by the attainment of the supreme region (*parama pada*) of Viṣṇu. The *parama pada* is likewise well-known from the most ancient Vedic hymns in connection with Viṣṇu in his capacity as Trivikrama, i.e. the 'Thrice-Strider', his three strides supposedly representing the three stations of the sun in its diurnal course. According to the lexical values of the word, which include 'step, footstep and place', the *parama pada* connotes at one and the same time the 'supreme place' carrying the footprint of the third step of Viṣṇu as the sun traversing the horizon.

We shall presently turn to the convergences and discrepancies evidenced in the allegories as they appear in each text, in order to evaluate whether the similarities occur in traits that are arbitrary enough to enhance the probability of borrowing, according to the criterion laid down previously.

In case borrowing should be deemed likely, its direction would still remain to be determined. Should Plato have borrowed the allegory from the *Kaṭha* or the other way round? As always, chronology does not help in an Indian setting, since the dating of Indian texts is, at best, aleatory and highly speculative.[23] The utmost that can be said is that the *Kaṭha* may very well be anterior to Plato, or roughly contemporary, without being able to absolutely rule out the possibility of the contrary.

[23] As one recent Upaniṣadic scholar puts it rather bluntly: 'any dating of these texts that attempts a precision closer than a few centuries is as stable as a house of cards' (Olivelle 1998: 12).

But one additional criterion may be resorted to, which finds ready application in the present circumstance, namely, the criterion of integrality, that might be conveniently expressed thus: the more an element appears to be organically integrated in its surrounding structure, the lesser the probability of its having been borrowed from somewhere else.

Now the allegory of the soul chariot is not particularly called for in the context of the *Phaedrus*: it works, but as far as I can see there is no compelling reason that makes it specially suitable to express the ruling function of the intellect over the other psychic faculties in the way Plato understands it, so that it is not unthinkable that he could have borrowed it from an external source. On the other hand, as we have seen, the allegory of the soul chariot in the *Kaṭha Upaniṣad*, with its attendant imagery of yoking and bridling, is conjured up by the very name of the Yoga doctrine it is meant to illustrate, so much so that it would be utterly unreasonable even to suppose that it might be of alien origin.[24]

The persuasiveness of this conclusion is reinforced if we extend the application of the criterion of integrality to the whole of the Greek and Indian scenarios. I have reviewed occurrences of the soul chariot allegory in both literatures elsewhere,[25] and space constraints do not permit to go over it now. I must be content with stating the conclusions: leaving hints of a questionable nature aside, a fully-fledged soul chariot allegory is unknown in Greece before Plato (with the possible exception of the *locus Parmenideus*, the allegorical nature of which, however, is moot).[26] On the other side, soul chariot allegories occur in India in at least three works belonging to the *Upaniṣad* genre – i.e. the *Mahaitareya*, the *Chāgaleya* and the *Kauṣitaki* – all of them probably antedating the *Kaṭha*; and two more – the *Śvetāśvatara* and the *Maitrāyaṇīya* – almost certainly more recent, but interesting nevertheless, in that both uphold Yoga as a means of deliverance and so corroborate the structural link obtaining between Yoga and the chariot allegory.

24 Richard Seaford alerts me to the concurrent option that it might be precisely the (preexisting) terminology of the Yoga doctrine that made the expression of the doctrine receptive to a possible influence of a chariot metaphor borrowed from elsewhere (e.g. Greece). Irrespective of the problems posed by chronology, here I subscribe to the tenet of the conceptual metaphor theory as advocated by Schlieter, according to which abstract thought is inherently metaphorical, and cognitive metaphors precede and structure (or are at least conterminous with) abstract thought. In other words, the verbal notion of *yoga*, having a literal meaning in the domain of activities concerning draught animals, could not have acquired its figurative meaning in the domain of activities concerning the human psyche, before the metaphor connecting both domains as source and target was in place.

25 Magnone 2012.

26 On the subject see Latona 2008.

Comparative assessment

The foregoing scrutiny has evidenced the following areas as most amenable to a comparison: in the first place, the correspondence of the distinct components of the chariot with certain psychic faculties; secondly, the discipline of the driving; and thirdly, the use of the chariot for the journey to the world beyond. Let us begin with the last one.

The chariot as a vehicle for the world beyond

Both in the Homeric epics and in the Vedic hymns the chariot is sometimes envisaged as a means of communication between the world of men and the world of gods;[27] likewise, in both literary traditions chariot imagery is employed as a metaphor of the poetic word granting the poet access to other planes of consciousness.[28] Because it is so, it is unnecessary to suppose external influences in this connection, as the *Phaedrus* and the *Kaṭha* allegories may very well have drawn on elements belonging to their respective traditions. Nevertheless, it is worthwhile pointing out some striking parallels in the two conceptions of the final goal of the journey:

a. The ὑπερουράνιος τόπος, the region above the heaven, is conceptually identical to the *parama pada*, the supreme region of Viṣṇu, for we have seen that the latter connotes at once the footprint (*pada*) of the third step (*pada*) of Viṣṇu 'whose eye is the sun'; at the same time, as representing the highest step, the *parama pada* corresponds to the zenith, or the ὑπουράνιος ἁψίς which is the threshold to the world beyond.
b. Besides, it may be no more than a baffling coincidence that the 'region above the heaven' is also qualified as the 'plain of truth', i.e. (ἀληθείας) πέδιον, where the word πέδιον is linguistically cognate to *pada* in *parama pada*.
c. According to the *Phaedrus*, in the ὑπερουράνιος τόπος the gods and their followers apply themselves to the contemplation of the true essences. In like manner in *Ṛgveda* 1.22.20 the *parama pada* is said to be perpetually contemplated by gods (or sages).[29]

[27] E.g. *Iliad* V, 355ff. (Ares and Aphodite); V, 720 ss. (Hera and Athena); VIII, 41 ss. (Zeus); VIII, 381 ss. (Hera and Athene); XIII, 23 ss. (Poseidon); on the Indian side, see Macdonell (1981: 18) and in the entries of individual deities about gods riding in chariots; Sparreboom (1986: 18) about chariots as vehicles for the world of heaven.

[28] On the Greek side, see, e.g., Simpson 1969; on the Indian side, Sparreboom 1986: 20f., also Magnone 2012: 102ff.

[29] RV 1.22.20: *tád víṣṇoḥ paramáṃ padáṃ sádā paśyanti sūráyaḥ*. *Sūri* may mean a god, a lord or a sage.

d. In the ὑπερουράνιος τόπος the gods and their followers enjoy the pleasures of the banquet; likewise in *Ṛgveda* 8.29.7 the gods and elsewhere (1.154.5) their worshippers rejoice in the *parama pada*, where flows the fountain of honey: 'O that I could reach that dear place where men sacred to the gods rejoice; for there, in Viṣṇu's supreme region, is the fountain of honey!'[30]
e. After reaching the ὑπερουράνιος τόπος the chariots come to a stand and are carried round by the revolution of the heavenly sphere; this reminds one of an (admittedly rather obscure) passage where the lord of the *parama pada* is said to have 'set his steeds in swift motion . . . like a turning wheel' (RV 1.155.6).

On the other hand, in the *Phaedrus* the ὑπερουράνιος τόπος can only be attained thanks to the horses' being provided with wings, and this undoubtedly constitutes the major discrepancy with respect to the image of the *Kaṭha*. Of course, winged hybrids are well-known to Greek mythology, so that we must look no further for an explanation.[31]

The steering of the chariot

Both the *Phaedrus* and the *Kaṭha* agree in stressing the need for disciplined steering of the chariot in order to reach the journey's destination. The notion of discipline is conveyed in the *Kaṭha* through the metaphor of the 'subjugated' (*yukta*) horses, and we have already drawn attention to the close lexical, semantic and conceptual relationship obtaining between the terms employed for subjugating and restraining the horses on the one hand and some key concepts of the burgeoning school of Yoga as a method for subjugating and restraining psychic faculties on the other. The seamless integration of the chariot imagery in the conceptual array of proto-Yoga, which is unparalleled in the *Phaedrus*, speaks for the native status of the metaphor in the *Kaṭha*, as we have already remarked.

However, we may perhaps discern some faint echo of it in the lexical usage of the Platonic dialogue. The Sanskrit term *yoga*, literally meaning a 'yoke', is linguistically cognate to the Greek ζεῦγος which designates the pair of divine horses harnessed to the chariot. Although the figurative meaning of 'subjugation'

30 RV 1.154.5: *tád asya priyám abhi pắtho aśyāṃ náro yátra devayávo mádanti / urukramásya sá hí bándhur itthắ víṣṇoḥ padé paramé mádhva útsaḥ.*

31 Nevertheless, the idea of wings as means to reach the supreme region is not unknown even in India: in the strophe immediately before the last quoted one, it is said that no one dares to approach Viṣṇu's third step, not even the birds flying with wings: *tṛtī́yam asya nákir ắ dadharṣati váyaś caná patáyantaḥ patatríṇaḥ*. (It is just a noteworthy curiosity that the word *patatrin*, literally 'winged', hence 'bird', is also attested in post-Vedic times in the meaning of 'horse').

is ostensibly absent in the Platonic passage, it may not be devoid of significance that, as we pointed out, Plato employs a different word (i.e. συνωρίς) to designate the unruly pair of human horses of opposite temperaments; so that by implication the word ζεῦγος seems to acquire the additional value of connoting the divine horses as unanimous and obedient to the charioteer: that is to say, 'subjugated' in the same sense as *yukta*.

But the most notable point of similarity with respect to the steering of the chariot is without doubt the one concerning the difficulty caused by the opposition between good and bad horses, although such opposition wears quite different aspects in either case, for in the *Phaedrus* one horse is congenitally good and the other the reverse, whereas the horses of the *Kaṭha* do not admit of an internal disparity, but they are only susceptible of being, all of them, well-behaved, or else ill-behaved. This divergence stems from the different symbolic function of the horses, and above all from the paramount difference in the underlying ontology, as we shall presently see; nevertheless, even the coincidence of the mere idea of the antithesis is worthy of note.

The chariot as an allegory of psychic functions

We finally come to the most important congruence, i.e. the application of the chariot imagery as a sustained allegory for the psychic functions. We have already observed that, although the motif of the chariot as a vehicle for a journey to the other world had been common to both literary traditions since hoary antiquity, on the contrary the motif of the 'soul chariot' appears to be more or less specific to the Indian literary tradition, at least in the earliest period, being attested in several *Upaniṣads*, whereas it is virtually unknown to the Greek literature before Plato (with the possible if controversial exception of Parmenides).

The table given in Appendix I outlines a synopsis of the correspondences between the single parts of the chariot and the constituents of the physio-psychic complex in some of the most meaningful texts, while the bottom line highlights the several goals of the journey in the same texts. Items appearing in all texts, albeit possibly in different connections, are marked in ALL CAPITALS; whereas correspondences of a more opinable nature by reason of not being expressly declared in the text, but only inferred from the context (or, in the case of Parmenides, from Sextus' interpretation) have been enclosed in square brackets.

What impresses one on first perusing the table is that, to start with, the correspondences are much more articulate in the Indian texts than in the *Phaedrus*, irrespective of their variability in the detail. The chariot is everywhere found to represent the body (albeit not explicitly in the Greek texts). The charioteer, on the other hand, severally corresponds to the mind (*manas*), the intellect (*buddhi*) or the soul in different texts both Indian and Greek. The alternation between *manas* and *buddhi* may be ascribed to a terminological indetermination characteristic of the older *Upaniṣads*. As for the equation of the charioteer with the soul, it occurs on the Indian side only in the *Chāgaleya*, which is peculiar in many respects, and seemingly cut off from the line of development connecting the *Mahaitareya* to the *Maitrāyaṇīya* through the *Kaṭha*.

What interests us more is that both in the *Kaṭha* and in the *Phaedrus* the charioteer represents the rational faculty: *buddhi* / *vijñāna* in the Indian text and νοῦς / διάνοια in the Greek one, viz. the intelligent (or 'intelligible', in Scholastic parlance) aspect of the soul (τὸ λογιστικόν, according to the psychology of the *Republic*).

The bridle, which represents the mind in the *Kaṭha*, is not expressly mentioned in the *Phaedrus*, but is implied in the Greek word for 'charioteer', which is ἡνίοχος,[32] i.e. 'he who holds the reins' (ἡνία).

As for the horses, their correlates are totally different in India and Greece, for in the Indian tradition they stand for the *indriyas*, i.e. the 'faculties' without distinction (in the earliest period), and later, at the time of the *Maitrāyaṇīya*, when the rising Sāṃkhya cosmo-psychology had started distinguishing between sense organs and action organs,[33] the latter ones. On the Greek side, in the *Phaedrus* the two horses represent the irrational aspects of the soul, which would later be called in scholastic parlance the irascible and the concupiscible (τὸ θυμοειδές and τὸ ἐπιθυμητικόν according to the psychology of the *Republic*). In the proem of Parmenides according to Sextus' interpretation, the mares likewise stand for desires and irrational impulses of the soul.[34]

The distinction of three aspects of the soul – τὸ λογιστικόν, τὸ θυμοειδές and τὸ ἐπιθυμητικόν – finds no equivalent in the ancient Upaniṣadic psychology. However, the rudiment of an analogous conception may perhaps be seen in the stereotyped pair *kāma* and *krodha* ('desire' and 'anger') which occurs several times in the *Bhagavad Gītā*[35] in the capacity of arch-enemies of *jñāna* ('knowledge'). For example, in a passage which calls to mind the chariot allegory through the use of certain words and images, Kṛṣṇa admonishes Arjuna as follows:

32 *Phdr*. 246a, 247b, 247e, 248a, etc. (ἡνίοχος); 246b (ἡνιοχέω, ἡνιόχησις). Elsewhere the charioteer is termed ἄρχων ('commander', 246b) and κυβερνήτης ('pilot', 247c).

33 The psychology of classical Sāṃkhya reckons, in addition to the five usual sense organs (*buddhīndriya*), also five action organs (*karmendriya*): speaking, grasping, going, ejaculating and evacuating.

34 See Latona 2008.

35 E.g. BG 2.62–3; 16.18; 16.21; 18.53, and especially the passage quoted below.

> This is desire (*kāma*), this is anger (*krodha*), fostered by the element of ardour (*rajoguṇa*) . . . as fire is enveloped by smoke and a mirror is clouded by dust . . . in the same way is knowledge obfuscated by this relentless opponent of the knower . . . the senses, the mind and the intellect are its abode, as they say, and through them it deludes the embodied [soul] by obfuscating knowledge. Therefore, restrain (*niYAM*) the senses in the first place, and then kill that iniquitous destroyer of knowledge and science. (*Bhagavad Gītā* 3.37–41)[36]

Admittedly, the *Bhagavad Gītā* properly speaking is no *Upaniṣad*, being embedded in the *Mahābhārata* epos, datable after the close of the Vedic period, and for that reason must on all likelihood be ascribed to a later time than the *Phaedrus*. Nevertheless, the couple of *kāma* and *krodha* already occurs in one of the most ancient *Upaniṣads*, in a passage enumerating as components of the (world-immanent) universal Self, in addition to the faculties and the elements, also *kāma-krodha* and their opposites (BU 4.4.5).

In general terms, it may be observed that the Indian tradition is more interested in articulating the physio-psychic complex in its entirety, in order to account for the ordinary, world-affirming sensory experience as well as for its opposite, the extraordinary, world-negating practice of sensory restraint (*yoga*) leading to the suprasensory. For its part, the allegory of the *Phaedrus* only contemplates the nature of the soul with its essential components, the intelligible, the irascible and the concupiscible, represented by the joint agency of the charioteer and the pair of horses.

Against the backdrop of all the varying degrees of similarity between the allegorical correlates examined above, one item of the allegory has been left unreviewed thus far, which appears in one way or another in all Indian texts, but is conspicuously absent in the Greek ones:[37] namely, the idle passenger on the chariot. In all of them (except for the odd *Chāgaleya*) its regular correlate is the soul: for the soul, according to the standard Indian view, coincides neither with any of the several psychic functions signified by the different parts of the chariots, nor with their joint agency (as is the case with the *Phaedrus*).

Indeed, here lies the paramount disparity between the Greek and Indian versions of the chariot allegory, which is rooted in the widely differing ontologies of Plato and of the school of Sāṃkhya-Yoga at its dawn in the *Kaṭha*. Those ontologies diverge essentially with respect to where they set the boundary line between the respective pertinences of body and soul. According to Plato, the soul is tripar-

[36] The strophe immediately following overtly quotes KaU 3.10, which speaks for the likelihood that the author had in mind the *Kaṭha* chariot allegory when he composed the passage in question.

[37] This difference is also discussed by Schlieter in this volume.

tite in its functions, this tripartition being reflected in the image of the charioteer and the pair of horses; but, according to the same image, it is up to the rational faculty to oversee the other two. On the other hand, in the Indian texts one meets the distinct figure of the *rathin*, that is to say, literally, the 'owner of the chariot', or he who makes use of the chariot as an instrument, while remaining distinct and detached with respect to it. The reason for this is that, according to the dualistic psychology of Sāṃkhya-Yoga, there exists a radical opposition between the soul (*puruṣa*), which is the pure luminosity of awareness as the horizon of the appearance of objects, and nature (*prakṛti*), which is the physical substrate of the outer world as well as of the inner physio-psychic complex, inclusive of the rational, volitional and desiderative faculties. To put it succinctly, the intellect is part (indeed, the best part) of the soul, according to Plato, whereas it is non-soul, but merely a part of the body, according to Sāṃkhya-Yoga.

Conclusion

The above tentative analysis, albeit needing further refinement, has brought to light both similarities and differences between the chariot allegories in the *Kaṭha Upaniṣad* and in the *Phaedrus*, which can be summed up as follows. We may count as points of similarity:

a. the overall idea of the chariot as an allegory of the psychic functions (for which there are more and still earlier instances on the Indian, but not on the Greek side);
b. the identification of the charioteer with the rational faculty;
c. the analogous characterisation of the *parama pada* and, respectively, the ὑπερουράνιος τόπος / ἀληθείας πέδιον as the final goal of the journey;
d. the general notion of the necessity of a 'subjugation' of the psychic faculties in order to reach the journey's end;
e. the broad concept of an opposition between good and bad horses (however differently declined in either case).

On the other hand, we can count as major discrepancies:

a. the different symbolic significance of the horses; and, above all,
b. the absence of the separate figure of the idle traveller in the *Phaedrus*;

both of them grounded in the crucial diversity of the underlying ontology of the two works.

It lies with the reader to judge for himself of the plausibility or otherwise of the considerations propounded; as for my own assessment, I am of the opinion that the similarities evinced may be momentous enough to justify the supposition, pending further research, that Plato might have been acquainted (either directly of indirectly) with the chariot allegory and the attendant doctrines of the *Kaṭha Upaniṣad*, and might have drawn inspiration from them, while contextually adapting them to the theoretical frame of his own ontological thought.

Appendix I

		Aitareya Āraṇyaka (2,3,8)	*Chāgaleya Upaniṣad*	*Kaṭha Upaniṣad* (1,3)	*Maitrāyaṇīya Upaniṣad* (2,3.6; 6,28)	**Parmenides** (B1)	*Phaedrus* (246)
soul / breath		traveller	impeller [CHARIOTEER]	traveller	impeller	[the 'mortal who knows']	
body		CHARIOT	CHARIOT	CHARIOT	CHARIOT	[CHARIOT]	[CHARIOT]
(body parts: tendons, bones, blood, skin)			(belts, supports, oil, hood)				
intellect				CHARIOTEER		– [the maiden 'immortal CHARIOTEERs' ἀθάνατοι ἡνίοχοι] – [Dike]	CHARIOTEER (ἡνίοχος)
mind		CHARIOTEER		reins	CHARIOTEER	[θυμός]	
sense organs	**eyes**	pair of HORSES	HORSES	HORSES	reins	[sun daughters]	
	ears	sides (wings)				[wheels]	
action organs					HORSES		
word		seat	noise				
natural disposition			whip (*karma*)		whip (*prakṛtimaya*)		
sensible experiences				paths			
irrational impulses						[MARES]	pair (ζεῦγος/συνωρίς) of winged HORSES
goal		destruction of worldly desires	death	Viṣṇu's 'highest footstep/abode' (*parama pada*)	to revolve (like a potter's wheel)	the Goddess's abode	– the 'region above the heaven' (ὑπερουράνιον τόπον) – the 'plain of truth' (ἀληθείας πεδίον)

11

'Master the chariot, master your Self': comparing chariot metaphors as hermeneutics for mind, self and liberation in ancient Greek and Indian sources

Jens Schlieter

In ancient Greece and India, the real use of chariots encompassed sports, cults, journeys and combat. These uses of the supposedly most complex mobile technology of early Greek and Indian culture suggest a potentially similar complex metaphorical or 'symbolic' use of the chariot. It can be assumed that steering fast chariots was a demanding and fascinating task: an intensive experience of speed and mid-distance travel, but also a dangerous device, as numerous reported instances of chariot accidents in ancient sources show. Thus, it should not astonish that chariots (and chariot rides) were taken as a source domain, forming a dynamic 'anthropo-therio-technological metaphor' for the interpretation of abstract target domains such as gods, or the philosophical reflection of body, soul and liberation. In fact, in both (and other Eurasian) traditions chariots were depicted as vehicles of gods such as the sun, i.e. as a symbol of cosmic stability; they were, moreover, used as symbols of royal power and social prestige, e.g. of kings and warriors (in the *Iliad*, Vedic hymns, and poetic literature); and, finally, chariots served as metaphors for the 'person', the 'mind' and the 'way to liberation'.

The parallel application of chariot imagery for the 'Self' and its salvific progress in both Greek and Indian contexts is indeed most astounding – yet it must be remarked that a certain Indian influence on pre-Alexandrian Greece is, although highly unlikely, theoretically possible, since the absolute (and even relative) chronology of the *Upaniṣads* is still a matter of academic dispute. Applying conceptual metaphor theory as a hermeneutic tool, I will try to outline subtle but important differences between the Greek and Indian chariot metaphors for 'mind', the 'Self' and 'liberation' – for instance in respect to a 'chariot passenger' able to descend from the 'chariot' at a final destination, or with regard to the 'horses' as either 'parts of the soul' or (neutral) 'senses', to be mastered by the charioteer. A cognitive analysis of chariot metaphors, may, in other words, be a valuable tool for highlighting those (sometimes hidden) philosophical preconceptions prevalent in abstract domains such as the 'mind', the connection of 'body and mind', the relationship between the 'rational' and the 'emotional' part of the 'mind', the relation between a 'steering mind' and the 'Self', etc.

Methodology: Hans Blumenberg and conceptual metaphor theory

Actually, there are as many different metaphor theories as there are – to apply a metaphor – grains of sand on the oceans' beaches. For my purpose, it will hopefully suffice to name some insights of the cognitive approaches towards metaphors (used also by Jurewicz in this volume), leaving aside theories that treat metaphor as a poetic or rhetorical device. The basic approach has been put forth by Mark Johnson and George Lakoff, namely, that mental activities, such as visualising problems, orientation in time and space, etc.,

> are metaphorical in nature. The metaphorical concepts that characterise those activities structure our present reality. New metaphors have the power to create a new reality. This can begin to happen when we start to comprehend our experience in terms of a metaphor, and it becomes a deeper reality when we begin to act in terms of it. If a new metaphor enters the conceptual system that we base our actions on, it will alter that conceptual system and the perceptions and actions that the system gives rise to'.[1]

Lakoff and Johnson distinguished between a 'source domain' that, grounded in human experience, is used to visualise a 'target domain', a more abstract realm – the human mind, the psyche, emotions, philosophical concepts, etc. The target domain, the authors hold, is 'constituted by the immediate subject matter', whereas the source domain

> provides the source concepts used in that reasoning. Metaphorical language has literal meaning in the source domain. In addition, a metaphoric mapping is multiple, that is, two or more elements are mapped to two or more other elements. Image-schema structure is preserved in the mapping – interiors of containers map to interiors, exteriors map to exteriors; sources of motion to sources, goals to goals, and so on.[2]

In their later work of 1999, *Philosophy in the Flesh*, Lakoff and Johnson champion three elementary principles: 'The mind is inherently embodied. Thought is mostly unconscious. Abstract concepts are largely metaphorical.'[3] However, only occasionally do they point to the fact that the 'embodiment' experience is, nevertheless, manipulated through the age-old use of technology

1 Lakoff and Johnson 2003: 146.
2 Lakoff and Johnson 2003: 266.
3 Lakoff and Johnson 1999: 3. These maxims can be followed without subscribing to the author's claim that 'reason' is to be fully 'naturalised' (cf. ibid.: 4).

and artefacts,[4] which provide, therefore, relevant metaphors, too. Accordingly, in the field of chariots one will find – as source domain – the metaphorical use of elements of the chariot as whole or in part (wheels, reins, centre/pivot, hub, body, horses), chariot riding (speed, road, sound and heat of the axle; wind; steering, etc.), or the broader use (sports, war, representation). As target domains, the chariot had been used to represent heroic virtues; the mind/soul; the movement of the sun and stars and the passing of time; air travel; etc. Declaring metaphors to be part of the 'cognitive unconscious', Lakoff and Johnson argue in line with a theory of 'primary metaphors' which are 'part of the cognitive unconscious':

> We acquire them automatically and unconsciously via the normal process of neural learning and may be unaware that we have them. We have no choice in this process. When the embodied experiences in the world are universal, then the corresponding primary metaphors are universally acquired. This explains the widespread occurrence . . . of a great many primary metaphors.[5]

A more recent development of the 'cognitive' (or 'conceptual') metaphor theory has been initiated by Gilles Fauconnier and Mark Turner as a theory of 'conceptual blending'.[6] Mental frames, they argue, may not only encompass a single 'source domain' but combine various 'input fields' which are 'blended' (or co-activated) in the metaphorical process. These input-domains may include senso-motoric schemata or triggers of certain emotions, and even incompatible 'input spaces' can be creatively combined in the 'blend'. The result is a more encompassing, complex model of a combination of metaphorical domains, which are held to be the original process of 'creative' thinking, because the mapping allows us to solve complex problems by fusing distinct realms to an integrated whole.

Highlighting the more existential meaningfulness of metaphors, I will turn to Hans Blumenberg, who, in the tradition of 'history of concepts' (*Begriffsgeschichte*), developed a 'Metaphorology' exemplified in various studies of philosophically meaningful metaphors (e.g. the metaphor of a 'book' or 'text' for the readability of the 'world'; or the metaphor of 'light' as imagery of 'truth'). Metaphors put themselves in place of the otherwise unimaginable reality of the 'world', 'life' or the human 'self'. In his early work, Blumenberg speaks of those metaphors that can principally not be reformulated as 'concepts'

4 Cf. the 'hard and soft energy' metaphors (Lakoff and Johnson 2003: 157), or their remark, that 'science' has been successful in extending 'our basic-level capacities for perception and manipulation via technology. Instruments like telescopes, microscopes', and, in addition, computers, have enlarged the capacities for 'manipulation' or 'calculation' (Lakoff and Johnson 1999: 91).

5 Lakoff and Johnson 1999: 59.

6 Cf. Fauconnier and Turner 2002.

as 'absolute metaphors': 'The absolute metaphor . . . springs into a void, projects itself on the tabula rasa of what cannot be fulfilled by theory; here it has taken the place of the no-longer living absolute will. Metaphysics often proved itself to us to be metaphorics taken literally; the disappearance of metaphysics calls metaphorics back to its place.'[7] A core function of those metaphors figures an 'existential' quality: to provide understanding of the 'non-conceptualisable', and, therewith, to reduce fear: 'absolute metaphors "answer" those supposedly naive, principally unanswerable questions whose relevance lies quite simply in the fact that they cannot be eliminated because we don't ask them but find them asked in the foundation of existence [*Daseinsgrund*]'.[8] For Blumenberg, metaphors fulfil functions of human survival and self-assertion strategies – metaphors do not reveal reality. Their function is to appease, because they help to reduce unknown (reality) to something known (within the lifeworld); they relieve the angst of 'the monstrous and outrageous'.[9] Metaphors allow us to speak of the powerful and frightening in indirect ways; in so doing they help to keep the fearful at a distance. In that respect, metaphors fulfil functions that have been explained by sociologists of religion as 'contingency formula' (Niklas Luhmann, Hermann Lübbe), i.e., to transform the contingent into something that can at least be addressed. Metaphors, therefore, describe the fundamental anthropological position of man, his relation to reality being 'indirect, complicated, delayed, selective, and, most prominently, "metaphorical"'.[10] How these ideas, sketched only roughly here, help to elucidate chariot imagery will be shown below. In addition to the 'grand theory', Blumenberg argues that metaphors assumed the negative image of being merely illustrative due to the fact that they appear to be 'genetically secondary', a pure ornamentation – however, 'the secondary significance of metaphors is only the pretence an author creates by the reversal of the genetic relationship in the representation'.[11] In other words: for the construction of meaning in abstract domains, metaphors are not secondary (even though they may be secondary in reference to the lifeworld domain, as seems obvious in the case of chariot imagery). On the contrary: they structure understanding right from the initial moment.

Significant for the case of chariot metaphors, the following observation of Blumenberg actually builds on the 'wagon': 'A metaphor demands a faithful interpretation of all of its functional moments; if this is violated, the metaphor regresses into allegory, in which the wheels of the wagon of any goddess may be

7 Blumenberg 1999: 23. All translations of Blumenberg are by myself.
8 Blumenberg 1981a: 15.
9 Cf. Blumenberg 2006: 10, 424.
10 Blumenberg 1981b: 115.
11 Blumenberg 2001: 179.

designated as the four cardinal virtues.'[12] This remark will prove to be helpful in analysing the phases of metaphor-use – allegory, for whatever reason, no longer takes the lifeworld-use seriously.

Sports, prestige, war: chariot and chariot use in Greece and India

In the first millennium BCE, to which the texts discussed below belong, charioty can be conceived as an already well-established technology in Greece and in India. Therefore it is not necessary to enter the intense and sometimes grim debate on the 'true origin' of the light and fast two-horse vehicle with one axle and spoked wheels. However, I would like to express sympathy with the view of Peter Raulwing, starting from evidence of the semantic field of chariots and their parts:

> If we take all the available philological, linguistic, archaeological, archaeo-zoological and cultural historical evidence into account, the most plausible solution seems to be that the chariot must be regarded as a product of the city states of the ancient Near East in the early 2nd Millennium BC.[13]

More relevant for my purpose is the technical structure, the supposed range of use, and the 'driving experience' of the chariot.

The chariot as a fast-moving car for usually one or two persons was, of course, dependent on several independent innovations: First, the revolutionary invention of spoked wheels (reinforced with a flat metal rim) replacing heavy and massive, tripartite wooden wheels; second, the breeding of horses able to provide motive power while bridled and yoked together (as a pair, or in the case of the quadriga, four); third, a light body-construction or basket with a D-shaped floor; fourth, a durable hub with an equally durable axis. The chariot complex as a whole, however, presupposes an environment in which there were tracks, roads, or, at least, a somehow 'drivable' ground. The latter remark may be trivial – nevertheless, it will be seen that chariot metaphors build on this aspect, too.

Comparing roughly Greek chariot constructions of the first millennium BCE with those of Indian chariots (known to us, apart from textual evidence, e.g. from depictions on the Buddhist stūpa in Sāñchī, first century BCE), the most obvious difference seems to be the wheel: Indian chariot wheels had a large number of thin spokes (in the earliest depictions of Sāñchī,[14] ca. 12–33 spokes), whereas Greek chariots, such as the Mycenaean box-chariot, were fitted with four-spoked wheels (compare, e.g., the Apulian Calyx krater with Helios riding a quadriga of

[12] Blumenberg 2001: 183.

[13] Raulwing 2000: 99.

[14] Cf. Sparreboom 1985: 14, 93–113.

four winged horses, ca. 430 BCE, now in the British Museum, London). In regard to functionality, this and other differences, such as the comparatively larger size of Indian chariots, seem to be of minor importance. Metaphorically relevant is the fact that chariots in Greece were more often steered by a single charioteer. Additionally, both in Greece and in India the individual shape of the chariot differed regionally and in regard to the intended usage: as racing vehicle, mobile platform in war, for royal festivals and ritual procession, or means of everyday transport for the aristocracy. Although the military usage was important and has been very often depicted (e.g. in Egypt or the Middle East), it has been argued by Peter Greenhalgh and others that its predominant early use was in sports and cults, whereas the military career came later.[15] There are famous early descriptions of chariot races in Homer (*Il.* 23.249–623) and in the Veda.[16] It was a highly demanding sport – due to the difficult high-speed interplay of horses, the artefact and the human charioteer – leading to various kinds of sometimes deadly accidents reported in the sources. Dangers of driving included the breakdown of the chariot itself (broken axes, spokes or wheels, etc.), runaway horses, clashes of chariots, and so on.

If I may add some more phenomenological comments on the experience of driving this 'anthropo-therio-technological' artefact, it seems that, in the epoch before riding of horses became common, nothing could equal the experience of speed offered in chariot rides. The swiftness of chariots, Max Sparreboom summarises, and their use as a racing car, are the most prominent element of chariot imagery in Vedic texts.[17] The Indian and Greek chariots were not fitted with suspension (some kind of basic suspension had been invented in Egyptian chariotry);[18] the off-road ride, leaving prepared tracks behind, must have been rather rough and bumpy. On sandy ground, turning the chariot at high-speed must almost inevitably lead, the pole being stiffly fixed to the chariot box, to a drifting chariot. Graphic illustrations are the famous chariot race scenes in movies such as *Ben Hur*. Tackling a narrow curve might even cause an overturn due to the centripetal force,[19] as can be acknowledged in replicas tested in experimental archaeology. Large jumps of the chariot box are equally attested. This lends plausibility to the ancient conceptualisation of 'flying' not only as an imagined bird's flight but also as a 'chariot ride'. For the driver – and probably even more so for a purely observing passenger not involved in steering – the experience of speed

15 Greenhalgh 1973: 29f.; Sparreboom 1985: 32f.
16 See Forte and Smith (in this volume); cf. Sparreboom 1985: 28–43.
17 Cf. Sparreboom 1985: 119f.
18 Cf., for the Greek chariot, Plath 1994.
19 Cf. Paipetis 2010: 74–6 (on Nestor's advice how to drive the chariot around the U-turn post).

must have been breath-taking. The same holds true for spectators of racing chariots. The thundering sound of hooves at full gallop, the cracking of the wheels and the whistling of the turning axles, initiated and controlled by a human charioteer: all this must have contributed to the prestigious image of chariots. Additionally, the chariot was not only one of the most complex technological artefacts of early civilisation – it was also a very expensive technology,[20] likewise in manufacture, maintenance, and in the fodder supply for the horses.

As a matter of fact, the chariot, 'a widespread symbol of élite transport for monarch and nobles', and 'the mystique of chariotry' as such, were to lose their prestige 'in favour of the ridden steed by the first millennium BC'.[21] Nevertheless, in the late antique world, the chariot continued to be of importance in some Eurasian regions, so that one should conceive of a long period of slow decline. And even after having lost most its everyday use, it was, for instance in the Roman period, still fashionable as a racing car. In India, Sparreboom observes, the chariot survived the Vedic period as an important literary device, while its lifeworld meaning had been marginalised, due to the fact that it had been advanced and transformed into slower, taller, more representative, and often four-wheeled vehicles (still named *ratha*).[22]

Chariots of the sun

A major metaphorical enrichment of the chariot (gr. ἅρμα; skt. *ratha*) had been its remarkably parallel application to the sun and its movement. In several ancient cultures including Greece and Vedic India, the sun had been conceptualised as a 'rotating wheel' (λάμπρος ἡλίου κύκλος; lat. *solis rota*; skt. *kālacakra*).[23] Sometimes, the golden, flamed wheel is the wheel and axis of the sun-god's chariot; in other depictions, it is the shining aureole or crown of the sun-god as the anthropomorphic chariot driver.[24] Of metaphorical benefit had been obviously the fast and steady drive of the celestial bodies from sunrise to sunset. In Greek mythology, there are various narrations of the four horses yoked in the early morning, whereas in the night, they are unharnessed and brought to a heavenly watering place with ambrosia.[25] In Orphic and Vedic hymns, the horses and the chariot of the sun are praised as fast and steady runners. In India, the sun-god Sūrya was closely connected to Kāla, 'time'. Apart from those

20 Cf. Piggott 1992, Littauer, Crouwel and Raulwing 2002.

21 Piggott 1992: 41.

22 Sparreboom 1985: 92f.

23 Cf. Roscher 1965, vol. III.2 (Phaethon), vol. I.2 (Helios), sp. 1996.

24 Cf. Gelling and Davidson 1969.

25 The question how the chariot returns from west to east in nighttime had been answered by a travel through the underworld.

depictions on the stūpa of Sāñchī, there is a second example, to be dated to the first century BCE, forming part of a relief at the Bhājā vihāra. Here Sūrya is shown on – or, as driving – a quadriga.[26] We have to refrain from delving into the details of sun-mythology here, but shall ask how this astonishing fact can be explained, that a human artefact, the chariot, was used to illuminate 'natural' activities of the gods. Obviously, the chariot drive was plausible in connection with the image of the 'celestial paths' of the sun and the moon. Accordingly, the sun-chariot is depicted as running on a 'heavenly' track. Sunrise and sunset had also – in Greece and India – been conceptualised involving an artefact, namely, as the opening of reinforced gates through which the chariots of dawn, sun and the moon pass while beginning or ending their daily journey.

Moreover, the chariot, being largely independent of the contingencies of natural movements (e.g. the *rhythm* of rivers), could be equipped with a human-like driver – human-like in respect of human intentions, namely, to drive along, to stop, or to deviate from a scheduled journey. By conceptualising them as god-driven chariots, the ancients were able to appeal to the sun-god not to deviate from the usual path. Any deviation, they thought, would lead to draughts, forest fires, etc., as depicted in the unauthorised use of Helios' chariot by his teenage son Phaethon. Heraclitus of Ephesus states: 'Helios (the sun) will not overstep his measures; if he were to do so, the Erinyes, handmaidens of justice, would seek him out for punishment' (22 DK B94). Another very interesting aspect can be seen in the description of the godly chariot drivers looking down on the world. In the *Ṛgveda* (hymn 1.50), we hear: 'Seven bay mares carry you in the chariot, O sun god with hair of flame, gazing from afar';[27] in Ovid's *Metamorphoses*, the chariot-driving sun-god is even called *mundi oculus* (4, 228) (cf. Plato *Politeia* 6, 508a–c). In Greece and in India the god of the sun is the 'bringer of light', and, as such, also a precondition for 'orientation'.

To summarise, the chariot, and the chariot ride as intentional, continuous travel on a given track, elevated from the sphere of the 'ordinary pedestrians', can be seen as a remarkable example of what we may call 'techno-therio-anthropomorphisation'. As can be seen from the descriptions of the chariots of emperors in the lifeworld, the imagined sun-chariot was soon to exert an inverse influence: representative chariots of emperors, kings and generals are variously described as gold-coloured or even gold-plated vehicles of incredible representative value, and it was obviously hoped that the qualities of the sun would be metonymically transferred to the chariot driver or passenger. We may assume that not only 'young gods' in heaven and earth were fascinated by this horse-

26 See Coomaraswamy 1927: pl. VII, fig. 24.
27 Doniger 1981: 190. Cf. RV 127.6, 128.1, 129.1.

driven machine and 'burning in ardent desire for [driving] the chariot' (lat. *flagratque cupidine currus*, Ovid *Metamorphoses* II, 104).

Chariots as 'anthropo-therio-technological' metaphor for Self and liberation: Parmenides, Plato and the *Kaṭha Upaniṣad*

The next move in chariot imagery that will be discussed here can be illustrated in Parmenides' famous proem, in which the Pre-Socratic philosopher describes a young man, probably himself, as driving a chariot from the 'halls of night' to the light. According to the approach chosen here, we will focus mainly on the metaphors used, and will try to elucidate them without referring in detail either to the respective author's philosophical propositions or to his poetic precursors: the metaphors shall, as far as possible, stand for themselves. The beginning of the proem narrates:

> The mares that carry me kept conveying me as far as ever my spirit reached, once they had taken and set me on the goddess' way of much discourse, which carries through every stage to meet her face to face, a man of understanding. On this I was carried, for on this the sagacious mares were carrying me, straining at the chariot and guided by maidens along the way. The axle in the naves kept blazing and uttering the pipe's loud note, driven onwards at both ends by its two metalled wheels, whenever the daughters of the sun made haste to convey me . . . There stand the gates between the journeys of night and day, enclosed at top and bottom by a lintel and threshold of stone, and themselves fitting closely to a great architrave in the aether . . . Whereupon the maidens drove the chariot and mares straight on through the gates along the road. And the goddess received me warmly, and taking my right hand in hers spoke as follows and addressed me: 'Welcome, O youth, arriving at our dwelling as consort of immortal charioteers and mares which carry you; no ill fate sent you forth to travel on this way, which is far removed indeed from the step of men, but right and justice. You must be informed of everything, both of the unmoved heart of persuasive reality and of the beliefs of mortals.'[28]

In these introductory verses, the philosopher describes a chariot journey to an extra-terrestrial place. A certain ambiguity remains as to whether the journey ascends to 'heavenly gates' or descends to the underworld, Tartaros.[29] The journey itself, on which he is accompanied by goddesses of the sun, obviously serves a narrative function – the young philosopher being 'initiated' (although the content of these initiations are rather philosophical insights) into a central idea of his famous philosophical vision: that being *is*, whereas the non-being not only *is not*, but cannot even be *thought*. While the 'daughters of the sun' guide and steer the chariot, the philosopher seems to perceive the impressive ride with all

[28] Coxon 2009: 50–4.
[29] Cf. Miller 2006: 18–24.

of his senses: the loud sound of the axle in the naves, the blazing – emitting heat and light. The wheels turn, on 'this way, which is far removed indeed from the step of men', beyond the human-inhabited world: Here again, we encounter the conception of an extra-terrestrial 'road' on which chariots drive. Interestingly, we encounter another artefact on the chariot's way: the obviously massive gates (of dawn and sunset, cf. Homer, *Il.*, 8.389–96) through which the chariot passes – again on a 'road' (ἀμαξιτὸς).

From Hermann Diels' study onwards[30] it has repeatedly been argued that the chariot ride is only an allegory for the travel of the 'soul', i.e. a 'shamanic flight'. Some hold that a travel to the underworld, again as 'flight of the soul', is depicted – e.g. of an initiate into secret mystery cults dying his 'spiritual' death.[31] In most interpretations, however, the chariot ride is only a literary device, paying tribute to the ecstatic motivation of visionary poetry.

As outlined above, and despite any poetic precursors, I would prefer to take the narrated experience of chariot riding more seriously. Parmenides' young man is a passenger (comparable, in that respect, to the detached and purely observing 'enjoyer', skt. *bhoktṛ*, of the Upaniṣadic chariot imagery discussed below). As such, the passenger 'desires', as do the horses, to start the ride. He enjoys his elevated position of observing the lifeworld of men. The ride in the chariot, intensively experienced, not only justifies the 'superhuman' truth-claims by the mode of travel to a 'transcendent' place (arrived at the divine place, the philosopher claims his insights to be disclosed by the goddess of truth) – the ride itself seems to be a preparatory part of the insights. Taking the ride seriously implies that real-world chariot rides exerted an impact on Parmenides and on the thoughts that he communicates. In other words, it bears characteristics of a technologically mediated, 'modernist' experience. We call it 'modernist' here to counter the tendency to read Pre-Socratic philosophy as a traditional and somehow naïve philosophy of nature.

Further, the chariot imagery had already been enriched by two other important input-domains: one being the aristocratic wealth, splendour and representative quality of a chariot in a technologically advanced environment (the fortified gates, the road). Depicting a chariot passenger, the 'proem' entrusts the 'observing' philosopher as traveller with aristocratic dignity. The second input-domain is the metaphorised travel of the celestial chariot, especially the chariot of the sun. In that respect, the chariot ride of Parmenides' young man is enriched by the quality of 'light' and 'vision from above' (long-standing metaphors of 'truth' and 'abstract overview'), but also by intentional steadiness, reliability and responsibility. Even if out of sight in cloudy, foggy or stormy

[30] Diels 1897: 46.
[31] Cf. Kingsley 1999: 115.

weather, the chariot of the sun moves on. Likewise the Parmenidean philosopher: he stays on track – being moved on a track, but unmoved in his thought that there *is* only being, or: *being* is all that is. In other words, being on the chariot of light itself, he *looks* from that perspective, the enlightened perspective being the light-emitting vision of all there is – which is equivalent to: of all there is to be seen. Therefore, the journey itself demonstrates already the highest view, which is fully achieved in the final conversation at the destination. It is not only a religio-philosophical justification strategy – it demonstrates what an elevated driving-experience may achieve. Although there are first hints that the chariot as an entire complex, including the driving sun-goddesses, interacts with the 'sagacious mares' in an almost intentional way, it is, in my view, not yet a full-fledged metaphor of the soul and its temporary or even final liberation.[32] The most prominent examples of this kind of metaphor-use are, in Greece, Plato's well-known chariot simile in the *Phaedrus*, and, in India, the Upaniṣadic chariot simile,[33] to both of which I will now turn.

As is well known, Plato uses the chariot imagery in a complex simile for describing the difference between the souls of humans and of gods by pointing to the ambivalent nature of the human soul's parts, its heavenly ascent, and its return to earth, i.e., rebirth (*Phdr.* 245c–256b). In Plato's dialogue, the chariot imagery is introduced by Socrates for proving the thesis that all souls are immortal, for 'she is the source of all motion both in herself and in others' (245c). Everything that moves itself must be immortal. If the soul is that which moves itself, it must be immortal. The Olympian gods may drive their chariot from the heights of the Olympus to a stable place outside of the revolving world (κόσμος), to the stable hyperuranian realm (ὑπερουράνιος τόπος) where they – after a turnaround, in which they cross the border of the moving fixed-star heaven towards the 'non-located location' at the back – can descend[34] from the chariot, take a rest, may look down at the world, and then return after a full turn of the sub-lunar heaven (cf. 274d) to their Olympian home.

In contrast, the human soul is compared to the 'composite nature' of a winged chariot and its driver. Whereas, however, the chariots and steeds of the

32 A defense of the full allegorical reading (such as Sextus Empiricus' reading of Parmenides) may be found in Latona 2008: 199–223.

33 Cf. Slaveva-Griffin 2003.

34 Forte and Smith (in this volume) are able to show, very convincingly, various parallels (or 'intertexts') of the Parmenidean poem and the *Iliad* (the chariot race in *Il.* 23). The only parallel that I would consider less plausible pertains to the equation of the Parmenidean 'path of thought' with a lap in a chariot race. To me, it seems very important that the outward journey arrives at a destination where the passenger descends and receives his philosophical insights, and returns only thereafter – whereas the racing charioteer will turn in high speed, without ever descending the chariot.

gods are of an excellent nature, the human chariot must cope with two very different steeds. One, the white one, the 'mindful' (possessing 'moderation', σωφροσύνη), is of noble descent; the other, the black one, of inferior descent. One is able to understand the commands of the charioteer, whereas the other, 'appetitive' part, or 'desire' (ἐπιθυμία), respects only the whip. While the chariots of the gods are equipoised and easy to handle, the human chariot is difficult to steer, in constant danger of crashing. Steering, therefore, is immensely difficult. The obnoxious steed of poor breeding wants to return to earth, to human desires, and gets inflamed and sexually agitated if the chariot meets other chariots in the sky. The noble steed, on the other hand, wants to ascend; if the charioteer could steer the whole complex accordingly, the chariot would leave the inner space and would enable the human soul to see being itself, reality, as it were.

Actually, the whole chariot imagery does not follow a coherent logic of lifeworld chariots in all details but alludes to a mythical picture (e.g. with its 'wings'), as G. W. F. Hegel already observed, commenting that this 'myth' has somehow an inconsistent 'potpourri' character.[35] Even though the cognitive analysis of the metaphors is still a valid undertaking, we have to note that Plato's chariots in some respect head into allegory. The imagery, however, is quite clear: it builds on a tripartite nature of the soul as the chariot-compound, made of the charioteer (as driver and passenger in one person) – who is the 'rational' (λογιστικόν), and whose bliss is realised in steering to the Imperishable; the 'mind' (νοῦς) is held to be the 'pilot of the soul' (ψυχῆς κυβερνήτης, 247c) – and of the two forces (τὼ δυνάμεις), symbolised in the horses: the innate nature of 'desire' (ἐπιθυμητικόν), aiming for lust and sensual pleasures, and the 'striving' or 'courageous' (θυμοειδές), aiming for the higher, the (cultivated) striving for the better. We may comment in passing that the imagery of an understanding, obedient, white steed (on the right-hand side, of course) and a low-breed black steed of stubbornness and sexual indulgence, unable to communicate (the white one understands and follows the *logos*!), seems to allude to the Greek conceptions of the 'barbarians' (e.g. of Ethiopia).[36] The human driver of the winged chariot must handle the antagonistic forces – only then will he realise autonomy and steer his life for the better; finally, he will be able to steer his soul after death to the immortal sphere of being. The simile, moreover, depicts what may happen when two chariots meet, but these details may not be followed here. Socrates concludes that, if the noble force within the winged chariot dominates, and self-control prevails, then

[35] Hegel 1986: 49.

[36] Cf. Phaethon's chariot travel that led to the 'nigrification' of the Aethiopians (Roscher 1965: sp. 2184). Belfiore, in contrast, argues that Plato alludes with the black horse to the 'satyr-like' characteristics of Socrates (Belfiore 2006: 201–5).

> they pass their lives in the greatest happiness which is attainable by man . . . But if they choose the lower life of ambition they may still have a happy destiny, though inferior, because they have not the approval of the whole soul. At last they leave the body and proceed on their pilgrim's progress, and those who have once begun can never go back. (255c–256a).[37]

Humans are not able to enjoy a steady view, because they are not able to reach the final destination of the heavenly journey, where the 'immortal souls' of the gods 'having travelled out stood upon the back of heaven' (ἔξω πορευθεῖσαι ἔστησαν ἐπὶ τῷ τοῦ οὐρανοῦ νώτῳ, 247b–c). Of course, in the context of the *Phaedrus*, the chariot imagery can be taken as an example of how to counter the challenge of a 'desire-driven life', but to decipher it only as a 'justification of the best life', as Elizabeth Schiltz does,[38] cuts off important soteriological dimensions.

As has been variously observed, this Platonic simile of the chariot as the soul has a very interesting parallel in the corpus of early Indian texts, namely, in the *Kaṭha Upaniṣad.* Before discussing the metaphorical dimensions of the simile, the relevant passage shall be quoted in full:

> Know the self (*ātman*) as a rider in a chariot,
> and the body, as simply the chariot.
> Know the intellect (*buddhi*) as the charioteer,
> and the mind (*manas*), as simply the reins.
> 4 The senses (*indriyāṇi*), they say, are the horses,
> and sense objects (*viśaya*) are the paths (*gocara*) around them;
> He who is linked to the body (*ātman*), senses, and mind,
> the wise proclaim as the one who enjoys (*bhoktar*).
> 5 When a man lacks understanding,
> and his mind is never controlled [*ajuktena*],
> his senses do not obey him,
> as bad horses, a charioteer.
> 6 But when a man has understanding,
> and his mind is ever controlled,
> his senses do obey him,
> as good horses, a charioteer.
> 7 When a man lacks understanding,
> is unmindful and always impure,
> he does not reach that final step,
> but gets on the round of rebirth (*saṃsāra*).

[37] Jowett 1871: 589. This soteriological ideal of life as a complex psychosomatic procedure of 'steering' to the border of the supra-empirical realm, detached from the realm of becoming, is in line with Plato's simile of the 'divided line' in the *Politeia* (509d–511e). The vertical ascent in the chariot-soul simile would then correspond to the 'c'-point of the simile of the line.

[38] Cf. Schiltz 2006.

8 But when a man has understanding,
is mindful and always pure,
he does reach that final step,
from which he is not reborn again.
9 When a man's mind is his reins,
intellect, his charioteer,
he reaches the end of the road,
that highest step of Viṣṇu . . .[39]

Looking at the Upaniṣadic simile, the thematic similarity with Plato is indeed remarkable. As astonishing may count not only the fact per se, that chariot imagery is used for exemplifying the human soul, but moreover, that it is done so in soteriological contexts. In the *Kaṭha Upaniṣad* the simile of the chariot and the horses aims at explaining the soul's way to liberation, i.e., immortality ('the highest step of Viṣṇu' depicts the place of final emancipation of transmigrating 'souls'). The *ātman*, the 'self', is the driver. The chariot, *ratha* – obviously the body of the wagon – metaphorises the human body. It is steered by the 'intellect' (*buddhi*), which is, by means of the 'mind'-reins, guiding the horses.[40]

But may we conclude that the authors of these similes are somehow dependent on each other, or did they use other common sources that did not survive? A closer comparative look reveals that both similes, while phenotypically quite close to each other, are, in terms of metaphorical systematics, rather distinct. The Upaniṣadic simile, presumably older than the Platonic simile,[41] presents a different anthropological model, as is shown in the table below.

	Phaedrus	***Kaṭha Upaniṣad***
chariot passenger [or 'serving commander', skt. *rathin*]	soul (*psyche*) [commander and driver one and the same person]	self (*ātman*), enjoyer (*bhoktṛ*)
charioteer (driver)	rational part of soul (*to logistikòn méros*)	reason / intellect (*buddhi*)
reins	[connection between soul and abilities]	mind (*manas*)
horses (steeds)	1. desire (*to epithymetikón*) 2. striving (*to thymoeidés*)	sense organs (*indriyāṇi*), i.e. touch, taste, smell, etc.
chariot (body)	[not metaphorically relevant]	body (*śarīra*)
path / road	[air-lane as road]	sense objects (*viṣaya*); i.e. perceptible world
end of road / end of travel	gods: back of heaven (intermediate station) humans: (epiphanic) vision of eternity [at death?]	the unborn; highest realm

39 KaU 3.3–9; Olivelle 1998: 238–40 (Sanskrit text and translation).
40 Cf. MaiU 3.2.6 (trans. e.g. Buitenen 1962).
41 Cf. Olivelle 1998; Lupaşcu 2008: 347.

While the highest command of the chariot is, in both similes, in the hand of the 'self', these 'selves' take on different roles. The Platonic 'soul', a skilled charioteer by himself, may only enjoy the travel's envisaged finish, the view of 'being'. The Upaniṣadic 'self' is purely a passenger (in that respect comparable to the Parmenidean simile), not involved in the steering, that is conducted by a second 'person', the charioteer.[42] The passenger is a detached observer, already enjoying the journey while still travelling to the place without return. In the Upaniṣadic simile, the 'self' is depicted as fully liberated at the arrival – if so achieved – or it has to return in the samsaric world. The latter, the Greek 'metempsychosis', seems to be an even more inescapable fate of the Platonic 'self'. However, the Indian 'self' is only loosely dependent on the chariot, and may leave the chariot in the final destination – just as the Olympian gods may do. In the Greek simile, the charioteer (the rational part of the soul) has to govern especially one side of his two-fold nature, namely, ruthless 'desire', the black steed. In the Upaniṣadic simile, the case is different, as it depicts the central task as 'controlling' the mind (i.e. the 'well-tensed [reins]', *yuktena*), whereas the horses – as the senses – are not in themselves 'bad', simply because their *behaviour can be* either 'good' (controlled) or 'bad' (uncontrolled). The worldly side of the charioteer, his body, senses, etc., is not in itself of an inferior, or 'evil', nature.[43]

Obviously, we may see at play here the yogic idea that the senses should be retrieved from their sense objects, and this is exactly the point where meditation techniques assume their indispensable function. The Upaniṣadic simile builds on continuous self-cultivation and self-transformation. It depicts the empirical mind, if not properly reined, as 'loose', which will result in unrestrained horses. By this, the 'senses' are handed over to their manifold sense objects, so that the chariot will not stay on track (*gocara*), and will therefore remain in Saṃsāra. In this respect, the Platonic simile offers a lower complexity: the horses are simply antagonistic forces; the reins, or the proper connection of the charioteer and the horses, do not come into the picture. The track, explicitly mentioned in the Indian case,[44] ensures that there is a road to be followed; the end of the road – as in Parmenides, an elevated place beyond the world of becoming – will be reached by the chariot on a track prolonged into heaven (leading to final liberation, *mokṣa*),[45]

42 This important difference, which is discussed by Magnone in this volume, is not mentioned in Schiltz 2006, and only noticed in passing in Lupaşcu 2008: 343, 349.

43 'It is like this – as a man driving a chariot would look down and observe the two wheels of his chariot, so he looks down and observes the days and nights, the good and bad deeds, and all the pairs of opposites. Freed from his good and bad deeds, this man, who has the knowledge of *brahman*, goes on to *brahman*' (KauU 1.5; Olivelle 1998: 329).

44 A more thorough interpretation of the philosophic background of the *Kaṭha Upaniṣad* can be found in Lupaşcu 2008.

45 Cf. Lupaşcu 2008: 341.

whereas the Platonic chariot seems to fly as a winged chariot right through the air. The Greek ‘soul’ profits as being a ‘pilot’, and his task is to overcome worldly desire;[46] his Indian counterpart, the ‘self’, profits from his chauffeur, a charioteer who is able to train ‘his’ mind and to cognise himself, so that he manages to steer the horses on their track into heaven. Andrew Domanski points out that the ‘Self (*ātman*), as the lord of, and passenger in the chariot, is the animating presence, the formless essence, the source which remains perfectly still, does nothing at all, and yet enables all the activity of the chariot and horses’.[47] Yet, the organic interplay of senses, mind and intellect in the Upaniṣadic simile should not obscure the fact that in yogic discourse it is repeatedly emphasised that the ‘intellect’ is unable to cognise itself. It cannot cognise that there is an inner ‘self’ that is sometimes, although not in the Upaniṣadic simile, called an ‘inner driver’.[48]

Chariot metaphors in India and Greece: historical dependency or coevolution?

In the form of a logical cascade, we may summarise the discussion above as follows:

The imagery (metaphorical systems) of chariots could unfold in India and Greece in parallel ways:

a. as myth of the travel of the chariot of the sun (and moon);
b. as chariot race in cult and sports;
c. as aristocratic symbol of power.

These three metaphorical systems enabled the use of:

d. The chariot imagery of the anthropologically and soteriologically meaningful simile of the chariot of the soul.

The latter (d.) developed largely autonomously in both traditions and had explanatory power as long as

e. the metaphorical systems of chariot imagery (input-domains a., b., c.) could convince.

Indeed, Parmenides, Plato and the author(s) of the *Upaniṣad* could build on the mythical metaphorisation of the sun-chariot and the lifeworld presence of real chariots. Obviously, the similes present ‘metaphorical blends’ of these

46 Cf., in contrast, the interpretation in Griswold 1986.
47 Domanski 2006: 50.
48 On the *ātman* as hidden inner driver cf. BU 3.7.

heterogeneous input-domains – to which in the case of the *Kaṭha Upaniṣad* one should add, as Alexander Forte and Caley Smith aptly demonstrate (in this volume), the intertextual dimension of chariot imagery in the Vedic sacrifice. By interpreting human psychology and soteriological philosophy with the chariot imagery, it becomes clear that they established an 'anthropo-therio-technological' idea of the human body-and-soul: it is the 'steerable soul' (Aristotle preferred the metaphor of the ship's pilot)[49] – a new, technologically mediated model of a 'kybernetic' soul (ψυχῆς κυβερνήτης), which, at least in Greece, made a career as a metaphorical model for steering any kind of complexity, e.g. the 'state' (cf. Plato's imagery of 'steering the ship of the state', e.g. *Republic* IV 488–9). But why apply technological metaphors in the first place? The 'manoeuvrability', such as it is, seems to reduce contingency. Applying the (in part) character of an artefact to the 'soul' and the 'self' makes it possible to discuss an objectifiable 'self' – a great cultural innovation (or, in more romantic terms, the beginning of the 'soul's' decline into the 'mechanics' of the 'psyche').

Surely, it seems tempting to think that Plato might have borrowed the chariot imagery from the East, given the 'identity of the religious logic which subtends *Phaidros* . . . and the *Kaṭha Upaniṣad*'.[50] However, by paying close attention to the metaphors used, we can also find remarkable differences. The most important aspect pertains to the agency handed over to the chariot driver, the 'intellect' (*buddhi*), in the yogic system of the *Kaṭha Upaniṣad*. The charioteer may, by concentration of the mind, rein the horses for reaching final emancipation, i.e. the accomplished goal. There, the passenger and chariot owner, the *ātman*, may descend. Arrived at his destination, he is no longer interested in any view of the world, even if very elevated. In comparison, Plato's simile offers full agency only for the gods. The human soul-chariot may only very rarely, if at all, catch a glimpse of the place where 'being' resides. While alive, the human 'soul' is ever absorbed with steering the bad-natured horse.

Although it is still tempting to construe an Eastern, Upaniṣadic influence on Plato, as Paolo Magnone does (in this volume), it is much more likely that the metaphorical use of chariots developed without direct historical dependency. Already scholars in the nineteenth century voiced the opinion that the chariot simile in Plato and the *Kaṭha Upaniṣad* may count as 'one of the most interesting examples of accidental correspondence'.[51] Yet, as argued above, I would not describe the correspondence as purely accidental. Seen from a greater distance, the two instances – and, we should add, the Parmenidean chariot ride – within the early Indian and Greek traditions should be construed, as Lupaşcu argues, as a

49 Cf. Aristotle *de anima* (On the Soul) 406a.

50 Lupaşcu 2008: 349.

51 Muir 1879: xxxviii.

result of open spaces of 'plurivalent, reciprocal communication, of the exchange of philosophical, moral, and religious values . . . between the Athenian intellectual milieu of the Vth–IVth centuries BCE and the milieu of ancient Hinduism'.[52] Both traditions share a mythical conceptualisation of the chariots of the sun, an aristocratic experience of chariot riding, and the pleasure of chariot technology. Therefore, each tradition could establish the 'chariot soul' for their specific psychological and soteriological purposes, which are parallel, though not, as Lupaşcu or Schiltz argued, nearly identical.

A final strikingly parallel development (to be discussed elsewhere) may be envisaged with the 'end' of the 'heroic' chariot imagery in both traditions (above: d.). Our assertion is that in late antiquity, which saw the end not only of the light and fast chariot but also of a certain ideal of embodied self-mastery, chariot imagery was no longer fully 'functional' (an early example of this can be seen in Sextus Empiricus' allegorical reading of the proem).[53] The Buddhist use of chariot imagery in India, and the Christian use in late antiquity, may, therefore, both best be described as a final allegorical phase, resulting in a rigorous deconstruction of the 'chariot (ride)' and of its metaphoric force for visualising the movement of the sun, human self-mastery, the soul, and the path to liberation.

52 Lupaşcu 2008: 348.
53 Cf. Latona 2008: 202–4.

12

New riders, old chariots: poetics and comparative philosophy

Alexander S. W. Forte and Caley C. Smith

Scholars have claimed that similarities between the Greek poem of Parmenides and the Indic *Upaniṣads* demand an explanation from either historical contact between Greece and other cultures, or a commonly inherited Indo-European philosophy.[1] Several striking similarities between Parmenides and the *Upaniṣads* supposedly reveal borrowing or a genetic relationship: first, monism, the idea of metaphysical unity;[2] second, the rejection of empirical knowledge;[3] third, the

[1] Editions are van Nooten and Holland 1994 (*Ṛgveda*), van Thiel 1996 (*Iliad*), Olivelle 1998 (*Upaniṣads*), Weber 1964 (*Śatapatha Brāhmaṇa*), Dumont 1951 (*Taittirīya Brāhmaṇa*), Palmer 2009 (Parmenides), and Inwood 2001 (Empedocles). Translations are our own unless noted. The editorial principles of the Diels-Kranz edition of Parmenides require re-examination; see Kurfess 2013, 2014.

[2] From a Greek perspective, the nature of Parmenides' monism is a source of scholarly debate, due to both the conceptual difficulties and fragmentary nature of the text. Parmenides is variously termed a strict monist (Guthrie 1965), a logical monist (Owen 1960), a speculative monist (Mourelatos 2008), a predicational monist (Curd 2004), a modal monist (Palmer 2009), or a mystic (Kingsley 1999). For an argument emphasising Parmenides' mystical affiliations and arguing against the analytic approach, see Gemelli 2008. For a useful treatment of the *status quaestionis* as regards Parmenides' affiliations, see Granger 2008 (thanks to John Bussanich for these two references). Therefore, making an *a priori* equation between the fragmentary representation of Parmenides' monism and a fully preserved external tradition is circular logic; even worse, the *Kaṭha Upaniṣad* is not monist. This is not an argument from *diaphonia*; it suggests that one needs to understand the intellectual culture of Parmenides before external comparison. Monism is a response to the ambiguity of 'the beginning' (e.g. Aristotle *Physics* 1.2.184b15–25). This is a controversial metaphysical question, but external explanation is unnecessary.

[3] Doubt relating to the reliability of empirical knowledge is present in Homer's *Iliad,* with which Parmenides clearly engaged, cf. *Il.* 2.484–93. One difference is that Parmenides provides an account of reliable knowledge, see Lesher 2008: esp. 472–6 *contra* Most 1999: 353. Cf. also *Il.* 23.450–98, where Idomeneus and Oelian Ajax break into a verbal quarrel in the stands based on their differing visual and intellectual judgements. Although

potential for allegory;[4] and fourth, the chariot imagery. This last similarity will be the focus of this chapter, which will argue that Parmenides' poem engages with the chariot race during Patroclus' funeral games in book 23 of the *Iliad*. Then, it will argue that the *Kaṭha Upaniṣad*'s chariot imagery draws on the use of chariots in the *Ṛgveda*.[5] Therefore, these supposedly anomalous chariots function perfectly well within their respective Greek and Indic intellectual traditions.[6]

We contend that there is no need to posit Indo-European philosophy to explain the striking, but ultimately incidental parallels between these two texts.[7] In short, an Indo-European explanation of the chariot in this case would only be applicable to Homeric poetry and the *Ṛgveda*. This itself is unlikely, because the

Parmenides' discussion of the senses is metaphysically sophisticated, this very sophistication is a development of pre-existing Greek thought. For a general account of Homeric phraseology in Parmenides, see Mourelatos 2008: 1–17. On the journeys of the *Odyssey* compared to the journey of the *kouros* in Parmenides, see Mourelatos 2008: 17–25, building on Havelock 1958. An account of Parmenides' thought as a development from his predecessors tempers some of the more extreme claims of Parmenides' 'big bang' of rationalism, e.g. Popper 1998: 71, 102. See B1.28–32, . . . χρεὼ δέ σε πάντα πυθέσθαι / ἠμὲν Ἀληθείης εὐκυκλέος ἀτρεμὲς ἦτορ / ἠδὲ βροτῶν δόξας, τῇς οὐκ ἔνι πίστις ἀληθής. / ἀλλ' ἔμπης καὶ ταῦτα μαθήσεαι, ὡς τὰ δοκοῦντα / χρῆν δοκίμως εἶναι διὰ παντὸς πάντα περῶντα. 'It is right for you to learn all things, both the unshaken heart of well-circled reality and of the opinions of mortals, in which there is no true trust; nevertheless you shall learn these as well, how it was right that the things that seem do seem, permeating all things from end to end.' It also must be recognised that λόγος in Greek philosophy is often assumed to be equivalent to 'logic', and its presence in Parmenides B7 is taken by some to indicate that he is an orthodox rationalist. This is problematic because λόγος in Plato and Aristotle frequently means 'explanatory account', see Moss 2014.

4 There is a tradition of allegory that precedes Parmenides in the Greek intellectual tradition, in the works of Pherecydes of Syros and Theagenes of Rhegium, both of whom were operative in the sixth century BCE. Parmenidean 'allegory' has clear antecedents in the Greek tradition, so explaining this as somehow being due to contact or Indo-European philosophy begs the question. On early allegorists and 'riddles', see Ford 2002: 67–89, Struck 2004: 21–9, Gemelli Marciano 2008: 22, Bierl 2014.

5 For students of philosophy, any intertextual relationship between a philosophical text and an antecedent or contemporary source provides additional empirical data that can help one to characterise how a given thinker 'does philosophy', or at the least, what sources he or she chooses to draw upon. On the importance of an understanding of intellectual history and culture as a precondition for philosophical analysis, see Mourelatos 2008: 350–63.

6 This chapter agrees with the conclusions in Staal 1955 and Bucca 1964, both of whom treat Greek and Indic philosophy as independent, with the latter focusing on the chariot imagery. For a cognitive approach to chariot metaphors, see Schlieter, in this volume.

7 This is *contra* Latona (2008: 208) and Ježić (1992), whose lexical evidence for inherited philosophy is overly general and unconvincing on linguistic grounds. For a helpful discussion on comparative methodology, see Barr 1995.

earliest evidence of the chariot in Greece (sixteenth century BCE) long post-dates any speaker of late Indo-European.[8]

There is perhaps even less of a reason to posit historical borrowing or 'diffusion' to account for the similarities in the chariot imagery.[9] There is no historically reliable evidence for an extended conversation between a Greek speaker and Indic speaker before the time of Alexander. Nor is there any historically reliable evidence that any Pre-Socratic philosopher had any contact with Iranian, let alone Indic priests.[10] Unless new primary source evidence from antiquity is discovered, there is no way to argue either point with probability.[11] Contextualisation is source criticism: one must examine what a document is, how it relates to other evidence, and how it has come to us.[12]

In the case of Parmenides, this chariot imagery, and indeed most of Parmenides' language, has been analysed in terms of earlier hexameter poetry.[13] However, there is an unrecognised density of intertexts between Parmenides' poem and a limited episode in the *Iliad*, the chariot race in Patroclus' funeral games.[14] The structure of the narrative is as follows: the organisation of the race (23.262–361), the race itself (23.362–447), a conflict between Idomeneus and Oelian Ajax in the stands (23.450–98), and the end of the race and the ensuing prize-ceremony (23.499–652). The didactic speech of Nestor to his son Antilochus before the race (23.301–50) shares several intertexts with Parmenides' poem:

τῶν δ' ἵπποι μὲν ἔασιν ἀφάρτεροι, οὐδὲ μὲν αὐτοὶ
πλείονα ἴσασιν σέθεν αὐτοῦ μητίσασθαι.

8 We, following Hooker (1999: 65–86), cannot agree with Drews 1988, which posits that Greeks 'arrived' on chariots based on linguistic evidence.

9 *Contra*, recently, Magnone 2012: 122–3 (and this volume); Kahn 2001: 19. McEvilley (2002) argues that monism and reincarnation diffused from India to Greece (122), but that the chariot allegory is an independent innovation owing to common heritage (185). For a review of McEvilley 2002, see Bussanich 2005. For a culturally situated treatment of Parmenides' ideas as related to monetary systems, see Seaford 2004: 185–9, 244–65. The concept of 'borrowing' itself is simplistic. Even if one is prepared to (re-)construct an unattested historical moment of contact, what would the cultural and personal preconditions of such a dialogue be?

10 See Seaford, this volume.

11 See Kahn 1979: 297–302, who says of the need to posit a 'historical' explanation for commonalities between Greek and Indo-Iranian thought: 'It also tends to produce historical fiction, as in West's (1971) concluding hypothesis . . . (299).'

12 As a young Frits Staal (1955: 82) pointed out, we must also consider ourselves. See Lincoln 1999: 209, 'If myth is ideology in narrative form, then scholarship is myth with footnotes.'

13 For Homeric poetry, see Coxon 2009: 9–12, Havelock 1958, Lesher 1984, Mourelatos 2008: 1–25; for Hesiodic poetry see, most recently, Pellikaan-Engel 1974.

14 Fränkel (1960a) omits the chariot race.

ἀλλ' ἄγε δὴ σὺ φίλος μῆτιν ἐμβάλλεο θυμῷ
παντοίην, ἵνα μή σε παρεκπροφύγῃσιν ἄεθλα.
μήτι τοι δρυτόμος μέγ' ἀμείνων ἠὲ βίηφι·
μήτι δ' αὖτε κυβερνήτης ἐνὶ οἴνοπι πόντῳ
νῆα θοὴν ἰθύνει ἐρεχθομένην ἀνέμοισι·
μήτι δ' ἡνίοχος περιγίγνεται ἡνιόχοιο.
ἀλλ' ὃς μέν θ' ἵπποισι καὶ ἅρμασιν οἷσι πεποιθὼς
ἀφραδέως ἐπὶ πολλὸν ἑλίσσεται ἔνθα καὶ ἔνθα,
ἵπποι δὲ πλανόωνται ἀνὰ δρόμον, οὐδὲ κατίσχει·
ὃς δέ κε κέρδεα εἰδῇ ἐλαύνων ἥσσονας ἵππους,
αἰεὶ τέρμ' ὁρόων στρέφει ἐγγύθεν, οὐδέ ἑ λήθει
ὅππως τὸ πρῶτον τανύσῃ βοέοισιν ἱμᾶσιν,
ἀλλ' ἔχει ἀσφαλέως καὶ τὸν προὔχοντα δοκεύει.

The horses of these men are faster, but they themselves do not
know how to be more crafty than you.
Remember then, dear one, to cast every kind of craft
into your mind, so that the prizes may not escape you.
The woodcutter is far better by craft than he is by force. It is by
craft that the pilot keeps true his swift ship,
though torn by winds, over the wine-faced sea. By craft
charioteer surpasses charioteer. He who is confident in his
horses and chariot and recklessly spins this way and that,
does not control them. But the man, although
driving the lesser horses, who knows his advantage, and constantly
watching the post turns closely, nor does it escape his notice,
how he first will pull with the ox-hide reins,
he holds steady, and watches the leader. (*Il.* 23.311–25)

In Parmenides' poem the mortals who do not understand the reality of the world are described using phraseology that is either inverted from that of Nestor's good charioteer (B1.39 ἐπιφραδέως ~ *Il.* 23.320 ἀφραδέως), or consistent with that of the poor charioteer (B8.54 ἐν ᾧι πεπλανημένοι εἰσίν ~ *Il.* 23.321 πλανόωνται).[15] Moreover, Parmenides' use of σῆμα as an indicator of knowledge, specifically referring to signs along the path of knowledge, recalls Nestor's polysemous use of this word in the middle of his speech to Antilochus:[16]

15 See Mourelatos 2008: 30 on 23.316–19, 20–1 and their relationship to Parmenides. Menelaus calls Antilochus' driving ἀφραδέως (23.426).

16 This is in agreement with the perceptive analysis of Latona 2008: 218–27, which sees Parmenides' poem in terms of a chariot race. Where this chapter differs is the identification of this race especially (but not exclusively) with that of *Iliad* 23, and a disagreement about Latona's definition of the term 'allegory' as an 'extended metaphor' (199), which does not reckon with the recent advances in the study of allegory, esp. Struck 2004: 1–20, see also note 4 above.

μόνος δ' ἔτι μῦθος ὁδοῖο
λείπεται, ὡς ἔστιν· ταύτῃ δ' ἐπὶ **σήματ'** ἔασι
πολλὰ μάλ', ὡς ἀγένητον ἐὸν καὶ ἀνώλεθρόν ἐστιν,
οὖλον μουνογενές τε καὶ ἀτρεμὲς ἠδ' † ἀτέλεστον,

Only one story of the way is still left: that (it) is. On this
way there are very many *signs*: that Being is ungenerated and
imperishable, entire, unique, unmoved and without end; (B8.1–4)

The 'signs' as the basis of understanding recall the centre of Nestor's extensive, didactic speech to his son:

σῆμα δέ τοι ἐρέω μάλ' ἀριφραδές, οὐδέ σε λήσει.
ἕστηκε ξύλον αὖον ὅσον τ' ὄργυι' ὑπὲρ αἴης
ἢ δρυὸς ἢ πεύκης· τὸ μὲν οὐ καταπύθεται ὄμβρῳ,
λᾶε δὲ τοῦ ἑκάτερθεν ἐρηρέδαται δύο λευκὼ
ἐν ξυνοχῇσιν ὁδοῦ, λεῖος δ' ἱππόδρομος ἀμφὶς
ἤ τευ **σῆμα** βροτοῖο πάλαι κατατεθνηῶτος,
ἢ τό γε νύσσα τέτυκτο ἐπὶ προτέρων ἀνθρώπων,
καὶ νῦν τέρματ' ἔθηκε ποδάρκης δῖος Ἀχιλλεύς.

I will tell you a distinct *sign*, and it will not escape you.
There stands a dry stump a fathom above the ground,
either oak or pine, which is not rotted away by rain,
and two white stones lean against it on either side,
at the joining place of the road, and there is a smooth track for horses around it.
Either it is the *grave-sign* of some long-dead man,
or was established as a racing mark by earlier men.
And now swift-footed, shining Achilles made it the turning-post. (*Il.* 23.326–33)

The σῆμα in both cases is the basis of knowledge, but used as a term of 'imagination' rather than vision. Nestor's instructions depend on Antilochus' ability to map the visual instructions onto a specific portion of the physical world, and the emphasis on the application of the 'sign' to Antilochus' actual sense perception differentiates Nestor's sign from Parmenides' signs. Although Parmenides' message is more abstract, the 'sign' in both poems is the instructional key, and located upon a path. Combined with other local lexical parallels, this suggests Parmenides' close engagement with book 23.[17] Both texts, moreover, share a similar internal audience: the addressee is a young man, in Parmenides' poem the anonymous *kouros* and in the *Iliad* Nestor's son Antilochus.

Parmenides' physical description of reality is highly reminiscent of language found elsewhere within the chariot race of book 23:

[17] On B8 see McKirahan 2009.

αὐτὰρ ἐπεὶ πεῖρας **πύματον, τετελεσμένον ἐστί**
πάντοθεν, εὐκύκλου σφαίρης ἐναλίγκιον ὄγκῳ,
μεσσόθεν ἰσοπαλὲς πάντῃ· τὸ γὰρ οὔτε τι μεῖζον
οὔτε τι βαιότερον πελέναι χρεόν ἐστι τῇ ἢ τῇ.

But since its limit is *final, it is completed from all sides,*
like the weight of a spherical ball, and similarly balanced in all ways
from the centre: for it must not become at all greater or at
all smaller in one way than in another. (B8.42–5)

This comparison of being to a sphere shares phraseology with the chariot race, including exact lexical parallels:[18]

Ἀλλ' ὅτε δὴ **πύματον τέλεον δρόμον** ὠκέες ἵπποι (≈ 23.768)
ἂψ ἐφ' ἁλὸς πολιῆς, τότε δὴ ἀρετή γε ἑκάστου
φαίνετ' . . .

But when the swift horses *were finishing the final run*
back towards the grey sea, then the virtue of each
was apparent . . . (*Il.* 23.373–5)

The three-dimensional circularity of the sphere can be in turn compared with the two dimensional circularity of the chariot race itself.[19] Parmenides characterises his own path of inquiry as recursive:

ξυνὸν δὲ μοί ἐστιν,
ὁππόθεν ἄρξωμαι· τόθι γὰρ πάλιν ἵξομαι αὖθις.

It is the same to me whence I begin,
for to that place I shall come back again. (B5)[20]

Therefore, one can envision Parmenides' 'path of thought' as being a *diaulos*, or a lap, just as a chariot race. In addition to the foregoing similarities, the case of Eumelus in the *Iliad* presents several points of comparison to Parmenides' proem:

18 Cf. *Il.* 23.410: ὧδε γὰρ ἐξερέω, καὶ μὴν **τετελεσμένον ἔσται**·, *Il.* 23.672: ὧδε γὰρ ἐξερέω, τὸ δὲ καὶ **τετελεσμένον ἔσται**·. See Mourelatos 2008: 31 discussing Onian's translation of τετελεσμένον ἔσται· 'it will be bound (to happen)'.

19 See Jameson 1958. Tarán (1965: 159) argues that Parmenides' being is not spherical, it is *compared* to that which is spherical.

20 The misguided inquiry of mortals employs similar language, B6.9: πάντων δὲ παλίντροπός ἐστι κέλευθος, 'but the journey of all men turns back on itself'. B6.4–6: αὐτὰρ ἔπειτ' ἀπὸ τῆς, ἣν δὴ βροτοὶ εἰδότες οὐδὲν / πλάζονται, δίκρανοι· ἀμηχανίη γὰρ ἐν αὐτῶν / στήθεσιν ἰθύνει πλακτὸν νόον . . . uses the same verb (ἰθύνει) as Nestor describing the captain who guides his ship (23.317). Likewise, as the bad charioteer's horses wander (πλανόωνται, 23.321), so do deceived mortals in Parmenides' poem (πλάζονται . . . πλακτὸν νόον).

> οὐδ' ἄρ' Ἀθηναίην ἐλεφηράμενος λάθ' Ἀπόλλων
> Τυδεΐδην, μάλα δ' ὦκα μετέσσυτο ποιμένα λαῶν,
> δῶκε δέ οἱ μάστιγα, μένος δ' ἵπποισιν ἐνῆκεν·
> ἣ δὲ μετ' Ἀδμήτου υἱὸν κοτέουσ' ἐβεβήκει,
> ἵππειον δέ οἱ ἦξε θεὰ ζυγόν· αἳ δέ οἱ ἵπποι
> ἀμφὶς ὁδοῦ δραμέτην . . .
>
> Nor did Apollo's obstruction of Diomedes escape Athena's notice, and especially quickly she aided the shepherd of the host, and gave his whip to him, and imbued his horses with vigour. But she angrily approached the son of Admetus, and the goddess broke the yoke of his horses: and his mares ran around the path . . . (*Il.* 23.388–93)

Eumelus is exceptional in the *Iliad* for having two mares as his horses.[21] So a young man driving a chariot pulled by two mares is sabotaged by a goddess. In Parmenides' proem, a young man on a chariot pulled by two mares (B1.1) is guided by a goddess (B1.22). It may also be relevant here that in the proems both of the *Iliad* (1.1) and of Parmenides' poem, the goddess (θεά) is anonymous.

Parmenides' engagement with book 23 of the *Iliad* puts him in good company, since a fragment of Empedocles' also engaged specifically with the chariot race:

> **στεινωποὶ** μὲν γὰρ παλάμαι κατὰ γυῖα κέχυνται,
> πολλὰ δὲ δείλ' ἔμπαια, τά τ' ἀμβλύνουσι μέριμνας.
> παῦρον δ' ἐν ζωῆισι βίου μέρος ἀθρήσαντες
> ὠκύμοροι καπνοῖο δίκην ἀρθέντες ἀπέπταν,
> αὐτὸ μόνον πεισθέντες ὅτωι **προσέκυρσεν** ἕκαστος,
> πάντοσ' **ἐλαυνόμενοι**, τὸ δ' ὅλον <πᾶς> εὔχεται εὑρεῖν·
> οὕτως οὔτ' ἐπιδερκτὰ τάδ' ἀνδράσιν οὔτ' ἐπακουστά
> οὔτε νόῳ περιληπτά . . .
> . . . σὺ <δ'> οὖν, ἐπεὶ ὧδ' ἐλιάσθης,
> πεύσεαι. οὐ πλεῖόν γε βροτείη **μῆτις** ὄρωρεν.
>
> For *narrow* devices are poured throughout their limbs,
> but many wretched things are embedded, and they blunt their meditations.
> And having seen [only] a small living in their lives,
> they swift-doomed soar and fly off like smoke,
> persuaded of only that very thing which *each crashes into*,
> being *driven* in all directions. But <each> boasts to have found the whole.
> In this way these things are neither seen by men nor heard
> Nor grasped with the understanding . . .
> . . . But you, then, since you have stepped aside here,
> you will learn. Mortal *craft* has certainly risen no further. (31 DK B2)

[21] The only other hero not to have a stallion is Iphinous, killed by Glaucus (*Il.* 7.13–16).

We have already seen how Nestor's advice regarding μῆτις ('craft') (*Il.* 23.311–18) features prominently in the lead up to the race, and Empedocles' mention of the limitations of craft here could be seen as an agonistic reference to Nestor's discourse. In moving to specifics, during the race itself, Antilochus' interpretation of his father's advice involves a dangerous manoeuvre to overtake Menelaus, who yells a warning to Nestor's son:

> Ἀντίλοχ' ἀφραδέως ἱππάζεαι, ἀλλ' ἄνεχ' ἵππους.
> **στεινωπὸς** γὰρ ὁδός, τάχα δ' εὐρυτέρη **παρελάσσαι**,[22]
> μή πως ἀμφοτέρους δηλήσεαι ἅρματι **κύρσας**.
>
> Antilochus, you are recklessly charioteering. Restrain your horses.
> For the road is *narrow*, and it will soon be wider *to pass*,
> lest you *crash* into my chariot and wreck both of us. (*Il.* 23.426–8)

We find here a significant overlap in lexicon with the Empedoclean passage: the adjective στεινωπός, 'narrow', and verb forms of ἐλαύνειν, 'drive', and κυρεῖν, 'strike'.[23] Antilochus' dangerous use of μῆτις, according to Menelaus, risks the disaster of mutual destruction, and it is in these terms that Empedocles discusses the limits of mortal craft (βροτείη μῆτις). By standing apart from the chaos, Pausanias, Empedocles' addressee, will learn precisely how to transcend these limitations.

The Iliadic chariot race also introduced a *topos* to post-Parmenidean and Empedoclean philosophical texts. Specifically, Nestor's speech to Antilochus is the *locus classicus* of Socratic ἐπαγωγή, usually termed 'induction', but perhaps more rightly, 'analogy'.[24] Later authors use the phraseology of Nestor's advice as the material for analogical arguments about knowledge and technique.[25] Eustathius' comments (on Nestor's speech) are as follows:

> Then, arguing inductively via a woodcutter (δρυτόμου) and a pilot (κυβερνήτου) and a charioteer (ἡνιόχου) that all things are achieved rightly by means of counsel and skill – for here first, they say, Homer uses induction like philosophers, namely, the argument establishing the general from specifics. (Eustathius *Commentary on the Iliad* 4:736.8–13)

22 We adopt West's (2000) reading of the aorist infinitive active.

23 Cf. στεινωπῷ ἐν ὁδῷ (*Il.* 23.416). Kingsley 2002: 360–6 is a more exhaustive treatment of the intertexts between Empedocles B2 and the chariot race of *Iliad* 23, emphasising the associations of Pausanias with Achilles and Empedocles with Apollo.

24 See Ausland 2002: 46–60, esp. 48 n28 for more on the relationship between the priamel, induction, and analogy; cf. Vlastos 1991: 267–9.

25 Ausland 2002: 49, n29, citing Eustathius *Commentary on the Iliad* 4:736.8–11, Aristotle *Top.* A.12, 105a13–16, Ovid *Ars Amatoria*, *incip.*, referencing Plato *Prot.* 318b1–d4, *Grg.* 448b4–c9.

This statement is borne out by the evidence when one turns to Plato's *Ion*, where Socrates' ultimate point is that a rhapsode does not have skill, but rather is inspired. Plato is not here engaging in induction, but analogy, since the rhapsode is negatively compared to skilled/artistic professions:

> Socrates: Why, does not Homer speak a good deal about arts, in a good many places? For instance, about chariot-driving (περὶ ἡνιοχείας): if I can recall the lines, I will quote them to you.
> Ion: No, I will recite them, for I can remember.
> Socrates: Tell me then what Nestor says to his son Antilochus, advising him to be careful about the turning-post in the horse-race in honour of Patroclus. (Plato *Ion* 537a5–7, trans. Lamb)

Now the *Ion* is specifically about Homeric recitation, so the presence of this passage would not necessarily be evidence for book 23's special place in Platonic thought were it the lone instance of charioteers and pilots appearing in Platonic arguments. However, Plato elsewhere uses the terms of book 23 to ask about the aptness of analogical comparisons between earthly rulers and the gods:[26]

> Athenian: But to which kind of rulers are they like? Or which are like to them, of those rulers whom we can fairly compare with them, as small with great? Would drivers (ἡνίοχοί) of rival teams resemble them, or pilots (κυβερνῆται) of ships? (Plato *Leges* 905e5–8, trans. Bury)

It is not just that charioteers are mentioned here, but that these are also compared to pilots of ships using the exact terminology of Nestor's speech. This does not necessarily imply a direct or intentional 'intertext' between Nestor's speech and the use of charioteers and pilots in inductive or analogical arguments in Classical philosophy. It more likely indicates that the authority of the *Iliad* created a *topos*, wherein the charioteer (ἡνίοχος) and the pilot (κυβερνήτης) were the default terms in induction/analogy. It also seemingly demonstrates that *Iliad* 23 was not as neglected in antiquity as it has been in modern scholarship. Aristotle, using the examples of both the pilot and the charioteer, similarly refers to this process as ἐπαγωγή:

> Induction (ἐπαγωγή) is the passage from specific things to the general; for example, if the knowledgeable pilot (κυβερνήτης) is best and likewise the charioteer (ἡνίοχος), generally speaking even the knowledgeable person is best concerning each thing. (Aristotle *Top*. A.12, 105a13–16)[27]

[26] Cf. Xenophon *Memorabilia* 1.1.9.7.

[27] See Polybius Sardianus *De Figuris* 614.4–10 Walz cited by Ausland 2002: 50, n30: 'It is induction (ἐπαγωγὴ δέ ἐστιν) when, having proposed something from similar things, we adduce the point for which we will persuade. For example . . . (citing *Il*. 23.315–18).'

Therefore, book 23 of the *Iliad* is a source of 'philosophical' authority for Classical philosophy. Nestor's examples of induction/analogy are precisely the same as Plato's and Aristotle's. Parmenides' engagement with the chariot race, therefore, aligns him with Empedocles as well as the later philosophical tradition.

One might speculate on the nature of Parmenides' conceptual relationship to the *Iliad*. Parmenides has used the metrical language of Homeric poetry, and specifically of the chariot race, in his metaphysical poem. Moreover, he specifically uses the competitive language of chariot racing:

> τόν σοι ἐγὼ διάκοσμον ἐοικότα πάντα φατίζω,
> ὡς οὐ μή ποτέ τίς σε βροτῶν γνώμη παρελάσσῃ.
>
> So I will tell you each thing, seemingly well-ordered,
> So that no judgement of mortals will ever surpass you. (B8.60–1)

In Homeric poetry, παρελαύνειν, 'to pass in one's chariot', appears only in the chariot race (*Il.* 23.382, 427, 527).[28] Based on Parmenides' use of verbs of competitive chariot racing, it is conceivable that he is portraying not only the conceptual journey of his philosophy, but also his *kouros* as participating in a race of insight against his contemporaries, predecessors and successors.[29] The conceptual metaphor of a chariot race, as a culturally prestigious and deeply embedded mental image of Parmenides' audience, might have been the perfect, to use I. A. Richards's term, 'vehicle' through which to impart knowledge.

To sum up, the precondition for assessing the degree of conceptual innovation or conservatism within Parmenides' poem is a nuanced understanding of the intellectual culture in which he lived. The contribution of this study is the idea that Parmenides' text is among the oldest instances of the reception of the chariot race in book 23 of the *Iliad*, with which Empedocles also directly engaged. Moreover, Nestor's advice to Antilochus in the lead up to the chariot race is the *locus classicus* for inductive reasoning and/or analogy in later philosophical writing. One cannot explain economically this chariot imagery via either a lost tradition of Indo-European philosophy or historical interaction with early Indic philosophy. Parmenides' interaction with Homeric poetry renders Indo-European or contact-based explanation of the role of the chariot in Parmenides and the *Upaniṣads* unnecessary. Regarding the correspondences between the chariots of Plato's *Phaedrus* and the *Kaṭha Upaniṣad*, we side with Jens Schlieter's judgement, in this volume, of 'coevolution' rather than any kind of diffusion. On the Greek side, it remains to be said that the representation of the soul as a chariot

[28] Noted by Lesher 1984: 23–8; Kingsley 2002: 364; Latona 2008: 219.

[29] The chariot race, the most culturally prestigious act of physical agonism within fifth-century Greek society, potentially reflects a competitive relationship between Parmenides and his poetic predecessors.

in *Phaedrus* potentially engages with the chariot in Parmenides' poem. Svetla Slaveva-Griffin (2003) has argued for a precise intertextual relationship between Parmenides and the *Phaedrus*, specifically focusing on their common use of Zeus' chariot ride in *Iliad* 8.41–52.[30] Moreover, Plato's wider attention to earlier poetry in this dialogue is well documented. As Moore (2014) has treated in detail, Socrates' quotation of Pindar at 227b6–10 reveals a more systematic relationship between the chariots of the *Phaedrus* and the chariot team of *Isthmian* 2. Furthermore, Pender (2007) has independently argued that Plato's *Phaedrus* engages intertextually with the poetry of Sappho and Anacreon.

The chariot also captured the imagination of the hieratic traditions of northern India. The Vedic texts routinely deploy the chariot journey as a metaphor for the sacrifice. The germ of this idea, seen already in the *Ṛgveda*, has been re-shaped by generations of Vedic theologians. It will be claimed in this chapter that the *Kaṭha Upaniṣad*, when restored to its proper canonical context, also uses the chariot as a metaphor for the sacrifice.

The *Upaniṣads* are a discrete genre of texts from the perspective of Śaṅkara, the great Advaita Vedānta philosopher of the eighth century CE. The earliest *Upaniṣads*, however, were not distinguished from their respective Vedic canons. Typically considered the oldest *Upaniṣad*, the *Bṛhadāraṇyaka Upaniṣad* is in fact the terminus of the White Yajurvedic canon, which begins with the *Vājasaneyi Saṁhitā*, a text containing all the sacrificial mantras. It is followed by the *Śatapatha Brāhmaṇa*, a text replete with variations and exceptions to ritual praxis as well as exegetical commentary. Placed at the end of the *Śatapatha Brāhmaṇa* is the *Bṛhadāraṇyaka Upaniṣad*.

The first chapters[31] of the *Kaṭha Upaniṣad*, a Black Yajurvedic text, would have been the capstone of Kaṭha education in its respective canon. Essentially, Parmenides, or his informants, would have had to be Vedic initiates and committed to memory the corpus of Kaṭha texts before instruction in an *Upaniṣad* would be permitted.[32] Outsiders to Vedic practice do not appear in depictions of

[30] On the particular relationship between Parmenides and the *Phaedrus*, see Slaveva-Griffin 2003: 244–9. She does not discuss the chariot race of *Iliad* 23 as a textual antecedent.

[31] A few remarks on the document's history will allow us to contextualise *Kaṭha Upaniṣad* within its own time, rather than through the lens of later Indian traditions. The consensus, based on thematic correspondences and manuscript divisions, is that the six chapters, or *vallīs*, consist of two halves. The latter three chapters are not reliably pre-Alexandrian. As the image of the chariot is located in the third *vallī*, it is the first half of the text which will receive attention. If indeed the first three chapters are pre-Alexandrian, then the text predates writing in India and must be an oral composition. Witzel (1977) suggests the first three *vallīs* originally belonged at the end of the lost *Kaṭha-Śīkṣā-Upaniṣad*.

[32] This is still true of Vedic transmission today. Knipe (2015: 32): 'In any case, if successful at memorizing passages from either the third or fourth section of the Taittiriya Samhita the student will persevere until he has mastered all seven sections before going on to the

studentship in the earliest *Upaniṣads*; only a senior student who has mastered the visible mechanics of the sacrifice is permitted to learn its arcane metaphysics. After all, these Vedic texts are the intellectual property of priestly clans and are orally transmitted exclusively within the family.

While the Saṁhitās were performed in public,[33] the *Āraṇyakas* and *Upaniṣads* were not. The *Āraṇyakas*, 'wilderness books', were studied privately away from settled populations.[34] The word *upaniṣad* is often translated as 'secret',[35] and indeed these texts were even less accessible. Their depiction of studentship is always master and pupil.[36] In the *Bṛhadāraṇyaka Upaniṣad*, Yājñavalkya only tells Janaka his secret after they go 'off-camera' such that the transmission is hidden even from the text itself.[37] As Parmenides would have encountered both linguistic and social barriers, a contact scenario is impractical. While this analysis treats the chariot imagery employed by the *Kaṭha Upaniṣad* and Parmenides, once restored to their respective intertextual relationships, any philosophical similarities become much more uncertain as well.[38]

In turning now to the chariot imagery, it merits pointing out that just as the *Upaniṣads* are the inheritors of Vedic traditions of ritual exegesis, they are also the inheritors of poetic and rhetorical traditions going back to the *Ṛgveda*.

next three major texts in his tradition, the *Taittiriya Brahmana*, *Taittiriya Āraṇyakas*, and *Taittiriya Upanisad*.'

33 In fact, there is a tradition of recitational acrobatics, still popular today at temples, in which the *Saṁhitā* is recited with word order transformed by algorithm. The more complex the recitation the more impressive and respectable.

34 Staal (2008: 116) notes that some Sāmavedic chants are *grāmageyagāna*, 'to be sung in the village', but a category of complex and powerful melodies are *araṇyageyagāna*, 'to be sung in the forest'. While the village was a public space, the forest was a remote, dangerous and private place. Concerning the *Āraṇyakas*, Staal (2008: 117) adds 'Renou characterized all these "Forest Compositions" as "meta-ritual esotericism", stressing their secretive character as well as the fact that they are still pervaded by ritual technicalities and often exhibit ritual structures."

35 The oldest of this stratum of texts, the *Jaiminīya Upaniṣad Brāhmaṇa*, clearly positioned itself in relation to the older *Jaiminīya Brāhmaṇa* as the 'secret Brāhmaṇa' of the Jaiminīya Sāmavedins.

36 Indeed, *Kaṭha Upaniṣad* depicts studentship this way; only in private does Death teach Naciketas how to pile the fire altar who recites the instructions back to him.

37 Staal (2008: 160) notes with irony: 'Secrecy is the last remnant of the originally secret oral traditions of families and clans. There is one paradox: the Upaniṣads became the most famous part of the Vedas.'

38 The specifics of Parmenides' monism are controversial, but the monism of *Kaṭha Upaniṣad* is no less problematic. The text claims a special relationship between the *ātman*, 'the self', and *brahman*, typically taken to be a panentheistic conception of the cosmos. These ideas are still developing, and to use these simple definitions bleaches the words of their ritual dimensions. If restored to their proper Vedic context, *ātman* and *brahman* are quite different from anything in Eleatic thought.

Already in the *Ṛgveda*, the chariot is a frequent locus of metaphor and simile for a number of reasons. We will enumerate a few here. Firstly, the root *yuj*, 'to yoke', is extended to new semantic domains much as the English verb 'to harness' can be; thus the chariot is used in the context of technique, for example RV 9.88.2a: *á īṃ rátho ná bhuriṣā́ḷ ayoji*, '(Soma) is yoked like a much-conquering chariot.' Secondly, the chariot is symbolic of competitive sport, so it is iconic of any agonistic endeavor. Employing both a metaphor and a simile is RV 9.94.3ab: *pári yát kavíḥ kā́viyā bhárate / śū́ro ná rátho bhúvanāni víśvā*, 'When the poet encompasses all poetics, like the champion chariot, [he encompasses] all worlds.' In this diptych, the winning poet is compared to a winning chariot, and not just any chariot, but the champion chariot who races in the largest track: the Sun. Thirdly, the chariot, being a constructed item, features in similes and metaphors of creation, sometimes called 'craft metaphors'. Consider examples such as RV 1.130.06ab: *imā́ṃ te vā́caṃ vasūyánta āyávo / ráthaṃ ná dhī́raḥ suápā atakṣiṣuḥ*, 'Seeking wealth, the Āyus fashioned this poetic speech for you, like an insightful artisan does a chariot.' The most famous iteration of chariot metaphor in the *Ṛgveda* may be that of 10.135.3, in which a boy mourning his deceased father hears a voice that tells him *yáṃ kumāra návaṃ rátham / acakrám mánasā́kṛṇoḥ / ékeṣaṃ viśvátaḥ prā́ñcam / ápaśyann ádhi tiṣṭhasi //* 'Boy, you have made a new chariot with your mind, wheel-less, single-axled yet facing all directions, without seeing you stand atop it.' This chariot may well be a metaphor for the sacrifice that has the power to reunite father and son, but because the son lacks vision, he cannot see the chariot and does not understand the sacrifice.

What follows is an attempt to demonstrate that the chariot in the *Kaṭha Upaniṣad* still refers to the sacrifice and constitutes a metaphysical theorisation of the operations of the fire altar. The *Kaṭha Upaniṣad*, like the *Maitrāyaṇīya Upaniṣad* and the *Taittirīya Upaniṣad*, belongs to a priestly *śākhā*, or school, of the *Black Yajurveda*. The chief representative of the *Black Yajurveda* on the ritual ground is the *adhvaryu* who is responsible for, among other things, piling the fire altar. A close examination of all three of these *Upaniṣads* reveals a focus on fire and the fire altar.[39] The first *vallī* of the *Kaṭha Upaniṣad* reimagines a dialogue in verse originally present in the lost *Kaṭha Brāhmaṇa*.[40] In the *Brāhmaṇa* account, a boy, Naciketas, goes to Death's house to discover the secrets of undiminishing merits and ritual. Death reveals that the secret is the proper piling of the *nāciketa* fire altar. Many altars take the sacrificer to heaven, but this fire altar allows one to avoid *punarmṛtyu*, 're-death', and remain in heaven indefinitely.

The text then describes how the altar is constructed. It utilises twenty-one

[39] Readings of KaU that ignore Bodewitz 1985 are intellectually moribund.

[40] Selections of the *Kaṭha Brāhmaṇa* survive as quotations in the *Taittirīya Brāhmaṇa*, see Witzel 1977: 140. Plato quotes neither text.

golden bricks in a ring as the base of the altar, called the *ātman*, upon which one piles a layer of clay bricks. The golden base establishes a golden, heavenly abode for the patron of the sacrifice, and this is explained through an aetiology of gold. The primordial sacrificer, Prajāpati, created *tapas*, 'heat', from which sprang gold. After tossing it into the fire, he is unsatisfied and casts it into two other fires. These three fires of the Vedic sacrifice still do not please him. He is only satisfied after placing the gold into the fire of his own heart, Agni Vaiśvānara.

The *Kaṭha Upaniṣad* repeats the same opening prose sentence as its source text before going into its poetic recreation. In oral texts in the Vedic tradition, the repetition of the *incipit*, or *pratīka*, immediately recalls the quoted text. This first *vallī* tells much the same story, focusing on Naciketas and Death. Naciketas visits Death who teaches him how to pile the *nāciketa* altar. Naciketas demonstrates his ability to memorise and repeat what Death instructs, and Death rewards him with a golden circle. Death repeatedly explains that the fire altar connects the *ātman*, hidden in the cave of the heart, to the *brahman* which is beyond. From the perspective of its source narrative, the *ātman* is Agni Vaiśvānara, the fire hidden in heart of Prajāpati. Rau argues that *brahman*'s 'birth' in the *Kaṭha Upaniṣad* refers to the Sun rising in the east:[41]

> *triṇāciketas tribhir etya sandhiṃ / trikarmakṛt tarati janmamṛtyū / brahma jajñaṃ devam īḍyaṃ viditvā / nicāyyemāṃ śāntim atyantam eti //*
>
> Uniting the three, he is the three *nāciketa* man. Doing the ritual threefold, he crosses birth and death, perceiving *brahman* as the one being born, as the god to be worshipped. Recognising this (golden disc), he goes to endless peace. (KaU 1.17)

Rau compares this passage with one found in an Atharvavedic hymn to the Sun, the *incipit* of which is *brahma jajñānáṃ prathamáṃ purástād*, 'the *brahman* first born in the East'.[42] Although Rau does not mention it, this verse also occurs in the piling of the fire altar.[43] The thesis of this *vallī*, read from the perspective of the Kaṭha canon, is that there is a latent connection between the internal fire, the fire altar and the Sun. That is why sacrifices work, and that is why they achieve the heavenly world. The reductive label 'monism' can hardly capture this ritual metaphysics, which joins microcosmic, mesocosmic and macrocosmic theatres. If anything, the text emphasises a threefold model of reality. We have already established the Ṛgvedic antiquity of the chariot as a metaphor for the sacrifice, but in the *Taittirīya Brāhmaṇa*, a Black Yajurvedic school closely related to the Kaṭhas, the *nāciketa* fire altar is directly likened to a chariot:

[41] Rau 1971: 162.
[42] *Śaunaka Saṃhitā* 4.1.1.
[43] *Taittirīya Saṃhitā* 4.2.8.2; *Kaṭha Saṃhitā* 16.15.

> *anantám̐ ha vā́ apārám akṣayyám̐ lokám̐ jayati*
> *yò 'gním̐ nāciketám̐ cinuté*
> *yá u ca enam evám̐ véda //*
> *átʰo yáthā ráthe tíṣṭhan pákṣasī páryāvártamāne pratyápekṣate*
> *evám ahorātré pratyápekṣate*
> *nā́syāhorātré lokám āpnutaḥ*
> *yò 'gním̐ nāciketám̐ cinuté*
> *yá u ca enam evám̐ véda //*

> He who knows this and piles the *nāciketa* fire (altar) wins a world beyond, one endless and undecaying. Just like one standing on a turning chariot looks down upon either side, he looks down upon Night and Day. He who knows this and piles the *nāciketa* fire (altar), Day and Night do not obtain his world. (TB 3.11.7.5)

The *Taittirīya Brāhmaṇa* informs us that the world beyond is one without spatial (*anantá*) or temporal (*akṣayyá*) boundaries. It lacks divisions of day and night. These qualities, however, apply excusively to the heavenly world gained through proper sacrifice using a *nāciketa* altar. It is not a theory of monism or masked by the illusion of plurality; these are separate worlds.

The following section of the *Kaṭha Upaniṣad* is particularly relevant since it opens the chapter featuring the chariot metaphor:

> *ṛtaṃ pibantau sukṛtasya loke / guhāṃ praviṣṭau parame parārdhe*
> *chāyātapau brahmavido vadanti pañcāgnayo ye ca triṇāciketāḥ*

> The *brahman*-knowers, who maintain the five fires and the triple *nāciketa* altar, say that shadow and light entered: (one) a cave (the other) yonder beyond. Both drinking in the world of proper ritual actions. (KaU 3.1)

Knowers of *brahman* assert there are two entities: one inside the heart and one in heaven. This could hardly be characterised as monism. While the two have a relationship, they are not identical, just as light and shadow have a relationship but are not identical. Further, this world is one of proper ritual; knowledge is useless without praxis.[44] The knowers of *brahman* are also maintainers of the five fires, which are the three used in sacrifice (*gārhapatya*, *āhavanīya*, *dakṣināgni*), as well as the domestic fire (*āvasthya*) and that of the king's court (*sabhya*).[45] Bodewitz (1973) argues that a doctrine of five fires is mapped to the five breaths as a way of internalising the sacrifice. Bodewitz (1985) argues that the triple *nāciketa* altar is not synonymous with the three fires of Vedic sacrifice, but rather

[44] Other readings of the text give *svakṛtasya*, 'one's own (ritual) actions'; both possibilities are captured by the translation 'proper', see Olivelle 1998: 606.

[45] This means they have done the *ādhana* ritual and become *āhitāgni*, 'one whose fires are set', a prerequisite to performing more advanced *śrauta* rituals like an *agniṣṭoma* or *agnicayana*. See Knipe 2015: 190–4.

three altars in three theatres.[46] Hardly rejecting Vedic orthopraxis, the *Kaṭha Upaniṣad* is theorising it. The text continues:

> *yaḥ setur ījānānām akṣaraṃ brahma yat param*
> *abhayaṃ titīrṣatāṃ pāraṃ nāciketaṃ śakemahi*
>
> May we master the *nāciketa* (fire altar), which is the bridge of those who have sacrificed, beyond which is unwithering *brahman*, for those who desire to cross to the far shore without fear. (KaU 3.2)

The speakers ('we') must be Kaṭha priests, those who can master the *nāciketa* to secure the heavenly shore for their financiers. No self-realisation or arcane knowledge about *brahman* is necessary for the patron of the sacrifice, only for the priests who must construct the altar correctly.

> *pra te bravīmi tad u me nibodha svargyam agniṃ naciketaḥ prajānan anantalokāptim atho pratiṣṭhāṃ u viddhi tvam etaṃ nihitaṃ guhāyām*
>
> I proclaim this to you, so pay attention Naciketas! Recognising the heavenly fire (altar) is one which attains an endless world – but know this: its foundation is hidden in the cave (of the heart). (KaU 1.14)

Here there is an explicit identification of *brahman* with the heavenly fire (altar), *svargya agni*, and the foundation, *pratiṣṭhā*, of that altar is in the cave (of the heart).[47] These are the two which the chapter opened with: Light and Shadow, *brahman* and *ātman*, the visible Sun and invisible altar in the heart; the *nāciketa* fire altar connects them.

Finally, in *Kaṭha Upaniṣad* 3.3, the players appear: the *ātman* is a *rathin*, 'chariot passenger', and the *śarīra*, 'body', is *ratham eva*, 'merely the chariot'. The *buddhi*, 'awareness', is *sārathi*, 'chariot driver'. The *manas*, 'thought', is *pragraham eva*, 'merely the bridle'. Finally, the *indriya*, 'senses', are the *haya*, 'horses'.[48] The Indian chariot is almost always depicted with a driver conveying a warrior or king, and so already different from its single-occupant Parmenidean

[46] Typically termed microcosmic, mesocosmic and macrocosmic, but perhaps better conceived of as internal, performative and universal. This emphasis on all three theatres, not simply microcosmic and macrocosmic, suggests that the internalisation of the ritual is a component of the ritual performance and not its replacement.

[47] KaU 2.20 tells us *ātmāsya jantor nihito guhāyām*, 'the *ātman* is hidden in the cave of this person'. A full treatment of the second *Vallī* is currently in preparation.

[48] Even this compositional metaphor, in which two wholes are homologised by the equation of their parts, has a precedent in the *Ṛgveda*, in which the sacrifice is equated to the year by equating its components to the seasons: *yát púruṣeṇa havíṣā / devā́ yajñám átanvata / vasantó asyāsīd ā́jyaṃ / grīṣmá idhmáḥ śarád dhavíḥ //* 'When the gods extended the sacrifice with the Puruṣa as the oblation, Spring was its butter, the kindling was its Summer, and Autumn was its oblation' (RV 10.90.6).

counterpart.[49] The chariot, as the method of conveyance of kings, suggests the *rathin* is of higher social station than the *sārathi*.[50] None of these nuances is present in the Greek metaphor. The *sārathi* has one task, then, to deliver the *rathin* safely to the destination:

> *vijñānasārathir yas tu manaḥ pragrahavān naraḥ /*
> *so 'dhvanaḥ pāram āpnoti / tad viṣṇoḥ paramaṃ padam //*
>
> A man who possesses the bridle of the mind, whose chariot-driver is discerning, he reaches the end of the road: Viṣṇu's ultimate step. (KaU 3.9)

What follows are three verses that describe a taxonomy of the consistent components of an individual. The lowest elements are the sense faculties, then the mental faculties, then the great *ātman*, then unmanifest, and then the cosmic man (*puruṣa*) which occupies the supreme position.

Definitions of *ātman* and *puruṣa* contoured by Vedic ritual reveal that the text describes the transmission of the terrestrial self to the heavenly self.[51] Passages of the *Taittirīya Brāhmaṇa* that describe the *nāciketa* fire altar portray the *ātman* of Prajāpati, synonymous with the cosmic man (*puruṣa*), as the fire inside his heart. Elsewhere the piling of the fire altar is depicted as the reassembling of Prajāpati, who sacrificed himself at the beginning of time to create the universe. Piling the altar reassembles his body and restores the universe to its proper state. The *Taittirīya Brāhmaṇa* claims that the altar will transport the patron of the sacrifice together with a body (*saśarīra*) to a world beyond.[52]

The chariot is indeed a metaphor, but one that is geared towards a theorisation of ritual success in the late Vedic period. For the sacrifice to work the *yajamāna*, the patron of the sacrifice, must become Prajāpati, the first sacrificer and cosmic man.[53] While the *yajamāna* has an invisible fire within his body, his *ātman*, the cosmic man has a great *ātman* within his body: the Sun. The bricks of the *nāciketa* fire altar are also a body for its *ātman*, which is the ring of gold at its

[49] ŚB (Mādhyandina) 5.3.1.8: *sáyonī vā́ aśvínau sáyonī savyaṣṭhṛsārathī́ samānaṃ hi rátham-adhitíṣṭhatastás*, 'Same-wombed are the Aśvins, and same-wombed both fighter and driver for they stand upon the same chariot.' Here the connection between chariot fighter and driver is given a charter in the Aśvins.

[50] Clear from later texts like the *Māhabhārata* where Karṇa is disrespected at the assembly as merely the son of a chariot driver. The *Bhagavad Gītā* inverts this paradigm by having Kṛṣṇa drive Arjuṇa's chariot just prior to revealing himself as God.

[51] This notion is wholly justified by the constant references to ritual executed through both narrative choice and style.

[52] *Kauṣītaki Upaniṣad* provides more details about this heavenly journey; however, the difficulties of travelling through heaven are also sources of anxiety in the *Ṛgveda*; see RV 10.135.

[53] See Gonda 1978: 376.

base.[54] Proper piling and pacifying of this altar produces the interpenetration of these three *ātmans* (self, gold, Sun) effecting the transit to heaven and preventing rebirth on earth.[55] The chariot, then, refers to the body of the *nāciketa* fire altar, which transports the sacrificer's *ātman* to a heavenly world.[56]

In conclusion, this study has been a collaborative demonstration that these two texts are contoured by their use of earlier sources. To ignore this intertextual dimension reduces the amount of empirical evidence that can inform scholarly analysis. The innovations of Parmenides and the *Kaṭha Upaniṣad* against their respective traditions deserve further treatment, but such an analytic process can only achieve the best results once these earlier sources are fully appreciated.

54 The dimensions of the altar and the sacrificial grounds are all relative to the physical measurements of the *yajamāna* himself; see Staal 2010: 196.

55 KaU 3.13 refers to three *ātmans*: a *jñāna*, 'recognitive', a *mahat*, 'immense', and a *śānta*, 'pacified', *ātman*, which in the Vedic context refers to the fire altar. Staal (2010: 508): 'It is believed that if the *adhvaryu* steps on the altar, he will die. The completed altar is now ferocious (*krūra*), vibrating with power, and dreadful (*ghora*). Its powers have to be channeled and it has to be pacified and made to be at peace (*śānta*).'

56 This is consistent with the early Vedic ideology of the fire altar. Proferes (2007) argues that the fire of the clan chief, known as Agni Vaiśvānara, is depicted as supreme over the individual fires of the allied clans just as the Sun is supreme over terrestrial fires.

13

The interiorisation of ritual in India and Greece

Richard Seaford

To the intriguing similarities that have been observed between Greek and Indian thought around the middle of the first millennium I will here add another: the *interiorisation* of ritual (specifically, the cosmic rite of passage), a process connected to the advent both of monism and of the all-importance of the inner self. The interiorisation of ritual is an idea that has been used by Indologists but not, so far as I know, by Hellenists. This is not to deny that there are differences between the two cultures in the way that the ritual is interiorised, and in the nature of the sources. But this chapter focuses on the basic similarity, and indicates a way of explaining why interiorisation occurred. I should add that, of the three kinds of explanation (listed in the Introduction) for the early similarities between Greek and Indian 'philosophical' thought, I favour – for the period before Alexander crossed the Indus – autonomous parallel development. Pre-Socratic and Upaniṣadic thought both exhibit *coherent internal* development, influenced in my view by the *monetisation* that made Greece and India (and China) different in this period from other societies. This is an argument that I will pursue in detail in a monograph. But the importance of monetisation will emerge even from within the relatively narrow confines of this chapter.

The interiorisation of Vedic sacrifice

Early Vedic sacrifice is based on a large series of imagined equivalences (or correspondences, or identifications) through which, especially in the *Brāhmaṇas*, what is within one's control (especially ritual control) corresponds with what is outside it. Ritual correspondence is defined by Clemens Cavallin as 'a relation between two or more entities, which connects them in a way that makes it possible to influence one of them through the ritual manipulation of the other (or to explain e.g. the use of one entity in terms of the other)'.[1] Such equivalences allowed sacrifice to be used as a means of encapsulating – so as to acquire or control – a wide range of phenomena.

However, this system of correspondences was not static. For the period of the *Brāhmaṇas* and early *Upaniṣads* the system of correspondences was transformed into *monism*, in a way that involved the *individualisation* and *interiorisation* of the sacrifice. I will describe how several scholars come to this view from different perspectives, so that my argument does not depend on the reliability of any one of them.

I begin with J. C. Heesterman. The sacrifice as presented in the *Brāhmaṇas* and *Śrauta Sūtras* centres on the single *yajamāna*, who is the sole beneficiary. But 'underneath the classical system', according to Heesterman, 'a different, older pattern can be discerned'.[2] The differences detected by Heesterman in the older pattern are threefold. It was characterised by *exchange*, by the participation of the *group*, and by *conflict or competition*. The marginalisation of these three characteristics within the sacrifice results in its *individualisation*, which has its mythical expression in the figure of Prajāpati: 'Prajāpati, the cosmic man and incorporation of the classical ritual doctrine, is the prototype of the single *yajamāna*, who performs without the intervention of a rival party and for his sole benefit the ritual of cosmic renewal.'[3]

The *Jaiminiya Brāhmaṇa* (2.69–70) narrates the victory of Prajāpati over Death through rival sacrifices: the result is that 'now there is no ritual competition (*saṃsava*); what was the second sacrifice (of Death), that waned; the sacrifice is only one; Prajāpati alone is the sacrifice'. Prajāpati wins by discovering the symbolical and numerical equivalences (*saṃpad, saṃhkyāna*). Heesterman describes the victory as follows:

> He managed in the end to win not because he was a stronger, better equipped contender and sacrificer – the two are explicitly said to be equally strong – but exclusively through his 'vision' of *saṃpad* or *saṃkhyāna* and the intricate arithmetic involved in establishing the symbolic equivalences.[4]

The result is that 'everything now depends on the correct execution of the automatically working ritual'.[5] The 'logical conclusion' of the process of individualisation is, Heesterman claims, 'the *interiorisation* of the ritual, which makes the officiants' services superfluous'. The knower of equivalences 'resumes in

1 Cavallin 2003a: 7–8.
2 Heesterman 1985: 26–44, 1993.
3 Heesterman 1985: 33.
4 Heesterman 1993: 54.
5 Heesterman 1985: 33–4, 1993: 3, 54–8.

himself the universe and performs in himself and by himself the sacrifice without any outside intervention'.[6]

Remarkable about this process of individualisation is that it might not – and sometimes did not – stop before everything was absorbed into the individual. What is required for an 'automatically working ritual' performed by an individual is neither reciprocity with other participants nor the intervention of deity but rather knowledge of its correct performance and of the equivalents. Knowledge of the equivalents is knowledge that *controls*, knowledge not only of the sacrifice but of the correspondence (or identification) of elements of the sacrifice with elements of the person and of the cosmos, extending to knowledge of the cosmos as a whole.

Individualisation advances to the point at which such knowledge amounts to absorption of the cosmos into the individual, identification of cosmos with individual self. 'The classical doctrine implies', notes Heesterman, 'that the *yajamāna*, through knowledge of the equivalences, becomes the integral cosmos, realizing in himself, and thereby mastering, the cosmic alternation of life and death.'[7]

My second scholar is Clemens Cavallin. Many of the correspondences expounded in the *Brāhmaṇas* are between elements of the ritual and the *prāṇa* (meaning basically breaths, then faculties or life forces generally). In his book-length study of these correspondences Cavallin[8] concludes that

> the tendency is that the sacrificer also becomes the goal of the ritual activity. It is, however, not only the sacrificer considered as self, as *ātman*, that is intended, but the focus is upon the constituent principles of the self, the breaths. The efficacy is thereby both dependent on the self – as knowledge of the correspondences is a prerequisite for the attaining of the fruits of the ritual actions – and, at the same time, directed towards it.

Given that many of the sacrificial correspondences are between ritual and man, more specifically the breaths of man (*prāṇa*), 'there is thus an anthropocentric tendency in Vedic ritualistic thought, something which could explain the final abandonment of the "outer" aspects of sacrifice in preference for its "inner" aspects'.[9] And there is in the *Brāhmaṇas* a development in reflection on the cor-

6 Heesterman 1985: 38–9.

7 Heesterman 1985: 39.

8 Cavallin 2003a: 230.

9 Cavallin 2003b: 20, citing *Mundaka Upanishad* 1.2.7–10 and *Prasna Upanishad* 1.9. Cavallin also distinguishes (2003b: 25–6) between three kinds of interiorisation: one is the ritual being performed within the body (for instance a food offering into the fires of the body), another is the ritual being performed mentally (imagined), and the third is intentionality and knowledge being considered as essential for ritual efficacy.

respondences: 'The logical outcome of a process in which interrelated objects more and more come to be considered as identical is some form of monism, and this tendency together with the focus on "breaths" prefigures the views expressed later in the Upaniṣads.'[10] Similarly, Brian Smith observes that:

> in the Upaniṣads, universal resemblance is brought to its logical terminus: universal identity. The complex system of connections between resembling phenomena, the web of *bhandus* integral to vedic ritualism, and hierarchical distinctions are collapsed in monistic thought into the ultimate connection: the equation of self and cosmos (without the ritual intermediary) formulated as the identity and full equality of *ātman* and the *brahman*.[11]

The collapse of connections between resembling phenomena into universal identity promotes and is promoted by the interiorisation of the sacrificial ritual, in which the complex system of connections is no longer sustained by the demands of actual practice. Interiorisation goes together with the development of monism and of the unitary inner self.

The process of individualisation of the sacrifice leading to its interiorisation is described also – with different material – by Herman Tull. He notes that there are a number of passages in the *Brāhmaṇas* that 'indicate that the Brahmanic thinkers recognized two types of sacrifice: the traditional sacrificial format and a form of sacrifice that emphasises the individual to the point of excluding the priests and perhaps even the gods'.[12] One such passage is *Śatapatha Brāhmaṇa* 11.2.6.13–14, which distinguishes between the one who sacrifices for the gods (*devayājin*, 'god-offerer') and the one who sacrifices for the self (*ātmayājin*, 'self-offerer').[13] Better is the *ātmayājin*:

> As to this they ask, 'Who is the better one, the self-offerer, or the god-offerer?' Let him say, 'The self-offerer;' for a self-offerer, doubtless, is he who knows, 'This my (new) body is formed by that (body of *Yagña*, the sacrifice), this my (new) body is procured thereby.'[14]

The *devayājin* on the other hand 'is as the inferior who brings tribute to the superior, or like a man of the people who brings tribute to the king: indeed, he does not win such a place (in heaven) as the other'. Whereas the *devayājin* attains the benefit of the sacrifice through the intercession of the gods, the *ātmayājin* attains it directly.

The distinction drawn between *devayājin* and *ātmayājin* is another symptom

[10] Cavallin 2003a: 227.
[11] Smith 1989: 194.
[12] Tull 1990: 39, Heesterman 1993: 82, 216.
[13] On this passage see Bodewitz 1973: 304.
[14] Translation by Eggeling.

of individualisation, and it introduces an *economic* dimension. If the *devayājin* is like the inferior who brings tribute to the superior, the implication is that the *ātmayājin*, whose body is created by the sacrifice, is like the economically autonomous individual. A similar idea[15] occurs in the *Bṛhadāraṇyaka Upaniṣad* (1.4.10), where he who knows 'I am *brahman*', and thereby becomes this all and the *ātman* of the gods, is contrasted with one who worships another deity, thinking 'he is one and I am another', does not know, and relates to the gods as livestock do to men; and so 'it is not pleasing to the gods when men know this'. Like those who pay tribute to their superiors, animals serve the economic interests of men, and some sacrificers benefit gods.

Another such passage (ŚB 9.5.2.12–13) fills out this picture by stating that the traditional sacrificer becomes poorer daily whereas the sacrificer for the self becomes richer daily. This suggests a world in which reciprocity (voluntary requital) has broken down: gifts do not necessarily elicit corresponding benefits in return, and so may impoverish the giver.[16]

The disadvantages of the economically less productive path arise from the facts that (a) the sacrificer's gifts to the priests ransom the sacrificial merit, which also however accrues to the priests,[17] and (b) the deceased must in the afterlife share both himself (with the gods, as food) and his accumulated store of sacrificial merit (with his ancestors): this is why

> he does not attain a full and lasting afterlife existence, but remains there 'only as long as there is a residue of sacrificial merit' and re-enters the cycle of generation. On the other hand, those who follow the interiorised path of sacrifice attain a lasting afterlife in the world of Brahmā.[18]

Tull, rightly concerned to emphasise the continuity between *Brāhmaṇas* and *Upaniṣads*, notes that at ŚB 10.5.4.16 the world attained by knowledge is the place where sacrificial gifts (for the priests) do not go.

This constitutes an 'experience independent of the ritual specialist', which in the *Upaniṣads* 'continues in the development of the interiorised sacrifice; its unfragmented nature, centering entirely on the individual, is thus mirrored in the conditions of the afterlife'.[19] Accordingly, the distinction between *pitṛyāna* and *devayana* is

> between a traditional path of worship, one that maintains the relationship between gods, priests, and sacrificers and a path that concentrates on the individual to the

[15] Tull 1990: 20.
[16] Cf. Heesterman 1993: 210.
[17] Cf. ŚB 4.3.4.6; 1.9.3.1.
[18] Tull 1990: 35.
[19] Tull 1990: 36.

> point of actually 'interiorising' the sacrifice . . . those who follow the interiorised path of sacrifice attain a lasting afterlife in the world of Brahmā.[20]

The distinction is consonant with the distinction we saw between *devayājin* and *ātmayājin*. And in both cases the new, superior form of sacrifice is associated with *knowledge*, focuses on the *individual self*, and implies *escape from the automatic cycle*.

The *knowledge* is mainly of the correspondences (as described earlier). Given also the focus on the individual self, the extreme outcome of such correspondences is the identity of self, sacrifice and cosmos. And indeed that is what we find in the figure of Prajāpati, who is sacrificer, sacrifice, creator of everything, and himself everything.[21] The individual in performing the sacrifice may be identified with Prajāpati, and may become everything.[22] The result is what I call *personal monism*: all things are one person.

The interiorisation of Greek mystic initiation

In Greece too, as in India at about the same time, we find the *interiorisation* of the ritual performed by the living to create well-being for themselves after death.

In India this ritual[23] was the Vedic sacrifice; in Greece however it was mystic initiation.[24] Indeed the Greek mystic initiand might, like the Indian sacrificer, be imagined as transported through the cosmos.[25] Both rituals may be described as *cosmic rites of passage*. It is also true however that in Greece animal sacrifice might (along with other rituals) be an important part of mystic initiation, and that the initiand might be imagined as a sacrificial victim.[26]

Heraclitus

Heraclitus belonged to the Ephesian royal family that – being descended from the Athenian royal family – held the priesthood of Demeter Eleusinia, the goddess of the Eleusinian mysteries.[27]

According to Heraclitus 'the mysteries practised among humankind are performed in an unholy way' (22 DK B14). Note that he does not say that the

20 Tull 1990: 34–5.
21 See the Brahmanic texts collected and discussed by Lévi 1898: 13–30.
22 E.g. ŚB 4.5.7.1; 3.3.4.5–11; 13.6.1.1; 13.7.1.1.
23 Or one such ritual: others may have vanished without trace.
24 The only instance that I have been able to find of an (implied) interiorised sacrifice in Greek texts is at Iamblichus, *The Mysteries of Egypt* 5.15.
25 Seaford 1986.
26 Seaford 1994: 282–4, Parker 2005: 342–3.
27 22 DK A1(6), A2; cf. B125.

mysteries are themselves unholy. And the specification 'among humankind' implies the existence of mysteries uncorrupted by human performance. Such imagined mysteries are, I suggest, in effect *interiorised.*

Wisdom comes through 'listening to the *logos*' (B50). A 'sacred *logos*' containing secret doctrine might be pronounced in the mysteries.[28] The *manner* in which Heraclitus presents his *logos*, and the *content* of his doctrine, each independently suggest that he envisages himself as pronouncing a *logos* that – though it does not depend on the performance of mysteries – is in some sense a *logos* of the mysteries. Mystic initiation gives to initiates access to the afterlife by rehearsing their death, and accordingly might involve transformation of their *understanding* (of life and death, of the cosmos). Heraclitus, in insisting on the importance of understanding the *logos*, envisages himself as transforming understanding (of life and death, of the cosmos) independently of the enactment of ritual. The kind of wisdom revealed in mystic ritual has – with Heraclitus – become detached from its *enactment*. This is both interiorisation and individualisation, inasmuch as elements of the ritual (performed by a group) exist only within each individual mind.

It remains to indicate the surviving evidence for my claim that Heraclitus' discourse resembled mystic doctrine both in the manner of its presentation and in its content.[29]

As for its presentation, Heraclitus' discourse is – like the language used in mystic initiation – riddling.[30] Accordingly – and this too resembles mystic discourse – the *logos* that he propounds is, he states, not understood at first hearing.[31] In a later text[32] the difficulty of Heraclitus' book is imagined as the initial darkness that is in the course of mystic initiation transformed into light.

A series of bone plates found at Olbia on the Black Sea seem to have been tokens of participation in sacrifices. Three of them, dating from the fifth century BCE, have inscriptions. One has the words 'life death life', 'truth', 'Dio(nysos)' and 'Orphic'. Another has 'peace war', 'truth falsehood' and 'Dio(nysos)', and a third has 'Dio(nysos)', 'truth' and 'soul' (*psuchē*) – possibly along with 'body' (*sōma*).[33] The bone plates were almost certainly membership tokens of a group constituted by Orphic-Dionysiac mystic initiation (including animal sacrifice).[34] These inscriptions are strikingly similar, in both form and content, to Heraclitean

[28] E.g. Herodotus. 2.51.4; many further refs. in Seaford 2004: 233 n18; see also Riedweg 1987: 5–14.

[29] For more detail see Seaford 1986: 14–20, Seaford 2004: 234–8, Schefer 2000.

[30] Seaford 2004: 184, 226 n36, 233 n19.

[31] B1, B34, Thomson 1961: 273–5, Schefer 2000: 56–62.

[32] *Anthologia Palatina* 9.540.

[33] Vinogradov (1991) believed he could detect it.

[34] West 1983: 17–19.

fragments such as B62 'immortals mortals, mortals immortals, . . .' or B67 'god is day night, winter summer, war peace, . . .'. The similarity is surely due to Heraclitus' use of the riddling style of mystery-cult, a hypothesis proposed well before the discovery of the Olbian incriptions (first published in 1978) and confirmed by them.

This brings us to what Heraclitean cosmology shares with the *content* of mystic doctrine, namely four things in particular: the idea that mortals are immortals (and vice versa), the general importance of the unity of opposites,[35] the idea that there are better and worse fates after death, and the importance of cosmological elements in the cyclical passage of the soul. The Olbian 'life death life' resembles Heraclitus in substance as well as in style, signifying as it does our transition (as immortal mortals or mortal immortals) through 'death' back to life, thereby also implying the unity of the opposites of life and death.[36] The content of the mystic *logos* was sometimes a myth, which might explain the unity of immortality and mortal suffering in humankind (we are Titans), but also might be interpreted as a riddling account of physical cosmology.[37]

Finally, besides providing the earliest extant Greek interiorisation of ritual, Heraclitus was an early exponent of Greek monism, and provides the earliest extant Greek account of the inner self or soul (*psuchē*) as an entity of comprehensive consciousness. As in India, this threefold combination is not coincidental. Moreover, he was also the first to object to the actual practice of ritual (mystic initiation, and purification by blood).[38] Plato, who – as we shall soon see – also interiorised mystic initiation, not only provided a supremely influential account of the central importance of the *psuchē* but was also the first extant writer to be critical of some kinds of sacrifice (without rejecting sacrifice *per se*).[39] Objections to the practice of sacrifice occur – along with the interiorisation of ritual and the emergence both of monism and of the central importance of the inner self (*ātman*) – in roughly the same period also in India.

Parmenides

The fragments of Parmenides contain a narrative in which he journeys through the gates of the paths of day and night, where a goddess reveals to him the content of his philosophy. The narrative has been shown to correspond in various

35 The mystic rite of passage involves the unity not only of the opposites of mortal and immortal, and of life and death, but also of male and female and of animal and human. See Seaford 1996: 43–4.

36 More detail in Seaford 1986: 17–20.

37 As in the Derveni papyrus. See Seaford 2004: 233–5.

38 In B14 and B5.

39 *Euthyphro* 14e, *Republic* 364b, *Laws* 716e, 885b, 905d–6d.

details to mystic initiation.[40] And there are reasons for believing that – as with Heraclitus – Parmenides' doctrine is influenced by mystery-cult not only in its presentation but also in its content.[41]

Mystic ritual is a performance by a group, whereas the mystic journey of Parmenides seems to be the mere vision of a mere individual, and as such it seems – as with Heraclitus – to individualise as well as to interiorise mystic ritual. With Parmenides the individualisation is unusually marked. He represents the wisdom of the goddess as revealed to himself alone, setting him apart from the ignorance of mortals.[42] As in mystic initiation, there is a right road and one or more wrong roads. Parmenides is carried, as 'the man who knows' (i.e. the mystic initiate),[43] along one road, 'far from the treading of humankind' (28 DK B1.2–3, 27), to the goddess, who warns him off other roads, one of which is followed by 'mortals knowing nothing' (B6.3–7).

Inasmuch as the journey imagined by Parmenides is a vision inspired by ritual, it represents the *interiorisation* of the ritual. There is interiorisation also in an aspect of his supposedly logical argumentation.

The goddess produces a chain of deductive argument to show that what exists is One, spherical, invariant in space and time (eternal, unchanging, unmoving, homogeneous), self-sufficient and limited. This bizarre conclusion is reached by *privileging the subjective*. Thinking, or its object, is identified by Parmenides with being. He imports into his argument an appeal to introspection: absent things present to the mind (i.e. objects of thought, imagined not perceived) are continuous (B4), and this assumption forms a premise from which the continuity and fullness of what exists can be deduced. But the assumption is in fact true only if the mind preconceives its contents as continuous.

Whence this preconception? And why does Parmenides privilege the supposed continuity and reality of what is imagined or thought (the subjective)? A complete answer cannot be given here. For now we emphasise that we have here a further *interiorisation* of mystic ritual: it is not just that mystic initiation is interiorised as a merely imagined revelation, but that moreover within the imagined mystic revelation there is a crucial appeal to *introspection*.

Moreover, the deduction of the continuity of what exists from the continuity of what is introspected, together with the use of the same terminology to express the continuity of each,[44] implies a degree of *assimilation* between the subjective (absent things present to the mind of Parmenides) and the objective (what exists).

[40] References in Seaford 2004: 185, 228–9.

[41] Seaford 2004: 228–9, 262–3.

[42] B1.2–3, 27, 30–2, 6.4–9, 7.2–6, 8.51–2.

[43] Thomson 1961: 289–90, Burkert 1969: 5.

[44] Cf. B4.2 with B8.23–5.

This is not the only instance of such assimilation in Parmenides.[45] He describes the One as 'whole and of a single kind and untrembling (ἀτρεμής) and complete' (B8.4). The rare word ἀτρεμής, though it describes here the objective One, also implies subjectivity, as it does also more clearly when describing the 'heart' of Truth at B1.29. The same word appears also in the passage of Plato's *Phaedrus* in which he describes pre-natal

> mysteries which it is right to call most blessed, which we celebrated ourselves whole (ὁλόκληροι) . . . with the gaze of our final initiation on whole (ὁλόκληρα) and simple and untrembling (ἀτρεμῆ) and blessed apparitions in a pure light, ourselves being pure. (250b8–c6)

The combination of 'whole' and 'untrembling' in both Parmenides and the explicitly mystic Platonic passage confirms that Parmenides is thinking of the goddess' revelation of the One in terms of mystic revelation. Further, 'blessed' (εὐδαίμων) in the Plato passage is a word used of the permanent happiness bestowed by mystic initiation on the initiates.[46] Its application here along with 'untrembling' to the apparitions, together with 'whole' and 'pure' describing both the initiates *and* what they see, corresponds with various passages of Plato and others[47] based on the idea *that the initiates are partially assimilated to what they see or contemplate in mystic initiation.* As for 'untrembling', trembling was a typical feature of the suffering of the mystic initiands before their transition to calm,[48] and Proclus describes mystic apparitions as 'full of calm'.[49]

And so mystic ritual, interiorised by Parmenides, might itself already contain some interiorisation of object by subject. The division between subject and object of the mystic vision was transcended by partial assimilation between the two, in both directions. In Parmenides, we have seen, the distinction between subject and object (Being) is transcended, both in his deductive argument and in his vision of the One. The vision results from the 'philosophical' interiorisation of the ritual interiorisation of what is seen by the mystic initiate. The positive psychological effect of the merging of subject with object, which I locate in mystic initiation (a rehearsal and overcoming of death), is described from a different perspective by Robbiano in this volume.

45 Seaford 2004: 227–9, 252.

46 E.g. Euripides *Bacchae* 902 with Seaford (1996) ad loc.

47 *Phdr.* 249c7, *Phaedo* 66e, 67ab, 69c, 79d, 81a, *Symp.* 212a, Plutarch *fragment* 178, Plotinus *Enneads* 6.9.11, Proclus *Commentary on Plato's Republic* 2.108.17–20 Kroll.

48 Seaford 2004: 229.

49 Proclus *Commentary* 2.185.3 Kroll.

Plato

In the many mentions and evocations of mystery-cult in Plato the *psuchē* has a central place. The allegory of the *psuchē* in his *Phaedrus* is full of evocations of mystery-cult.[50] A metaphor in the *Republic* (560e) speaks of purifying the *psuchē* of the person being initiated preparatory to the transformative arrival of a crowned chorus. In *Cratylus* (400c) the followers of Orpheus are said to have taught that the *psuchē* is punished by being imprisoned in the body. The doctrine of the persistence of the immortal *psuchē* through death and rebirth is attributed by Plato (*Meno* 81ab) to a *logos* told by priests and priestesses (probably in mystery-cult). Plato's *Symposium* is explicit in describing philosophical development in terms of mystic initiation (210a1, etc.).

The *Phaedo* refers four times explicitly to doctrine propounded in mystic ritual concerning the passage of the *psuchē* to the next world (62b, 69c, 81a, 108a). The *psuchē* should withdraw from the senses and 'trust nothing except itself in its thought by itself of what exists by itself', in a manner reminiscent of Parmenides. In doing so the *psuchē* 'sees the intelligible and invisible' (83b). The *psuchē* contains its own abstract object of thought, which it sees only when it achieves the purity of withdrawal from the senses, rather as mystic initiation requires exclusive focus on the object to which the inner self of the purified initiate is assimilated.

In the *Phaedrus* (249b8) we remember our pre-natal vision by understanding 'a general conception going from many sense-perceptions into a unity (εἰς ἓν) collected by reasoning. This is a memory of those things which our *psuchē* once saw when it journeyed with god . . . (i.e. in its mystic vision).'[51] This helps to explain why shortly afterwards Plato insists – we saw – on the *wholeness* of the mystic initiate. His account in *Phaedo* of the soul *gathering itself from all parts of the body*[52] may be one of the ideas that this passage of Plato has taken from mystery-cult.[53] It seems to have inspired Plotinus' account (*Enneads* 1.6.5) of the longing to 'gather yourselves away from your body' with an excitement that he calls a 'bacchic revel'. In Neoplatonic philosophy the dismemberment and reconstitution of Dionysos is taken as an *allegory* for the fragmentation of the soul or mind (resulting from its fall into the sensible world) and its subsequent gathering of itself so as to recover its original unity.[54] In the *Epinomis* (attributed to Plato)

50 Riedweg 1987: 30–69.

51 For the importance of mystic initiation throughout this passage of *Phaedrus* see Riedweg 1987: 30–69.

52 67c; similarly 80e, 83a.

53 Riedweg 1987: 11, 19, 27, 53.

54 Olympiodorus *In Phaedonem* 111, 4–19. Norvin; further refs. and discussion in Seaford 1998: 142.

a blessed person is described as having been initiated truly and really, 'participating, being one, in one thinking (μεταλαβὼν φρονήσεως εἷς ὢν μιᾶς)' (986d).

The sacrificial dismemberment and reconstitution of Dionysos, and of Pentheus in Euripides' *Bacchae*, in fact derives from mystic initiation.[55] Of course the mystic initiand was not in fact physically dismembered: there are indications[56] that the idea of physical fragmentation may rather have inspired or expressed a terrifying experience of *mental* fragmentation that was – in the mystic transition from anxious ignorance to knowledge and belonging – replaced by a joyful sense of internal unity. After all, mental fragmentation was perhaps most easily expressed by the idea of bodily fragmentation, especially in the pre-Platonic era, in which the mind was imagined as – however tenuous – corporeal.[57] Similarly, the assimilation of the sacrificer to the dismembered Prajāpati implied mental fragmentation.

In Plato's *Symposium* the mystic assimilation of subject to object combines with the philosopher's ascent from the multiplicity of particular objects of sense to a vision of a single unitary abstraction of absolute, eternal beauty, through which he finally becomes 'if any other of mankind, he too immortal' (212a). The perception of abstract unity beyond the appearance of multiplicity is salvational also in India.[58]

Plato interiorised mystery-cult and drew on its doctrine in propounding a coherent and influential ethics that dispensed with ritual, emphasising instead a subtle combination of understanding with freedom from desire. (For Indian parallels see Bussanich in this volume.)

What caused the interiorisation?

None of the scholars who describe the individualisation and interiorisation of Indian sacrifice can explain why it occurred. Any explanation based on the internal logic of the sacrificial system is bound to be at best insufficient, because it can explain neither why a system that needed to change came into being nor why it needed to change when it did. What is also required is attention to *external* developments. I have in my *Money and the Early Greek Mind* (2004) described the influence of monetisation on the earliest Greek philosophy (including Heraclitus and Parmenides), including an account of how money merges with

55 West 1983: 140–75, Seaford 1996.

56 E. *Ba*. 968–9 with Seaford 1998: 135, Plato *Laws* 672b: cf. Plut *Mor*. 389a, Seaford 2004: 309, Seaford 1998: 136–7.

57 Indeed one ancient citation of Parmenides B8.4 has οὐλομελές (rather than μουνογενές), denoting the wholeness of the *body*. Cf. Empedocles B62.4, Seaford 2004: 252.

58 E.g. BU 4.4.19.

mystic doctrine in influencing the imagining of the cosmos. Here I confine myself to indicating briefly ways in which monetisation may have promoted the individualisation and interiorisation of the cosmic rite of passage, in both cultures, although for detail here I confine myself here to India.

Money was a new form of power quite different from – and potentially a threat to – the ritual power of the Brahmins. It must be emphasised that a general measure of value, especially if it is also a general means of exchange, *requires for its highly convenient effectiveness* that the everyday life of ever more people is pervaded with something new, the impersonal power of uniform value. Money tends to pervade everything.

In the *Brāhmaṇas* gold (or occasionally silver) given to the priests might be specified as of a certain weight,[59] and it might be given in pieces of a certain weight.[60] In an early *Upaniṣad* Janaka, king of Videha, plans a sacrifice, at which he intends to give lavish gifts to the priests, and to the assembled Brahmins he declares that the most learned man of them should drive away a thousand cows, to the horns of each of which are attached ten pieces[61] of gold.[62] This goes beyond anything in the *Ṛgveda*, but is not yet money in the full sense. These texts are produced by a highly traditional rural elite (Brahmins), and in a period of urbanisation are hostile to urban forms of life and ignore towns. But this did not prevent the wealth once *given* to priests from now being *paid*. My argument would be enhanced by discussion of the complex issue of the chronology of monetisation (and of the relevant texts) in India, which I must postpone to my monograph.

The monetisation of the sacrifice can be illustrated by a passage in which Heesterman describes the earlier phase of sacrifice as one in which 'the issue and outcome – the redistribution of the "goods of life" – are clear and for all to see. The munificent sacrificial patron may, moreover, hope that reciprocity will reward him over time.' This is succeeded by a 'ritualism' that by contrast

> is not dependent on the participation of others . . . It stands apart in sovereign independence . . . it transcends the surrounding world . . . deals with the invisible (*adṛṣṭa*). The effect, the 'fruit' it promises to the faithful sacrificer, comes about in an invisible way, and the promised effect is said to be invisible, namely heaven. The expert officiants who receive the *daksinā* wealth are not held to any reciprocity. The Mīmāmsa rejects the view that the *daksinā* should be considered a gift that

59 E.g. ŚB 12.7.2.13; 13.2.3.2; 13.4.1.6–7; 13.4.2.10; 13.4.2.13; TB 1.8.9.1; 1.7.8.2; TS 2.3.11.6; *Maitr. Sam.* 1.6.4; 2.2.2; etc.: Prasad 1966: 165.

60 ŚB 5.4.3.26; 5.5.5.16; *Pancavimsa Brāhmaṇa* 18.3.2.

61 Sanskrit *pāda* (meaning foot, both part of body and measurement, as in English; also means a quarter). 'Gold' is understood.

62 BU 3.1.1. The combination of pastoral with metallic wealth (expressing a transition from the former to the latter?) occurs also in Greek mythology, for instance in the famous golden fleece.

> would consequently oblige the recipient. Instead it is viewed as a salary for services rendered. When the service is rendered and the salary received there is no longer reciprocity or mutual obligation . . . The ritual is supposed to produce its result automatically, be it cattle, health and long life, male progeny, or headmanship, but the way in which the effect should come about is hidden from our view . . . It [*śraddhā*] has come to mean the unquestioning faith in the efficacy of the ritual. As such it has no social content. But the connection it still shows with the *daksinā* points in the direction of an original social context of gift-giving and alliance.[63]

It would – unbeknownst to its author – be difficult to think of a better account than this of what *monetisation* brings to society. Money replaces the interpersonal links created by gift-exchange (reciprocity) with a new unitary power that is individually owned, universal, transcendent, invisible, automatic (impersonal), and dependent on a generalised confidence that replaced the interpersonal confidence attached to the gift. Another aspect of monetary influence may be in the cosmic *cycle* implicit in the sacrifice; and central new features of money that are easily interiorised are its *abstractness* and its *unlimitedness*.[64] But I cannot discuss all these characteristics here. Instead I will say something more about what Heesterman calls the 'fruit' of the sacrifice, and conclude by sketching the relation of monetisation to the *individualisation* and *interiorisation* of ritual.

In the doctrine of the two paths as described above by Tull the performer of economically less productive sacrifices has eventually to return to the cycle of generation when his sacrificial merit in the afterlife runs out (just as running out of money may mean returning to the commercial cycle). The concepts of *sukṛta* and *iṣṭāpūrta* each refers to the merit that the sacrificer accumulates for himself in the next world. Instead of being gifts for the gods, sacrifices now produce stores of something like money for the sacrificer. Similarly, the meaning of the word *karma* passed from ritual action to an ethicised substance-power that is accumulated by action in general and determines the well-being of the actor (like a store of money). *Iṣṭāpūrta* is etymologically connected with sacrifice, and could refer to the totality of merit accumulated (not only by sacrifice[65]) in the addressee's life,[66] or to material wealth in this world.[67]

63 Heesterman 1993: 77–8.

64 Just as for Heraclitus – in the context of the interiorisation of mystery-cult and its denigration as *practised* – the soul has an unlimited *logos* (B45), so for instance at BU 3.1.3–10 the *brahman* priest wins an unlimited world (*loka*) with the unlimited mind, whereas the other priests by sacrificing win only one or another *loka*.

65 Halbfass 2000: 59, Krishan 1997: 4–5.

66 Biardeau and Malamoud 1976: 165, Keith 1925: 250, 409, 478. Krishan 1997: 5: 'It appears to be a synonym for *nidhi* (treasure), deposit in heaven, consisting of religious merit, something on a man's credit side in the invisible world or in the life hereafter.'

67 Source references in Krishan 1997: 33.

I proceed to *individualisation*. The ease with which metal money is stored, preserved, concealed, transported and exchanged makes it highly suitable for possession and use by the autonomous individual. The isolating effect of money has been confirmed by empirical psychology.[68] In practice of course the monetised individual may need, even if wealthy, to call on the loyalty of friends and relatives. But the overall effect of monetisation is undoubtedly to increase the potential or actual autonomy of the individual. Whereas gifts tend to leave donor connected to recipient, a monetised transaction concerns only the equivalence of money with goods, and *qua* monetised transaction leaves the transactors unrelated to each other. Each transactor is completely separated from what the other transactor has received and from the other transactor himself. The monetised transactor is *individualised.* Older forms of social relationship – gift-exchange, kinship, communal possession of land and so on – unite individuals, whereas money tends to make them autonomous. To the extent that what was once *given* by the sacrificer becomes *payment* he tends to become an isolated individual.

What then of the process by which this individualisation leads to *interiorisation*? Whereas gifts acquired embody some relation (such as memory, gratitude or obligation) to the donor, money acquired belongs absolutely to its owner. The invisible power of money is impersonal and universal, but expresses the will of its individual owner. Indeed, it is through the seemingly invisible power of his money, without any intermediary such as ritual or gift, that the individual enacts his will. There is anthropological and historical evidence for the role of individual property in shaping the very idea of the (autonomous, unitary) individual.[69] In Greek texts there is evidence indicating that the inner self is to some extent modelled on the abstract power-substance of money.[70] The universal, invisible power of money may seem to belong to the inner self of its owner. Money is interiorised in Plato.[71] *Karma* is imagined internal as well as external. The power of money may be interiorised.

The interiorisation of the Vedic sacrifice requires, we remember, knowledge rather than officiants or gods – knowledge especially of the correspondences by which ritual controls the external world; the sacrifice is increasingly directed towards the self; and each correspondence tends to collapse into identity, and their plurality ultimately into the fundamental identity of *ātman* with *brahman.*

How might this development be related to monetisation? In the pre-monetary sacrifice the sacrificer gave gifts to the priests, and the equivalences (or correspondences) embodied various forms of ritual control over various things in the

[68] E.g. Vohs et al. 2006.

[69] E.g. LiPuma 1998: 74, Macpherson 1962: 3.

[70] Seaford 2016.

[71] *Phaedo* 69a; *Republic* 416e.

world. But with the advent of money, the individual may in principle use it to obtain all goods and services, and do so more successfully than with ritual. By accumulating money he is more obviously (than when he gives gifts) himself the goal of his economic activity, and because he can acquire a wide variety of goods by means of a single thing (money), all the various goods may seem to be manifestations of the monetary value that embodies his will. This dual process promotes monistic collapse (of money and inner self with world).

We have observed that this very same dual process promoting monistic collapse occurred in the sacrifice – promoted, I suggest, by the advent of money;[72] for even if the sacrificer continued to sponsor the sacrifice in the traditional way (with goods in kind), the goods were not immune to acquiring monetary value.

The series of sacrificial equivalences – the individual sacrificer using *b* to control *c*, *d* to control *e*, *f* to control *g* – corresponds to the required series of interpersonal relationships (with various men and deities) in the pre-monetary world. But money is a single thing (*x*) that can in principle control all things, which seem therefore to merge into *x*; and because the power of the individual seems identical to the power of *x*, he too merges with *x*. Such a process in the sacrificial sphere promotes and is promoted by its interiorisation.[73] The invisible power of money – individualising but universal, interiorised but direct – comes to influence the way in which the traditional power of the individual sacrificer is imagined. The mythical embodiment of the individual sacrificer, Prajāpati, prevails – we remember – exclusively through his vision of the intricate *arithmetic* involved in establishing the symbolic equivalences. The traditional power of the sacrificer to obtain *lokas* (often translated 'worlds'), together with the *interiorised universal* power of money, promotes the idea of an inner self that is identified with the universe.

I do not claim that monetisation was the only factor in the interiorisation of the Vedic sacrifice.[74] But it was an important factor, and has been entirely ignored. Finally, I suggest that monetisation was also a factor in the interiorisation of Greek mystic initiation, but here I must postpone detailed argument to my monograph.[75]

72 For the similarity between monetary payment and ritual action see Seaford 2012: 125–7.

73 As a small example of how this might work, several passages of ŚB 'suggest a subtle shift in the meaning of *bandha*, from the physical binding of the animal to that of a metaphysical binding of the animal to the sacrificer' (Tull 1990: 74).

74 Other factors may have included the need for a merely symbolic death for the sacrificer, and resentment of the Brahminic monopoly.

75 See also Seaford 2016.

14

Rebirth and 'ethicisation' in Greek and South Asian thought

Mikel Burley

Underlying many speculations about the origins of beliefs in rebirth or reincarnation is an assumption about the relation between metaphysics and ethics. Roughly speaking, the assumption is that ethical outlooks are grounded in metaphysical beliefs or theories, and hence that, in any given case, a metaphysical conception of the world is prior, logically and chronologically, to the ethical outlook. I call this the *assumption of metaphysical priority*. Among the theories in which we see this assumption at work is that developed by the anthropologist Gananath Obeyesekere in several publications since the late 1960s, which concerns how conceptions of rebirth evolved from 'non-ethicised' to 'ethicised' forms.[1] Equating 'ethicised' with 'karmic', Obeyesekere posits a transition from 'rebirth eschatologies' to 'karmic eschatologies'. According to this view, rebirth eschatologies are conceptions of what happens after death that involve rebirth but lack a distinctive ethical dimension, whereas karmic eschatologies incorporate into their conception of what happens after death the idea that rebirth is conditioned or determined by the ethical quality of one's actions in the preceding life. Although his thesis applies primarily to traditions deriving from South Asia – most notably Hindu, Buddhist and Jain traditions – Obeyesekere acknowledges similarities with conceptions of transmigration among certain Greek thinkers, noting for example that Pythagorean theory 'perhaps' constitutes a karmic eschatology.[2]

The assumption of metaphysical priority is, however, questionable. It has been poignantly challenged by Catherine Osborne, who argues that certain metaphysical theories of transmigration might in fact have emerged from the ethical commitments that their proponents held prior to devising the metaphysical the-

[1] See esp. Obeyesekere 1968, 1980, 1994, 2002.

[2] Obeyesekere 1994: xx.

ories.[3] Although Osborne's claim is made with specific reference to ancient Greek philosophers and is not advanced as a direct response to Obeyesekere, the challenge it represents has wider implications. It forces us to question whether metaphysical conceptions *must* precede and undergird ethical values and practices, and thereby obliges us, when clear historical evidence is lacking, to refrain from simply assuming that they do have this undergirding role.

My purpose in this chapter is, after outlining Obeyesekere's ethicisation thesis, to follow Osborne in disrupting the aforementioned assumption of metaphysical priority, and then to go further by re-evaluating the idea that there must be an order of priority between metaphysics and ethics at all. A viable alternative is that worldviews involving a belief in rebirth comprise both metaphysical and ethical dimensions, neither of which is logically or chronologically prior to the other. Indeed, in at least some instances, the supposed bifurcation between metaphysical theory and ethical outlook is thoroughly misleading, and we should think more in terms of what Clifford Geertz spoke of as *syntheses* between metaphysical worldview and 'ethos' or 'style of life'.[4] An implication of this latter contention is that the coherence of talk of a transition from *non*-ethicised to ethicised versions of rebirth belief ought not to be taken for granted, for what is apt to be at issue would be better characterised as a transition from one ethically imbued conception to another.

Although the debate with which this chapter is concerned – over the relation between ethics and metaphysics in worldviews involving rebirth – cannot directly shed light on the historical relationship between eschatological thinking in ancient Greece and ancient South Asia, it does bring into sharper focus important conceptual issues that, while strongly influencing reflections upon that historical relationship, tend to go largely unnoticed.

The ethicisation thesis

Obeyesekere is far from unique in assuming that conceptions of rebirth involving notions of retributive *karma* and ethical evolution are higher or more advanced than those which do not. G. R. S. Mead, for example, writing in the early twentieth century and subscribing to a broadly Theosophical model of human spiritual progress, distinguishes what he sees as the more philosophically refined versions of rebirth belief from those of so-called 'primitive tribes'.[5] In view of the wide

3 See Osborne 2007: 43–62. Since publishing this work, its author has reverted to using her maiden name, Catherine Rowett. To avoid confusion, however, I refer to her as Osborne in this chapter.

4 Geertz 1973: chs 4 and 5.

5 Mead 1912: 170.

distribution of rebirth beliefs among diverse human societies, Mead infers that the idea of rebirth 'must . . . be due to elementary experience of some sort'.[6] It is, he avers, 'in the comparatively highly cultured nations of India and Greece' that, from the seventh century BCE onwards, more sophisticated and systematic conceptions developed; these were characterised in particular by the idea that the human soul progresses morally and spiritually over a long series of lives like 'a warrior or divine adventurer' towards the ultimate goal of realising one's unity with all living beings.[7]

Indian philosophers, too, have remarked upon the supposed fact that, when 'advanced religions' adopted the notion of rebirth – paradigm cases being Buddhism, Jainism and Brahmanical Hinduism – 'they added a rider thereto that the soul carries with it the results of the good or bad acts done by it'.[8] We thus see a common conceptual and historical picture in play, according to which purportedly pre-ethical and pre-soteriological notions of rebirth were refined by more 'highly cultured' or 'advanced' peoples, who devised conceptions evincing greater ethical and philosophical nuance. It is this picture that Obeyesekere inherits, and he designates the alleged transition from relatively uncultivated to full-blown karmic versions of rebirth a process of *ethicisation*.

Obeyesekere articulates his ethicisation thesis in bold terms, contending that the historical process he is adumbrating has the force of logical necessity. 'When ethicization is systematically introduced into any rebirth eschatology', he writes, 'that rebirth eschatology must logically transform itself into a karmic eschatology.'[9] It should be noted that Obeyesekere uses the term 'eschatology' not in the strict sense of a conception of the final destination or goal of humankind and of the world but rather to denote any conception of what happens to a person after death. Had he been aware of it, he could have borrowed John Hick's term 'pareschatology' (which Hick himself attributes to his colleague Michael Goulder). 'Whereas eschatology is the doctrine of the *eschata* or last things, and thus of the ultimate state of man', Hick writes, 'pareschatology is, by analogy, the doctrine of the *para-eschata*, or next-to-last things, and thus of the human future between the present life and man's ultimate state.'[10] In Obeyesekere's terms, a rebirth eschatology is any system of beliefs incorporating the view

6 Mead 1912: 170.

7 Mead 1912: 162, 177–9.

8 Tatacharya 1967: 48. See also Radhakrishnan's contention that, 'While the conceptions of karma and rebirth are unquestionably the work of the Aryan mind, it need not be denied that the suggestions may have come from the aborigines [i.e. pre-Aryan inhabitants of the Indian subcontinent], who believed that after death their souls lived in animal bodies' (Radhakrishnan 2008: 104).

9 Obeyesekere 2002: 78.

10 Hick 1976: 22.

that at least some people, and perhaps some animals as well, will be reborn in a new form after their present life. This construal, taken on its own, says nothing about the ethical content of the beliefs at issue. But when Obeyesekere is drawing a contrast between rebirth eschatologies and karmic eschatologies the difference that he means to highlight is the specifically ethical one, that while a karmic eschatology remains a form of rebirth eschatology, it is one that has been ethicised. This means that the conception of rebirth has become one in which each person's future life is conditioned by the moral quality of the individual's present-life actions.[11]

Obeyesekere's narrative of transformation from simple rebirth eschatologies to specifically ethicised karmic eschatologies comprises two main steps. The first step is to form the belief that entry into the after-death world is dependent not exclusively on correct performance of religious rites but upon 'the ethical nature of one's this-worldly actions'. An element of this first step is that the 'other world' is conceived as being conducive to the appropriate reward or punishment of the deceased individual: 'Heavens and hells have to be invented in any ethicized eschatology.'[12] The second step is to speculate that, beyond sojourning in the 'other world', one's future earthly lives will also be 'ethically conditioned', taking forms consistent with and at least partially determined by the quality of one's moral behaviour in a previous life or lives.[13] Once the two steps of this conceptual shift have occurred, Obeyesekere maintains, 'a concomitant epistemological shift takes place', which involves viewing rebirth not as '*a thing in itself*' but as '*a product of the ethical nature of one's actions*'. From this new perspective, 'Rebirth cannot be divorced from ethics; it looks as if it is generated *from* ethics.'[14]

Obeyesekere frames his presentation of this two-step narrative as an 'imaginary experiment', an approach that he derives from Max Weber, who speaks of using imagination to extrapolate from experientially acquired knowledge to historical claims that are at least 'objectively possible'.[15] In contrast with Weber's talk of objective possibility, however, Obeyesekere's suggestion of logical necessity seems inapposite. On the face of it his imaginative model, with its two main steps and their respective ramifications, constitutes a speculative reconstruction of how *karma*-imbued conceptions of rebirth emerged in South Asia around the middle centuries of the first millennium BCE. So it comes as a surprise when he implies that the emergence 'must logically' have happened

11 Obeyesekere 2002: 79–80, 247.
12 Obeyesekere 2002: 79.
13 Obeyesekere 2002: 80.
14 Obeyesekere 2002: 82; original emphasis.
15 Weber 1949: 174–5; cf. Obeyesekere 2002: 18.

this way. By using this vocabulary, Obeyesekere blurs the distinction between an account of the historical (diachronic) development of particular beliefs and practices and an account of the logical (synchronic) relations between different conceptual features of those beliefs and practices.

What Obeyesekere says about a karmic eschatology's having become ethicised in the way he describes makes most sense when understood as an analytic description of what a particular conception of rebirth *is*; as an analysis, that is, of the strands of interconnected thought and practice that constitute the religious and cultural phenomenon that Obeyesekere terms 'karmic eschatology'. When understood in this way, it provides what some philosophers, influenced by Ludwig Wittgenstein and Gilbert Ryle, have called a conceptual 'map', or what others have termed 'connective analysis'.[16] As characterised by Peter Hacker, the latter kind of analysis 'is concerned with describing and clarifying the concepts we employ in discourse about ourselves and about the world, and in elucidating their relationships – their forms of relative priority, dependency, and interdependency'.[17] Admittedly, the concepts that Obeyesekere seeks to describe and clarify, being specifically those concerning rebirth, might not be ones that *we* employ, since many of his readers will not be believers in rebirth themselves. But if 'we' in the passage from Hacker is expanded to encompass any given human community, then Hacker's sketch of connective analysis seems to fit what Obeyesekere is up to fairly well.

Even when considered under the aspect of conceptual connective analysis, Obeyesekere's use of the logical 'must' may still sound too categorical to many philosophical readers. This is because he implies that if certain basic conceptual factors are in place then, regardless of the details of any particular cultural milieu, certain other factors will necessarily also be there. The approach displays what Wittgenstein would call a 'craving for generality' modelled on the explanatory methods of natural science, carrying with it the danger of overlooking what is important in particular cases.[18] Fortunately, Obeyesekere avoids an exclusive preoccupation with schematic generalisations by also devoting attention to specific textual sources, such as the *Upaniṣads*, and to religious traditions such as Buddhism and the Ājīvika sect.[19] When examining these sources and traditions there is no problem with presenting one's account as historical, since relevant historical evidence is available. The problem with Obeyesekere's treatment of

[16] For the term 'connective analysis', see, e.g., Strawson 1992: ch. 2. For discussion of conceptual 'maps' or 'the metaphor of logical or conceptual geography', see Baker and Hacker 2005: 284.

[17] Hacker 2004: 352.

[18] See Wittgenstein 1969: 17–18.

[19] For discussion of the Ājīvikas, see Obeyesekere 2002: 102–8.

rebirth on which I have focused is his insistence that a speculative historical account – an 'imaginary experiment' – has the force of logical necessity. This insistence, and the assumption of metaphysical priority that underlies it, will be challenged in the remainder of this chapter.

Challenging the assumption of metaphysical priority

In an essay on Pythagoras, Empedocles and Plato, Catherine Osborne examines these three philosophers' ideas on the relation between transmigration and ethical attitudes towards animals. The thesis for which she argues has a negative and a positive aspect. Its negative aspect is that, contrary to a common presupposition, it is not the case that each of the philosophers first devised a theory of transmigration according to which human souls can be reborn as members of other species and then, on that basis, developed a moral outlook advocating vegetarianism and respectful treatment of animals. This presupposition is a version of what I have termed the assumption of metaphysical priority. Though Osborne does not herself name any particular exemplars, we see the assumption typified in numerous places. For instance, it is often claimed of the Orphic religion, which is commonly held to have been a forerunner of Pythagorean thought, that its prohibition of eating meat is based on a belief in transmigration. As William Guthrie puts it:

> The reasoning was this. If the soul of a man may be reborn in a beast, and rise again from beast to man, it follows that soul is one, and all life akin. Hence the most important Orphic commandment, the commandment to abstain from meat, since all meat-eating is virtually cannibalism.[20]

Whether or not this *was* the line of reasoning, most modern commentators certainly assume it to have been, not only in the case of the Orphics but also in the thought of the philosophers with whom Osborne is concerned.[21] There are exceptions, such as Radcliffe Edmonds, who writes in a recent book that 'the earliest references to vegetarianism associated with Orpheus stress purity with no hint of the idea of reincarnation', adding that 'we must not let the assumption of a doctrine of reincarnation distract us from other interesting possibilities'.[22] But such openness to other possibilities deviates from the predominant interpretive trend. Obeyesekere accords with the trend when he takes it for granted that belief in animal rebirth 'explains' the Pythagorean 'injunction against consuming

[20] Guthrie 1993: 196.

[21] See, e.g., Walters and Portmess 2001: 2, Simons 2010: 159.

[22] Edmonds 2013: 290.

flesh'.[23] It is even occasionally asserted by some that belief in transmigration 'leads logically to vegetarianism',[24] an assertion that faces many historical counter-examples, one especially poignant instance being the Jewish Kabbalists who maintain that the ritual slaughter of an animal for human consumption 'is an act of compassion' because it enables the animal's soul to rise to the human sphere where it can attain a conception of God as ruler of the earth.[25]

The positive aspect of Osborne's thesis requires some clarification, as I argue below; but its gist is articulated in the following passage:

> The claim that these beasts have human souls, and that they are related to us as close family members, is an *expression* of a distinctive outlook on the world, in which one can come to hold such creatures dear and find oneself as one of them (but temporarily in human form). The theory does not ground the moral advice; rather, the moral outlook generates the theoretical justification.[26]

Underlying Osborne's thesis is a more general contention regarding the asymmetrical relation between theories and evaluative judgements. According to Osborne, while any theory or collection of information about the respective biological or psychological characteristics of humans and animals cannot avoid being guided by value judgements, the theory or body of information itself lacks any power to guide our evaluative perceptions and activities. So, for example, a taxonomy of animal species based on similarities and differences between them will inevitably be guided by judgements concerning which features of the respective species are important for classificatory purposes; yet the taxonomy itself cannot usefully inform our estimations of how different species ought to be treated. 'There is', Osborne writes, 'no reason to suppose that the lines of division drawn up for a taxonomy of species include any differences that are morally relevant.'[27]

In the light of this underlying conception of the relation between theories and evaluations, Osborne's thesis regarding Pythagoras, Empedocles and Plato can be read as the claim that, irrespective of what these philosophers *thought* they were doing, it cannot be the case that their dedication to animal welfare derived from value-neutral reflection upon psychological resemblances between humans and animals, with these resemblances in turn being taken to indicate cross-species transmigration. This cannot be so because such reflection is invariably guided by evaluative commitments while being impotent to generate any

23 Obeyesekere 2002: 191.
24 Spencer 1996: 74.
25 Rabbi Nosson Sternhartz of Breslov (1780–1844), *Likkutei Halachos, Eiver Min HaChai* 2:1, quoted in Sears 2003: 289.
26 Osborne 2007: 45.
27 Osborne 2007: 60.

such commitments itself. Osborne is not denying that a link exists between the philosophers' advocacy of vegetarianism and their belief in the transmigration of souls; rather, as the passage quoted above indicates, she is reversing the routinely assumed order of logical and chronological priority. Instead of its being the metaphysical theory that grounds the moral outlook, it is the 'moral outlook that generates the theoretical justification'.

Although I, too, want to question the assumption of metaphysical priority, there are two doubts that I have concerning Osborne's way of doing this. First, her thesis relies on an equivocation over notions such as 'values' and 'evaluation'; and second, the thesis remains uncertain whether to merely reverse the standard order of priority between metaphysics and ethics or instead to abandon the assumption that there need be any order of priority at all. I shall elaborate each of these doubts in turn, and in discussing the second of them it will become clear that my own sympathies favour the downplaying of any supposedly sharp distinction between metaphysical theory and moral or ethical outlook.

Equivocating on 'values'

It is plainly true that taxonomical theories regarding similarities and differences between various animal species, including humans, will be guided (albeit normally implicitly rather than explicitly) by evaluative judgements or attitudes about which features of the species concerned should be attended to. But it does not follow that these judgements or attitudes are themselves *ethical* in nature. By analogy, my decision to go shopping may depend on a logically prior evaluation that my food cupboard needs restocking, but this does not entail that the latter evaluation is an ethical one. While there remains room for debate over where the boundaries of the ethical lie, it would be tendentious to extend the boundary so far that every evaluative judgement became eo ipso an expression of ethics.[28] Thus it sounds suspicious when Osborne moves from the non-contentious claim that 'How we classify the animals and plants that are the subject of biology will depend upon the needs that the system of classification is required to serve' to the contentious proposal that, when Pythagoras, Empedocles and Plato emphasise the commonality of 'capacities and origins' between ourselves and other creatures, 'Their claims were based on a revised moral understanding of how the world is divided.'[29]

Admittedly, there is an intermediate step in Osborne's argument. This involves citing a particular example from the *Timaeus* of how, in offering 'a

[28] In common with both Obeyesekere and Osborne, I am not drawing a distinction between 'ethics' and 'morality'.

[29] Osborne 2007: 60, 61.

taxonomy according to the habitat that a creature occupies', Plato 'builds a set of value judgements into that classification by suggesting that one gets closer to the earth the more disabled one's intellectual powers'.[30] Osborne submits that, rather than having first observed the intellectual powers of various creatures and then inferred the correlation between these powers and the creatures' proximity to the earth, Plato's deliberations were imbued from the outset with evaluative associations such as those of 'higher' and 'lower'. Plato assigns, for example, weaker intellects to worms than to birds 'because he despises the weaker intellects, and because he thinks that worms are low on the *scala naturae*'.[31] In other words, he has already decided which animals are least (morally) valuable before he contrives a system that ranks them according to their alleged intellectual capacities and proximity to the earth.

While the example just cited pertinently illustrates Osborne's thesis, the thesis' generality relies on the underlying contention that systems of classification are substantially influenced by value judgements and that these judgements are specifically moral. It is still not obvious that this is so; and even in the exemplary case of Plato the situation may be more complicated than Osborne allows. Might he not have had other reasons for assigning weaker intellects to worms than to birds, over and above his ranking them lower in the scale of nature? One might, for example, consider the behaviour of birds to be more complex than that of worms and hold complexity of behaviour to be correlated with intellectual capacity. If someone such as Plato had taken this view, it might remain true that he despised weaker intellects, but it would become less credible that his judging worms to have weaker intellects than birds was *due to* (or at least partially due to) his underlying evaluation of worms as less morally worthy than birds. Whether this latter suggestion applies to Plato himself is hard to determine, yet the fact that it *might* should forestall our assuming that his verdict on worm intellects must be a consequence of his moral attitude. Clearly, Plato's conception of intellectual capacity is bound up with his understanding of moral worth, but it is the idea that one of these must precede and undergird the other that is questionable.

While discussing Plato, we should also note the uncertainty about how seriously to take his remarks on animals and transmigration. Some commentators surmise that the whole passage from *Timaeus* 91d to 92a is intended to be humorous. According to Alfred Taylor, for example, Plato's 'lumping together' of various sea creatures into one category 'should show that we are dealing with humour, not with science'.[32] Osborne, while not deeming Plato's taxonomy to be merely humorous, would not deem it to be merely scientific either; and I concur

[30] Osborne 2007: 60.
[31] Osborne 2007: 61.
[32] Taylor 1928: 644.

with her on that. Part of what she takes Plato to be doing is encouraging his readers to see the positions of relative height and proximity to the earth as value-laden, and these identifications – of height with goodness and lack of height with badness – are 'not written into nature to be discovered by science'.[33] We might add that Taylor's dichotomy between humour and science leaves out the live possibility that the taxonomy's significance is best characterised neither as humour nor as science, but as something that combines playfulness with other purposes, such as serious allegory or an ontology that fuses biological with spiritual and ethical qualities.

Whether Plato was himself a vegetarian and whether he actually believed in transmigration both remain disputed matters. With regard to the first issue, after considering the textual evidence Daniel Dombrowski goes no further than 'to reserve the possibility that Plato was a vegetarian, or, at the very least, was supportive of vegetarian thought'.[34] With regard to the second, the principal bone of contention is whether Plato used the idea of transmigration only 'as a myth to convey ethical admonition' or whether his belief went deeper than that.[35] Again on the basis of close textual analysis, Dorothy Tarrant concludes that, on the whole, the topic of transmigration is treated with sufficient seriousness in those of Plato's dialogues in which it is discussed to substantiate 'the view that he did believe in the doctrine itself'.[36] Few scholars deny, however, that the body of Plato's works hardly presents a consistent perspective on the issue.[37] Though I cannot enter into these disputes here, they illustrate the knot of difficulties that confronts anyone trying to settle the question of whether ethics or metaphysics has logical priority in Plato's worldview. Difficulties of comparable severity – compounded all the more by the relative unavailability of primary textual material – hamper the exegetical task in the cases of Pythagoras and Empedocles.[38]

Reversing the order of priority – or abandoning it?

Turning now to my second worry concerning Osborne's thesis, this was that the thesis betrays uncertainty over whether to merely reverse the standard order of priority between moral outlook and rebirth theory or instead to dispense with the

33 Catherine Rowett (formerly Osborne), personal communication, 24 January 2012.
34 Dombrowski 1984: 62.
35 Tarrant 1948: 32.
36 Tarrant 1948: 32.
37 For discussion of the primary sources, see Ehnmark 1957.
38 See Kahn 2001, esp. ch. 1, for a lucid account of why Pythagoras is 'one of the most fascinating and mysterious figures of antiquity' (1). The same author discusses salient difficulties associated with the interpretation of Empedocles' fragments in Kahn 1960.

idea of an order of priority altogether. Osborne seems principally to be saying of the philosophers she discusses that, instead of regarding their conception of rebirth as grounding their moral outlook, we should see their moral outlook as grounding their conception of rebirth. She says, for example, that 'To change whom we see as kin, we must first change our moral outlook',[39] thereby implying that the moral outlook can change independently of whom we see as kin but that changing whom we see as kin requires changing our moral outlook. Osborne proceeds to say of Pythagoras, Empedocles and Plato that they 'give us a story to explain how souls can transmigrate and how we might all be kin, but the story is there to defend and promote a revisionary moral outlook', again implying that the moral outlook precedes the story of transmigration.

Earlier, however, in a passage that I have quoted already, Osborne asserts of the claim that animals 'have human souls, and . . . are related to us as close family members', that this 'is an *expression* of a distinctive outlook on the world, in which one can come to hold such creatures dear and find oneself as one of them (but temporarily in human form)'. Here, Osborne's emphasis on 'expression' suggests not that the 'distinctive outlook on the world' preexists the theory of human-to-animal transmigration, but that the outlook *takes the form of* or *is articulated in terms of* this theory. Under this description, we are not forced to say that if the theory of animal–human relations is to be changed 'we must first change our moral outlook', for there is a sense in which the theory and moral outlook are one. There is no logical gap between them: we see what the theory of transmigration means *in* the forms of ethical judgement and action that constitute the moral outlook. For this reason it would make no less sense to describe the moral outlook as expressing the claim that animals have human souls than it does to say that the claim that animals have human souls expresses the moral outlook. We could also describe both of these as expressions of one integrated picture.

If Osborne would agree with the points I have just made, then her real thesis could be formulated by saying that the transmigration theories of Pythagoras, Empedocles and Plato are infused with moral value and commitments from the outset. It is not that the theory is logically and chronologically prior to the moral outlook, but neither need it be that 'the moral outlook generates the theoretical justification'. Rather, what we have is a unified way of being with, and responding to, animals in the world – an outlook that views animals and humans as a community of commonly 'ensouled' creatures.[40]

Wittgenstein, in his 'Remarks on Frazer's *Golden Bough*', makes a point

[39] Osborne 2007: 62.

[40] Cf. Osborne's remark that Empedocles, Plato and Pythagoreans conceive of animals not merely as ensouled (*empsucha*), but as possessing '*exactly the same* kind of souls as we have' (2007: 59).

that resembles the one I have just been making. What Wittgenstein is objecting to is James Frazer's purported explanation of the ancient rite of succession at Nemi, in which the successor had to kill the incumbent priest-king. More precisely, Wittgenstein is not so much criticising the particular explanation that Frazer offers, as questioning Frazer's assumption that an explanation must disclose a belief upon which the action is based. Wittgenstein writes of Frazer that,

> When, for example, he explains to us that the king must be killed in his prime, because the savages believe that otherwise his soul would not be kept fresh, all one can say is: where that practice and these views occur together, the practice does not spring from the view, but they are both just there.[41]

This remark was written in 1931 shortly after Wittgenstein's first acquaintance with Frazer's text. In a later manuscript from 1945 Wittgenstein makes a similar point with reference to cultures in which people hold what, when rendered into a European language, is expressed as the belief that they are descended from an animal (such as a snake). In response to those who would then describe various practices of the culture as 'based on this belief', Wittgenstein asks rhetorically: 'But why should we not say: these customs and laws are not *based* on that belief, but they show *to what extent*, in what sense, such a belief exists.'[42]

Although Wittgenstein is writing in condensed form, he is evidently resisting the assumption that we must postulate an order of priority between belief and practice – an order in which the belief, or view, provides the rationale for the practice. How far Wittgenstein is going in the direction of rejecting all attempts at explanation is a moot point.[43] For present purposes all that needs to be noted is that he is identifying the absence of any necessity to suppose that the practice is based on a prior belief. Both the belief and the practice – or, better, the belief–practice nexus – may, to use Osborne's phrase, express 'a distinctive outlook on the world'. It follows from this that neither are we forced simply to reverse the direction of influence and say that the belief is based on the practice (or on the moral outlook).

It is worth pausing to register the philosophical dangers associated with using the term 'expression' in these contexts. For when Osborne says that the transmigration claims of Pythagoras and others are 'an *expression* of a distinctive outlook on the world', some critics will hear this as a denial that these philosophers 'really' believed in transmigration at all, and will assume that in debates such as those to which I alluded in the previous section, concerning

[41] Wittgenstein 1993: 119.

[42] Wittgenstein 2000: MS 116, p. 283; my translation.

[43] For discussion of what Wittgenstein is up to in his remarks on Frazer, see Clack 1999, esp. chs 4 and 5, Needham 1985: ch. 7, and Burley 2012: ch. 1.

whether Plato for instance treated transmigration merely 'as a myth to convey ethical admonition', Osborne is coming down firmly on the side of those who maintain that he did. In short, such critics will perceive Osborne as offering a reductive, non-realist, non-cognitivist analysis of the philosophers' transmigration-talk: non-realist in the sense that the talk does not entail belief in the reality of transmigration, and non-cognitivist in the sense that it does not aim to articulate knowledge about the world but merely to express value judgements. It is thus reductive inasmuch as, by eliminating any cognitive or truth-apt content from the transmigration-related pronouncements of the philosophers, it reduces those pronouncements to 'mere' expressions. Although I doubt whether Osborne would look favourably upon this construal of her thesis, her claim that 'the moral outlook generates the theoretical justification' may unwittingly invite it.

One way of reclaiming Osborne's thesis from the reductive reading involves rejecting the dualistic conception of facts and values on which the reading depends. To construe in non-realist or non-cognitivist terms the assertion that transmigration-claims express moral values, one would have to assume that moral values are incapable of connecting with reality in ways that are true or knowledge-bearing. Relinquishing *this* assumption facilitates our conceiving of transmigration-claims as true, without necessarily affirming that the criteria for their being true must conform to those that apply to, say, statements of empirical science. We may, for example, allow that they could be *morally* true or *metaphysically* true without our thereby implying that transmigration beliefs are empirically testable. A further, related, way of resisting the reductive reading of Osborne's thesis would be to reject the Cartesian metaphysical assumption that states of mind (including beliefs and value-commitments) are logically independent of and prior to the actions and responses that they are supposed to causally initiate. If, as argued by Wittgenstein and Gilbert Ryle for example, it is *in* our actions and responses that our beliefs and values are characteristically seen, then the picture of an expression of a belief or value being logically (conceptually) detachable from the belief or value itself loses its appeal.[44]

These latter thoughts are taking us further than my purposes in this chapter require. My principal reason for discussing Osborne's proposal has been to indicate how a certain presupposition might be brought into question, the presupposition being that the relation between a theory of rebirth or transmigration and a moral outlook must be one of logical and historical priority, wherein it is the theory that holds the prior position. Osborne displaces this presupposition by, apparently, switching the order of priority. What I have argued is that even this switching presupposes a division of roles between 'theory' and 'outlook', or 'belief' and 'practice', that need not be present. At the very least, we should

[44] See, e.g., Ryle 2009: 116–18. For discussion of Wittgenstein, see Churchill 1984.

question the viability of this postulated division rather than simply accepting that it is there.

Conclusions

A way of misreading the present chapter would be to see it as proposing a thoroughgoing scepticism about explanation in matters of religious or metaphysical belief. I have not been arguing that there is anything necessarily misguided about seeking explanations for how particular forms of belief, such as beliefs in *karma* and rebirth, came about in specific historical circumstances. What I have been arguing is that, in cases where clear evidence is lacking, there are certain assumptions that we should be wary of making. Central among these is the assumption that belief in rebirth – that is, the belief that in some sense each of us undergoes not a single lifetime but a series of lifetimes either in human or in some other form – must preexist and give rise to the systems of ethics that come to be associated with it. This is an instance of the more general assumption that metaphysical beliefs are logically and chronologically prior to ethical values and practices; or, more concisely, that metaphysics necessarily precedes ethics. It is an assumption of this sort, I have argued, that underlies Obeyesekere's speculative reconstruction of the process by which 'rebirth eschatologies' became 'karmic eschatologies' in ancient South Asian religious traditions – a process that Obeyesekere terms 'ethicisation'. While not claiming that this account is necessarily false, I have argued that it lacks the force of logical necessity that Obeyesekere attributes to it.

An implication of accepting Obeyesekere's thesis would be that the extent to which non-karmic conceptions of rebirth are also bound up with ethical values and practices is liable to be missed. This is because, by characterising the transition from rebirth eschatology to karmic eschatology in terms of ethicisation, the impression is given that the non-karmic conceptions must be non- or pre-ethical. The truth is that these conceptions are very rarely, if ever, dissociable from ethical values and practices, and hence the term 'ethicisation' as used by Obeyesekere is a misnomer.[45]

By adducing Osborne's contention concerning the relation between ethics and metaphysics in the thought of Pythagoras, Empedocles and Plato, I have

[45] I discuss this matter at greater length in Burley 2013 and in Burley 2016: ch. 4. The present chapter expands and refines early portions of the argument advanced in those two publications. See also Mills (1994: 17): 'One problem with Obeyesekere's distinction between the Buddhist/Hindu/Jain concepts of reincarnation as "ethicized" and tribal concepts . . . as "unethicized" is that it masks the fact that tribal eschatologies also contain ethical premises.'

illustrated one way of challenging the assumption of metaphysical priority upon which the sort of thesis advanced by Obeyesekere depends. By highlighting an apparent equivocation in Osborne's argument and discussing an ambiguity in the alternative picture of the metaphysics–ethics relation that she is putting forward, I have sought to develop a clearer version of that alternative picture. Drawing upon the thought of Wittgenstein, the picture is one in which the relation between metaphysical beliefs or theories on the one hand and ethical values, practices or outlook on the other is not one of logical or chronological priority; the former do not generate the latter and neither do the latter generate the former, 'but they are both just there'. This picture is intended not to explain how any particular conception of rebirth in fact came about, but rather to loosen the grip of competing pictures by which we might otherwise be held captive, pictures according to which not only must a clear division obtain between metaphysics and ethics but there must also be an order of priority between them.[46]

As for the relation between the respective conceptions of rebirth in ancient Greece and India, my purpose has not been to say anything directly about it. What we can say, however, is that the tasks of comparing them and theorising about their possible historical connections depend upon clear-sighted hermeneutical investigations of the conceptions in question. These investigations are prone to vitiation if we bring with us suspect assumptions concerning how ethics and metaphysics 'must' be related. Freeing ourselves from those assumptions can at least play a part in setting the conditions for the kind of inquiry that is demanded.

[46] I borrow the well-known metaphor of being held captive by a picture from Wittgenstein 1967: §115.

15

On affirmation, rejection and accommodation of the world in Greek and Indian religion

Matylda Obryk

Since its coinage by Jaspers, scholars have been looking for an explanation for the changes that Indian and Greek cultures (and many others) seem to have gone through in the so-called Axial Age.[1] This is the time in which the so-called Greek Enlightenment and the Upaniṣadic turn in Indian philosophy took place (roughly a period of several centuries from the eighth to the second century BCE). I will apply to this development a typology coined by Roy Wallis, a sociologist working on new religious movements in the 1980s. Wallis analyses *par excellence* new religious movements from a static perspective. However, his typology might be understood even more broadly and provide a frame within which even the dynamics of the development of cultures may find a plausible explanation. We will also see that light on the similarities between Axial Age developments may be shed by an Indian concept of human development[2] concerning the attitudes of humans towards their environment in a widest possible sense. We should also note from the beginning that in the most ancient cultures there is no way to draw a sharp distinction between the secular and religious spheres of life, and therefore issues of both religious and philosophical character will be discussed in parallel here.[3]

Wallis divides religious movements into three categories according to their attitudes towards the values and settings of the surrounding world. Wallis's first category is the world-affirming type wherein the world is being embraced and accepted as it appears in order to achieve goals that are immanently connected

[1] Jaspers 1949: passim.

[2] That the Indian philosophy includes three paths to salvation (*karma-marga*, *jñana-marga* and *bhakti-marga*) is widely known (Sikora 2002: 15). Within the Vaishnava Bengali tradition there is to be spotted a notion of the progress from one to the other (see below).

[3] Cf. McPherran 1996: 20.

with the life within this world as such – happiness, prosperity and so on.[4] The second type would then encompass the world-rejecting movements. They reject the values and mind-sets that derive from the world, and very often strongly renounce and negate all that comes from the world of senses.[5] And finally the third type is the world-accommodating type wherein the world is understood and moulded in such a way that it has to be neither rejected nor fully embraced but just seen from a new perspective or engaged in a new attitude.[6]

Wallis' concern is with the attitudes towards the *values* of the society wherein a particular movement develops. However, a case could be made for widening the perspective so as to examine the attitudes towards the world and its components. The question of the main relation (either affirming, rejecting or accommodating) of each philosophy or religious movement to the world will be therefore central.

The Indian paradigm

As already mentioned, those three attitudes towards the world correspond to a paradigm found in the Indian scriptures. The Vedas contain a vast amount of different instructions. The first portion of them (the *Ṛg-*, *Sāma-*, *Atharva-* and *Yajur-veda* which make up about 90 per cent of the Veda) pertain to the path of *karma* and are therefore technically speaking *karma-kāṇḍa*. The oldest text (the *Ṛgveda*) is traditionally dated back to BCE 1450–1350 and the whole Vedic period spans a time frame of roughly 1,000 years.[7] *Karma-kāṇḍa* is the science of ritualistic acts and sacrifices, and aims at controlling the gods, who then become bound by the very performance of the rituals to act as requested by the worshippers.

For instance in the *Śatapatha Brāhmaṇa* (the *brāhmaṇas* are the part of the Veda that describes rituals) it is said:

> And when he offers in the morning before sunrise, then he produces that (sun-child) and, having become a light, it rises shining. But, assuredly, it would not rise, were he not to make that offering: this is why he performs that offering. (ŚB 2.3.1, 5)

The aim of the ritual is therefore to make the world – through the medium of diverse divinities – function according to one's needs and desires. The performer of the ritual is considered to have power over the world. The ritual is used as a somewhat mechanical technology that ensures the world's functioning: the

4 Wallis 1984: 20–35.
5 Wallis 1984: 9–20.
6 Wallis 1984: 35–9.
7 Witzel 2003: 68.

performance of a certain ritual forces the gods to comply with the sacrificer's wish. The polytheistic structure of the divine sphere is on this path immanently embedded into the concept of rituals.[8] The ultimate goal of performing these sacrifices appears therefore to be a 'happy life' that is basically understood as having better opportunities for enjoyment. On this path the heavenly planets, which in their depictions vividly resemble Western ideas of paradise, are the highest goal.[9] Within this realm the environment and the world are used as a tool for achieving one's own ends and are therefore accepted as they appear. The main characteristics of this path are therefore rituals aimed at satisfying different divinities in order to achieve one's personal goals. The divinities are prevalently regarded as being immanent, embedded in this very sphere of the world where the humans dwell, and resemble humans in almost all personal features. They therefore enable human beings to establish a relationship with them similar to that with the powerful personalities of this world (cf. the personal relationship of Odysseus with Athena in Homer's *Odyssey*). This path and its outlook resemble Wallis' world-affirming type.

Another portion of the Veda deals with the liberation that is to be achieved on the path of cultivating knowledge about the suffering that derives from the very contact with the world.[10] The *Upaniṣads* are the main source for this path, called *jñāna*. The *Upaniṣads* are a part of the Vedas, but in them the philosophical attempt at understanding the world became prominent, and they are commonly regarded as being anti-ritualistic. Traditionally they are dated to the period of BCE 800–200, which corresponds smoothly with the Jasperian Axial Age and the rationalistic revolution in Greece.[11] As simply being in this world is considered to be the cause of suffering, adherents to this path claim it is necessary to free oneself from the bondage of this world. This liberation is to be achieved through the cessation of all *karma*. *Karma* means action and therefore work. The law of *karma* dictates that every action enforces a reaction: as long as there is action, a reaction in the form of either enjoyment or suffering will follow. As long as a reaction is to be experienced, the living entity is bound to remain in the world and always pursue a new body after the previous one has worn out. As the path of *karma* is *par excellence* action and therefore produces reactions (even

8 Siegel 1978: 420.

9 Cf. Keith 1925: 581.

10 For the *Upaniṣads* as the main literature for the person pursuing the *jñana*-path, cf. *Aruni Upaniṣad* 7; Olivelle 1992: 228 n10; Olivelle 2014: 10. For the conflict of the values between the ritualistic (*Brahminic/karmic*) and the renouncer path (*jñana-marga*) of the Hindu tradition see Olivelle 2003: passim, esp. 275–7.

11 Cf. Witzel 2003: 83–6. Olivelle points to the fact that any dating of the *Upaniṣads* is as stable as a house of cards (2014: 12). But this roughly dated period of six centuries corresponds with the opinion of most scholars.

if good or predominantly good, but nevertheless binding), it is rejected. On the path of *jñāna* the goal is considered to be lasting[12] and transcendental (liberation from the world), and therefore it cannot be achieved by mundane means.[13] On this path the search for the divine reaches into transcendence and is achieved through the means of rejection. The concept of divinity becomes increasingly impersonal. The yoga path sees the *iśvara*, god, as being totally distinct from nature and removed from everyday experience. The concept of *brahman*, as the supreme force is called in *jñāna*, is pantheistic in its outline. Finally the Sāṃkhya school and then the Buddhist school arrive at a somewhat atheistic conception of the divine. They arrive at the notion that the supreme is Nothing.[14] This is a perfected rejection that corresponds clearly with Wallis' second type.

Finally, there is the path of reconciliation. Reconciliation comes from the realisation of the fact that negation is ultimately bound to what is negated (to say non-A, one first has to think of A) and therefore it cannot lead to the Absolute. Furthermore, the realisation that the rejection demanded by *jñāna* is ultimately a false renunciation[15] leads to the path of *upāsanā* (which means meditation, as this is the process of getting into contact with a new type of divine) as Ramanuja[16] called it – or in later literature – *bhakti* (devotion). The *bhakti* reconciliation entails an engagement with the world and its components – for instance the para-

[12] The reactions enjoyed or suffered on the *karma*-path are regarded as temporal and compared to a bank account that can simply be used up.

[13] Or even described by any mundane means. Therefore the definition by negation is prevalent on this path. Similar notions occur in the KaU 1.2.10: 'By non-permanent works the Permanent is not obtained', or MuU 1.2.7: 'Frail indeed are those boats, the sacrifices'. Therefore the injunction is to seek *jñana*: MuU 1.2, 12.13: 'Let a Brahmana, after he has examined all these worlds that are gained by works, acquire freedom from all desires. What is not made cannot be gained by what is made . . .'

[14] Cf. Siegel 1978: 420.

[15] *Bhaktirasāmṛta Sindhu*, by a seventeenth-century author of the Bengali Vishnuite tradition, Rupa Goswami, makes the distinction between right and wrong renunciation: *anāsaktasya viṣayān yathārham upayuñjataḥ / nirbandhaḥ kṛṣṇa-sambandhe yuktaṁ vairāgyam ucyate* ('Things should be accepted for the Lord's service and not for one's personal sense gratification. If one accepts something without attachment and accepts it because it is related to Krishna [Supreme God], one's renunciation is called *yukta-vairāgya*.') . . . *prāpañcikatayā buddhyā hari-sambandhi-vastunaḥ / mumukṣubhiḥ parityāgo vairāgyam phalgu kathyate* ('When persons eager to achieve liberation renounce things related to the Supreme God, thinking them to be material, their renunciation is called incomplete' (Bhaktivedanta Swami 2004, CC. Madhya 19.170–1, quoting *Bhaktirasamrta Sindhu* 1.2.255–6).

[16] Ramanuja, a theologian of the Sri Vishnuite tradition of the eleventh/twelfth century, makes in his commentary on the first verse of the *Vedanta Sūtra* the point that ultimately the goal is to achieve happiness that in turn is to be found only when desires cease. This cessation of desires is only possible when the senses are properly engaged in meditation that is combined with work for the sake of the Supreme (Thibaut 1904: 18).

phernalia of worship – in the service of a transcendent yet immanent Supreme.[17] The goal is similar to that of the *jñāna* path: termination of mundane existence.[18] *Bhakti* is therefore supposed to transcend the sentimental affirmation of *karma* and the cynical rejection of *jñāna*. As *bhakti* encompasses a service towards the Supreme that is ultimately a symptom of a developing genuine loving relationship with the divine, it encourages a highly personal attitude towards the divinity.[19] Interestingly, Wallis also recognised that the personal feature is a special characteristic of the accommodating type of religious movements. The personal aspect of the third type will also become central in our discussion of its Greek equivalent.

The Hindu Vaishnava tradition of Bengal (Caitanyaite) claims that all cultures move along a progression: from *karma*, the world-affirming, through *jñāna*, the world-rejection, to *upāsanā*, or *bhakti*, the world-accommodating worldview.[20] An illustration of this progression can be found on a micro-scale in the *Bhagavad Gītā*, the central Hindu scripture. The *Gītā* is the key part of the *Mahābhārata*, an Indian epic that narrates the story of the conflict between two factions of one family: the Kurus and the Pandavas. The sons of two brothers – Dhṛtaraṣtra and Pandu – fight over the kingdom on the battlefield of Kurukṣetra. Just before the battle starts, Arjuna, one of the Pandavas and commander in chief of the Pandava army, asks his chariot driver, who happens to be Krishna (the Supreme God as becomes clear in due course) to drive him into the midst of the armies so he can have a look at his opponents. Seeing on the other side his cousins, grandfather and teacher, Arjuna breaks down and lays aside his bow (BG 1.46). He presents arguments for his desired withdrawal from the battlefield, but Krishna instructs him and explains in roughly 700 verses both the ultimate goal of life and the real and proper relationship of a human being to both the world and the Supreme.

17 About the transcendence and immanence of God on the path of *bhakti* (especially its late Bengali version of the Caitanyaites): 'God had to be transcendent because He was too great to be limited, and he had to be immanent, distinct from the self and personal, because He demanded love, passionate love' (Siegel 1978: 422).

18 On the highest stages of spiritual understanding on this path this liberation is solely a by-product of the love of God. And the attainment of that love is the real aim and goal of every *bhakta* (follower on the path of *bhakti*). On this path the revival of a dormant relationship with the Supreme Person is the goal and means by which all happiness is to be achieved (Siegel 1978: 422).

19 Raj Singh 2006: 19.

20 Correctly understood, *bhagavat-dharma*, as presented in the Bengali tradition by its prophet Caitanya and explicated by his followers Sanatana, Rupa and Jiva, is the all-inclusive religion, the religion of religion, in that it gives us a fruitful framework for grasping the whole range of human spiritual endeavours, both in their successes and their failures (from an email conversation with William Deadwyler aka Ravindra Svarupa Dasa, a scholar and practitioner of the *bhakti* path, from 14 October 2014; cf. also Deadwyler 1987: passim).

Gītā illustrates here a specific development. Dhṛtaraṣtra, the chief enemy of the Pandavas, is violating justice and the social order and therefore stands for sinful action. Arjuna, responding to the situation and having just suffered from a breakdown, tries to find the right response to the given circumstances. However, he considers restoring righteousness to be an action of the same type as violating it: he claims that it would be equal to performing duties with the goal of enjoying the fruits of action (BG 1.31). He rejects therefore the path of *karma*, the world-affirming process, and turns out of frustration and despair, to the opposite, which is considered to be higher by the scriptures themselves (BG 2.5).[21] He wants to renounce (reject) everything and head for the forest to live by begging. However, ultimately Krishna assures him that the path of rejection is not going to bring him full peace and satisfaction. The whole *Bhagavad Gītā* consists of Krishna persuading Arjuna to take to the path of accommodating his duties in the world in order to engage everything in the service of the Supreme, Krishna himself.[22] Therefore the tension between work as understood by Arjuna as being *karma*, and knowledge as a reflection of the cessation of action (*jñāna*), makes up the whole of the *Bhagavad Gītā*.[23]

This is in fact the very same progression: Arjuna first considers (and rejects) the path of *karma* – performing one's duties in order to enjoy the kingdom – and consequently feels attracted to the path of *jñāna*, the path of rejection, and tries renounce all his life and duties. It takes Krishna 700 verses to explain to him the value of reconciliation of both of them, *bhakti*, for an even higher purpose: service to the Supreme. And that promises him the ultimate fulfilment.

This development can also be discerned in a historical perspective. The Vedic period emphasised *karma-mīmāṃsā* or *karma-kāṇḍa*,[24] followed by the rise of *uttara-mīmāṃsā* (also called Vedānta) which makes up the Upaniṣadic

[21] The question of the value of each path can be found as well in the *Bhagavad Gītā* itself. In the beginning of chapter 5 Arjuna asks about the difference between *jñāna* and *bhakti*: 'O Krishna, first of all you ask me to renounce work (*karma*), and then again you recommend work with devotion. Now will you kindly tell me definitely which of the two is more beneficial?' And Krishna answers: 'The renunciation of work (*jñāna*) and work in devotion are both good for liberation. But, of the two, work in devotional service is better than renunciation of work' (BG 5.1–2). Further (5.3) it is stated that only one who is free from dualities of accepting and renouncing is completely liberated. Only one who has transcended the path of affirmation and rejection is truly free.

[22] This is most clearly stated in the last instruction Krishna gives to Arjuna (BG 18.66): *sarva-dharmān parityaja, mām ekaṁ śaraṇaṁ vraja / ahaṁ tvāṁ sarva-pāpebhyo, mokṣayiṣyāmi mā śucaḥ* ('Abandon all varieties of dharma and just surrender unto Me. I shall deliver you from all sinful reactions. Do not fear.').

[23] This tension is repeatedly voiced in the *Gītā*: the beginnings of chapter 3, 5 and 12.

[24] The Vedas in the traditional understanding encompass the *Ṛg*, *Sāma* and *Yajur Veda* and are called *śruti*; in Sanskrit: revealed scriptures (the root *śru* means to hear).

view on *brahman* and the world, and then by the rise of *bhakti*, initiated in South India in the seventh and eight centuries CE and swept northwards in a wave of devotion that engulfed India from about the twelfth to the fifteenth century.[25]

The Greek counterpart

The aim of this chapter is to test whether the progression I have described is to be discerned in Greek culture as well. Greek thought and culture seem to move along the path of ritualistic state religion with the immanent gods of the myths (corresponding to the *karma*-path); in the next step the rituals and gods meet with a scientific rejection (*jñāna*); finally there is a specific reconciliation of both, which can be traced for instance in the personal religion of Socrates or the theurgy of the Neoplatonists, both of which have a strong personal attitude towards the (nevertheless) transcendental divinity (*upāsanā* or *bhakti*).[26]

Polis religion

The religion of the *polis* provides a frame for the social structure and simultaneously, through rituals and sacrifices, claims to win control over the gods, who are therefore bound to perform according to the requests of their worshippers.[27]

Sacrifices played a central role in the life of every Greek citizen. They provided a timeframe, leisure and opportunity to accentuate one's social position, and – last but not least – the rare portion of sacrificial meat in the assembly of the feasters. Attendance at and the performance of such sacrifices were the central practices of the religion. Not *orthodoxy*, therefore, but *orthopraxy* was the criterion for being a good citizen and person.[28] The family altar and hearth was the centre of the micro-cosmos, as the city temples were the centres of civic life. Sacrifices were performed because they were a part of the inherited family tradition, and violating this tradition was considered to be a major breach of one's

25 Krishna in the *Bhagavad Gītā* (2.45) considers the three Vedas to be the core of the *karma-kāṇḍa* path. However, Olivelle (2014: 3) claims that the *Upaniṣads* are the major ancient influence on Hinduism. The progression from one path to the other is marked clearly in the commentary of Bhaktivedanta Swami on BG 2.45: 'When the activities for sense gratification, namely the karma-kāṇḍa chapter, are finished, then the chance for spiritual realisation is offered in the form of the Upaniṣads, which are part of different Vedas.'

26 For a similar depiction of this kind of progression – at least chronological – note Bruit Zaidmann and Schmitt Pantel 1992: 233–4.

27 Sourvinou-Inwood 2000: 24.

28 Bruit Zaidman and Schmitt Pantel (1992: 27) stress that not the acceptance of a specific dogma or belief was what held the community together but rather the right performance of ritual. The Vedic period with its rituals is also called the phase of *orthopraxy* (cf. Witzel 2003: 86).

duties. But besides their importance in perpetuating tradition, the rituals seem to have had a tangible outcome that was widely believed in and apparently experienced: prosperity both on the micro and the macro scale.

Isocrates speaks about the outcomes of the performed sacrifices with firm confidence:

> καὶ πρῶτον μὲν τὰ περὶ τοὺς θεοὺς . . . οὐκ ἀνομάλως οὐδ᾽ ἀτάκτως οὔτ᾽ ἐθεράπευον οὔτ᾽ ὠργίαζον· . . . καὶ γὰρ τοι καὶ τὰ παρὰ τῶν θεῶν οὐκ ἐμπλήκτως οὐδὲ ταραχωδῶς αὐτοῖς συνέβαινεν, ἀλλ᾽ εὐκαίρως καὶ πρὸς τὴν ἐργασίαν τῆς χώρας καὶ πρὸς τὴν συγκομιδὴν τῶν καρπῶν. (Isocrates *Areopagiticus* 29–30)
>
> First of all as to their conduct towards the gods they were not erratic or irregular in their worship of them or in the celebration of their rites; . . . And so also the gifts of the gods were visited upon them, not fitfully or capriciously, but seasonably both for the ploughing of the land and for the ingathering of its fruits. (trans. G. Norlin)

The performance of sacrifices, then, was necessarily one of the most important obligations of every citizen. And, if done properly, the results were supposed to be immediately tangible: the gods provided their gift in the forms of rain and dry weather according to the needs of their dependants.

Not only the weather depended on the performance of sacrifices. So did the well-being of whole states. We hear from Lysias that due to the strict following of laws the ancestors managed to bring forth a prosperous city. The state's good fortune depends solely on the rituals (τὰ ἱερά):

> οἱ τοίνυν πρόγονοι τὰ ἐκ τῶν κύρβεων θύοντες μεγίστην καὶ εὐδαιμονεστάτην τῶν Ἑλληνίδων τὴν πόλιν παρέδοσαν, ὥστε ἄξιον ἡμῖν τὰς αὐτὰς ἐκείνοις θυσίας ποιεῖσθαι, καὶ εἰ μηδὲν δι᾽ ἄλλο, τῆς τύχης ἕνεκα τῆς ἐξ ἐκείνων τῶν ἱερῶν γεγενημένης. (Lysias 30.18)
>
> Now our ancestors, by sacrificing in accordance with the tablets, have handed down to us a city superior in greatness and prosperity to any other in Greece; so that it behoves us to perform the same sacrifices as they did, if for no other reason than that of the success, which has resulted from those rites. (trans. W. R. M. Lamb)

One must (as Lysias himself insists) sacrifice according to the tradition of the homeland in order to assure its prosperity:

> ὅστις ἀξιῶ πρῶτον μὲν κατὰ τὰ πάτρια θύειν, ἔπειτα ἃ μᾶλλον συμφέρει τῇ πόλει (Lysias 30.19).
>
> First that our sacrifices be performed according to our ancestral rules, and second that they be those which tend to promote the interests of the city. (trans. W. R. M. Lamb)[29]

[29] These results are also the ultimate proof for the very existence of gods. By sacrificing according to the tradition one gets what one wanted. It follows that someone has to be there to be able to grant these benedictions (cf. Parker 2011: 3).

This process seems to be rather mechanistic: one has to perform a certain action in order to achieve the desired result.[30] There is no room for consideration of the inner attitude. The action itself is the key to the result. Therefore, it clearly resembles in this particular feature the path of *karma* of the Indian tradition.[31] In both cultures the rituals are employed to reach one's own ends and goals, which are understood as gaining prosperity for oneself and the city one was born in. The environment and the rituals have their role and function solely in the context of earthly existence and are directed towards divinities, who are considered to be immanent and personal. All these characteristics hint at the similarity between this form of Greek religion and the Indian phase of *karma*.

Philosophical rejection

Relatively early on in the development of Greek thought there seems to occur a departure from the mythological view of the world and the at times all-too-human gods and strictly ritualistic approach to divinity. This rejection is mainly connected with the philosophical search for the one primordial element. This one primordial element takes the place of the manifold Olympus of the polytheistic religion.

The earliest extant explicit critique of the traditional view starts with Xenophanes, who dismisses the anthropomorphic images of the gods and seeks after a transcendent (or monistic) god. A god who is unlike anything humans can experience on earth. Xenophanes dismisses in regard to gods everything that is based on everyday experience and pleads for an uncompromising monism that quite vividly resembles the Upaniṣadic tradition. In the following famous lines, he criticises the traditional views on gods as being relative and dependent on the given circumstances of the people creating them:

> ἀλλ' οἱ βροτοὶ δοκέουcι γενν̣ᾶcθαι θεοὺc,
> τὴν cφετέρην δ' ἐcθῆτα ἔχειν φωνήν τε δὲμαc τε. (21 DK B14)
>
> But mortals suppose that gods are born,
> wear their own clothes and have a voice and body.
>
> ἀλλ' εἰ χεῖραc ἔχον βόεc <ἵπποι τ'> ἠὲ λέοντεc
> ἢ γράψαι χείρεccι καὶ ἔργα τελεῖν ἅπερ ἄνδρεc,
> ἵπποι μέν θ' ἵπποιcι βόεc δέ τε βουcὶν ὁμοίαc
> καί <κε> θεῶν ἰδέαc ἔγραφον καὶ cώματ' ἐποίουν
> τοιαῦθ' οἷόν περ καὐτοι δέμαc εἶχον <ἕκαcτοι> (B15)

30 Apparently it worked as well the other way around: Suetonius tells that after the death of Germanicus the temples of the gods were destroyed, for they (the gods) did not provide the requested protection for the beloved Germanicus (Suetonius *Life of Caligula* 5).

31 This way of practising religion is encoded in the famous Latin phrase commenting on the religious attitudes of Romans: *do ut des* ('I give that you may give': cf. Rüpke 2007: 149).

But if horses or oxen or lions had hands
or could draw with their hands and accomplish such works as men,
horses would draw the figures of the gods as similar to horses and the oxen as similar to oxen,
and they would make the bodies
of the sort which each of them had.

Αἰθίοπέϲ τε <θεούϲ ϲφετέρουϲ> ϲιμοὺϲ μέλανάϲ τε
Θρῆκέϲ τε γλαυκοὺϲ καὶ πυρρούϲ <φαϲι πέλεϲθαι> (B16)

Aithiopians say that their gods are snub-nosed and black,
Thracians that they are blue-eyed and red-haired. (trans. J. H. Lesher)

Having rejected the traditional gods, he presents a constructive theology of a strict monism that resembles the Upaniṣadic view. Xenophanes claims that god is transcendent, completely unlike men: εἷϲ θεόϲ, ἐν δὲ θεοῖϲι καὶ ἀνθρώποιϲι μέγιϲτοϲ / οὔτι δέμαϲ θνητοῖϲιν ὁμοίιοϲ οὔδε νόημα, 'One god is greatest among gods and men, / not at all like mortals in body or in thought' (B23); that he does not have the necessity to move, as he moves the universe by his thought (B25–6); and that he sees, thinks and hears in his wholeness (B24). This divinity appears to be so different from the traditional gods that no relationship is possible between him (it?) and the world as such.[32]

Besides Xenophanes there were other philosophers who tended towards monism. Heraclitus for instance talks about the One God through opposites in a way that marks vividly the monistic approach – a breach from earthly dualism:[33]

ὁ θεὸϲ ἡμέρη εὐφρόνη, χειμὼν θέροϲ, πόλεμοϲ εἰρήνη, κόροϲ λιμόϲ· ἀλλοιοῦται δὲ ὅκωϲπερ πῦρ ὁπόταν ϲυμμιγῇ θυώμαϲιν ὀνομάζεται καθ' ἡδονὴν ἑκάϲτου [πῦρ]. (22 DK B67)

God is day and night, winter and summer, war and peace, plenty and want. But he is changed, just as when incense is mingled with incense, but named according to the pleasure of each. (trans. G. T. W. Patrick)[34]

32 Cf. Feyerabend 1987: 16.

33 Interestingly, such a definition through opposites is also found in the *Isopaniṣad* Mantra 5: *tad ejati tan naijati / tad dūre tad v antike / tad antar asya sarvasya / tad u sarvasyāsya bāhyataḥ* ('The Supreme Lord walks and does not walk. He is far away, but He is very near as well. He is within everything, and yet He is outside of everything.') And 8: *sa paryagāc chukram akāyam avraṇam / asnāviram śuddham apāpa-viddham / kavir manīṣī paribhūḥ svayambhūr / yāthātathyato, rthān vyadadhāc chāśvatibhyaḥ samābhyaḥ* ('Such a person must factually know the greatest of all, the Personality of Godhead, who is unembodied, omniscient, beyond reproach, without veins, pure and uncontaminated, the self-sufficient philosopher who has been fulfilling everyone's desire since time immemorial.') (trans. A. C. Bhaktivedanta Swami).

34 Here god is so much unlike men that any meaningful talk about him is impossible. The Platonic Parmenides (134e 2–4) makes the point very clear and marks the first step towards

Xenophanes and Heraclitus both claimed that there is one god. But this divinity took on different shapes in the hands of the various philosophers. Interestingly, out of similar considerations the *Upaniṣads* arrived at the (almost pantheistic) notion that everything is spirit (*brahman*). The Ionian philosophers and their followers deified the elements of nature: water, fire, air and so on. In that way the philosophers did not reject the idea of divinity but acknowledged that basically everything may be of divine nature. This notion was further developed by Anaxagoras, who saw the ἀρχή in the Mind and – having deified it – arrived at a strongly impersonal image of a deity.[35]

However, the gods were not rejected without taking into consideration the rituals that go along with them. Heraclitus criticises for instance the practice of prayer in front of images of the deity and compares it to having a conversation with or trying to talk to houses without understanding the true nature of gods (cf. B5). The idea of there being a true nature of the gods is a hint that they are considered by him not as immanent, belonging to the earthly realm, but rather as coming from a different dimension.

Plato goes a step further and calls sacrifices bribery.[36] However, this Platonic view, and the resulting notion that the attitude of the worshipper is far more important than the sacrifice itself, points towards an attempt at a personal relationship with the divinity and therefore to the next step in the development: the level of reconciliation (see below).

This turn to a monistic but rather impersonal view of the now transcendent divinity, coupled with the notion of its ineffability in comparison to the mythological gods suited to narrative, is a shared step in the development of Greek and Indian thought. Interestingly, they happened roughly in the same time-span (the earliest *Upaniṣads* are dated around 600–500 BCE; the Greek explosion of [so-called] rationalism starts around the same time).

Among the sages of the East this particular development is connected with a kind of frustration deriving from the realisation that the happiness achieved through the means of traditional religion is impermanent and shallow. The immediate reason for the Greek development is difficult to discern, although we

the development of apophatic theology: ἀλλὰ ὁμοίως ἡμεῖς τ' ἐκείνων οὐκ ἄρχομεν τῇ παρ' ἡμῖν ἀρχῇ οὐδὲ γιγνώσκομεν τοῦ θείου οὐδὲν τῇ ἡμετέρᾳ ἐπιστήμῃ ('we do not rule the gods with our authority, nor do we know anything of the divine with our knowledge' – trans. H. N. Fowler).

35 Cf. Price 1999: 129 and Muir 1985: 196.

36 *Leg.* 10.885b 7–9: '. . . or he believes that they (*scil.* the gods) are easily to be won over when bribed by offerings and prayers' (trans. R. G. Bury). Apparently Saint Paul had exactly the same criticism of this kind of religious behaviour. Businesslike religion, he claimed, has nothing to do with spirituality or developing a loving attitude towards the divine (Romans 4: 4).

can detect a similar frustration about the all-too-human relations with the gods and a longing for an all-encompassing explanation of the world and a monistic yet transcendent dimension.

Reconciliation: towards a personal religion

The third and last step in the development, which is represented in the Indian tradition by *bhakti*, is characterised through an attempt at establishing personal contact with the divinity by means of loving or devotional service towards god. This service consists of engaging the world in the worship of the Supreme. On this path it is not one's own satisfaction and pleasure that are central, but the pleasure of the divine. Within the Greek tradition it will be possible to detect similar reflections.

Besides calling traditional sacrifices bribery, Plato stressed that through the means of ritual and incantation one can win power.[37] Plato makes a strong case that those who perform these kinds of rituals in order to achieve their own goals are hypocritical criminals hiding their utmost impiety under the semblance of religious behaviour (εἰρωνικοί; *Leg.* 10.908e1): they do not pay attention to the divine but just want their desires fulfilled. In simply doing some business with the gods they do not seek a deeper relationship with them (*Leg.* 10.908e–909c). He also recognised that it was not the rituals *per se* that were reproachable but the attitudes of the performers of the sacrifice. He stressed in a passage of the *Laws* that men have to commune with the gods continually in order to achieve real happiness in life:

> τῷ μὲν ἀγαθῷ θύειν καὶ προcομιλεῖν ἀεὶ τοῖc θεοῖc εὐχαῖc καὶ ἀναθήμαcιν καὶ cυμπάcῃ θεραπείᾳ θεῶν κάλλιcτον καὶ ἄριcτον καὶ ἀνυcιμώτατον πρὸc τὸν εὐδαίμονα βίον καὶ δὴ καὶ διαφερόντωc πρέπον. (*Leg.* 4.716d)

> To engage in sacrifice and commune with the gods continually, by prayers and offerings and devotions of every kind, is a thing most noble and good and helpful towards the happy life, and superlatively fitting also for the good person. (trans. R. G. Bury)

Against the tradition of *polis* religion Plato claims that in the course of the sacrifice performance what is crucial is not the ritual itself but rather the attitude of the sacrificer. He opts for rituals to be performed primarily for the sake of the gods themselves. The satisfaction and happiness of the people who perform those acts is seen as a by-product of the satisfaction of the gods. Being lovingly worshipped, the gods ensure through their goodwill and gratitude that their subjects

[37] *Republic* 2.364b 6–8: 'begging priests and soothsayers go to rich men's doors and make them believe that they by means of sacrifices and incantations have accumulated a treasure of power from the gods' (trans. P. Shorey).

are provided with all that is needed (*Leg.* 11.931a). The ritual begins therefore to cease to be a business-like enterprise. It rather appears to be a symptom of a budding relationship with the divine.

A similar notion is found in Porphyry, who is in the first place concerned with the ways to please the gods and claims that they are not as much satisfied with abundant meat offerings (for the people probably have in mind mostly the feast afterwards) as with offerings of the first fruits done in a devotional attitude (Porphyry *De Abstinentia* 2.16).[38] And even more so it is not the sacrifice itself that is the key process of worship but the contemplation of god, as Porphyry claims along with Pythagoreans.[39] Meditation as central to religious practice is found also in Apuleius. Lucius, after having been transformed back into human form, promises Isis, his saviour, that he will enclose her image in his heart – the very meaning of a meditative relationship:

> *ergo quod solum potest religiosus quidem, sed pauper alioquin, efficere curabo: divinos tuos vultus numenque sanctissimum intra pectoris mei secreta conditum perpetuo custodiens imaginabor.* (Apuleius *Metamorphoses* 11.25)

> Howbeit as a good religious person, and according to my poor estate, I will do what I may: I will always keep Thy divine appearance in remembrance, and close the imagination of Thy most holy godhead within my heart. (trans. W. Adlington).

However, this kind of personal religious commitment is rarely institutionalised or widespread in Greece.[40] As we have already mentioned, *orthopraxy* was considered to be the crucial element of the *polis* religion. In the early days it was in particular Orphics (and Pythagoreans) who demanded personal involvement, and offered in exchange a religious identity.[41] Renunciation (especially of meat), coupled with a personal commitment to the deity, provided a revolutionary aspect in religious life: externally and internally encompassing commitment.

The philosophical longing for a monistic and transcendent divinity – which we recognised as characteristic on the *jñāna*-path of Indian thought – is also

38 Price (1999: 140) notes that Porphyry is an example of an extreme spiritualisation of conventional piety.

39 Price 1999: 140.

40 In the Indian tradition there is also a notion of a pyramid when it comes to the distribution of each of the paths in the society. For all three paths, despite being put in an order of development, coexist with each other. The first one, *karma*-path, is acknowledged as having the most followers and the *bhakti*-path the least, as it is as well connected with a somewhat higher demand on the individual development.

41 Price 1999: 141. Dodds called the Orphics and Pythagoreans 'Puritans' and world-renunciants in the sense that they had strict rules of conduct and believed strongly in purification as the main goal of life: 'Purity, rather than justice, has become the cardinal means of salvation' (1951: 154).

present in this type, but with an interesting personal twist. This can be seen in the person of Socrates, who made traditional offerings[42] but at the same time carefully listened to what he called *to daimonion*. Muir claims that Socrates recognised in it a being who has supreme wisdom and intelligence and is responsible for the order of the world, and that this divinity has much in common with Anaxagoras' idea of the Mind as the controlling power of the universe.[43] Socrates admitted to having been in his youth a disciple of Anaxagoras, but rejected him as he was dissatisfied with looking solely into Nature herself without inquiring about the duties and roles of human beings (Plato *Phaedo* 97d). Socrates acknowledged therefore the achievements of the Ionian philosophers of Nature but tended to go further – investigating not only the question of how we should live but also the supreme power behind the realities described by the philosophers of nature (cf. *Phaedo* 98c–99d: Socrates' second voyage). Therefore, it seems that in Socrates (as in Arjuna in the *Gītā*) there can be detected a kind of development from one level of religious experience to the next.

This interesting merging of the philosophical and religious approaches finds its most striking example in the Neoplatonic theurgy. Iamblichus states in *de mysteriis* that not reason but ritual, some unspeakable act beyond comprehension, is the means for attaining salvation, which is understood to be a union with the divinity:

> . . . οὐδὲ γαρ ἡ ἔννοια cυνάπτει τοῖc θεοῖc τοὺc θεουργούc· ἐπεὶ τί ἐκώλυε τοὺc θεωρητικῶc φιλοcοφοῦνταc ἔχειν τὴν θεουργικὴν ἕνωcιν πρὸc τοὺc θεούc; νῦν δ' οὐκ ἔχει τό γε ἀληθὲc οὕτωc· ἀλλ' ἡ τῶν ἔργων τῶν ἀρρήτων καὶ ὑπὲρ πᾶcαν νόηcιν θεοπρεπῶc ἐνεργουμένων τελεcιουργία ἥ τε τῶν νοουμένων τοῖc θεοῖc μόνον cυμβόλων ἀφθέγκτων δύναμιc ἐντίθηcι τὴν θεουργικὴν ἕνωcιν. (Iamblichus *De Mysteriis* 96, 13 Parthey)
>
> It is not thought that links the theurgist with the gods: what would hinder those who are theoretical philosophers from enjoying theurgic union with gods? But the situation is not so: it is the accomplishment of acts not to be divulged and beyond all conception, and the power of the unutterable symbols, understood solely by the gods, which establishes theurgic union. (trans. E. C. Clarke / J. M. Dillon / J. P. Hershbell)

Apparently the ritual of the theurgist is of a different kind than that of traditional religion. The theurgist, as the name suggests (θεόc and ἔργον), does not talk about the gods but rather acts upon them. Dodds points out that whereas the deeds in the environment of the *polis* aimed at worldly and oftentimes profane ends, here the same ritual is not abandoned but engaged in a different way. It per-

[42] Cf. the famous 'we owe a cock to Asklepios' (Plato *Phaedo* 118a) and the statement of Xenophon about his religious behaviour conforming with the ways of his fellow citizens (*Memorabilia* 1.1–3).

[43] Muir 1985: 208–9.

tains to the solely religious ends of satisfying the divine or achieving a mystical theurgic union with the gods – ἕνωσις.[44]

Theurgy also used highly sophisticated magical enchantments to animate the statues of gods, which was considered the highest level of deity worship. Theurgists developed these techniques to such a point that they claimed to be able to ask the deities for oracles and in that way free themselves from fate[45] and ensure for themselves τῆς ψυχῆς ἀπαθανατισμός ('the immortalisation of the soul': Proclus *Commentary on Plato's Republic* 1.152, 10). So the performance of the ritual and religious acts had a different aim than that of the common state religion: the goal was not prosperity and fulfilment of immediate desires but rather liberation in the experienced union with the beloved divinity.[46] Theurgy thus 'may be described more simply as magic applied to a religious purpose and resting on a supposed revelation of a religious character', as Dodds puts it.[47]

This form of worship of the gods and engagement in a ritual with a strictly religious purpose of pleasing the gods is comparable with what we have seen described as *bhakti* in the Indian tradition. Theurgy, combining philosophical reflection, the search for a transcendent divinity, and ritual directed at a personal god who is to be pleased, is the closest the Greek tradition gets to the Indian version of the third step of the development.

Conclusion

The notion of the Axial Age puts a spell on thinkers and scholars of various creeds and denominations. Diverse reasons for the parallel developments in the greatest cultures of the world between the eighth and the third centuries BCE have been put forward.[48] The Indian paradigm of a progression from *karma* through *jñāna* to *upāsanā* (or *bhakti*) seems to have its counterpart in Greek culture.

[44] Dodds 1951: 291.

[45] οὐ γὰρ ὑφ' εἱμαρτὴν ἀγέλην πίπτουσι θεουργοί (*Chaldean Oracles*, p. 59 Kr.): 'the theurgists do not fall under the fate-fixed mass of people'.

[46] Of course we hear as well famous stories about producing thunderstorms in order to save the Roman army (cf. Suidas s.v. Ἰουλιανός) or even ending pestilence (cf. reference in Dodds 1951: 301), which might remind us of the traditional (in our scheme) *karma* approach to ritual. Using the ritual and worship for profane ends and not as a means to please the divine has in fact nothing to do with the path of real theurgy (in our scheme *bhakti*) as presented in Iamblichus. This development or abuse of theurgical acts might be considered a deterioration of their pure purpose as they were developed in the first place for the sake of establishing a meaningful relationship with the divine.

[47] Dodds 1951: 291.

[48] For instance the theory that universal philosophies came into being in universal and multi-cultured empires (Christian 2004: 319) or the view that coinage had a decisive influence on the development of new ways of thinking (Graeber 2011, drawing on Seaford 2004).

Greek culture moves along the path from a mythological understanding of the world, through a rationalistic one, towards an attempt at an apparent reconciliation between the two. The elements of each step are consistent with the characteristics of the Indian counterpart. Immanent polytheistic gods and the rituals designed to control them correspond with the first step (*karma*) of the Indian development. The search for a primordial monistic force underlying the universe and the ways of expressing it (apophatic theology) is analogous with the Upaniṣadic attempts at achieving *jñāna*. Finally the third step of the Indian paradigm, the *bhakti* stage, seems to have some elements that are analogous with the Neoplatonistic theurgy (and to some extent with the personal development of Socrates).

The Indian paradigm offers yet another approach to the question of the development of cultures. In its Vaishnava Bengali version it even claims a universality as it points out that not only individuals (cf. Arjuna in the *Bhagavad Gītā*) but whole cultures go through an affirming, rejecting and then finally accommodating phase in their development. From that perspective the changes that different cultures underwent at the point of the so-called Axial Age would be just a natural development from the first to the next step. The third step would then still await its Jaspers to name it.

16

The justice of the Indians

Richard Stoneman

Περὶ τῶν Ἰνδῶν, ὅτι δικαιότατοι, καὶ περὶ τῶν ἐθῶν καὶ νομίμων αὐτῶν.

Ctesias claims that the Indians are very just people; he also describes their customs and manners. (Ctesias fragment [= F] 45.16)

Πολλὰ δὲ λέγει (sc. Ctesias) περὶ τῆς δικαιοσύνης αὐτῶν καὶ τῆς περὶ τὸν σφῶν βασιλέα εὐνοίας καὶ τῆς τοῦ θανάτου καταφρονήσεως.

Ctesias says a great deal about their justice, their goodwill towards their king, and their contempt for death. (Ctesias F45.30)

(Οἱ Κυνοκέφαλοι) . . . δίκαιοι δέ εἰσι καὶ μακροβιώτατοι πάντων ἀνθρώπων.

The Dogheads . . . are just men who enjoy the greatest longevity of any people. (Ctesias F45.43)

Greek accounts

These three passages are almost the only references to the customs of any Indian peoples in what survives of Ctesias' account of India.[1] Ctesias of Cnidus was a physician who held a post at the court of the Persian King Artaxerxes I, probably from 415 to 398/7 BCE. He wrote an extensive account of Persian history in twenty-three books and a much shorter description of India in one book. His history of Persia is regarded as extremely unreliable, not least where it contradicts his predecessor Herodotus, but it probably contains much that was in oral circulation in Persian court circles. Ctesias' *Indica* is the first monograph devoted in Greek (or any other language) to India: he did not visit India but recorded what he had learned from merchants, some of them Bactrian, visiting Persia from the Indus

[1] F45.23 has a similar report of the Pygmies of India; the Dog-heads are described at length in F45.37–43.

Valley and the 'Silk Road'.[2] His works are lost, but we possess long excerpts from both of them in the reading diary of the tenth-century Byzantine bishop Photius, as well as scattered quotations in other writers, notably Aelian. Most of the Indian extract is devoted to hydrography, to zoological and botanical marvels – griffins, poisonous birds, manticores – and to bizarre races like the Dog-headed people. By contrast, Megasthenes, who spent time at the court of Chandragupta Maurya in the early third century BCE, wrote a book which included extensive information on manners and customs, including (F27 Schwanbeck = FGrH 715F32) their simplicity and the infrequency of lawsuits among them.[3]

Is this what Ctesias meant by calling the Indians 'very just'?[4] The question requires some investigation of the meaning of 'justice' for Greek writers, in particular in its ethnographic application. Distant (or 'primitive') peoples are often described as 'just' or something similar by Greek writers, beginning with the 'blameless Ethiopians' of Homer. The Augustan writer Nicolaus of Damascus (FGrH 90F103m)[5] also wrote of the Ethiopians that they ἀσκοῦσι δὲ εὐσέβειαν καὶ δικαιοσύνην, ἄθυροι δὲ αὐτῶν αἱ οἰκίαι. Και ἐν τοῖς ὅδοις κειμένων πολλῶν οὐδὲ εἶς κλέπτει, 'They practice piety and justice, and their houses have no doors. No one steals any of the many things lying around in the streets.' They are also said by Stephanus to have been the first people to create laws (s.v. Αἰθίοψ).

Aeschylus, if he is the author of *Prometheus Unbound*, mentioned the Gabii,

Δῆμον ἐνδικώτατον
<βροτῶν> ἁπάντων καὶ φιλοξενώτατον (F196 Lloyd-Jones),

'a people of all mortals most just and hospitable', who need never plough the earth for it brings forth all they need of its own accord. These are no doubt the same as the Abii of Homer (*Iliad* 13.6). Their justice and hospitality are part of a Golden Age scenario in which nature provides men's needs without work, like the Garden of Eden, expulsion from which entailed that 'in the sweat of thy brow shalt thou eat bread'.

2 F45.51; on Bactria F45.6 and 26; Karttunen 1989: 85, Nichols 2011: 21–7.

3 Karttunen (1989: 97) is of the opinion that Ctesias imposes less interpretation than Megasthenes, who makes India into a Utopia. But is he right? Strabo 2.1.9 rates Megasthenes' reliability lower than that of Patrocles, but only on geographical matters. Cf. Democritus 68 DK A18 (Taylor 1999: 61 = Strabo 15.1.38): Strabo, discussing the River Sila(s), on which it is said nothing floats, notes that Megasthenes asserts this and that Democritus denies it, and he also refers to Aristotle for the denial.

4 There is probably an implied contrast, in their loyalty to their kings, with the relationship of the Persian Great King to his peoples. See Lenfant 2004: clviii.

5 Stobaeus 44.25 (IV.142). Photius calls Nicolaus' work παραδόξων ἐθῶν συναγωγή, which implies a work of paradoxography rather than ethnography; he adds to a number of weird tales collected by Conon (no. 186 in Wilson). See Wilson 1994: 129. Edith Parmentier in her edition of *Nicolas de Damascus* (2011), xxviii–xxxii follows the geographical order of these ethnographic snippets rather than the Byzantine 'moral' order.

Other peoples are described in similar terms. Agatharchides (*Periplus of the Red Sea* 49) says that the Fish-Eaters of the Red Sea are notable for the absence of greed among them, and for this reason they neither inflict evil on others nor incur it. Strabo (11.4.4) says of the Albanians of the Caucasus that they are ἁπλοῖ, not so much simple as straightforward: they use barter not money and because they are 'uncivilised' they do not engage in business. Similar qualities are sometimes attributed also to the Scythians[6] and to the Seres.[7]

Such qualities verge on the Utopian.[8] Onesicritus, who travelled with Alexander, described the kingdom of Musicanus on the Lower Indus (FGrH 134F24 = Strabo 15.1.34), 'lauding it rather at length for things of which some are reported as common also to other Indians, as, for example their length of life . . . their healthfulness, their simple diet . . .'; they do not use gold or silver; there is no slavery (since the young men perform the duties of public servants, like the helots of Sparta [see also F25]); they regard science as wickedness (except for medicine); 'they have no process at laws except for murder and outrage, for it is not in one's power to avoid suffering these, whereas the content of contracts is in the power of each man himself'. Much the same is reported of the definitely fabulous people described in the novel of Iambulus: they also live in India (somewhere), are notably long-lived and have no private property.[9]

All this raises the suspicion that Greek writers about India simply foisted on its inhabitants a set of qualities that they associated with what later came to be called the 'noble savage'. Even Megasthenes, who wrote some fifty years after Alexander's expedition, has been accused of *interpretatio Graeca*, with perhaps less justification than most authors.[10] Karttunen in fact states that Ctesias is less prone to this vice than other Greeks.[11] Indians were conveniently 'other' and could be used as a stick to beat Greeks, as for example in Eratosthenes (Strabo

6 Strabo 7.3.7, Dio Chrysostom *Orations* 69.6. Σκύθαι γοῦν οὐδὲν κωλύονται οἱ νομάδες μήτε οἰκίας ἔχοντες μήτε γὴν σπείροντες ἢ φυτεύοντες δικαίας καὶ κατὰ νόμους πολιτεύεσθαι. ἀνεὺ δὲ νόμου καὶ δικαίου μὴ κακῶς ζῆν ἀνθρώπους καὶ πολὺ τῶν θηρίων ὠμότερον οὐ δυνατόν, 'The Scythians, at any rate, nomads who have no houses and do not sow or plant land, are not precluded from living justly and according to laws. It is not possible for men without law and justice not to live a bad life, and one much more savage than that of animals.'

7 *Epistula Alexandri ad Aristotelem* 22.

8 See Ferguson 1975: 18–19 on all this. In general, Lovejoy and Boas 1935: 287–367 on 'the Noble Savage'. The standard work is now Winiarczyk 2011. At pp. 247–50 he collects all the instances of justice as a utopian *topos*, but omits *Epistula Alexandri ad Aristotelem* 22.

9 See Winiarczyk 2011: 190 (Taprobane), 238 (long-livedness), 250 (commonality of property) for these markers of Utopia.

10 Karttunen 1989: 97, who asserts that Herodotus also makes use of *interpretation Graeca*, while Ctesias listens to everything 'with attention and credulity' (80).

11 Karttunen 1989: 80.

1.4.9) who wrote that 'not only are many of the Greeks bad, but many of the barbarians refined (ἀστεῖοι)[12] – Indians and Arians [from the region of Herat], for example'. Aelian (*Varia Historia* 10.14) says that the Indians and Persians are 'brave and free'. However, there is also material in the Greek sources that indicates a serious attempt to report on Indian conditions, even before Megasthenes, and I propose to explore some of the connotations of the idea of Indian 'justice' through Indian material also.

It is worth noting that in the sixth century CE the Chinese traveller Xuan Zang reported in similar terms on the Indian peoples:

> With respect to the ordinary people, although they are naturally light-minded, yet they are upright and honourable. In money matters they are without craft, and in administering justice they are considerate. . . . They are not deceitful or treacherous in their conduct, and are faithful to their oaths and promises . . . with respect to criminals or rebels, these are few in number, and only occasionally troublesome.[13]

Xuan Zang goes on to enumerate the rules of trial and forms of punishment. This may be regarded as independent testimony, from nearly a millennium later, of a general view of the Indians as a law-abiding people.

Justice in Greek philosophy

If we look beyond the ethnographic perspective, it is clear that Justice is a key concept in Greek philosophy, and if I were to summarise Plato's philosophy in a couple of sentences I could do worse than describe it as an exploration of the nature and conditions of justice. The *Republic* begins from the insight that 'no man is an island' and that to live in society entails getting along with one's fellow-man; the *Laws* is an exploration of the way that a just society might be created in the teeth of man's natural propensity to injustice and personal advantage. Justice is social justice: but that can be interpreted in different ways. Heraclides Ponticus in his lost work περὶ δικαιοσύνης (F50 Wehrli), describing the collapse of the Milesian *polis*, described it in terms of political strife of rich and poor, perhaps implying that his definition of justice includes a measure of political equality. Much later, Philostratus in his *Life of Apollonius of Tyana* (3.25), has an Indian reprove the philosopher: 'You seem to think avoidance of

12 The meaning of *asteioi* here is not perspicuous. Probably 'refined', 'gracious' is the correct translation, rather than a specific reference to being city-dwellers.

13 Beal 1884: I. 83. Cf. also I. 177 on the bravery and justice of the Kullu people. The first passage is also included in Devahuti 2001: 132. Xuan Zang is also spelled Hsüan Ts'ang, and other variants, in older scholarship. See also Waley 1952, for a lively account of Xuan Zang's journey.

wrong is the same as Justice', which implies that social equality, not just the rule of law, is required.

Plato's society, however, is to be ruled by philosopher kings, embodiments of wisdom, who control both the spirited part of the soul and of society and that dominated by desire. No conception of social equality here. John Ferguson declared without argument[14] that Plato based this idea on the threefold division of Indian society into Brahmins (wisdom), Kshatriyas (temper) and traders (desire), while the Sudras were the equivalent of slaves in Plato's construction. This idea, Ferguson averred, Plato had got from Pythagoras following the latter's travels in India where he also picked up the idea of metempsychosis and so on. We need not take this idea very seriously in this form,[15] even while we admit that earlier Greeks had acquired some knowledge of India. Plato's older contemporary, Democritus, in particular was said to have travelled to India (and practically everywhere else in the known world as well).[16] Both Aelian[17] in the second century CE and Bishop Hippolytus[18] in the fourth have him visiting India and the 'naked sages'.[19] He seems to have had views on the origins of civilisation, perhaps based on observation of polities less 'advanced' in organisation than that of contemporary Greeks. Most of the anthropogony in Diodorus' *History* I. 35–42, which is the reverse of any Golden Age concept, probably derives from Democritus.[20]

Law

Plato believed it was necessary to create a Utopia to ensure a just society, and that justice could only be ensured by extensive and detailed laws. Indian society in the period before and around Alexander is characterised by both Nearchus and Megasthenes as having no written laws,[21] which would qualify it as a natural Utopia. However, if we examine this phrase further, it is clear that these authors are not saying that there are no laws in India. In fact, if there was, as it seems,

14 Ferguson 1975: 63–4.

15 Plato's suggestion may, however, be taken to imply some awareness of the kind of tripartite division of Indo-European society argued for by Georges Dumézil

16 68 DK A7 = T7 in Taylor 1999: 59.

17 *Varia Historia* 4.20 = T22 Taylor.

18 *Refutatio* 1.12–13 = T78.

19 T6 Taylor = DL 9.35.

20 Cole 1967: 186, Cartledge 1998: 20–1.

21 Nearchus FGrH 133F23 = Strabo 15.1.66; Megasthenes F27 Schwanbeck = FGrH 715F32 = Strabo 15.1.53. See also Onesicritus FGrH 134F24 who says that in the kingdom of Musicanus there was no process of law.

no writing, there could be no written laws.[22] This does not preclude there having been extensive laws. The detailing in these authors of various severe punishments for certain crimes (mutilation for false witness, the loss of a hand for maiming another person, death for causing another to lose a hand or eye)[23] makes clear that there were laws to be applied. In writing about the absence of slavery Megasthenes (as paraphrased by Diodorus)[24] states that 'it is silly to make laws on the basis of equality for all persons, and yet to establish inequalities in social intercourse'.[25] Though our surviving Indian texts all belong to a later period, the tradition of Indian law-making goes back at least to the sixth century BCE. Romila Thapar writes of the emergence of kingdoms in this period that one of the responsibilities of kings was to maintain the laws (and to collect taxes).[26] Authority was required to combat the 'law of the fish', which is that big fish eat little fish. This took place when the religious forms of Vedic society began to be modified by the rise of kingships, clan-states and republics.[27] Ctesias, notably, never mentions kings, perhaps reflecting a backward-looking view of Indian society.

Indians, like Plato, recognised that society was impossible without a sense of justice. So the *dharma* was established at the moment of creation, when the gods dismembered the cosmic giant.[28]

> From that sacrifice in which everything was offered, the verses and chants were born, the metres were born from it, and from it the formulas were born. Horses were born from it, and those other animals that have two rows of teeth; cows were born from it, and from it goats and sheep were born. . . . With the sacrifice the gods sacrificed to the sacrifice. These were the first ritual laws (the *dharmas*, archetypal

22 The evidence is somewhat contradictory. Megasthenes says that the Indians 'have no written laws, but are ignorant of writing' (Strabo 15.1.53 = Megasthenes F27 Schwanbeck = FGrH 715F32), while Nearchus says that 'they write missives on linen cloth' (Strabo 15.1.67 = FGrH 133F23). Modern scholars are equally divided, with Romila Thapar (2002: 163) conceding the existence of writing in the fifth century and Richard Gombrich (2013: 17) adamant that there is no writing before Aśoka. For a fuller discussion see Stoneman (forthcoming).

23 Megasthenes FGrH 715F32 = Strabo 15.1.54. The delightful tenth-century CE book of travellers' tales by Buzurg ibn Shahriyar (1928: no. 99, 137f) notes that 'theft among the Indians is a very serious offence', and is punishable by death.

24 Diod. 2.39 = Megasthenes FGrH 715F4.39.

25 'Social intercourse' translates the conjecture συνουσίας (Capps); the mss. have οὐσίας ('properties'). The existence of judges is also mentioned at FGrH 715F4.42.

26 Thapar 2002: 153.

27 Cf. Avari 2007: 86ff. Gore Vidal also shows awareness of this social development in his novel about Xerxes, *Creation* (1981: 214, 219–20), in which Jains and Buddhists pose a threat to society by their rejection of caste rigidities.

28 Doniger 1981: 31.

patterns of behaviour). These very powers reached the sky where dwell the Sadhyas, the ancient gods. (RV 10.90.9–16)

Righteousness is the first need of all: 'What is needful? Righteousness, and sacred learning and teaching' (TU 1.9). This is then followed by Truth, Meditation, Self-control, Peace, Ritual and Humanity. Another statement about justice in the *Upaniṣads* comes in the *Chāndogya Upaniṣad*: 'in my kingdom there are no thieves, no misers, no one who drinks; no one without learning or a sacred fire, no lecher, much less a whore!' (ChU 5.11.5).[29] Again, theft ranks high among the blemishes on a just or righteous society. However, *dharma* varies according to caste and status,[30] and the duty of Krishna expressed in the *Bhagavad Gītā* is not necessarily the same as that of non-heroic mortals. It also progresses through a historical development.

Can *dharma* be the concept that the Greeks had in mind when they extolled Indian *dikaiosyne?* When the British ruled India they took *dharma* to be the equivalent of Law and attempted to introduce the *Laws of Manu* as a law-code for India.[31] However dubious this enterprise, the *Laws of Manu* and its predecessor texts, the *Dharmasūtras*, are a repository of information about laws that may go back at least to the sixth century BCE. They are both descriptive and prescriptive.[32] The earliest of the *Dharmasūtras* have sometimes been attributed to the sixth century.[33] That of Gautama has sometimes been regarded as the earliest, but its references to Yaunas (Greeks) may preclude its being earlier than the middle of the third century.[34] Patrick Olivelle[35] regards that of Apastamba as being somewhat earlier than this, while Doniger[36] is of the opinion that the earliest of the *Dharmasūtras* belong to the fourth century BCE. Most of the provisions in Apastamba's work relate to ritual rather than social interaction, though from 2.10 onwards there are discussions of class, marriage and inheritance. From 2.25 the duties of the king include taxes, crime and punishment and judicial process. It is the king's rod (*danda*) that symbolises authority and the power of coercion.

These basics are much more developed in the *Laws of Manu*, which certainly belongs to a later period, but the range of topics is similar. Book 7 (12–18) begins from a consideration of justice, emblematised in the rod, as a duty of kings in

29 The passage is discussed by Agrawala 1953: 485–7.

30 Thapar 2013: 339.

31 Doniger and Smith 1991: lx.

32 Doniger and Smith 1991: x and lvi.

33 Olivelle 1999: xxxi.

34 Indians may have known of Greeks as subjects of the Achaemenid empire before they encountered the army of Alexander.

35 Olivelle 1999: xxi.

36 Doniger 1981: xxxv.

order to avoid social collapse. Book 8 includes discussion of such matters as interest (140–3), contracts (163), the necessity of impartial judgement (174), deception (224), livestock, boundaries, irreligion (310), theft (314), assault (345), adultery (352).

It is interesting to examine how far such topics, which are not specified in the earliest *Dharmasūtras*, are nevertheless reflected in the reports of Greek writers. The Greeks might thus prove to be witnesses for adherence to law and social customs from the sixth century, prior to their encoding in the written law codes. Let us take some examples.

Piety

As was made clear above, the moment of creation was marked by the establishment of the rule of sacrifice and reverence towards the gods. Aelian writes:

> Who could fail to admire the wisdom of the barbarians? None of them has lapsed into atheism, and none argue about the gods – whether they exist or do not exist, and whether they have any concern for us or not . . . neither the Indian, nor the Celt, nor the Egyptian. The barbarians I have just mentioned say that gods exist, that they provide for us, that they indicate the future by omens and signs, by entrails and by other forms of instruction and teachings. (*Varia Historia* 2.31)

Aelian contrasts the barbarians in this matter with the sophisticated Greek intellectuals such as Euhemerus and Epicurus who deny the gods. While Aelian does not refer exclusively to Indians, and not all his characteristics belong to Indian religion (e.g. divination by entrails), he certainly makes them a prominent example. It is probable that this passage, like many of Aelian's unattributed snippets of information about India, derives ultimately from Ctesias. In fact, religious dissent and scepticism are found as early as the sixth century, when shramanas begin to reject animal sacrifice and other Vedic practices; their attitudes may have influenced Pyrrhonian scepticism in the generation after Alexander.[37]

Honesty

If we turn now to matters of human interaction, there are a number of traits reported by Greeks that exemplify justice. A long excerpt from Megasthenes preserved by Strabo begins by observing the frugality of the Indians, and goes on:

[37] Frenkian 1957: 75ff.: see the German summary review in *Bibliotheca Classica Orientalis* 4 (1958), 212–49; Flintoff 1980: 88–108, Kuzminski 2010, Beckwith 2015. See note 27 above on ascetics as the enemy of traditional religion.

> Theft is of very rare occurrence. Megasthenes says that those who were in the camp of Sandrokottos, wherein lay 400,000 men, found that the thefts reported on any one day did not exceed the value of two hundred drachmae, and this among a people who have no written laws, but are ignorant of writing, and must therefore in all the business of life trust to memory.[38]

Below, he writes 'Their houses and property they generally leave unguarded.' This description of Indian manners recalls the behaviour of the idealised Ethiopians mentioned by Nicolaus (above, note 5), who are able to leave property lying about in public places. However, an identification of Nicolaus' Ethiopians with Indians seems precluded by the fact that he has another passage specifically about Indians (F103y), in which he writes:

> Among the Indians, if anyone is deprived of money he has lent or deposited, there is no trial, but the creditor accuses him personally. He who deprives an artisan of the use of his hand or his eye is punished by death. By order of the king, the greatest offenders have their heads shaved, since this is the extremity of shame among them.

This may be set alongside a passage just following in Strabo's report of Megasthenes: 'The simplicity of their laws and their contracts is proved by the fact that they seldom go to law. They have no suits about pledges or deposits, nor do they require either seals or witnesses, but make their deposits and confide in each other.' All these passages bear witness to the honesty of Indians, the unusualness of theft and their reluctance to go to law.

Elsewhere Aelian (*Varia Historia* 10.14) quotes Socrates (!) as saying that Indians are 'brave and free but idle in commerce', a description which recalls that of Heraclides Ponticus (F55 Wehrli) who says that Indians don't work, because they are given over to *tryphe*. Both passages may perhaps be taken to imply a kind of negative honesty, in the sense that these alleged Indians are too lazy to rob or cheat you.

The mention of pledges and deposits prompts consideration of usury and rates of interest. Aelian (*Varia Historia* 45.1) writes: 'The Indians do not lend money, nor do they have any notion of accepting a loan. For an Indian it is not right (*themis*) to commit an injustice or to be the victim of one. Hence they make no written contracts or deposits' (οὐδὲ ποιοῦνται συγγραφὴν ἢ καταθήκην, a difficult clause to translate). The second sentence seems vapid, though perhaps suggesting a religious underpinning of their honest behaviour, but the key point, that Indians do not or should not lend at interest, is a *topos* of the Vedic texts.[39] Usury is also condemned in the *Jatakas*, though money-lending is accepted as an honest trade, though not one to be engaged in by Brahmins and Kshatriyas.

[38] F27 = FGrH 715F32 = Strabo 15.1.53–6.

[39] Jain 1929: 3.

A rate of 15 per cent is commonly mentioned. The *Arthashastra* (3.11.1–9)[40] devotes a substantial section to loans, termed 'debt', *rina*, specifying a rate of 15 per cent on 'normal' transactions, but much more for commercial transactions (5% per month, i.e. 60% p.a.), and even more for risky travel by sea or through forests. The *Laws of Manu* also devoted a substantial section (8.140–62) to debt, interest and contract.

Plato regarded usury and lending at interest as undesirable and forbade them in his ideal society in *Laws* (742c). While the idea in Plato is a Utopian one, it may nonetheless recall what was believed to be the case in an actually existing society which Greeks regarded as in some ways ideal, namely India. But the writers either confused ideal with reality, taking a prohibition on such practice for members of higher castes as a general rule, or were misled by their idealisation of the barbarian. A third possibility is that they are describing old-fashioned Vedic-age ideas rather than the situation in the more complex societies they (presumably) actually encountered. Ctesias, reporting what he heard from visitors to Persia,[41] may be telling what those people thought ought to be the case, as it had been in the good old days. If Aelian is using Ctesias, then he too reflects practices from those good old days before Ctesias' activity at the very end of the fifth century BCE and in the early fourth.

Violence and non-violence

Non-violence, that most iconic of Indian practices[42] (though non-Vedic, and associated with asceticism), is enshrined in numerous places in the *Laws of Manu* (e.g. 6.75) but is largely absent from the ethnographer Megasthenes. However, Onesicritus, in his account of his interview with the Naked Philosophers (F17a, Strabo 15.1.64), writes that Dandamis/Mandanis described Alexander as 'the only philosopher in arms that he ever saw, and that it was the most useful thing in the world if those men were wise who have the power of persuading the willing, and forcing the unwilling, to learn self-control'. The two men go on to discuss vegetarianism, Onesicritus explaining to Mandanis that this is also a Pythagorean custom (because of the transmigration of souls). These hints are expanded in the *Alexander Romance*, which may be the earliest surviving Alexander text, when (3.6) the philosophers reply to Alexander's question 'What is the wickedest of creatures?', that the answer is 'Man . . . Learn from yourself the answer to that. You are a wild beast, and see how many other wild beasts you have with you,

40 Rangarajan 1992: 425.
41 F45.6 and 45h; see above, note 2.
42 Chapple 1993.

to help you tear away the lives of other beasts.' Later they ask Alexander 'Since you are a mortal, why do you make so many wars?'

This passage is developed in the somewhat later Cynic diatribe, the Geneva papyrus,[43] into an attack on meat-eating, and this in turn in the much later *Life of the Brahmans*[44] by the fifth century CE author Palladius[45] into an attack on the wild beast shows of the Roman Empire. These authors were well aware of Indian non-violence, and its specific manifestation as vegetarianism, as well as making it part of their own philosophical approach to life. It seems that this motif would not have developed if they had not found it expressed in the earliest Greek writers about India, even though the fragments we have are silent on the matter. The *Alexander Romance* appears to reflect more up-to-date information than Megasthenes, who describes Vedic conditions.

Drunkenness also forms part of the diatribe in Palladius, and is a major crime for Manu (9.235).

Marriage

Aristobulus (who travelled with Alexander) described how in Taxila the unmarried daughters of poor families were shown in the market place to find husbands for them.[46] A related tale is that of Nearchus who describes how brides may be won in fist-fights.[47] Some historians have supposed that this is a reference to sale of brides, a practice explicitly forbidden by Manu (3.31), in which case Aristobulus would be either wrong, or evidence for a custom at odds with later Indian law-making. However, as Karttunen points out, 'it seems to have been customary somewhere as there was the need to grant a wife's status to women married in this way', as the passage of Manu makes clear. He goes on to state that the custom is still alive, and quotes Sir John Marshall for the practice in parts of the Himalayas. However, Aristobulus does not actually say that the brides were purchased, unlike Herodotus in his comparable account of bride-sale in Babylon (1.196).

Under the heading of marriage, adultery is naturally an important issue for Manu (8.352), though it is unmentioned in the Greek writers except for a line in

43 Martin 1959.

44 The naked philosophers are not actually Brahmins. Megasthenes understood this. See Stoneman 1995; the reference is to p. 102.

45 Ed. Berghoff 1967, Derrett 1960: 77–135. A new edition of this text will appear in volume III of *Il Romanzo di Alessandro*, ed. Richard Stoneman and Tristano Gargiulo (forthcoming).

46 Aristobulus FGrH 139F42. See Karttunen 1989: 223.

47 Nearchus FGrH 133F23 = Strabo 15.1.66.

Megasthenes[48] stating that 'the wives prostitute themselves unless they are compelled to be chaste'. Widow-burning is however mentioned by Onesicritus (F21), who attributes it to a people called the Cathaeans, located between the rivers Hydaspes (Jhelum) and Acesines (Chenab). The same practice is attributed more generally to 'the Indians' by Aelian (*Varia Historia* 7.18).

Suicide

Suicide by fire may be mentioned here since Onesicritus (F17, end) states that this is normal among Brahmins who feel their end approaching, as in the case of the renegade Calanus who accompanied Alexander to Babylon. Philo[49] regards this as the normal view of philosophers. Megasthenes however denies this. He seems right to do so, but, as I wrote in 1994, it looks as if this conflict in the sources reflects a genuine controversy in ancient India about suicide by fire:

> Such suicide was practised by some Indian ascetics, but orthodox Hinduism [I would now write mainstream Brahmin opinion] would be opposed to it, and this is the view that Megasthenes reflects. That there were accounts of Calanus with a different tendency is clear from the account in Philo which has Calanus praise suicide without any hint of controversiality.[50]

Megasthenes reflects an older state of affairs, perhaps because he talked to Brahmins and had his attention drawn to the *Ṛgveda*.

Basham (1951) makes it possible to be more precise about the nature of this controversy. Though Jains, for example, disapproved of suicide, a breakaway group known as the Ajivikas practised voluntary death and went so far as to detail forty-eight different ways of seeking death. Ajivikas were known for their skill in fortune-telling. Though both Jains and Ajivikas were known as *ekadandin* ('carrying a single staff'), a word which recalls the name of the leader of the Naked Philosophers in the *Alexander Romance*, Dandamis, Ajivikas were regarded as 'bad' ascetics, because hypocritical in both diet and sexual matters. Much of our information about the Ajivikas comes from the Buddhist text, the *Samannapala Sutta*, which is hostile to both ascetics and Brahmins (not as good as Buddhists), and details the numerous forms of Ajivika hypocrisy.[51] The conclusion to be drawn is that the Naked Philosophers may be Jains, or something very like them, expressing their hostility to the

48 F27 Schwanbeck = FGrH 715F32 = Strabo 15.1.54.

49 *Quod omnis probus liber* 96.

50 Stoneman 1994: 505.

51 See e.g. Ling 1981: 18–22 (paras 46–61 of the *Samannapala Sutta*). The classic study of the Ajivikas (Basham 1951: 124) details their misdemeanours (as a Buddhist/Jain saw them).

Ajivika Calanus, who breaks away from them to accompany Alexander (telling his fortune and enjoying his food) and ultimately to commit suicide in spectacular fashion.

Slavery

Megasthenes says that slavery is unknown among the Indians,[52] while Onesicritus states that it is peculiar to the Indians in the kingdom of Musicanus,[53] and is just one aspect of the excellent government of this country. Manu however regards the existence of slavery as a datum, and at 8.415 specifies the seven ways in which slaves can be made: through warfare, out of poverty, through being born in a household, by purchase, by gift, by inheritance, or as a punishment.[54] It looks as if Megasthenes' information here is simply wrong. Romila Thapar writes:

> Slavery was a recognized institution . . . Megasthenes may have been confused by the caste status cutting across the economic stratification. Technically, there was no large-scale slavery for production. Greek society made a sharp distinction between the freeman and the slave, which distinction was not apparent in Indian society. A slave in India could buy back his freedom or be voluntarily released by his master . . . What was immutable in Indian society was not freedom or slavery, but caste.[55]

In this case, therefore, the Greek writer seems to be imposing an idealising view of India on the facts, partly through misunderstanding.

Conclusion

The picture that has emerged is a complex one. Greeks regarded India as a particularly just society. In part this was due to an idealising tendency that made the distant people an example of Utopia, and reinforced this by finding examples of social equality in Indian conditions. However, the Greek writers do also provide evidence of legal practices and social customs resembling those described by the later Indian law codes, and thus have the right to be regarded as genuine witnesses for Indian society in the period before Alexander. Paradoxically, information in the *Alexander Romance* and Onesicritus seems to be more up-to-date than that in either Ctesias (who preceded them but relied on non-Indian informants) or Megasthenes (who was a generation later but seems to have derived his

52 A Utopian motif: Winiarczyk 2011: 255

53 F22, 24 and 25, Strabo 15.1.54.

54 A similar account is in Rangarajan 1992: 453. See also Ray 2000: 265–6 (non vidi).

55 Thapar 2002: 77.

information mainly from conservative Brahmin intellectuals). The evidence of all these authors must be treated critically and with caution, but is not to be dismissed as mere idealisation. The Justice of the Indians was a reality in the fifth and fourth centuries BCE.

17

Nietzsche on Greek and Indian philosophy

Emma Syea

This chapter aims to use Nietzsche as a prism for examining the parallels between ancient India and ancient Greece. As Mervyn Sprung maintains, ideas of Greece and India are viewed by Nietzsche very much through a 'powerful Nietzschean lens'[1] in that he mines these cultures for concepts, attitudes and *Weltanschauungen* which will provide him with alternatives to the life-denying Christian morality he so deplored. I would like to suggest, however, that the interpretations Nietzsche offers are by no means redundant. The parallels between ancient Indian and ancient Greek philosophy have frequently been noted by commentators, and various theories have been put forward to account for them. One prevalent theory is the idea of parallel autonomous intellectual development in these countries. I would like to suggest here that the genealogical approach Nietzsche advances in *On the Genealogy of Morality* (1887) complements this notion of parallel autonomous intellectual development in Greece and India. The genealogical method asserts that the value systems which emerge in societies are driven by and supported by certain physiological, psychological and sociological trends. There is no sole origin for values; instead we see a conjunction of diverse lines of development and a multiplicity of origins. In this way it seems very possible that we would see parallels between Greek and Indian thought if certain conditions obtained in both cultures.

In particular this chapter will examine the idea of value systems arising in India and Greece in part due to the emergence of city-states, and the ever present threat of war. Such conditions cultivated a spirit of *agon* (ἀγών, often translated as conflict, strife, competition),[2] at both a personal and societal level, leading

1 Nietzsche's 'trans-European eye saw India through a powerful Nietzschean lens' (Sprung 1996: 83).

2 The concept of the agon was especially prevalent amongst the Pre-Socratics, most notably Empedocles, Hesiod and Heraclitus.

to a certain set of values. The idea of conflict and *agon* preoccupied Nietzsche across his oeuvre. I would like to suggest that such themes are manifest not only in Greek thought – we need only think of Homer's *Iliad*, Hesiod's two Erises and Heraclitean strife – but also in Indian texts such as the *Mahābhārata* and the *Ramayana*, both of which Nietzsche was acquainted with from as early on as his school days.[3] This chapter will: 1) examine how Nietzsche found cultures which he believed offered viable models of self and state; 2) suggest that these models were born out of an agonal context; and 3) propose that Nietzsche came to see 'Greek' and 'Indian' as *modes of being*, which informed his own ideas on normativity, providing an alternative to the Christian slave morality he so despised.

Nietzsche's project

In *Human, all too Human* (1878) Nietzsche declares that the defining feature of truly original thinkers is their ability to see the old and the familiar as though it were new, to look past the obvious, and to re-examine the overlooked. In the aphorism titled 'Estranged from the Present', he uses ocean metaphors to convey the distance he deems necessary for cultivating this ability:

> There is a great advantage to be gained in distantly estranging ourselves from our age and for once being driven as it were away from its shores back to the ocean of the world-outlooks of the past. Looking back at the coast from this distance we command a view, no doubt for the first time, of its total configuration, and when we approach it again we have the advantage of understanding it better as a whole than those who have never left it. (HH I 616)[4]

Turning to other cultures – '*das Fremde*' – provides Nietzsche with this requisite 'distance'.

We should note that this distance is not merely the idea of space but rather involves a notion of superiority. For Nietzsche nineteenth-century Germany was in a crisis. Around him he witnessed a stagnant, decadent society, corrupted by a Christian slave morality,[5] which could benefit from emulating concepts belong-

3 See Figl 1996. These epics were mentioned in a draft for a school essay on 'the characterisation of Kriemhild in the Nibelungen Song' on 8 December 1862 (BAW 2.445 Nachbericht).

4 A list of abbreviations and works by Nietzsche referred to can be found at the end of this chapter.

5 Nietzsche first discusses the notion of slave morality (which is contrasted with master morality) in *On the Genealogy of Morality*. Slave morality promotes values of humility, patience, compassion, pity, altruism. Such a morality, according to Nietzsche, is born from a sense of *ressentiment* against those who are stronger (the masters), forcing the masters' natural set of values such as 'pride, strength, power, nobility' to become regarded as degenerate and harmful. In this way slave morality is a reactive, negative morality designed to

ing to the vastly superior Hellas. He took ancient Greece, as did many others in German Philhellenist circles,[6] to be the pinnacle of culture, and indeed mankind (although the reasons why Nietzsche praises Greece differ greatly from those of his Philhellenist predecessors, as I shall discuss later). Nietzsche consistently emphasises the alterity of Hellas from modern Germany, and sees within Greek culture the seeds for the regeneration of his own. In the Greeks Nietzsche found a 'surplus of a wise and harmonious conduct of life' (HH II 173).

Ancient India too held many admirable traits for Nietzsche. Upon reading the *Laws of Manu* the Brahmins emerged in his eyes as 'a species of human being a hundred times more gentle and rational' than the oppressive Christian slave morality with its 'sick house and dungeon atmosphere' (TI, 'The Improvers of Mankind', 3). As Scheiffele suggests, unlike the eighteenth century with its concept of the 'Noble Savage', Nietzsche does not value 'alien cultures because of their close ties with nature, their "primordality", or because they were morally unspoiled'. Instead, he admired them for what he perceived as an 'intellectual, artistic, and practical *superiority*'.[7]

Viewing Germany from the Greek or Indian standpoint provides Nietzsche with what he calls a 'pathos of distance'.[8] These cultures offered vitalising models of the self and the state which he believed would pave the way for cultural dominance and lay the foundations for a strong German identity. Contrasting them

level out natural differences in society. Nietzsche views slave forms of morality as inimical to the flourishing of *Kultur* and art.

6 German Philhellenism reached its peak in the late eighteenth and nineteenth centuries, and went hand in hand with a resurgence in Neo-Classicism. Art historians such as Johann Winckelmann and Gotthold Lessing idealised fifth-century classical Greek art and architecture, with Winckelmann coining the phrase '*edle Einfalt, stille Größe*', 'noble simplicity, quiet grandeur', to capture the spirit of Hellenic art. Jacob Burckhardt later offered a very different interpretation of classical Greece and evoked a more violent, cruel image of Greek society.

7 Scheiffele 1996: 42.

8 BGE 25: 'Every enhancement so far in the type "man" has been the work of an aristocratic society – and that is how it will be, again and again, since this sort of society believes in a long ladder of rank order and value distinctions between men, and in some sense needs slavery. Without the pathos of distance as it grows out of the ingrained differences between stations, out of the way the ruling caste maintains an overview and keeps looking down on subservient types and tools, and out of this caste's equally continuous exercise in obeying and commanding, in keeping away and below – without this pathos, that other, more mysterious pathos could not have grown at all, that demand for new expansions of distance within the soul itself, the development of states that are increasingly high, rare, distant, tautly drawn and comprehensive, and in short, the enhancement of the type "man", the constant "self-overcoming of man" (to use a moral formula in a supra-moral sense).'

with the life-denying, nay-saying Christian culture[9] he perceived in Germany allows him to reinforce his attack against Christianity and to acquire a greater self-knowledge – he is 'looking *back at his own from the respective counterpositions*'.[10] Greece and India are therefore enlisted by Nietzsche in his polemical project. Consequently his primary concern is not to offer the most accurate or faithful readings of the texts. Having begun his career as a philologist, Nietzsche was very well acquainted with the Greek texts. In the case of the Indian texts, however, his knowledge is far from extensive. Much of it is second-hand from figures such as Schopenhauer and Paul Deussen,[11] and more often than not, he makes use of poor translations, for example Louis Jacolloit's *Les législateurs religieux. Manou, Moïse, Mahomet* (1876).[12] He is therefore prone to making broad generalisations on the basis of insufficient knowledge, and is at times somewhat cavalier with his use of the texts, compiling quotations from the originals and composing them into one single quotation to intensify his argument. Essentially Nietzsche plays fast and loose with the sources.

This is not say, however, that the interpretations he offers should be dismissed. Nietzsche may make use of Greece and India primarily for advancing his critique of the ideas of his own time, but he often hits upon crucial similarities, and there is a certain intuitiveness in some of his insights into these cultures. At times, he identifies, as it were, the spirit rather than the letter of the concepts that arise in these cultures.

The state

Perhaps the most obvious (and impressive) parallel Nietzsche saw in Greece and India was the idea of the aristocratic state. According to Nietzsche, the efficacious society is the artistic society; it is through art that we measure and assess a culture. It is paramount that the artistic individuals – the so-called 'higher types' – should be permitted to flourish. In his unpublished essay 'The Greek State' (1871/2) Nietzsche declares that: 'in order for there to be a broad, deep, fertile soil for the development of art, the overwhelming majority has to be slavishly subjected to life's necessity in the service of the minority' (GSt 166). The pyramidal structure of the aristocratic society, whereby, through rigid stratification, the bottom stratum enables the elite to prosper, is therefore highly desirable. For

9 Nietzsche consistently emphasises the idea that Christian morality 'encouraged man to consider himself even blacker and more evil than is actually the case' (HH I: 124).

10 Scheiffele 1996: 42.

11 For example Deussen 1883.

12 For discussion relating to this problematic translation see Etter 1987: 340–52 and Smith 2004: 37–56.

Nietzsche, the model of the Greek *polis*, as envisaged by Plato in the *Republic*, was the sine qua non of the Greeks' creative achievements:

> *Plato's perfect state* . . . the actual aim of the state, the Olympian existence and constantly renewed creation and preparation of the genius, compared with whom everyone else is just a tool, aid, and facilitator, is discovered here through poetic intuition and described vividly. (GSt 173)

Similarly the caste system outlined in the *Laws of Manu* greatly appealed to Nietzsche. In *The Anti-Christ* (1895) he states that 'to draw up a law book such as Manu means to permit oneself to get the upper hand, to become perfection, to be ambitious of the highest art of living' (A 57). This is because the divisions of the four *varnas* in Manu (from lowest rank to highest: the Sudras [labourers and service providers], the Vaishyas [merchants, agriculturists, artisans], the Kshatriyas [warriors and kings], and the Brahmins [priests and scholars]) safeguard 'the higher types'.

In both the *Republic* and the *Laws of Manu* every individual has to perform the function best suited to their nature, with each stratum having its own particular obligations and rights. This principle of specialisation facilitates a division of labour to ensure the smooth running of the state, and ensures that the various classes within society remain in fixed relations of power and influence. The divisions are sustained and sanctioned by Noble Lies.[13] In the *Republic* Socrates adduces the 'myth of the metals', whilst in the *Laws of Manu* a reference to the *Puruṣa* myth in the Vedic 'Hymn to Creation' is made.[14] Both these Noble Lies propagate the view that despite the partitions in society, there is ultimate unity. Socrates is careful to make mention of the fact that the citizens of the *polis* are 'all akin' and 'brothers', whilst the *Puruṣa* myth sees all the *varnas* spring from the same fundamental material via the dismemberment of the divine primordial being. Through reference to the divine, these divisions are grounded in an unquestionable authority and individuals are seen to serve a higher purpose, thereby strengthening the model, and sugaring the pill which the lower divisions must swallow.

The *Laws of Manu* go a step further than Plato by implying that these

[13] In *The Birth of Tragedy* Nietzsche highlights art's restorative properties and terms it 'the great enabler of the possibility of life', 'the great seducer to life' – without it life would be rendered unbearable. The myths and legislation which constitute the *Republic* and Manu's Noble Lies ennoble and justify any suffering encountered in the state, providing us with a clear illustration of why, for Nietzsche, art is worth more than truth: cf. KSA 11.587, 13.194.

[14] Radhakrishnan and Moore 1957: 1.31: 'But for the sake of the prosperity of the worlds he caused the Brahmana, the Kshatriya, the Vaisya, and the Sudra to proceed from his mouth, his arms, his thighs, and his feet.'

societal divisions have an ontological status – the *varnas* are quasi-biological: 'he was created by the Self-existent to be the slave of a *brahmin*' (414); 'a *sudra*, though emancipated by his master, is not released from servitude; since that is innate in him, who can set him free from it?' (415). As Nietzsche puts it in *The Anti-Christ*: '*Caste-order* . . . is just the sanction of a *natural order*' (A 57). In this way Manu appears to be closer to Aristotle in the *Politics* when he suggests that an individual's societal role is determined by his inherent nature: 'from the hour of their birth, some are marked out for subjection, others for rule' (1254a22–3). For Aristotle social status has a biological basis and necessarily cannot be altered. Unlike the *Republic*, which does allow for some social mobility – Socrates observes that on occasions a golden child may be born from a silver parent, and in that event rulers should give such a child 'the position in society his nature deserves' (415b) – Aristotle does not allow for any promotion within the classes. Similarly Manu explicitly bans any miscegenation between *varnas*, effectively breeding individuals for their assigned societal roles, thereby preserving the purity of the higher castes.

What Nietzsche admires in these models of the state is the acknowledgement of the fundamental heterogeneity of individuals comprising the state; difference is not denied and there are no attempts to level mankind. This is in line with his theory of 'types' whereby individuals are classified according to their psycho-physical constitution. Additionally an individual's type will determine the values he adopts. In this way Nietzsche denies any fundamental parity amongst men. Furthermore we see an active promotion of these intrinsic differences via the ordering of society, or *Rangordnung* as Nietzsche terms it. In *On the Genealogy of Morality* Nietzsche maintains that in societies with a clear *Rangordnung*, the values which will be generated will be so-called 'noble' values – values of strength, power, pride – all of which he contrasts with the weaker 'slave' values such as humility and sympathy, espoused by Christianity. This is because those belonging to the highest ranked class – the so-called 'noble' types – are permitted to cultivate a positive sense of self, feel themselves to be superior to the other classes, and subsequently propagate their own values. The *Rangordnung* facilitated by aristocratic societies is, according to Nietzsche, the sole reason for the cultural achievements of these societies, and is that which allows the higher types to flourish: 'every enhancement so far in the type "man" has been the work of an aristocratic society' (BGE 257).

The agonal context

Something which particularly preoccupied Nietzsche was the fact that Greek city-states often existed against a background of *bellum omnium contra omnes* ('the war of all against all'). War was a structural component in these societies, and something which was reflected at a personal, societal and cosmic level. Regarding Greece, the prevailing Philhellenist view at the time held by figures such as Johann Winckelmann painted a picture of a beautified Hellas, which encompassed spiritual nobility, clarity, composure, self-restraint and harmony. This Neo-Classical idea was encapsulated by the leitmotiv '*edle Einfalt, stille Größe*' (noble simplicity, calm grandeur). Following Jacob Burckhardt, who characterised the *polis* as a *città dolente* (a city of pain), Nietzsche proposed a revaluation of Greece and emphasised its agonal spirit, championing Sparta over Athens. He glorified 'the bloody jealousy of one town for another . . . this murderous greed of those petty wars, the tiger-like triumph over the corpse of the slain enemy' (GSt 169), and accentuated conflict and disunity rather than centralisation and stability. The Hellas depicted by Winckelmann and his followers – a serene, moderate and harmonious Hellas – was, according to Nietzsche, a gross misrepresentation. The fact that the *poleis* were in constant competition with each other and that war often seemed more prevalent than peace was an inescapable factor for Nietzsche in assessing ancient Greece. As Porter notes: 'the background that ultimately matters to him is not metaphysical but anthropological and cultural; and the violence of the politics is only one of the arenas in which the ramifications of cultural violence make themselves felt'.[15] Heidegger's assertion that Nietzsche was 'the discoverer of the Greeks' demonstrates how he moved away from seeing the Greeks as a product of 'cheerfulness',[16] à la Winckelmann et al., and instead proposed that their philosophy came into being through an excess of the agonistic cultural sphere.

In Greece war was considered not only as a way of life, but as a means of bringing out the best in men; victory was seen as an expression of manly excellence.[17] In the *Rhetoric* Aristotle declares: 'victory is pleasant too, not only for those who are competitive, but for everyone; for there arises a sense (*phantasia*) of superiority, for which everyone has a passion, whether less or more' (1371b14–15). War was thus seen to elevate the entire *polis*, allowing both the individual and the state to forge a strong identity born out of this feeling of superiority. It was precisely this sense of superiority which Nietzsche pinpointed as the driving force behind Greece's cultural achievements. And he saw war as the necessary catalyst. In 'The Greek State' he explicitly refers to the relationship between war and culture:

> this mysterious connection . . . between the state and art, political greed and artistic creation, battlefield and work of art . . . the concentrated effect of that *bellum*, turned

[15] Porter 2000: 142.
[16] Luchte 2011: 16.
[17] Tritle 2007.

> inwards, gives society time to germinate and turn green everywhere, so that it can let the radiant blossoms of genius sprout forth as soon as warmer days come. (GSt 170)

And in a notebook of 1887 he proposes that 'a dominating race can only grow up out of terrible and violent beginnings'.[18] In this way we can see how he draws on Heraclitus' claim that 'war is father of all and king of all' (22 DK B53), viewing it as a fundamentally productive phenomenon. Moreover in *Human, all too Human*, he calls for Germany to exercise its own destructive urges: 'the present-day Europeans require not merely war but the greatest and most terrible wars – thus temporary relapses into barbarism – if the means to culture are not to deprive them of their culture and of their existence itself' (HH I 477). The war he speaks of is not a physical war, but a cultural war against the decadence and Christian slave morality he saw prevailing in Germany; instead he hopes to reinstate the agonal, virile, noble values of the ancients.

If we turn to ancient India, a similar social context and cultural attitude to war can be seen. Reception of Indian philosophy in the West has, for the most part, tended to focus on the rejection of violence, with texts such as the Buddhist *darśana* – in this way we have come to associate Indian philosophy with quietism and pacifism. But of course this says nothing about the reality of peace and war. Just like the Greek *poleis*, city-states in India fought for power and control. According to Unto Tähtinen, in ancient India 'peace is merely the interval between two wars . . . war is a permanent institution'.[19] This is reflected in the Sanskrit term for peace, *shanti*, which has several nuances. As Salomon suggests,[20] the sense in which it would approximate to the English 'peace' – i.e. with connotations of 'welfare, prosperity, good fortune, ease, happiness, comfort, bliss, concord, cordiality' – is not its most customary meaning. Instead, rather than referring to external circumstances, *shanti* relates to inner states of mind or spirit such as the calmness of mind, absence of passion, averting of pain, indifference to objects of pleasure or pain, alleviation, cessation, abatement, extinction. *Shanti* then, is far more concerned with inner peace than outer peace, perhaps suggesting that the latter is not the norm. Moreover such an inner peace created ideal Kshatriyas (warriors/kings), with a strong sense of self-control and clarity of mind – both important qualities for military strategy and combat.

Moral codes

Given the caste divisions in the Indian city-states, and the perception of such divisions as being natural, and divinely ordained, it follows that there would be

[18] WP 868: November 1887–March 1888.

[19] Tähtinen 1976: 91–2.

[20] Salomon 2007: 58.

no universal code of conduct pervading the state. Instead moral codes emerge which are specific to these castes.

This can be seen with the caste specific notion of *dharma* (a notoriously difficult term to translate – connotations include virtues, principles, duties, all of which determine a person's relationship to (a) himself/herself, (b) the gods, and (c) the cosmos).[21] The struggle we see in the *Bhagavad Gītā* between universal *dharma* which dictates that one should not kill, and *svadharma* which is caste-specific and holds that Arjuna, as a Kshatriya, ought to fight and kill in order to fulfil his *dharma*, illustrates the more nuanced understanding of moral codes present in Indian thought. *Dharma* and *adharma*, 'that which is not in accordance with the *dharma*', are relative terms – one person's *dharma* may be another person's sin. There is no Manichaeism here. In this way we can see how this would tie in with Nietzsche's theory of types. Given that he believed there was no universality amongst men due to the presence of types, a universal code of morality is unrealistic and inappropriate. As Leiter (2002) suggests, Nietzsche claims that, like nutrients, *values* can also be good or bad (nutritional or non-nutritional, even harmful) for different types of people, depending on their nature. The relativity of *dharma* according to castes in Indian thought would therefore have greatly appealed to him.

Similarly in Greece there evolved a code of conduct and a set of virtues achievable only by certain types. If these normative standards are not met, just as the Kshatriya risks accumulating *adharma*, so the Homeric hero risks incurring shame, *aidos*. Crucially, Homeric ethics revolves around – as the Spartan Tyrtaeus puts it – 'the man good in war'.[22] Courage is highly prized and deemed necessary for the common good along with a respect for one's enemy. As Konstan (2007) highlights, there is a clear distinction between a *polemios* (a 'military enemy') and an *ekhthros* (a 'personal enemy'), which comes from the noun '*ekhthra*' meaning 'enmity'. It is only with the former, a *polemios*, that warfare should be conducted. In the *Iliad*, after a duel, it is not hatred which Hector displays towards Ajax but rather noble courtesy and respect:

21 This notion of *dharma* as being specific to caste and as something to which individuals must strictly adhere is best exemplified in the *Bhagavad Gītā* where Arjuna and Krishna discuss the duties of the Kshatriya caste, and how contravening these duties would amount to gathering karmic demerit.

22 'This is courage, this is the finest possession of men, the noblest prize that a young man can win. This is the common good for the city and for all the people, when a man stands firm and remains unmoved in the front of the rank and forgets all thought of disgraceful flight, steeling his spirit and heart to endure, and with words encourages the man standing beside him. This is the man good in war' (Tyrtaeus fr. 12.13–20 West).

> Come then, let us give each other glorious presents, so that any of the Achaians or Trojans may say of us: 'These two fought each other in heart-consuming strife, then joined with each other in close friendship, before they were parted.' (*Il.* 7.299–302; trans. Lattimore)

We may see this reflected in Nietzsche's claim in *Ecce Homo* (1908) that: 'equality before the enemy: the first presupposition of an *honest* duel. Where one sees something beneath oneself, one has no business waging war' (EH 'Why I am so wise' 7), so emotions such as contempt or pity should not feature.[23] That one may only engage in warfare with one's equals where mutual respect exists is indicative of the presence of different types of men within the state.

The focus on the moral codes of the warrior classes present in both Greek and Indian texts suggests that not only was conflict seen as a normal feature of life; it was also exalted as 'an instrument of policy and a means of releasing heroic and praiseworthy human qualities'.[24] The warrior classes are venerated. In Plato's *Republic* only the philosopher-kings are placed a class above the Guardians; similarly in the *Laws of Manu*, the Kshatriyas are only superseded in importance by the intellectual and priestly Brahmins. Society looks to the Guardians and the Kshatriyas as defenders of the state. With their high-ranking position in society comes a strict code of conduct or *dharma*. In the *Mahābhārata* (2.59.11) it is made clear that 'honest men carry on war without crookedness or cunning' – we can see here that there is a strong element of honour that goes along with conducting warfare. In *Salya Parva* it is stated that if a Kshatriya is killed in battle, 'there is great merit in it'. Similarly there is great sin if he flies from the field. Just like the champions in Greek epics like the *Iliad*, the main 'heroes' in the Indian epics are warriors engaging in warfare, providing us with laudable exemplars. The values of these exemplars are explicitly cultivated in the context of warfare.

In both Greece and India moral codes were forged (a) out of perceived natural differences amongst individuals, and (b) against a background of war and conflict. For Nietzsche, both the content and the context that generated these moralities were infinitely superior to those of a Christian slave-based morality. These ancient moralities acknowledged and promoted natural differences, har-

[23] Cf. Acampora 2013: 19: 'One can defeat an opponent in at least two ways: either by summoning a superlative performance from oneself, thereby winning by surpassing one's opposition, or by diminishing the capacities of one's opponent, thereby undercutting his excellence and overcoming by diminishing one's opposition. An effect of the latter is to lower the bar for what stands as the best.' Emotions such as contempt or pity would amount to the latter method, by diminishing both the enemy and oneself. In *The Anti-Christ* Nietzsche appears scathing about pity: 'pity stands in antithesis to the tonic emotions which enhance the energy of the feeling or life: it has a depressive effect. One loses force when one pities . . . it preserves what is ripe for destruction' (A 7).

[24] Derrett 1961: 143–4.

nessed these differences to create efficient and cohesive states, and promulgated 'noble' values based on strength and superiority. That these moralities were born out of conflict and *agon* is for Nietzsche central to their appeal.

The self

The idea of conflict also infiltrates the model of the self in Greece and India. It is noticeable that in both cultures the image of the chariot is used to depict the self – we need only think of Plato's *Phaedrus* or the *Kaṭha Upaniṣad* (see the contributions by Forte and Smith, Magnone and Schlieter in this volume). Such an image provides us with a useful metaphor to illustrate the composite nature of the psyche and the *ātman*; in both the Greek and Indian traditions we see the soul being divided up into parts relating to reason, appetite and spirit. In all individuals these various parts vie for control but in the ideal individual the more contemplative, cognitive aspect will prevail and maintain order in the psychological economy: i.e. the driver must control and steer the chariot. The chariot also appears in the *Iliad* and the *Ṛgveda* as an emblem of power and a vehicle of battle; the choice of an instrument of war to represent the self is surely noteworthy.

Such depictions of the self may be aligned with some of Nietzsche's views on the self; he envisages the self as a plurality of 'drives' and 'affects' which must be continuously ordered into a hierarchy. In *Beyond Good and Evil* he proposes that the soul is a 'social structure of the drives and affects' (BGE 12), and in *Human, all too Human* he declares 'the self has become, not an *individuum*, but a *dividuum*, an "oligarchy", "a multiplicity" where the drives or affects are continually competing with and against each other leading to a dynamic state of continual change' (HH I 57). Here we can see how the composite nature of the self present in Greek and Indian thought would appeal to him. Crucially we also witness how the *agon* is turned inwards with this idea of aspects of the self competing against one another: 'the highest man would have the greatest multiplicity of drives, in the relatively greatest strength that can be endured. Indeed, where the plant "man" shows himself strongest one finds instincts that conflict powerfully (e.g. in Shakespeare), but are controlled' (WP 966; cf. BGE 212, TI 9).[25] The notion of gaining mastery over this plurality of drives is therefore paramount for Nietzsche; the individual must be able to exercise control over the drives in

[25] The idea that the drives occur in their strongest form is also crucial – we can relate this to the model of *agon* and recall that the noble man must always seek his strongest opponent. Here Zarathustra's recommendation, 'for the worthier enemy, O my friends, you shall save yourselves; therefore you must pass much by' (Z II 12.21), suggests that the greater the challenge, the more worthy the contest.

the sense of 'giving style to one's character', as is suggested in *The Gay Science* (1882).[26] The competing drives must be moulded into a hierarchy, and arranged into configurations such that the individual will be able to flourish. The chariot metaphor is therefore apt to capture Nietzsche's understanding of the conflictual nature of the individual: for Nietzsche, man is nothing more than 'dissonance'.[27] Thus, aligning the individual with something which experiences warfare and which requires a skilful mastery goes hand in hand with his interpretation of the self.

Conclusion

In conclusion, it seems that the agonal spirit Nietzsche hits upon in his interpretations of ancient Greece, and the importance he attaches to the role of conflict within the culture, could also be extended to ancient India. In this way factoring in conditions such as warfare amongst the city-states, through a genealogical method, can be a useful way of explaining an autonomous parallel intellectual development in Greece and India. Understanding the models of the self and ideas on normativity which emerge in Greece and India against this background of conflict provide us with an insight into the *Weltanschauung* of these two cultures. For Nietzsche such a *Weltanschauung* appears far superior to the attitudes prevailing in nineteenth-century Germany, and makes the failings of Christian-based morality with its misconceptions regarding the nature of man all the more acute. In this way he considers 'Greek' and 'Indian' as modes of being[28] – identifiable with certain outlooks, codes of values and ways of assessing and implementing these codes. Such modes of being are, according to Nietzsche, conducive to higher types and a vibrant, virile *Kultur*.

26 Unlike the Greek and Indian models, Nietzsche does not wish to privilege reason or conscious thought in the mental economy.

27 'If we could imagine dissonance become man – and what else is man?' (BT 25). In this way the self appears as a scaled-down Heraclitean cosmos – cf. Heraclitus 22 DK B10: 'Couples are things whole and not whole, what is drawn together and what is drawn asunder, the harmonious and discordant. The one is made up of all things, and all things issue from the one.'

28 Nietzsche seems to use terms like 'orientally', 'Indian' or 'Greek' in such a manner that a mode of being or thinking is suggested: 'I must learn to *think more orientally* about philosophy and knowledge. *Oriental* [Morgenländischer] overview of Europe', (notebook from 1884: KSA 11, 26 [317]); 'I fear that we do not understand these people in a sufficiently "Greek" way, indeed, that we would shudder were we to understand them for once in a genuinely Greek way' (HC 175; in KSA 1 783–92); 'so patient do I become, so happy, so Indian, so settled' (CW I: i).

Acknowledgements

I am very grateful to my supervisors Dr Sacha Golob and Professor Michael Silk at King's College London, and to the organisers and participants at the 'Atman and Psyche: Cosmology and the Self in Ancient India and Ancient Greece' conference at the University of Exeter for their feedback on this paper.

Abbreviations

A	*The Anti-Christ*
BAW	*Werke und Briefe: Historisch-kritische Gesamtausgabe*
BGE	*Beyond Good and Evil*
BT	*The Birth of Tragedy*
CW	*The Case of Wagner*
D	*Daybreak*
EH	*Ecce Homo*
GSt	'The Greek State'
HC	'Homer's Contest'
HH	*Human, all too Human*
KSA	*Friedrich Nietzsche: Sämtliche Werke: Kritische Studienausgabe*
TI	*Twilight of the Idols*
WP	*The Will to Power*
Z	*Thus Spake Zarathustra*

Works by Nietzsche

Reference edition of Nietzsche's works: *Friedrich Nietzsche: Sämtliche Werke, Kritische Studienausgabe in 15 Bänden*, herausgeben von G. Colli, und M. Montinari, Munich: Walter de Gruyter, 1967–77.

Beyond Good and Evil: Prelude to a Philosophy of the Future (1886), trans. W. Kaufmann, New York: Vintage, 1966.

Daybreak (1881), trans. R. J. Hollingdale, Cambridge: Cambridge University Press, 1997.

Ecce Homo (1908), trans. R. J. Hollingdale, London: Penguin, 1979.

'Homer's Contest' (1872), in *On the Genealogy of Morality*, trans. C. Diethe, Cambridge: Cambridge University Press, 2006.

Human, all too Human (1878), trans. R. J. Hollingdale, Cambridge: Cambridge University Press, 1986.

On the Genealogy of Morality, trans. C. Diethe (2010), Cambridge: Cambridge University Press, 2006.

The Anti-Christ (1895), trans. R. J. Hollingdale, London: Penguin, 1968.

The Birth of Tragedy (1872), trans. R. Speirs, Cambridge: Cambridge University Press, 1999.

The Case of Wagner (1888), trans. W. Kaufmann, Toronto: Random House, 1967.

The Gay Science (1887), trans. W. Kaufmann, New York: Vintage, 1974.

'The Greek State' (1871/2), in *On the Genealogy of Morality*, trans. C. Diethe, Cambridge: Cambridge University Press, 2006.

The Will to Power, trans. W. Kaufmann and R. J. Hollingdale, New York: Vintage, 1967.

Thus Spake Zarathustra (1892), trans. A. Del Caro, Cambridge: Cambridge University Press, 2006.

Werke und Briefe. Historisch-kritische Gesamtausgabe, 5 vols, ed. Hans-Joachim Metre et al., München: Beck, 1933–.

Bibliography

Acampora, C. (2013), *Contesting Nietzsche*, Chicago: University of Chicago Press.

Adam, C. and P. Tannery (eds) (1964–76), *Oeuvres de Descartes*, rev. edn, Paris: Vrin/CNRS.

Adluri, V. and J. Bagchee (2012), 'From Poetic Immortality to Salvation: Ruru and Orpheus in Indic and Greek Myth', *History of Religions* 51:3, 239–61.

Agrawala, V. S. (1953), *India as Known to Panini: A study of the Cultural Material in the Ashṭādhyāyī*, Lucknow.

Albinus, L. (2000), *The House of Hades: Studies in Ancient Greek Eschatology*, Aarhus: Aarhus University Press.

Allen, N. J. (1998), 'The Indo-European Prehistory of Yoga', *International Journal of Hindu Studies* 2:1, 1–20.

Allen, N. J. (2000), *Categories and Classifications: Maussian Reflections on the Social*, Oxford: Berghahn Books.

Allen, N. J. (2005a), 'Asceticism in some Indo-European traditions', *Studia Indo-Europæa* 2, 37–51.

Allen, N. J. (2005b), 'Thomas McEvilley: The Missing Dimension', *International Journal of Hindu Studies* 9:1–3, 59–75.

Allen, N. J. (2007), 'The Close and the Distant: A Long-term Perspective', in G. Pfeffer (ed.), *Periphery and Centre: Studies in Orissan History, Religion and Anthropology*, Delhi: Manohar, 273–90.

Allen, N. J. (2012), 'Tetradic Theory and Omaha Systems', in P. White and T. Trautmann (eds), *Crow-Omaha: New Light on a Classic Problem of Kinship Analysis*, Tucson: University of Arizona Press, 51–66.

Allen, N. J. (2015), 'Vedic Sacrifice and the Pentadic Theory of Indo-European Ideology', *Religions of South Asia* 9:1, 7–27.

Alonso, V. (2007), 'War, Peace, and International Law in Ancient Greece', in K. A. Raaflaub (ed.), *War and Peace in the Ancient World*, Oxford: Blackwell.

Andrade, G. (2015), 'Immortality', *The Internet Encyclopaedia of Philosophy*, ISSN 2161-0002, http://www.iep.utm.edu

Annas, J. (1999), *Platonic Ethics, Old and New*, Ithaca, NY: Cornell University Press.

Apte, V. M. (1942), 'Ṛta in the Ṛgveda', *Annals of the Bhandakar Oriental Research Institute*, vol. XXIII, 55–60.

Armstrong, K. (2006), *The Great Transformation: The Beginning of our Religious Traditions*, New York: Knopf.

Ausland, H. W. (2002), 'Forensic Characteristics of Socratic Argumentation', in G. A. Scott (ed.), *Does Socrates Have a Method?: Rethinking the Elenchus*, University Park: Pennsylvania State University Press, 36–60.

Avari, B. (2007), *India: The Ancient Past*, Oxford: Routledge.

Bader, J. (1990), *Meditation in Sankara's Vedanta*, Delhi: Motilal Banarsidass.

Baker, G. P. and P. M. S. Hacker (2005), *Wittgenstein: Understanding and Meaning, Part 2*, 2nd edn, Oxford: Blackwell.

Barker, A. (1989), *Greek Musical Writings, Volume II: Harmonic and Acoustic Theory*, Cambridge: Cambridge University Press.

Barr, J. (1995), 'The Synchronic, the Diachronic and the Historical: A Triangular Relationship', in J. C. de Moor (ed.), *Synchronic or Diachronic: A Debate on Method in Old Testament Exegesis*, Leiden: E. J. Brill, 1–14.

Basham, A. L. (1951), *History and Doctrines of the Ajivikas*, London: Luzac.

Beal, S. (1884), *Si-Yu-Ki. Buddhist Records of the Western World*, translated from the Chinese of Hiuen Tsang (AD 629), London: Trübner and Co.

Beckwith, C. I. (2015), *Greek Buddha*, Princeton: Princeton University Press.

Belfiore, E. (2006), 'Dancing with the Gods: The Myth of the Chariot in Plato's Phaedrus', *The American Journal of Philology* 127:2, 185–217.

Belvalkar, S. K. and R. D. Ranade (1974) [1927], *History of Indian Philosophy. The Creative Period*, Delhi: Oriental Books Reprint.

Benveniste, E. (1969), *Le vocabulaire des institutions indo-européennes*, 2 vols, Paris: Minuit.

Bergaigne, A. (1963) [1883], *La Religion védique d'après les hymnes du Rig Veda* (tome III), Paris: Honoré Champion.

Berghoff, W. (1967), *Palladius de gentibus Indiae et Bragmanibus*, Meisenheim: Hain.

Bernabé, A. (2002), 'Orphisme et présocratiques: bilan et perspectives d'un dialogue complexe', in A. Laks and C. Louguet (eds), *Qu'est-ce que la Philosophie Présocratique?, What is Presocratic Philosophy?*, Villeneuve d'Ascq: Presses Universitaires du Septentrion, 205–47.

Bernabé, A. and J. Mendoza (2013), 'Pythagorean Cosmogony and Vedic Cosmogony (RV 10.129). Analogies and Differences', *Phronesis* 58:1, 32–51.

Betegh, G. (2004), *The Derveni Papyrus. Cosmology, Theology and Interpretation*, Cambridge: Cambridge University Press.

Bhaktivedanta Swami, A. C. (1974), *Sri Isopanishad*, New York/Los Angeles: Bhaktivedanta Book Trust.

Bhaktivedanta Swami, A. C. (2004), *Caitanya Caritamrta, Madhya-lila I-II*, Los Angeles/Stockholm: Bhaktivedanta Book Trust.

Bhaktivedanta Swami, A. C. (2012), *Bhagavad-Gita As It Is*, Watford: Bhaktivedanta Book Trust.
Biardeau, M. and C. Malamoud (1976), *Le Sacrifice dans l'Inde Ancienne*, Paris: Presses Universitaires de France.
Bierl, A. (2014), '"Riddles over Riddles": "Mysterious" and "Symbolic" (Inter) textual Strategies: The Problem of Language in the Derveni Papyrus', in I. Papadopoulou and L. Muellner (eds), *Poetry as Initiation: The Center for Hellenic Studies Symposium on the Derveni Papyrus*, Hellenic Studies Series 63. Washington, DC, and Cambridge, MA: Harvard University Press, 187–210.
Black, B. (2007), *The Character of the Self in Ancient India. Priests, Kings and Women in the Early Upanishads*, Albany: SUNY Press.
Bloomfield, M. (1908), *The Religion of the Veda: The Ancient Religion of India rom Rig Veda to Upanishads)*, New York: G.P. Putnam's Sons.
Blumenberg, H. (1981a), *Die Lesbarkeit der Welt*, Frankfurt am Main: Suhrkamp.
Blumenberg, H. (1981b), *Wirklichkeiten, in denen wir leben*, Stuttgart: Reclam.
Blumenberg, H. (1999), *Paradigmen zu einer Metaphorologie*, Frankfurt am Main: Suhrkamp.
Blumenberg, H. (2001) [1976], 'Geld oder Leben: Eine metaphorologische Studie zur Konsistenz der Philosophie Georg Simmels', in *Ästhetische und metaphorologische Schriften*, ed. Anselm Haverkamp, Frankfurt am Main: Suhrkamp, 177–92.
Blumenberg, H. (2006), *Arbeit am Mythos*, Frankfurt am Main: Suhrkamp.
Bodewitz, H. W. (1973), *Jaiminīya Brāhmana 1.1–65: Translation and Commentary, with a Study of Agnihotra and Prāṇāgnihotra*, Leiden: E. J. Brill.
Bodewitz, H. W. (1985), 'Yama's Second Boon in the Kaṭha Upaniṣad', *Wiener Zeitschrift für die Kunde Südasiens und Archiv für indische Philosophie* 29, 5–26.
Bodhi, B. (2011), 'What Does Mindfulness Really Mean?', *Contemporary Buddhism* 12, 19–39.
Bostock, D. (1986), *Plato's Phaedo*, Oxford: Clarendon Press.
Bremmer, J. (2001), *The Rise and Fall of the Afterlife. The 1995 Read-Tuckwell Lectures at the University of Bristol*, London: Routledge.
Brereton, J. (1990), 'The Upanishads', in W. T. DeBary, and I. Bloom (eds), *Approaches to the Asian Classics*, New York: Columbia University Press, 115–35.
Brereton, J. (2004), 'Dharman in the Rig Veda', *Journal of Indian Philosophy* 32, 449–89.
Brickhouse, T. C. and N. D. Smith (1994), *Plato's Socrates*, Oxford: Oxford University Press.
Brisson, L. (2000), *Plato the Myth Maker*, Chicago: Chicago University Press.
Brisson, L. (2004a), 'Myths in Plato's Ethics', in M. Migliori, L. M. Napolitano Valditara and D. Del Forno (eds), *Plato Ethicus: Philosophy is Life. Proceedings of the International Colloquium, Piacenza (Italy) 2003. Lecturae Platonis; v. 4*, St Augustin: Academia Verlag, 63–76.

Brisson, L. (2004b), *How Philosophers Saved Myths*, Chicago: Chicago University Press, based on *Introduction à la philosophie du mythe*, Paris: Librairie Philosophique Vrin, 1996.

Brisson, L. and F. W. Meyerstein (1995), *Inventing the Universe*, Albany: SUNY Press, translation of *Inventer l'Univers*, Paris: Les Belles Lettres, 1991.

Brobjer, T. (1995), *Nietzsche's Ethics of Character: A Study of Nietzsche's Ethics and its Place in the History of Moral Thinking*, Uppsala: Uppsala University Press.

Bronkhorst, J. (1993), *The Two Traditions of Meditation in Ancient India*, Delhi: Motilal Banarsidass.

Bronkhorst, J. (2007), *Greater Magadha*, Leiden: Brill.

Brown, W. N. (1942), 'The Creation Myth of the Ṛg Veda', *Journal of the American Oriental Society* 62, 85–98.

Bruit Zaidmann, L. and P. Schmitt Pantel (1994), *Religion in the Ancient Greek City*, Cambridge: Cambridge University Press, translation of *La religion grecque*, Paris: Armand Colin, 1989.

Bruno, V. J. (1977), *Form and Color in Greek Painting*, New York: Norton.

Bryant, E. F. (2009), *The Yoga Sūtras of Patañjali: A New Edition, Translation, and Commentary*, San Francisco: North Point Press.

Bucca, S. (1964), 'La Imagen del Carro en el Fedro de Platon y en la Katha-Upanisad', *Anales de Filología Clásica* 8, 5–28.

Buitenen, J. A. B. van (1962), *The Maitrāyaṇa Upaniṣad: A Critical Essay with Text, Translation and Commentary*, The Hague: Mouton.

Burckhardt, J. (1818–1897), *Griechische Kulturgeschichte*, Berlin: Spemann.

Burkert, W. (1969), 'Das Proōmiom des Parmenides and die Katabasis des Pythagoras', *Phronesis* 14, 1–30.

Burkert, W. (1972), *Lore and Science in Ancient Pythagoreanism*, Cambridge, MA: Harvard University Press.

Burkert, W. (1991), *Antike Mysterien. Funktionen und Gehalt*, Munich: C. H. Beck.

Burkert, W. (2008), 'Prehistory of Presocratic Philosophy in an Orientalizing Context', in P. Curd and D. W. Graham (eds), The *Oxford Handbook of Presocratic Philosophy*, Oxford: Oxford University Press, 55–85.

Burley, M. (2007), *Classical Sāṃkhya and Yoga: An Indian Metaphysics of Experience*, London: Routledge.

Burley, M. (2012), *Contemplating Religious Forms of Life: Wittgenstein and D. Z. Phillips*, New York: Continuum.

Burley, M. (2013), 'Reincarnation and Ethics', *Journal of the American Academy of Religion* 81, 162–87.

Burley, M. (2016), *Rebirth and the Stream of Life: A Philosophical Study of Reincarnation, Karma and Ethics*, New York: Bloomsbury.

Burnet, J. (ed.), (1902), *Platonis Opera*, Oxford: Clarendon Press.

Burnyeat, M. F. (2009), 'Eikos muthos', in C. Partenie (ed.), *Plato's Myths*, Cambridge: Cambridge University Press, 167–86.

Bussanich, J. (2005), 'The Roots of Platonism and Vedānta: Comments on Thomas McEvilley', *International Journal of Hindu Studies* 9:1, 1–20.
Bussanich, J. (2013a), 'Rebirth Eschatology in Plato and Plotinus', in V. Adluri (ed.), *Philosophy and Salvation in Greek Religion*, Berlin: De Gruyter, 243–88.
Bussanich, J. (2013b), 'Socrates' Religious Experiences', in J. Bussanich and N. D. Smith (eds), *The Bloomsbury Companion to Socrates*, London: Bloomsbury, 276–300.
Calaprice, A. (2005), *Quotable Einstein*, Princeton: Princeton University Press.
Calvo, T. and L. Brisson (eds) (1997), *Interpreting the Timaeus and Critias*, St Augustin: Academia Verlag.
Capra, F. (1975), *The Tao of Physics: An Exploration of the Parallels Between Modern Physics and Eastern Mysticism*, Boston: Shambhala Publications.
Carrithers, M., S. Collins and S. Lukes (eds) (1985), *The Category of the Person: Anthropology, Philosophy, History*, Cambridge: Cambridge University Press.
Carroll, S. M. (2010), 'Time and Change in an Eternal Universe', in R. D. Mohr, and B. M. Sattler (eds), *One Book, The Whole Universe: Plato's Timaeus Today*, Las Vegas: Parmenides Publishing.
Cartledge, P. (1998), *Democritus*, London: Phoenix.
Cavallin, C. (2003a), *The Efficacy of Sacrifice*, University of Gothenburg: Department of Religious Studies.
Cavallin, C. (2003b), 'Sacrifice as Action and Actions as Sacrifice', in T. Ahlbäck and B. Dahla (eds), *Ritualistics*, Abo, Finland: Donner Institute for Research in Religious and Cultural History, 19–35.
Chakrabarti, D. K. (1999), *India: An Archaeological History. Paleolithic Beginnings to Early Historic Foundations*, Delhi: Oxford University Press.
Chapple, C. K. (1993), *Non-violence to Animals, Earth and Self in Asian Traditions*, Albany: SUNY Press.
Christian, D. (2004), *Maps of Time: An Introduction to Big History*, Oakland: University of California Press.
Churchill, J. (1984), 'Wittgenstein on the Phenomena of Belief', *International Journal for Philosophy of Religion* 16, 139–52.
Clack, B. R. (1999), *Wittgenstein, Frazer and Religion*, Basingstoke: Macmillan.
Clooney, F. X. (1990), *Thinking Ritually: Rediscovering the Pūrva Mīmāṃsā of Jaimini*, Vienna: Institut für Indologie der Universität Wien.
Cohen, S. (2008), *Text and Authority in the Older Upanisads*, Leiden: Brill.
Cole, T. (1967), *Democritus and the Sources of Greek Anthropology*, Philadelphia: American Philological Association Monographs 25.
Collins, S. (1998), *Nirvana and Other Buddhist Felicities*, Cambridge: Cambridge University Press.
Coningham, R. A. E. (1995), 'Dark Age or Continuum? An Archaeological Analysis of the Second Emergence of Urbanism in South Asia', in F. R. Allchin (ed.), *The Archaeology of Early Historic South Asia*, Cambridge: Cambridge University Press, 54–74.
Conze, E. (1951), *Buddhism: Its Essence and Development*, London: Bruno Cassirer.

Conze, E. (1956), *Buddhist Meditation*, London: Unwin.

Conze, E. (1962), *Buddhist Thought in India*, London: Routledge.

Coomaraswamy, A. (1927), *History of Indian and Indonesian Art*, London: Edward Goldston.

Cooper, J. M. (ed.) (1997), *Plato: Complete Works*, Indianapolis: Hackett Publishing Company.

Cooper, J. M. (2007), 'Socrates and Philosophy as a Way of Life', in D. Scott (ed.), *Maieusis: Essays in Ancient Philosophy in Honour of Myles Burnyeat*, Oxford: Oxford University Press, 20–43.

Cooper, J. M. (2012), *Pursuits of Wisdom: Six Ways of Life in Ancient Philosophy from Socrates to Plotinus*, Princeton: Princeton University Press.

Cornford, F. M. (1997) [1935], *Plato's Cosmology*, London: Routledge (reprint, Indianapolis: Hackett).

Cottingham, J. (ed. and trans.) (1985), *The Philosophical Writings of Descartes,* Cambridge: Cambridge University Press.

Cousins, L. S. (1992), 'Vitakka/Vitarka and Vicara: Stages of Samadhi in Buddhism and Yoga', *Indo-Iranian Journal* 35, 137–57.

Coxon, A. H. (1986), *The Fragments of Parmenides: A critical text with introduction and translation, the ancient* testimonia *and a commentary*, Assen: Van Gorcum.

Coxon, A. H. (2009), *The Fragments of Parmenides: Revised and Expanded Edition*, 2nd edn, Las Vegas: Parmenides Publishing.

Crangle, E. F. (1994), *The Origin and Development of Early Indian Contemplative Practices*, Wiesbaden: Harrassowitz.

Cross, R. C. (1965), 'Logos and Forms in Plato', in R. E. Allen (ed.), *Studies in Plato's Metaphysics*, London: Routledge, 13–21.

Curd, P. (2004), *Parmenides: Eleatic Monism and Later Presocratic Thought*, 2nd edn, Las Vegas: Parmenides Publishing.

Dandekar, R. N. (1967), *Some Aspects of the History of Hinduism*, vol. 3, Poona: University of Poona.

Dasgupta, S. (1922), *A History of Indian Philosophy*, vol. I (of V), Cambridge: Cambridge University Press.

Dasti, M. R. and E. F. Bryant (eds) (2014), *Free Will, Agency and Selfhood in Indian Philosophy*, Oxford: Oxford University Press.

Day, T. P. (1982), *The Conception of Punishment in Early Indian Literature*, Waterloo: Wilfrid Laurier University Press.

Deadwyler, W. (1987), 'The Contribution of Bhagavata-Dharma Toward a "Scientific Religion" and a "Religious Science"', in T. D. Singh and R. Gomatam (eds), *Synthesis of Science and Religion*, San Francisco-Bombay: Bhaktivedanta Book Trust, 366–81.

Derrett, J. D. M. (1960), 'The History of "Palladius on the Races of India and the Brahmans"', *Classica et medievalia* 21, 64–99.

Derrett, J. D. M. (1961), 'The Maintenance of Peace in the Hindu World: Practice and Theory', *Recueils de la Société Jean Bodin* 14, 143–4.

Detienne, M. (1963), *La Notion de Daïmôn dans le Pythagorisme ancien*, Paris: Les Belles Lettres.
Detienne, M. (1996), *The Masters of Truth in Archaic Greece*, Cambridge, MA: Zone Books.
Deussen, P. (1883), *Das System des Vedânta*, Leipzig: F. A. Brockhaus.
Deussen, P. (1897), *Sechzig Upanishad's des Veda*, Leipzig: F. A. Brockhaus.
Deussen, P. (1966) [1906], *The Philosophy of the Upanishads*, trans. A. S. Geden, Edinburgh: T. & T. Clark (reprint, New York: Dover).
Deussen, P. (1999) [1898 in German], *The Philosophy of the Upanishads*, Delhi: Motilal Banarsidass.
Deutsch, E. (1973), *Advaita Vedānta: A Philosophical Reconstruction*, Hawaii: University of Hawaii Press.
Deutsch, E. and R. Dalvi (2004), *The Essential Vedānta: A New Source Book of Advaita Vedānta*, Bloomington: World Wisdom.
Devahuti, D. (2001), *The Unknown Hsüan-Tsang*, New Delhi: Oxford University Press.
Diels, H. (1897), *Parmenides Lehrgedicht. Griechisch und Deutsch*, Berlin: Reimer.
Diels, H. and W. Kranz (1903), *Die Fragmente der Vorsokratiker. Griechisch und Deutsch*, vol. I, Berlin: Weidmannsche buchhandlung.
Diels, H. and W. Kranz (1951), *Die Fragmente der Vorsokratiker*, 6th[h] edn, Berlin: Weidemann.
Dodds, E. R. (1951), *The Greeks and the Irrational*, Berkeley: University of California Press.
Domanski, A. (2006), 'The Journey of the Soul in Parmenides and the Katha Upanishad', *Phronimon* 7:2, 47–59.
Dombrowski, D. A. (1984), *The Philosophy of Vegetarianism*, Amherst: University of Massachusetts Press.
Doniger, W. (1981), *The Rig Veda: An Anthology*, New York: Penguin Books.
Doniger, W. and B. K. Smith (1991), *The Laws of Manu*, Auckland: Penguin Books.
Dover, K. J. (1980), *Plato: Symposium*, Cambridge: Cambridge University Press.
Drews, R. (1988), *The Coming of the Greeks: Indo-European Conquests in the Aegean and the Near East*, Princeton: Princeton University Press.
Dumézil, G. (1954), 'Ordre, fantaisie, changement dans les pensées archaiques de l'Inde et de Rome (à propos du latin mos)', *Revue des études latines* 32, 139–60.
Dumézil, G. (1958), *L'Idéologie Tripartie des Indo-Européens*, Brussels: Latomus.
Dumézil, G. (1968), *Mythe et épopée, I: l'idéologie des trois fonctions dans les épopées des peuples Indo-Européens*, Paris: Gallimard.
Dumézil, G. (1979), *Mariages Indo-Européens*, Paris: Payot.
Dumézil, G. (1981), 'Entretien', in J. Bonnet and D. Pralon (eds), *Georges Dumézil*, Paris: Centre Georges Pompidou et Pandora, 15–44.
Dumézil, G. (1986), 'Le messager des dieux', entretien avec François Ewald, *Le magazine littéraire*, April, 16–21.
Dumont, P.-E. (1951), 'The Special Kinds of Agnicayana', *Proceedings of the American Philosophical Society* 95:6, 628–75.

Dundes, A. (1986), 'The Anthropologist and the Comparative Method in Folklore', *Journal of Folklore Research* 23: 2/3, 125–46.

Dundes, A. (ed.) (1988), *The Flood Myth*, Berkeley: University of California Press.

Edelglass, W. (2013), 'Buddhist Ethics and Western Moral Philosophy', in S. Emmanuel (ed.), *A Companion to Buddhist Philosophy*, Oxford: Blackwell, 476–90.

Edmonds, R. G. (2013), *Redefining Ancient Orphism: A Study in Greek Religion*, Cambridge: Cambridge University Press.

Eggeling, J. (1882), *The Śatapatha-Brāhmana: According to the Text of the Mādhyandina School, Part 1, books I & II, Sacred Book of the East 12*, Oxford: The Clarendon Press.

Eggeling, J. (1897), *The Śatapatha-Brāhmana, part 4 of 5, Books VII, IX, X: According to the Text of the Mâdhyandina school*, Oxford: The Clarendon Press.

Ehnmark, E. (1957), 'Transmigration in Plato', *Harvard Theological Review* 50, 1–20.

Einstein, A. (1954), *Ideas and Opinions*, New York: Random House.

Einstein, A. (1956, reprint 1996), *Out of My Later Years*, New York: Random House.

Eliade, M. (1978), *The Forge and the Crucible: The Origins and Structure of Alchemy*, Chicago: Chicago University Press.

Elizarenkova, T. Ya. (1989), *Rigveda. Mandaly I-IV*, Moskva: Nauka.

Elizarenkova, T. Ya. (1995), *Language and Style of the Vedic Ṛṣis*, New York: State University of New York Press.

Etter, A. (1987), 'Nietzsche und das Gesetzbuch des Manu', *Nietzsche-Studien* 16, 340–52.

Falk, H. (1986), 'Vedisch upaniṣád', *Zeitschrift der deutschen morgenländischen Gesellschaft* 136:1, 80–97.

Falk H. (1989), 'Soma I and II', *Bulletin of the School of Oriental and African Studies* 52:1, 77–90.

Fauconnier, G. and M. Turner (2002), *The Way We Think: Conceptual Blending and The Mind's Hidden Complexities*, New York: Basic Books.

Ferguson, J. (1975), *Utopias of the Classical World*, London: Thames and Hudson.

Festugière, A.-J. (1975), *Contemplation et Vie Contemplative Selon Platon*, Paris: Vrin.

Feyerabend, B. (1984), 'Zur Wegmetaphorik beim Goldblättchen aus Hipponion und dem Proemium des Parmenides', *Rheinisches Museum* 127, 1–22.

Feyerabend, P. (1987), 'Reason, Xenophanes and the Homeric Gods', *The Kenyon Review*, New Series 9.4, 12–22.

Figl, J. (1996), 'Nietzsche's Early Encounters with Asian Thought', in G. Parkes (ed.), *Nietzsche and Asian Thought*, Chicago: University of Chicago Press, 51–64.

Finney, G. L. (1973), 'Harmony or Rapture in Music', *Dictionary of the History of Ideas*, vol. II, New York: Charles Scribner & Sons.

Flintoff, E. (1980), 'Pyrrho and India', *Phronesis* 25, 88–108.

Ford, A. (2002), *The Origins of Criticism*, Princeton: Princeton University Press.

Foucault, M. (1988), *Technologies of the Self: A Seminar with Michel Foucault*, ed. L.H. Martin, H. Gutman and P. H. Hutton, Boston: University of Massachusetts Press.

Fränkel, H. (1960a), 'Parmenidesstudien', in Fränkel 1960b: 157–97 [= *Göttingische Gelehrte Anzeigen*, 30, 1930, 153–93].

Fränkel, H. (1960b), *Wege und Formen frühgriechischen Denkens*, 2nd edn, Munich: C. H. Beck.

Franklin, J. C. (2002), 'Harmony in Greek and Indo-Iranian Cosmology', *The Journal of Indo-European Studies* 30:1, 1–26.

Frede, D. and B. Reis (eds) (2009), *Body and Soul in Ancient Philosophy*, Berlin: De Gruyter.

Frenkian, A. M. (1957), *Scepticismul grec şi filozofia indiană*, Bucharest: Academiei Republicii Populare Romîne.

Friedländer, P. (1964), *Platon*, Band I: Seinswahrheit und Lebenswirklichkeit, Berlin: Walter de Gruyter & Co.

Ganeri, J. (2007), *The Concealed Art of the Soul: Theories of Self and Practices of Truth in Indian Ethics and Epistemology*, Oxford: Oxford University Press.

Ganeri, J. (2012a), *The Self: Naturalism, Consciousness, and the First-Person Stance*, Oxford: Oxford University Press.

Ganeri, J. (2012b), *Identity as Reasoned Choice: A South Asian perspective on the reach and resources of public and practical reason in shaping individual identities*, New York: Continuum.

Geertz, C. (1973), *The Interpretation of Cultures*, New York: Basic Books.

Gelling, P. and H. R. E. Davidson (1969), *The Chariot of the Sun, and other Rites and Symbols of the Northern Bronze Age*, New York: Frederick A. Praeger.

Gemelli Marciano, M. L. (2008), 'Images and Experience: At the Roots of Parmenides' Aletheia', *Ancient Philosophy* 28, 21–48.

Gemelli Marciano, M. L. (2014), 'The Pythagorean Way of life and Pythagorean Ethics', in C. A. Huffman (ed.), *A History of Pythagoreanism*, Oxford: Oxford University Press, 131–48.

Gernet, L. (1981), *The Anthropology of Ancient Greece*, Baltimore and London: Johns Hopkins University Press.

Gerson, L. (2003), *Knowing Persons*, Oxford: Oxford University Press.

Gerson, L. (2013), *From Plato to Platonism*, Ithaca, NY: Cornell University Press.

Gethin, R. (1998), *The Foundations of Buddhism*, Oxford: Oxford University Press.

Gethin, R. (2004), 'On the Practice of Buddhist Meditation According to the Pali Nikāyas and Exegetical Sources', *Buddhismus in Geschichte und Gegenwart* 10, 17–37.

Gethin, R. (2011), 'On Some Definitions of Mindfulness', *Contemporary Buddhism* 12, 263–79.

Gill, C. (2001) [1991], *The Person and the Human Mind. Issues in Ancient and Modern Philosophy*, Oxford: Oxford University Press.

Gill, C. (2006), *The Structured Self in Hellenistic and Roman Thought*, Oxford: Oxford University Press.

Gimello, R. (1978), 'Mysticism and Meditation', in S. M. Katz (ed.), *Mysticism and Philosophical Analysis*, Oxford: Oxford University Press, 170–99.

Glucklich, A. (2008), *The Strides of Vishnu: Hindu Culture in Historical Perspective*, Oxford: Oxford University Press.

Gocer, A. (2000), 'Hesuchia, a Metaphysical Principle in Plato's Moral Psychology', in M. McPherran (ed.), *Recognition, Remembrance and Reality: New Essays on Plato's Metaphysics and Epistemology*, Kelowna: Academic Printing and Publishing, 17–36.

Gombrich, R. (1996), *How Buddhism Began: The Conditioned Genesis of the Early Teachings*, London: Athlone Press.

Gombrich, R. (2013), *What the Buddha Thought*, revised reprint, London: Equinox.

Gonda, J. (1963), *The Vision of the Vedic Poets*, The Hague: Mouton & Co.

Gonda, J. (1965), 'Bandhu in the Brāhmaṇas', *Adyar Library Bulletin* 29, 1–29.

Gonda, J. (1972), *The Vedic God Mitra*, Leiden: Brill.

Gonda, J. (1977), 'Postscript on Mitra', *Annals of the Bhandarkar Oriental Research Institute*, 137–150.

Gonda, J. (1978), *Die Religionen Indiens I Veda und älterer Hinduismus*, 2nd edn, Stuttgart: W. Kohlhammer.

Gonda, J. (1985), 'Some Notes on Prajāpatir aniruktaḥ', *Münchener Studien zur Sprachwissenschaft* 44 (Festgabe für Karl Hoffmann I), 59–75.

Goodman, C. (2013), 'Buddhist Meditation: Theory and Practice', in S. Emmanuel (ed.), *A Companion to Buddhist Philosophy*, Oxford: Blackwell, 555–71.

Graeber, D. (2011), *Debt: The First 5000 Years*, Brooklyn: Melville House Press.

Graham, D. W. (2010), *The Texts of Early Greek Philosophy: The Complete Fragments and Selected Testimonies of the Major Presocratics*, Cambridge: Cambridge University Press.

Granger, H. (2008), 'The Proem of Parmenides' Poem', *Ancient Philosophy* 28, 1–20.

Grassmann, H. (1875), *Wörterbuch zum Rig Veda*, Leipzig: F. A. Brockhaus.

Greenhalgh, P. A. L. (1973), *Early Greek Warfare: Horsemen and Chariots in the Homeric and Archaic Times*, Cambridge: Cambridge University Press.

Gren-Eklund, G. (1978), *A Study of Nominal Sentences in the Oldest Upaniṣads*, Stockholm: Acta Universitatis Upsaliensis.

Grimes, J. (2004), *The Vivekacūḍāmaṇi of Śaṅkarācārya Bhagavatpāda: An Introduction and Translation*, Aldershot: Ashgate Publishing Limited.

Griswold, C. J. (1986), *Self-Knowledge in Plato's Phaedrus*, New Haven, London: Yale University Press.

Guthrie, W. K. C. (1962), *A History of Greek Philosophy, Volume I: The Early Presocratics and the Pythagoreans*, Cambridge: Cambridge University Press.

Guthrie, W. K. C. (1965), *The Presocratic Tradition from Parmenides to Democritus, Vol. II of A History of Greek Philosophy*, Cambridge: Cambridge University Press.

Guthrie, W. K. C. (1971), 'Plato's Views on the Nature of the Soul', in G. Vlastos (ed.), *Plato II*, New York: Anchor.

Guthrie, W. K. C. (1993), *Orpheus and Greek Religion*, Princeton: Princeton University Press.

Hacker, P. (1965), 'Dharma im Hinduismus', *Zeitschrift für Missionswissenschaft und Religionswissenschaft* 49, 93–106 ('Dharma in Hinduism', trans. R. Davis, *Journal of Indian Philosophy*, 34:5, 2006, 479–96).

Hacker, P. M. S. (2004), *Wittgenstein: Connections and Controversies*, Oxford: Oxford University Press.

Hadot, P. (1995), *Philosophy as a Way of Life: Spiritual Exercises from Socrates to Foucault*, Oxford: Blackwell.

Hainsworth, J. B. (1998), *The Iliad: A Commentary*, vol. III (Books 9–12), Cambridge: Cambridge University Press.

Halbfass, W. (1988), *India and Europe*, Albany: SUNY Press.

Halbfass, W. (2000), *Karma und Wiedergeburt im Indischen Denken*, Munich: Diederichs.

Havelock, E. A. (1958), 'Parmenides and Odysseus', *HSCP* 63, 133–43.

Havelock E. A. (1983), 'The Linguistic Task of the Presocratics', in K. Robb (ed.), *Language and Thought in Early Greek Philosophy*, Chicago: Open Court Publishing Company.

Heesterman, J. (1985), *The Inner Conflict of Tradition*, Chicago: Chicago University Press.

Heesterman, J. (1993), *The Broken World of Sacrifice: an Essay in Ancient Indian Ritual*, Chicago: Chicago University Press.

Hegel, G. W. F. (1986), *Vorlesungen über die Geschichte der Philosophie*, vol. II. (*Werke*, vol. XIX), Frankfurt: Suhrkamp.

Heisenberg, W. (1974), *Across the Frontiers*, New York: Harper and Row.

Herrero de Jáuregui, M. (2013), 'Salvation for the Wanderer: Odysseus, the Gold Leaves, and Empedocles', in V. Adluri (ed.), *Philosophy and Salvation in Greek Religion*, Berlin: De Gruyter, 29–57.

Hick, J. (1967), *Death and Eternal Life*, London: Collins.

Hooker, J. T. (1999), *The Coming of the Greeks*, Claremont: Regina Books.

Horsch, P. (1967), 'Vom Schoepfungsmythos zum Weltgesetz', *Asiatische Studien: Zeitschrift der Schweizerischen Gesellschaft für Asienkunde* 21, 31–61 ('Creation Myth to World Law: the Early History of Dharma', trans. J. Whitaker, *Journal of Indian Philosophy* 32:5–6, 2004, 423–48).

Hume, R. E. (1921), *The Thirteen Principal Upanisads*, Oxford: Oxford University Press.

Husserl, E. (1965) [1935], 'Philosophy and the Crisis of European Man', trans. Q. Lauer, in *Phenomenology and the Crisis of Philosophy*, New York: Harper Torchbooks, 149–92.

Ibn Shahriyar, Buzurg (1928), *Book of the Marvels of India*, London: George Routledge.

Ilievski, Petar H. (1993), 'The Origin and Semantic Development of the Term Harmony', *Illinois Classical Studies* 18, 19–29.

Inwood, B. (2001), *The Poem of Empedocles: A Text and Translation with an Introduction*, rev. edn, Toronto: University of Toronto Press.

Jain, L. C. (1929), *Indigenous Banking in India*, London: Macmillan.

Jameson, G. (1958), '"Well-Rounded Truth" and Circular Thought in Parmenides', *Phronesis* 3, 15–30.

Jamison, S. W. and J. P. Brereton (2014), *The Rigveda: The Earliest Religious Poetry of India*, 3 vols, Oxford: Oxford University Press.

Jaspers, K. (1949), *Vom Ursprung und Ziel der Geschichte*, München: Piper.

Iežić, M. (1992), 'Parmenides and Uddalaka: The Upaniṣads and the Presocratics', *Synthesis Philosophica* 14, 427–40.

Johansen, T. K. (2004), *Plato's Natural Philosophy. A Study of the Timaeus-Critias*, Cambridge: Cambridge University Press.

Jowett, B. (1871), *The Dialogues of Plato*, vol. I, Oxford: The Clarendon Press.

Jurewicz, J. (2007), 'The Fiery Self. The Ṛgvedic Roots of the Upaniṣadic Concept of Ātman', in D. Stasik and A. Trynkowska (eds), *Teaching on India in Central and Eastern Europe*, Warsaw: Dom Wydawniczy Elipsa, 123–37.

Jurewicz J. (2010), *Fire and Cognition in the Ṛgveda*, Warsaw: Dom Wydawniczy Elipsa.

Jurewicz J. (2014), 'The Cow's Body as the Source Domain of Philosophical Metaphors in the Ṛgveda. The case of "udder" (ū́dhar)', in M. Brenzinger, I. Kraska-Szlenk (eds), *The Body in Language Comparative Studies of Linguistic Embodiment*, Leiden: Brill, 98–116.

Jurewicz, J. (forthcoming), *Fire, Death, and Philosophy: A History of Ancient Indian Thinking*, Warszawa: Dom Wydawniczy Elipsa.

Kahn, C. H. (1960), 'Religion and Natural Philosophy in Empedocles' Doctrine of the Soul', *Archiv für Geschichte der Philosophie* 42, 3–35.

Kahn, C. H. (1979), *The Art and Thought of Heraclitus: An Edition of the Fragments with Translation and Commentary*, Cambridge: Cambridge University Press.

Kahn, C. H. (1997), *Plato and the Socratic Dialogue: The Philosophical Use of a Literary Form*, Cambridge: Cambridge University Press.

Kahn, C. H. (2001), *Pythagoras and the Pythagoreans: A Brief History*, Indianapolis: Hackett.

Kahrs, E. (1998), *Indian Semantic Analysis: The Nirvacana Tradition*, Cambridge: Cambridge University Press.

Kane, P. V. (1941), *History of Dharmaśāstra (Ancient and Mediaeval Religious and Civil Law)*, 2.2, Poona: Bhandarkar Oriental Research Institute.

Kapstein, M. (2013), 'Stoics and Bodhisattvas: Spiritual Exercise and Faith in Two Philosophical Traditions', in S. Clark, M. McGhee and M. Chase (eds), *Philosophy as a Way of Life Ancient and Modern. Essays in Honor of Pierre Hadot*, Oxford: Blackwell, 99–115.

Karttunen, K. (1989), *India in Early Greek Literature*, Helsinki: Finnish Oriental Society.

Keith, A. B. (1925), *The Religion and Philosophy of the Veda and the Upanishads*, 2 vols, Cambridge, MA: Harvard University Press. Re-issued 1989, Delhi: Motilal Banarsidass.

Kenoyer, J. (1995), 'Interaction Systems, Specialized Crafts and Culture Change: The Indus Valley Tradition and the Indo-Gangetic Tradition in South Asia', in G. Erdosy (ed.), *The Indo-Aryans of Ancient South Asia*, Berlin and New York: Walter de Gruyter, 213–57.

Killingley, D. (1986), 'Oṃ, the Sacred Syllable in the Veda', in J. L. Lipner (ed.), *A Net Cast Wide: Investigations into Indian Thought in Memory of David Friedman*, Newcastle: Grevatt and Grevatt, 14–33.

Kingsley, P. (1999), *In the Dark Places of Wisdom*, Inverness, CA: Golden Sufi Center.

Kingsley, P. (2002), 'Empedocles for the New Millennium', *Ancient Philosophy* 22, 333–413.

Knipe, D. M. (2015), *Vedic Voices*, Oxford: Oxford University Press.

Konstan, D. (2007), 'War and Reconciliation in Greek Literature', in K. A. Raaflaub (ed.), *War and Peace in the Ancient World*, Oxford: Blackwell.

Kranz, W. (1912), 'Die ältesten Farbenlehren der Griechen', *Hermes* 47, 126–40.

Kranz, W. (1974), *The Dual Deities in the Religion of the Veda*, Amsterdam: North Holland Publishing Company.

Krishan, Y. (1997), *The Doctrine of Karma*, Delhi: Motilal Banarsidass Publishers.

Kulikov, L. (2007), 'The Reflexive Pronouns in Vedic: A diachronic and typological perspective', *Lingua* 117.8, 1412–33.

Kurfess, C. (2013), *Restoring Parmenides' Poem*, PhD dissertation, University of Pittsburgh.

Kurfess, C. (2014), 'Verity's Intrepid Heart: The Variants in Parmenides, DK B1.29 (and 8.4)', *Apeiron* 47:1, 81–93.

Kuzminski, A. (2010), *Pyrrhonism: How the Greeks Reinvented Buddhism*, Lanham, MD: Lexington Books.

Kuznetsova, I., J. Ganeri and C. Ram-Prasad (eds) (2012), *Hindu and Buddhist Ideas in Dialogue: Self and No-Self*, Farnham: Ashgate.

Lakoff, G. (1993), 'The Contemporary Theory of Metaphor', in A. Ortony (ed.), *Metaphor and Thought*, Cambridge: Cambridge University Press, 202–51.

Lakoff, G. and M. Johnson (1999), *Philosophy in the Flesh: The Embodied Mind and its Challenge to Western Thought*, New York: Basic Books.

Lakoff, G. and M. Johnson (2003) [1980], *Metaphors We Live By*, Chicago: University of Chicago Press.

Lakoff, G. and M. Turner (1989), *More than Cool Reason: A Field Guide to Poetic Metaphor*, Chicago: University of Chicago Press.

Larson, G. J. (1979) [1969], *Classical Sāṃkhya: An Interpretation of its History and Meaning*, Delhi: Motilal Bạnarsidass.

Latona, M. J. (2008), 'Reining in the Passion: The Allegorical Interpretation of Parmenides B Fragment 1', *American Journal of Philology* 129:2, 199–230.

Lee, E. N. (1976), 'Reason and Rotation: Circular Movement as the Model of Mind in Later Plato', in W. Werkmeister (ed.), *Facets of Plato's Philosophy. Phronesis*, Suppl. vol. 2. Assen, 70–102.

Lee-Stecum, P. (2006), 'Dangerous Reputations: Charioteers and Magic in Fourth-Century Rome', *Greece & Rome* 53:2, 224–34.

Leggett, A. J. (2010), 'Plato's Timaeus: Some Resonances in Modern Physics and Cosmology', in R. D. Mohr and B. M. Sattler (eds), *One Book, The Whole Universe: Plato's Timaeus Today*, Las Vegas: Parmenides Publishing.

Leiter, B. (2002), *Routledge Philosophy Guidebook to Nietzsche on Morality*, London: Routledge.

Lenfant, D. (2004), *Ctésias de Cnide*, Paris: Les Belles Lettres.

Lesher, J. H. (1984), 'Parmenides' Critique of Thinking: The Poluderis Elenchos of Fragment 7', *Oxford Studies in Ancient Philosophy* 2, 1–30.

Lesher, J. H. (2002), 'Parmenidean Elenchos', in G. A. Scott (ed.), *Does Socrates Have a Method? Rethinking the Elenchus*, University Park: Pennsylvania State University Press, 19–35.

Lesher, J. H. (2008), 'The Humanizing of Knowledge in Presocratic Thought', in P. Curd and D. W. Graham (eds), *The Oxford Handbook of Presocratic Philosophy*, Oxford: Oxford University Press, 458–84.

Lévi, S. (1898), *La Doctrine du sacrifice dans les Brahmanas*, Paris: Leroux.

Lincoln, B. (1991), *Death, War, and Sacrifice: Studies in Ideology and Practice*, Chicago: University of Chicago Press.

Lincoln, B. (1999), *Theorizing Myth: Narrative, Ideology, and Scholarship*, Chicago: University of Chicago Press.

Lincoln, B. (2012), 'Theses on Comparison', in C. Calame and B. Lincoln (eds), *Comparer en histoire des religions antiques: controverses et propositions*, Liège: Presse universitaire, 99–110.

Ling, T. (1981), *The Buddha's Philosophy of Man*, London: Everyman.

LiPuma, E. (1998), 'Modernity and Forms of Personhood in Melanesia', in M. Lambek and A. Strathern (eds), *Bodies and Persons*, Cambridge: Cambridge University Press, 53–79.

Littauer, M. A. and J. H. Crouwel (1979), *Wheeled Vehicles and Ridden Animals in the Ancient Near East*, Leiden: Brill.

Littauer, M. A., J. H. Crouwel and P. Raulwing (2002), *Selected Writings on Chariots and Other Early Vehicles, Riding and Harness*, Leiden: Brill.

Lloyd, A. B. (1996), *Battle in Antiquity*, Swansea: Duckworth.

Lloyd, D. R. (2006), 'Symmetry and Asymmetry in the Construction of "Elements" in the Timaeus of Plato', *Classical Quarterly* 56, 459–71.

Lloyd, D. R. (2007), 'The Chemistry of Platonic Triangles: Problems in the Interpretation of the Timaeus', *HYLE* 13, 99–118.

Long, A. A. (1996), 'Parmenides on Thinking Being', Paper presented at the Proceedings of the Boston Area Colloquium in Ancient Philosophy, 12:1, 125–51.

Long, A. A. (2015), *Greek Models of Mind and Self*, Cambridge, MA: Harvard University Press.

Lovejoy, A. O. and G. Boas (1935), *Primitivism and Related Ideas in Antiquity*, Baltimore: Johns Hopkins University Press.

Luchte, J. (2011), *Early Greek Thought Before the Dawn*, London: Continuum.
Lüders, H. (1959), *Varuna und das Ṛta*, vol. II, Göttingen: Vandenhoeck & Ruprecht.
Lupaşcu, S. (2008), 'The Chariot of the Soul. A Commentary on Plato, Phaedrus, 246a–254b and Kaṭha-Upaniṣad I, 3.3–9', *Archæus. Studies in the History of Religions* XI–XII, 337–50.
McDermott, J. J. (1978), *The Writings of William James*, Chicago: University of Chicago Press.
Macdonell, A. A. (1981) [1898], *Vedic Mythology*, Delhi: Motilal Banarsidass.
McEvilley, T. (2002), *The Shape of Ancient Thought: Comparative Studies in Greek and Indian Philosophies*, New York: Allworth Press.
Macfie, J. M. (1924), *Myths and Legends of India: An Introduction to the Study of Hinduism*, Edinburgh: T. & T. Clarke.
Machleidt, R. (2005), 'Plato's Timaeus and Modern Particle Physics', *American Physical Society*, Abstract # R13.001.
McKirahan, R. (2009), 'Signs and Arguments in Parmenides B8', in P. Curd and D. W. Graham (eds), *The Oxford Handbook of Presocratic Philosophy*, Oxford: Oxford University Press, 189–229.
McPherran, M. L. (1996), *The Religion of Socrates*, University Park: Pennsylvania State University Press.
Macpherson, C. B. (1962), *The Political Theory of Possessive Individualism*, Oxford: Oxford University Press.
Magnone, P. (ed.) (1999), *Aforismi dello Yoga (Yogasūtra)*, Torino: Promolibri.
Magnone, P. (2000), 'Floodlighting the Deluge: Traditions in Comparison', *Studia Indologiczne* 7, 233–44.
Magnone, P. (2004), 'Floodlighting the Deluge: Traditions in Comparison', in P. Balcerowicz and M. Mejor (eds), *Essays in Indian Philosophy, Religion and Literature*, Delhi: Motilal Banarsidaas, 137–48.
Magnone, P. (2009), 'La Alegoría del Carro del Alma en Platón y en la Kaṭha Upaniṣad', in O. Cattedra (ed.), *El carro. Imágenes y símbolos en oriente y occidente*, Mar del Plata: Argentina, 133–64.
Magnone, P. (2012), 'La Alegoría del Carro del Alma en Platón y en la Kaṭha Upaniṣad', in G. Rodríguez (ed.), *Textos y Contextos (II)*, Mar del Plata, Argentina: Universidad Nacional de Mar del Plata, 87–125.
Mahoney, W. L. (1998), *The Artful Universe: An Introduction to the Vedic Religious Imagination*, New York: State University of New York Press.
Malamoud, C. (1989), *Cuire le Monde: Rite et Pensée dans l'Inde Ancienne*, Paris: La Découverte.
Martin, V. (1959), 'Un Recueil de Diatribes Cyniques: Papyrus Genève inv. 271', *Mus. Helv.* 16, 77–115.
Mauss, M. (1968–9), *Oeuvres*, 3 vols, ed. V. Karady, Paris: Minuit.
Mayrhofer, M. (1992), *Etymologisches Wörterbuch des Altindoarischen*, vol. I, Heidelberg: Carl Winter Universitätsverlag.
Mead, G. R. S. (1912), 'The Doctrine of Reincarnation Ethically Considered', *International Journal of Ethics* 22, 158–79.

Miller, M. (2006), 'Ambiguity and Transport: Reflections on the Proem to Parmenides' Poem', in David Sedley (ed.), *Oxford Studies in Ancient Philosophy*, vol. XXX, Oxford: Clarendon Press, 1–47.

Mills, A. (1994), 'Reincarnation Belief among North American Indians and Inuit: Context, Distribution, and Variation', in Mills and Slobodin 1994: 15–37.

Mills, A. and R. Slobodin (eds) (1994), *Amerindian Rebirth: Reincarnation Belief among North American Indians and Inuit*, Toronto: University of Toronto Press.

Moore, C. (2014), 'Pindar's Charioteer in Plato's Phaedrus (227B9–10)', *The Classical Quarterly* 64, 525–32.

Morgan, M. (1990), *Platonic Piety*, New Haven: Yale University Press.

Moss, J. (2014), 'Right Reason in Plato and Aristotle: On the Meaning of Logos', *Phronesis* 59, 181–230.

Most, G. W. (1999), 'The Poetics of Early Greek Philosophy', in A. A. Long (ed.), *The Cambridge Companion to Early Greek Philosophy*, Cambridge: Cambridge University Press, 332–61.

Mourelatos, A. P. D. (1970), *The Route of Parmenides: A Study of Word, Image and Argument in the Fragments*, New Haven: Yale University Press.

Mourelatos, A. P. D. (2008), *The Route of Parmenides: A New Revised Edition with a New Introduction, Three Additional Essays and a Previously Unpublished Paper by Gregory Vlastos*, 2nd edn, Las Vegas, Zurich, Athens: Parmenides Publishing.

Muir, J. (1879), *Metrical Translations from Sanskrit Writers*, London: Trübner & Co.

Muir, J. V. (1985), 'Religion and the New Education', in P. E. Easterling and J. V. Muir (eds), *Greek Religion and Society*, Cambridge: Cambridge University Press, 191–218.

Murray, A. T. (1924), *Homer, The Odyssey*, 2 vols, London: W. Heinemann.

Murray, A. and F. Wyatt (1924), *Homer, The Iliad*, 2 vols, London: W. Heinemann.

Mus, P. (1935), *Barabudur: Esquisse d' une histoire du Bouddhisme fondée sur la critique archéologique des textes*, Hanoi: Ecole Française d'Extrême Orient.

Needham, R. (1985), *Exemplars*, Berkeley: University of California Press.

Nichols, A. (2011), *Ctesias on India*, London: Bristol Classical Press.

Nightingale, A. N. (2004), *Spectacles of Truth in Classical Greek Philosophy: Theoria in its Cultural Context*, Cambridge: Cambridge University Press.

Nooten, B. A. van and G. B. Holland (1994), *Rig Veda: A Metrically Restored Text with an Introduction and Notes*, Harvard Oriental Series (50), Cambridge, MA: Harvard University Press.

Oberlies, T. (1998), *Die Religion des Ṛgveda. Erster Teil. Das religiöse System des Ṛgveda*, Vienna: Publications of the De Nobili Research Library, vol. XXVI.

Oberlies, T. (1999), *Die Religion des Ṛgveda. Zweiter Teil. Kompositionsanalyse der Soma- hymnen des Ṛgveda*, Wien: Institut für Indologie der Universität Wien.

Obeyesekere, G. (1968), 'Theodicy, Sin, and Salvation in a Sociology of Buddhism', in E. R. Leach (ed.), *Dialectic in Practical Religion*, Cambridge: Cambridge University Press, 7–40.

Obeyesekere, G. (1980), 'The Rebirth Eschatology and Its Transformations: A Contribution to the Sociology of Early Buddhism', in W. Doniger O'Flaherty (ed.), *Karma and Rebirth in Classical Indian Traditions*, Berkeley: University of California Press, 137–64.

Obeyesekere, G. (1994), 'Foreword: Reincarnation Eschatologies and the Comparative Study of Religions', in Mills and Slobodin 1994: xi–xxiv.

Obeyesekere, G. (2002), *Imagining Karma: Ethical Transformation in Amerindian, Buddhist, and Greek Rebirth*, Berkeley: University of California Press.

Oguibenine, B. (1983), 'Bandhu et dakṣiṇā. Deux termes védique illustrant le rapport entre le significant et le signifié', *Journal Asiatique* 271, 263–75.

Oldenberg, H. (1888), *Die Hymnen des Rigveda*, Berlin: Wilhlem Hertz.

Olivelle, P. (1992), *Samnyasa Upaniṣads*, Oxford: Oxford University Press.

Olivelle, P. (1996), *Upaniṣads*, Oxford: Oxford University Press.

Olivelle, P. (1998), *The Early Upaniṣads. Annotated Text and Translation*, Oxford: Oxford University Press.

Olivelle, P. (1999), *Dharamsūtras. The Law Codes of Ancient India*, Oxford: Oxford University Press.

Olivelle, P. (2003), 'The Renouncer Tradition', in G. Flood (ed.), *The Blackwell Companion to Hinduism*, Oxford: Blackwell Publishing, 271–87.

Olivelle, P. (2008), *Upaniṣads*, Oxford World's Classics, New York: Oxford University Press.

Olivelle, P. (ed.) (2009), *Dharma: Studies in its Semantic, Cultural and Religious History*, Delhi: Motilal Banarsidass Publishers.

Olivelle, P. (2011), *Language, Texts, and Society: Explorations in Ancient Indian Culture and Religion*, London: Anthem Press.

Olivelle, P. (2014), *The Early Upanisads: Annotated Text and Translation*, 2nd edn, Oxford: Oxford University Press.

Osborne, C. (2007), 'On the Transmigration of Souls: Reincarnation into Animal Bodies in Pythagoras, Empedocles, and Plato', in C. Osborne, *Dumb Beasts and Dead Philosophers*, Oxford: Oxford University Press, 43–62.

Owen, G. E. L. (1960), 'Eleatic Questions', *The Classical Quarterly* 10, 84–102.

Paipetis, S. A. (2010), *The Unknown Technology in Homer*, New York: Springer Dordrecht.

Palmer, J. (2009), *Parmenides and Pre-Socratic Philosophy*, Oxford: Oxford University Press.

Panaino, A. (2003), 'Some Remarks Upon the Initiatic Transmission in the Later Avesta', in C. G. Cereti and F. Vajifdar (eds), *ĀTAŠ-E DORUN The Fire Within: Jamshid Soroush Soroushian Commemorative Volume*, vol. II, Bloomington: First Books Library, 333–9.

Parker, R. (2005), *Polytheism and Society at Athens*, Oxford: Oxford University Press.

Parker, R. (2011), *On Greek Religion*, Ithaca, NY: Cornell University Press.

Pellikaan-Engel, M. (1974), *Hesiod and Parmenides: A New View on Their Cosmologies and on Parmenides' Proem*, Amsterdam: Adolf M. Hakkert.

Pender, E. E. (2007), 'Sappho and Anacreon on Plato's Phaedrus', *Leeds International Classical Studies* 6:4, 1–57.

Piggott, S. (1992), *Wagon, Chariot and Carriage Symbol and Status in the History of Transport*, London: Thames and Hudson.

Pinault, G.-J (2001), 'Védique tanū- et la notion de personne en indo-iranien', *Bulletin de la Société de Linguistique de Paris* 96:1, 181–206.

Pinchard, A. (2009), *Les langues de sagesse dans la Grèce et l'Inde anciennes*, Genève: Droz.

Plath, R. (1994), *Der Streitwagen und seine Teile im frühen Griechischen. Sprachliche Untersuchungen zu den mykenischen Texten und zum homerischen Epos*, Nürnberg: H. Carl.

Pontillo, T. (2003), 'Il prototipo e le regole specifiche della letteratura rituale come modello della tecnica di sostituzione di Pāṇini: il verbo lup- e il sostantivo lopa nei kalpa-sūtra', *Annali della Facoltà di Lettere e Filosofia dell' Università di Cagliari, Nuova Serie* XXI, vol. LVIII, 5–42.

Popper, K. R. (1998), *The World of Parmenides: Essays on the Presocratic Enlightenment*, London and New York: Routledge.

Porter, J. L. (2000), *The Invention of Dionysus: An Essay on The Birth of Tragedy*, Stanford: Stanford University Press.

Prasad, M. (1966), 'Literary Evidence on the Chronology of Punch Marked Coins', in A. Narain and L. Gopal (eds), *Seminar Papers on the Chronology of Punch Marked Coins*, Varanasi: Banaras Hindu University, 161–70.

Pregadio, F. (2014), *The Way of the Golden Elixir: An Introduction to Taoist Alchemy*, Mountain View, CA: Golden Elixir Press.

Price, S. (1999), *Religions of the Ancient Greeks*, Cambridge: Cambridge University Press.

Principe, L. M. (2012), *The Secrets of Alchemy*, Chicago: University of Chicago Press.

Proferes, T. (2007), *Vedic Ideals of Sovereignty and the Poetics of Power*, American Oriental Series 90, New Haven: American Oriental Society.

Puett, M. (2002), 'Humans and Gods: The Theme of Self-Divinization in Early China and Early Greece', in S. Shankman and S. W. Durrant (eds), *Thinking Through Comparisons: Ancient China and Ancient Greece*, Albany: SUNY Press, 55–74.

Radhakrishnan, S. (1994) [1953], *The Principal Upaniṣads*, Delhi: HarperCollins.

Radhakrishnan, S. (2008), *Indian Philosophy*, vol. I, 2nd edn, New Delhi: Oxford University Press.

Radhakrishnan, S. and C. A. Moore (1957), *A Sourcebook in Indian Philosophy*, Princeton: Princeton University Press.

Raj Singh, R. (2006), *Bhakti and Philosophy*, Lanham: Lexington Books.

Raju, P. T. (1985), *Structural Depths of Indian Thought*, Albany: SUNY Press.

Rangarajan, L. N. (1992), *Kautilya – The Arthashastra*, India: Penguin Books.

Rau, W. (1971), 'Versuch einer deutschen Übersetzung der Kāṭhaka-Upaniṣad', *Asiatische Studien* 25, 158–74.

Raulwing, P. (2000), *Horses, Chariots and Indo-Europeans: Foundations and methods of Chariotry research from the viewpoint of comparative Indo-European linguistics*, Budapest: Archaeolingua Alapítvány.

Raveh, D. (2008), 'Ayam aham asmīti: Self-consciousness and identity in the eighth chapter of the Chāndogya Upaniṣad vs. Śankara's bhāṣya', *Journal of Indian Philosophy* 36:2, 319–33.

Ray, N. (ed.) (2000), *A Source Book of Indian Civilisation*, Hyderabad (A.P.), India: Orient Longman.

Rees, A. and B. Rees (1961), *Celtic Heritage: Ancient Tradition in Ireland and Wales*, London: Thames and Hudson.

Remes, P. and J. Sihvola (eds) (2008), *Ancient Philosophy of the Self*, Berlin: Springer.

Renou, L. (1946), '"Connection" en védique, "cause" en bouddhique', in *Dr. C. Kunhan Raja, Presentation Volume: A Volume of Indological Studies*, Madras: Adyar Library, 55–60.

Renou, L. (1949), 'Un hymne à énigmes du Ṛgveda', *Journal de Psychologie Normale et Pathologique* 42, 266–73.

Renou, L. (1952), 'On the Word Ātmán', *Vak*, II, Poona, 151–7.

Renou, L. (1956), *Hymnes Spéculatifs du Véda: Traduits et Annotés*, Paris: Gallimard.

Renou, L. (1961), *Études védiques et pāṇinéennes*, vol. X, Paris: De Boccard.

Renou, L. (1964), *Études védiques et pāṇinéennes*, vol. XII, Paris: De Boccard.

Reynolds, C. (1981), 'Toward a History of Religions in South and Southeast Asia. Some reflections on the work of Paul Mus', *Religious Studies Review* 7:3, 228–33.

Reynolds, F. E. and M. B. Reynolds (1982), *Three Worlds According to King Ruong: A Thai Buddhist Cosmology*, Berkeley: Asian Humanities Press.

Riedweg, C. (1987), *Mysterienterminologie bei Platon, Philon und Klemens von Alexandrien,* Berlin and New York: De Gruyter.

Riedweg, C. (2005), *Pythagoras. His Life, Teaching, and Influence*, Ithaca, NY: Cornell University Press, translation of *Pythagoras: Leben, Lehre, Nachwirkunge. Eine Einführung*, Munich: C.H. Beck, 2002.

Robbiano, C. (2006), *Becoming Being: On Parmenides' Transformative Philosophy*, St Augustin: Academia Verlag.

Robbiano, C. (2016), 'Parmenides' and Śaṅkara's Nondual Being Without Not-Being', *Philosophy East and West* 66:1, 290–327.

Robbiano, C. (forthcoming), 'Being is Not an Object: An interpretation of Parmenides' fragment DK B2', *Ancient Philosophy*.

Robin, L. (ed.) (1970) [1933], *Phèdre*, Paris: Bibliothèque de la Pléiade.

Robinson, J. V. (1990), 'The Tripartite Soul in the Timaeus', *Phronesis* 35:1, 103–10.

Roebuck, V. (trans.) (2014), *Upanishads*, London: Penguin.

Roscher, W. H. (1965), *Ausführliches Lexikon der griechischen und römischen Mythologie*, Hildesheim: Olms.

Ruben, W. (1947), *Die Philosophen der Upanishaden*, Berne: E. Francke.

Rüpke, J. (2007), *Religion of the Romans*, Cambridge: Polity Press.

Ryle, G. (2009) [1949], *The Concept of Mind*, London: Routledge.

Sagan, C. (1980), *Cosmos*, New York: Random House.

Salomon, R. (2007), 'Ancient India: Peace Within and War Without', in K. A. Raaflaub (ed.), *War and Peace in the Ancient World*, Oxford: Blackwell.

Sauzeau, P. and A. Sauzeau (2012), *La Quatrième Fonction: Études d'idéologie Indo-Européenne*, Paris: Les Belles Lettres.

Schefer, C. (2000), 'Nur für Eingeweihte! Heraklit und die Mysterien', *Antike und Abendlan* 46, 46–75.

Scheiffele, E. (1996), 'Questioning One's "Own" From the Perspective of the Foreign', in G. Parkes (ed.), *Nietzsche and Asian Thought*, Chicago: Chicago University Press, 31–50.

Schiltz, E. A. (2006), 'Two Chariots: The Justification of the Best Life in the Katha Upanishad and Plato's Phaedrus', *Philosophy East and West* 56:3, 451–68.

Seaford, R. (1986), 'Immortality, Salvation, and the Elements', *HSCP* 90, 1–26.

Seaford, R. (1994), *Reciprocity and Ritual*, Oxford: Oxford University Press.

Seaford, R. (1996), *Euripides Bacchae*, Warminster: Aris and Phillips.

Seaford, R. (1998), 'In the Mirror of Dionysos', in S. Blundell and M. Williamson (eds), *The Sacred and the Feminine in Ancient Greece*, London and New York: Routledge, 128–46.

Seaford, R. (2004), *Money and the Early Greek Mind*, Cambridge: Cambridge University Press.

Seaford, R. (2012), *Cosmology and the Polis*, Cambridge: Cambridge University Press.

Seaford, R. (2016), 'The Psuchē from Homer to Plato: A Historical Sketch', in R. Seaford, J. Wilkins and M. Wright, *Selfhood and the Soul: Essays on Ancient Thought and Literature in Honour of Christopher Gill*, Oxford: Oxford University Press.

Sears, D. (2003), *The Vision of Eden: Animal Welfare and Vegetarianism in Jewish Law and Mysticism*, Spring Valley, NY: Orot.

Sedley, D. (2000), 'The Ideal of Godlikeness', in G. Fine (ed.), *Plato 2: Ethics, Politics, Religion, and the Soul*, Oxford: Oxford University Press, 309–28.

Sedley, D. (2009), 'Three Kinds of Platonic Immortality', in Frede and B. Reis 2009: 145–61.

Shaw, S. (2006), *Buddhist Meditation: An Anthology of Texts from the Pali Canon*, London: Routledge.

Siderits, M., E. Thompson and D. Zahavi (eds) (2010), *Self, No Self? Perspectives from Analytical, Phenomenological and Indian Traditions*, Oxford: Oxford University Press.

Siegel, L. (1978), 'Commentary: Theism in Indian Thought', *Philosophy East and West* 28:4, 419–23.

Sikora, J. (2002), *Religions of India*, San Jose and New York: Writers Club Press.

Silburn, L. (1955), *Instant et Cause: Le discontinu dans la pensée philosophique de l'Inde*, Paris: Librairie Philosophique J. Vrin.

Silburn, L. (1989), *Instant et Cause: Le discontinu dans la pensée philosophique de l'Inde*, Paris: De Boccard.

Simons, J. (2010), 'Meatless Diets Before Vegetarianism', in M. Puskar-Pasewicz (ed.), *Cultural Encyclopedia of Vegetarianism*, Santa Barbara: Greenwood, 159–62.

Simpson, M. (1969), 'The Chariot and the Bow as Metaphors for Poetry in Pindar's Odes', *Transactions and Proceedings of the American Philological Association* 100, 437–73.

Singh, U. (2013), *A History of Ancient and Early Medieval India*, New Delhi: Pearson.

Slaveva-Griffin, S. (2003), 'Of Gods, Philosophers, and Charioteers: Content and Form in Parmenides' Proem and Plato's Phaedrus', *TAPA* 133:2, 227–53.

Smith, B. (1989), *Reflections on Resemblance, Ritual and Religion*, Oxford: Oxford University Press.

Smith, D. (2004), 'Nietzsche's Hinduism, Nietzsche's India: Another Look', *Journal of Nietzsche Studies* 28, 37–56.

Smith, G. (1873), 'The Chaldean Account of the Deluge', *Transactions of the Society of Biblical Archaeology* 2, 213–34.

Snell, B. (1986) [1946], *Die Entdeckung des Geistes. Studien zur Entstehung des europäischen Denkens bei den Griechen*, Gottingen: Vandenhoeck und Ruprecht.

Sorabji, R. (2006), *Self. Ancient and Modern Insights about Individuality, Life and Death*, Oxford: Oxford University Press.

Sourvinou-Inwood, C. (2000), 'What is Polis Religion?', in R. Buxton, *Oxford Readings in Greek Religion*, Oxford: Oxford University Press, 13–37.

Sparreboom, M. (1985), *Chariots in the Veda*, Leiden: Brill.

Spencer, C. (1996), *The Heretic's Feast: A History of Vegetarianism*, Hanover: University Press of New England.

Sprung, M. (1996), 'Nietzsche's Trans-European Eye', in G. Parkes (ed.), *Nietzsche and Asian Thought*, Chicago: Chicago University Press, 76–91.

Srinivasan, D. (1973), 'The Myth of the Panis in the Rig Veda', *Journal of the American Oriental Society* 93, 44–57.

Staal, F. J. (1955), 'Parmenides and Indian Thought', *Philosophical Quarterly* (India) 28, 81–106.

Staal, F. J. (1986), *Agni: The Vedic Ritual of the Fire Altar*, 2 vols, Delhi: Motilal Banarsidass.

Staal, F. J. (2008), *Discovering the Vedas*, New York: Penguin Books.

Stoneman, R. (1994), 'Who are the Brahmans?', *Classical Quarterly* 44, 500–10.

Stoneman, R. (1995), 'Naked Philosophers', *JHS* 115, 99–114.

Stoneman, R. (forthcoming), *The Greek Experience of India, from Alexander to King Menander*, Princeton: Princeton University Press.

Strawson, P. F. (1992), *Analysis and Metaphysics: An Introduction to Philosophy*, Oxford: Oxford University Press.

Struck, P. (2004), *Birth of the Symbol*, Princeton: Princeton University Press.

Struycken, P. (2003), 'Colour Mixtures According to Democritus and Plato', *Mnemosyne* 56:3, 273–305.

Stuhrmann R. (2006), 'Capturing Light in the Ṛgveda: Soma seen botanically, pharmacologically, and in the eyes of the Kavis', *Electronic Journal of Vedic Studies* 13:1, 1–93 (http://www.ejvs.laurasianacademy.com).

Stunkel, K. R. (1979), *Relations of Indian, Greek and Christian Thought in Antiquity*, Washington, DC: University Press of America.

Sweetser, E. (1990), *From Etymology to Pragmatics: Metaphorical and Cultural Aspects of Semantic Structure*, Cambridge: Cambridge University Press.

Tähtinen, U. (1976), *Ahimsa: Non Violence in Indian Tradition*, London: Rider.

Tandy, D. W. and W. C. Neale (1996), *Hesiod's Works and Days: A Translation and Commentary for the Social Sciences*, Berkeley: University of California Press.

Tarán, L. (1965), *Parmenides: A Text with Translation, Commentary, and Critical Essays*, Princeton: Princeton University Press.

Tarrant, D. (1948), 'Style and Thought in Plato's Dialogues', *Classical Quarterly* 42: 28–34.

Tatacharya, A. R. (1967), 'Philosophy of Karma and Rebirth', *Indian Philosophical Annual* 1, 45–9.

Taylor, A. E. (1928), *A Commentary on Plato's Timaeus*, Oxford: Clarendon (reprint, New York: Garland, 1967).

Taylor, C. (1989), *Sources of the Self: The Making of the Modern Identity*, Cambridge, MA: Harvard University Press.

Taylor, C. C. W. (1999), *The Atomists: Leucippus and Democritus. Fragments: A Text and Translation with a Commentary*, Toronto: University of Toronto Press.

Thapar, R. (2002), *Early India: From the Origins to AD 1300*, London: Allen Lane.

Thapar, R. (2013), *Readings in Early Indian History*, New Delhi: Oxford University Press.

Thibaut, G. (1904), *The Vedanta-Sutras with the Commentary by Ramanuja, Sacred Books of the East*, vol. XLVIII, Oxford: Oxford University Press.

Thiel, H. van (1996), *Homeri Ilias*, Hildesheim: Georg Olms Verlag.

Thieme, P. (1968), 'Ādeśa', in *Mélanges d'Indianisme à la mémoire de Louis Renou*, Paris: De Boccard, 15–23 (reprinted in P. Thieme, *Kleine Schriften*, vol. I, 1984, 259–67).

Thieme, P. (1982), 'Meaning and Form of the "Grammar" of Pāṇini', *Studien zur Indologie und Iranistik* 8–9, 1–34 (reprinted in P. Thieme, *Kleine Schriften*, vol. II, 1995, 1170–1201).

Thomson, G. (1961), *The First Philosophers*, 2nd edn, London: Lawrence and Wishart.

Tritle, L. A. (2007), '"Laughing for Joy": War and Peace Among the Greeks', in K. A. Raaflaub (ed.), *War and Peace in the Ancient World*, Oxford: Blackwell.

Tsong Kha-Pa (2000), *The Great Treatise on the Stages of the Path to Enlightenment*, Ithaca, NY: Snow Lion Publications.

Tull, H. W. (1990), *The Vedic Origins of Karma*, Delhi: Sri Satguru Publications.
Tuncel, Y. (2013), *Agon in Nietzsche*, Milwaukee: Marquette University Press.
van Binsbergen, W. M. J. (2012), 'Before the Presocratics: cyclicity, transformation, and element cosmology: the case of transcontinental pre- or protohistoric cosmological substrates linking Africa, Eurasia and North America', *Quest: an African Journal of Philosophy/Revue Africaine de Philosophie*, 23–4:1–2, 1–398.
Velardi, R. (ed.) (2002), *Platone. Fedro*, Milano: BUR.
Vernant, J.-P. (2006), *Myth and Thought Among the Greeks*, Cambridge, MA: Zone Books.
Vetter, T. (1988), *The Ideas and Meditative Practices of Early Buddhism*, Leiden: Brill.
Vidal, G. (1981), *Creation*, New York: Random House.
Vinogradov, J. G. (1991), 'Zur sachlichen and geschichtlichen Deutung der Orphiker-Plättchen von Olbia', in P. Borgeaud (ed.), *Orphisme et Orphée en l' honneur de J. Rudhardt*, Geneva: Recherches et Rencontres 3, 77–86.
Vlastos, G. (1991), *Socrates: Ironist and Moral Philosopher*, Ithaca, NY: Cornell University Press.
Vohs, K. D., N. L. Mead et al. (2006), 'The Psychological Consequences of Money', *Science* 314 (5802), 1154–6.
Waley, A. (1952), *The Real Tripitaka*, London: Allen and Unwin.
Wallis, R. (1984), *The Elementary Forms of the New Religious Life*, London: Routledge and Kegan Paul.
Walters, K. S. and L. Portmess, (2001), 'Introduction: Ambiguous Permission, Journeying Souls, Resplendent Life', in K. S. Walters and L. Portmess (eds), *Religious Vegetarianism: From Hesiod to the Dalai Lama*, Albany: SUNY Press.
Wasson, R. G. (1968), *Soma: Divine Mushroom of Immortality*, New York: Harcourt, Brace, Jovanovich.
Waterfield, R. (trans.) (2009), *Plato: Timaeus and Critias*, with an introduction and notes by A. Gregory, Oxford: Oxford University Press.
Watkins, C. (1995), *How to Kill a Dragon: Aspects of Indo-European Poetics*, Oxford: Oxford University Press.
Weber, A. (1964), *The Çatapatha-Brāhmaṇa in the Mādhyandina-Çākhā*, 2nd edn, Varanasi: Chowkhamba Sanskrit Series Office.
Weber, M. (1949), *The Methodology of the Social Sciences*, New York: Free Press.
West, M. L. (1971), *Early Greek Philosophy and the Orient*, Oxford: Oxford University Press.
West, M. L. (1983), *The Orphic Poems*, Oxford: Oxford University Press.
West, M. L. (2000), *Homeri Ilias II Volumen Alterum, Rhapsodiae XIII–XXIV*, Munich, Leipzig: KG Saur.
West, M. L. (2007), *Indo-European Poetry and Myth*, Oxford: Oxford University Press.

Wilson, N. G. (1994), *Photius: The Bibliotheca*, London: Duckworth.
Winckelmann, J. J. (1755), *Gedanken über die Nachahmung der griechischen Werke in der Malerei und Bildhauerkunst*, Hamburg: Tredition Classics.
Winiarczyk, M. (2011), *Die hellenistischen Utopien*, Berlin: De Gruyter.
Wittgenstein, L. (1967), *Philosophical Investigations*, 3rd edn, Oxford: Blackwell.
Wittgenstein, L. (1969), *The Blue and Brown Books*, 2nd edn, Oxford: Blackwell.
Wittgenstein, L. (1993), 'Remarks on Frazer's *Golden Bough*', in J. C. Klagge and A. Nordman (eds), *Philosophical Occasions*, 1912–1951, Indianapolis: Hackett, 118–55.
Wittgenstein, L. (1995) [1922], *Tractatus Logico-Philosophicus*, London: Routledge.
Wittgenstein, L. (2000), *Wittgenstein's Nachlass: The Bergen Electronic Edition*, Oxford: Oxford University Press.
Witzel, M. (2014), 'Textual Criticism in Indology and in European Philology During the 19th and 20th Centuries', *Electronic Journal of Vedic Studies*, 21:3, 9–91 (http://www.ejvs.laurasianacademy.com).
Witzel, M. (1977), 'An Unknown Upaniṣad of the Kṛṣna Yajurveda: The Kaṭha-Śīkṣā-Upaniṣad', *Journal of the Nepal Research Centre* 1, 139–53.
Witzel, M. (2003), 'Vedas and Upanishads', in G. Flood (ed.), *The Blackwell Companion to Hinduism*, Oxford: Blackwell Publishing, 68–101.
Witzel, M. and T. Gotō (2007), *Rig-Veda: Das Heilige Wissen. Erster und Zweiter Liederkreis*, Frankfurt: Weltreligionen.
Wynne, A. (2007), *The Origin of Buddhist Meditation*, London: Routledge.
Wynne, A. (2009), *Mahabharata Book Twelve, Vol. III, Peace: 'The Book of Liberation'*, Clay Sanskrit Library, New York: New York University Press.
Yeats, W. B. and S. P. Swami (trans.) (1975) [1937], *The Ten Principal Upanishads*, New York: Macmillan.

Index

Note: Page numbers followed by the letter 'n' refer to notes.

absolute metaphors, 171
absolute reality, 7, 132; *see also brahman*
abstract concepts, 28, 35, 39; *see also ásat*; *harmonia*; *ṛtá*; *sát*
abstraction, 1, 4
action *see karma*
adharma, 273
Aditi, 44–5, 45n
Ādityas, 44–5, 46, 48; *see also* Mitra; Viṣṇu
adultery, 261–2
Aelian, 254, 258, 259, 260
Aeschylus, 252
Agatharchides, 253
agency, 57, 66, 164, 184
Agni, 46, 83–4
Agni Vaiśvānara, 199
agnicayana ritual, 109–15, 156n, 198–203
agonal spirit, 11, 265–6, 270–2, 275
ahaṃkāra, 21
Aitareya Āraṇyaka (AiA), 167
Ajivikas, 262
ākāśa, 23
Albanians of the Caucasus, 253
alchemy, 104
Alexander Romance, 260–1
Ambā, 16
Ambālī, 16
Ambikā, 16n
a-mita, 26
Amitaujas, 16–17
anangkē, 73, 73n
Anaxagoras, 245
animal rebirth, 225–9, 230
'Anna-Virāj' (Mauss), 24–5
anṛtá, 45, 46, 47, 51
antarjyotiḥ, 60
anthropo-therio-technological metaphor, 8, 176–83, 184
Anti-Christ, The (Nietzsche), 269, 270
áp, 32
a-peiron, 26
ar1 and *ar2*, 40n
Āra, 15
Āraṇyakas, 197
archaeological evidence, 67–9
Arete, 17
Aristobulus, 261
aristocratic state, 268–70
Aristotle, 119, 125, 130, 194, 270, 271
Arjuna, 19, 19n
arkhē, 24n
art, 268, 269n
art of living, 87
Arthashastra, 260
Aryaman, 46, 48
as, 5
ásat, 28, 44, 45, 46, 47
assimilation, 212–13
assumption of metaphysical priority, 200
  challenges to, 225–7
  ethicisation theory, 221–5
Athena, 15
ātman, 1–2, 4–5, 113, 131, 142, 199
  chariot allegory, 81, 183
  chariot imagery, 181
  cosmogonic entry into the world, 60–5
  definitions, 55, 56–60, 76
  in the fire altar, 202
  individualised entry into the world, 65–7
  influence of material/social conditions, 67–9
  Kaṭha Upaniṣad (KaU), 203n
  relation between *brahman* and, 76–9, 138
ātmayājin, 207–8
attunement, 53
autonomy, 118, 118n, 218
Axial Age, 1

Basham, A. L., 262
becoming, 72

being, 7, 72, 124, 212
  undivided, 135, 139, 140, 141–2, 143–5
  see also sát; self
beliefs versus practice, 231
Belvalkar, S. K., 149
Benveniste, E., 12, 40
Bernabé, A., 118n
Beyond Good and Evil (Nietzsche), 275
Bhagavad Gītā (BG), 163–4, 202n, 239–41, 240n, 241n, 273
bhagavat-dharma, 239n
bhakti, 238–9
Bhaktirasāmṛta Sindhu (Rupa Goswami), 238n
bhāvanā, 91–4
bhavati, 63
bhū, 5
Birth of Tragedy, The (Nietzsche), 269n
Black Yajurveda, 198
Blumenberg, H., 170–2
Bodewitz, H. W., 200
body, 65
Böhtlingk *Wörterbuch* (1928), 42
boundaries, 7, 134, 135
  epistemological weakness of, 138–41
  existential consequences of, 142–3
  ultimate, 143–4
bow, 52–3
Brahmā, 15, 17, 18
brahman, 21, 63, 129, 145n, 200, 201, 238
  as liberation, 145–6
  meanings, 7, 24, 76
  relation to *ātman*, 76–8, 79, 138, 142
Brāhmaṇas, 128, 205, 206–7, 216
  Katha Brāhmaṇa, 9, 198–9
  Śatapatha Brāhmaṇa (SB), 109, 111–13, 116, 208, 236
  Taittirīya-Brāhmaṇa (TB), 202
Brahmins, 68–9
breath, 76
Bremmer, J., 105–6
Bṛhadāraṇyaka Upaniṣad (BU)
  ātman, 57–8, 59, 60, 65, 66, 77, 80
  being and becoming, 5
  brahman, 21, 77, 80
  identification, 120
Brown, W. N., 44–5, 45n
buddhīndriyas, 22–3
Buddhism, early, 6
Buddhist yogic tradition, 88, 91–4
bulls, 33, 34, 35
Burkert, W., 106

calm meditation, 92, 93
Cartesian doubt, 136
caste system, 269–70, 272–3
cattle *see* bulls; cows
Caucasian Albania, 253
cause, 73
Cavallin, C., 204, 206
certainty, 135–7
Chāgaleya Upaniṣad, 167
Chāndogya Upaniṣad (ChU), 25
  enjoyment, 122
  gods, 120
  immortality, 84–5
  justice, 257
  self, 128
  victory, 121
chariot allegory, 7–8, 149–50, 167
  chariot as a vehicle for the world beyond, 160–1
  chariot as an allegory of psychic functions, 162–5
  Kaṭha Upaniṣad (KaU), 155–9, 196
  Phaedrus, 153–5
  steering of the chariot, 161–2
chariot imagery, 8–9, 90, 168–9, 187
  Iliad, 188–9, 190, 191–2, 193, 195
  Kaṭha Upaniṣad (KaU), 198–200
  Parmenides, 188, 189–90, 190–1, 192, 195
  Phaedrus, 178–80
chariot metaphors, 8, 168–9, 171–2, 176–83, 202–3, 275–6
  anthropo-therio-technological metaphor, 176–83
  chariot of the soul, 80–1
  chariots of the sun, 174–6
  historical dependency or coevolution, 183–5, 188
  Kaṭha Upaniṣad (KaU), 180–1, 201–2
  Ṛgveda (RV), 198
chariot racing, 195n
charioteers, 194
chariots, 38n
  as anthro-therio-technological metaphor, 176–83
  use, 168, 172–4
Christian morality, 268n
class system, 269–70
code of conduct, 273, 274
coevolution, 2, 183–5, 195–6
cognition, 29, 34–5
cognitive linguistics, 29
Collins, S., 89n
comparative mythology, 152–3
compassion, 146
completeness, 63, 64
concentration, 89, 101, 102
conceptual metaphor theory, 29, 169–72
conflict, 266, 274; *see also* war
connections, Vedic system of, 112–13
connective analysis, 224
contemplative virtues, 90–1
contingency formula, 171
Conze, E., 92
Cornford, F. M., 71–2n, 74n
cosmic order, 5, 83–4
cosmic rite of passage, 9
cosmogony, 5, 23–4, 60–5, 74–9
cosmology, 5, 44, 45, 46–50, 60–5, 85–6, 86n
  Timaeus, 71–4, 75, 79–80
  Upaniṣads, 79–80
cosmos, 43
courage, 273
cowherdess, 31
cows, 30–2, 33–4, 35–6
  body parts, 37–9
Coxon, A. H., 144–5
Cratylus, 214
creation myths, 46–7
cross-cultural contacts, 2, 150–3

Ctesias, 10, 251–2, 260
culture, 271–2

Danavas, 44–5, 46
Danu, 44–5, 45n
Daoist alchemy, 104
dawn, 30, 31, 32
death, 69–70
deity *see* divinity; gods
deluge myth, 152–3
dēmiourgos, 79, 83
Descartes, R., 7, 29, 136, 137, 141
desire, 7, 75, 131, 132
devayājin, 207–8
devayāna, 14, 208–9
devotion, 238–9
dharma, 84, 256–7, 257, 273, 273n
Dharmasūtras, 257
dhyānas, 93–4
dialectic, 98
dianoia, 98
Dionysos, 214, 215
discipline, 161
discursive knowledge, 98–9
divinisation, 96–7
divinity, 53, 80, 82, 83, 126, 155
  personal contact with, 246–9
  see also gods
Domanski, A., 183
doxeiē, 125n
drunkenness, 261
Dumézil, G., 3, 12–13, 20
dynamic principle of order, 47

early Buddhism, 6
earth, 23, 24
Ecce Homo (Nietzsche), 274
economic interests, 208; *see also* monetisation
Edmonds, R., 225
ego-principle, 21, 22
eight-limbed yoga, 88
Einstein, A., 82n
elements, 23–4, 26, 45, 73, 245
Empedocles
  chariot imagery, 192, 193
  cosmology, 44, 45
  harmonia, 42, 48–50, 53
  immortality, 122, 126
  self-divinisation, 107
energy, 38, 39
enjoyment, 121–2
Epinomis, 214–15
episteme, 113
epistemological weakness of boundaries, 135, 138–41
Eratosthenes, 253–4
ether, 24
ethical virtues, 90–1
ethicisation theory, 9, 221–5, 233
ethics, 220, 227, 273
Ethiopians, 252, 259
Eumelus, 191–2
Eustathius, 193
evil, 78

excluded middle, principle of the, 132
existence, 4–5
experiences, 140, 142
expression, 231–2

faith, 88
Fauconnier, G., 170
fire, 23, 24, 30, 32–3, 37, 200–1
fire altar ritual, 109–15, 156n, 198–203
Fish-Eaters, 253
fiveness, 25–6
floods, 152–3
folklore, 151, 152–3
Forms, 96n, 98–9
Forte, A. S. W., 150n, 151n, 156n, 157n
Foucault, M., 105
fours, 26
fragmentariness, 152
Franklin, J. C., 53n
Frazer, J., 231
freedom, 57, 145–6
Friedländer, P., 150
functions, 20–6

Gabii, 252
Gay Science, The (Nietzsche), 276
genealogy, 11, 265
Geneva papyrus, 261
German Philhellenism, 267n
Germany, 272
God, 239n, 244; *see also* divinity; monism
god of the sun, 175
gods, 120, 243
  and the *brahman*, 129
  in chariot allegory, 155
  in chariot imagery, 178, 179
  in chariot metaphors, 175
  and cosmogony, 75
  and immortality, 107–8, 122
  River God, 15
  and *ṛtá*, 36–7, 46
  see also divinity
gold, 216
Gonda, J., 43
goodness, 72–3, 78, 82–3
Greek accounts of Indian justice, 251–4
  honesty, 258–60
  law, 255–8
  marriage, 261–2
  piety, 258
  slavery, 263
  suicide, 262–3
  violence and non-violence, 260–1
Greek language, 12
'Greek State, The' (Nietzsche), 268–9, 271–2
Gren-Eklund, G., 67n
guṇas, 22

harmonia, 4, 40, 48–9, 51–2, 73
  as dynamic and ontologically independent principle, 52–3
  etymology, 41–2
  hidden, 47, 52
  similarities between *ṛtá* and, 43

harmony, 41, 53, 73, 79, 82, 83
Havelock, E. A., 28
Heesterman, J. C., 205, 216
Helios, 175
Heraclides Ponticus, 254, 259
Heraclitus of Ephesus
  chariot metaphors, 175
  cosmology, 47–8
  harmonia, 42, 52–3
  monism, 244, 245
  mystic initiation, 209–11
  opposites, 45
Hick, J., 222
hidden *harmonia*, 47, 52
higher mind, 90
highest knowledge, 120–1, 127
historical documentation, 151
Homer, 144n; *see also Iliad*
Homeric ethics, 273
homology, 27
homoplasty, 26–7
honesty, 258–60
honey, 38, 59
hrada, 15
Hsüan Ts'ang *see* Xuan Zang
Human, all too Human (Nietzsche), 266–7, 272, 275
human souls, 108–9, 154, 155, 178–9, 222
Husserl, E., 118, 119, 122, 123–4

Iamblichus, 248
identification, 112–13, 120
ideology, 12
Iliad (Homer)
  chariot imagery, 9, 188–9, 190, 191–2, 193, 195
  Gabii, 252
  harmonia, 41
Ilievski, P. H., 41n
Ilya, 16, 18–19
imaginary experiment, 223, 225
immortal self *see ātman*
immortal souls, 125n, 180
immortality, 6, 107n
  Chāndogya Upaniṣad (ChU), 84
  in chariot imagery, 178
  chariot metaphors, 181
  models of, 104, 104n
  Plato, 81–2, 83, 96–7, 107, 115–16, 154–5, 214
  as a rational choice, 105–9, 115–16, 116–17
  ritual construction of, 109–15, 116, 117
  through philosophy, 122–8
  through self-knowledge, 121
  see also ātman
incompleteness *see* completeness
Indian justice, 10–11, 251–4
Indian society
  honesty, 258–60
  law, 255–8
  marriage, 261–2
  piety, 258
  slavery, 263
  suicide, 262–3
  violence and non-violence, 260–1
Indica (Ctesia), 251–2
individual souls, 73–4, 77, 82, 83
individualisation, 9, 205–6, 207–8, 210, 212, 218
individuality, 61, 62
individuation, 65–7
Indo-European protolanguage, 12
Indo-European trifunctional ideology, 3, 12–13, 20
Indra, 46–7
inductive reasoning, 195
inner light, 60
inner self *see ātman*
insight meditation, 92, 94
intellect, 81, 126n
intellective knowledge, 126
intellectual activity, 102
intellectual virtue, 96, 101
interiorisation of ritual, 9, 206n
  causes, 215–19
  Greek mystic initiation, 209–15
  Vedic sacrifice, 204–9
introspection, 212
intuition, 29, 124
intuitive knowledge, 99
invulnerability, 144
Ion (Plato), 194
Ionian philosophers, 245
Isocrates, 242
iṣṭāpūrta, 217

Jagatī, 16
Jaiminiya Brāhmaṇa, 205
Jains, 262
Janaka, 216
jñāna, 10, 237, 238, 238n, 240, 240n, 241
Johnson, M., 169–70
journeys, 14–20
Jurewicz, J., 55
justice, 10–11
  Greek accounts of Indian, 251–4
  in Greek philosophy, 254–63

Kahn, C. H., 52
karma, 10, 217, 218, 237–8, 240
karma-kāṇḍa, 236–7
karmendriyas, 22–3
karmic eschatologies, 220, 223, 224, 233
kartā, 66
Karttunen, K., 252n, 253n, 261
Kaṭha Brāhmaṇa, 9, 198–9
Kaṭha Upaniṣad (KaU), 196–7, 196n, 197n, 201–2
  chariot allegory, 7–8, 149–50, 155–8, 159, 160–5, 167
  chariot imagery, 9, 90, 184, 187, 198–200
  chariot metaphors, 81, 180–3
Kauṣītaki Upaniṣad (KauU), 3, 76, 89, 121, 123
  ātman, 203n
  similarities with Odysseus, 14–20
Keith, A. B., 149
kena, 58n
Kenoyer, J., 67–8
knowing, 7, 135, 139, 140, 142
knowledge, 98–9, 119, 124, 126, 139, 206, 209
  highest, 120–1, 127
  moral, 142

mystic, 122, 128, 130–2
of reality, 136
ritual, 127
scientific, 142
of the self, 79–80, 121, 122, 132

Lakoff, G., 169–70
language, 12
Latona, M. J., 189
law, 255–8
Laws (Plato), 100, 246, 254
Laws of Manu, 257–8, 261, 263, 269–70, 269n, 270, 274
leading cow *see* cows
Lee, E. N., 101
liberation, 145–6, 237–8
Life of Apollonius of Tyana (Philostratus), 254–5
Life of the Brahmans (Palladius), 261
Lincoln, B., 13n
'Linguistic Task of the Presocratics, The' (Havelock, 1983), 28
literacy, 28
living, art of, 87
loans, 259–60
locations, 17–18
logical necessity, 223–4, 225
logos, 52, 52n, 210, 211, 214
lower mind, 90
lyre, 52–3
Lysias, 242

McEvilley, T., 24, 150, 150n
Mahābhārata, 70, 90–1, 239–41, 274
Mahoney, W. L., 51
Maitrāyaṇīya/Maitrī Upaniṣad (MaiU), 80, 167
marriage, 261–2
material changes, 67–9; *see also* monetisation
Mauss, M., 24–5
Mead, G. R. S., 221–2
meditation, 6, 91–6, 182, 247; *see also* Platonic recollection
Megasthenes, 252, 252n, 253, 256, 258–9, 262, 263
Mendoza, J., 118n
metaphor theory, conceptual, 29, 169–72
Metaphorology, 170–2
metaphors, 4
absolute, 171
anthropo-therio-technological, 176–83
see also chariot metaphors
metaphysical priority, assumption of, 220–1
challenges to, 225–7
ethicisation theory, 221–5
mind, 90
Mitra, 46, 48, 50
monetisation, 9, 26, 215–19; *see also* economic interests
money, 9, 68, 70
Money and the Early Greek Mind (Seaford), 215–16
money-lending, 259–60
monism, 1, 186n, 197n, 207, 243–5, 247–8
moral codes, 272–5
moral knowledge, 142
moral opposites, 45–6
moral outlook versus rebirth theory, 229–30
moral realism, 5
moral values, 232
mortals, 155
moving cow *see* cows
Muhūrta, 15
Mus, P., 114
Musicanus, kingdom of, 253, 263
mysteries, 126, 128
mystic initiation, 209–15
mystic knowledge, 128, 130–2
mythology, 152–3

Naked Philosophers, 260, 261n, 262–3
Nambudiri Brahmins, 110
nature, 45–50, 165
Nearchus, 261
Nemi, 231
neoplatonic theory, 248–9
Nestor, 188–9, 190, 193, 195
Nicolaus of Damascus, 252, 252n
Nietzsche, F., 11, 265–8
Greek agonal spirit, 270–2
moral codes, 272–5
self, 275–6
state, 268–70
noble value, 270
noeîn, 124
non-being *see ásat*
non-violence, 260–1
not-being, 143; *see also ásat*
numerology, 25–6

Obeyesekere, O., 9, 220, 221–5
challenges to, 225–6
Odysseus, 3, 14–20; *see also Iliad*
Olbia, 210–11
oṃ, 24
On Nature (Philolaus of Croton), 48
On the Genealogy of Morality (Nietzsche), 11, 265, 265–7n, 270
Onesicritus, 253, 260, 262, 263
opposites, 43–5, 47, 48
order, 4, 5, 40, 41, 74
in human life, 50–2
in nature, 45–50
see also harmonia; *ṛtá*
ordering of society, 270
original thinkers, 266
Orphic religions, 225
Orphic-Pythagorean virtues, 96
Osborne, C., 9–10, 220–1, 225–7
critique, 227–33
otherworld journeys, 14–20

painters, 50
Pali Canon, 91
Palladius, 261
Paṇis, 46
parama pada, 158
pareschatology, 222
Parmenides, 134, 134n
chariot allegory, 167
chariot imagery, 188, 189–91, 192, 195, 196

Parmenides, 134, 134n (*cont.*)
chariot metaphors, 176–8
empirical knowledge, 186–7n
immortality, 122
monism, 186, 186n
mystic initiation, 211–13
stillness, 98
undivided being, 7, 135, 136–7, 139, 141–2, 143–5
particle physics, 86n
pathos of distance, 267, 267n
paths, 30–1, 33
Patroclus, 188
peace, 272
pentadic ideology, 20–3, 24
pentadic structure, 3, 20
pentadic theory, 25–6, 26–7
perfection, 144, 145
Persians, 254
personal religion, 246–9
personhood, 57
Phaedo (Plato), 97, 214
Phaedrus (Plato)
chariot allegory, 149–50, 153–5, 159, 167, 181, 182, 183
chariot imagery, 184
chariot metaphor, 80–1
comparison with *Kaṭha Upaniṣad* (KaU), 7–8, 160–5, 195–6
mystic initiation, 213, 214
Pherecydes, 23–4
Philolaus of Croton, 45, 48, 53
philosophical rejection, 243–6
philosophy, 1, 106–7, 118, 119, 132
immortality through, 122–8
Philosophy in the Flesh (Lakoff and Johnson), 169–70
Philostratus, 254–5
Photius, 252n
physical world, 5
piety, 258
pilots, 194
Pindar, 80, 81
pitṛyāna, 208–9
Plato
art of living, 87
chariot imagery, 178–80
immortality, 126n
interiorisation, 214–15, 218
Ion, 194
Laws, 100, 246, 254
money lending, 260
mystic initiation, 211
Phaedo, 97, 214
on sacrifice, 245, 246–7
social justice, 255
Symposium, 102, 214, 215
see also Ion; *Laws*; *Phaedrus*; *Republic*; *Timaeus*
Platonic recollection, 6, 96–103
polis, 241–3, 269
political equality, 254
Politics (Aristotle), 270
poplar grove, 16, 18–19
Porphyry, 247
Porter, J. L., 271
Poseidon, 17–18
power, 120, 216, 217
practice versus beliefs, 231
Prajāpati, 75, 78, 113, 130, 202, 205
prakṛti, 21, 22, 165
prāṇa, 206
pratiloma, 157
Pre-Socratic cosmology, 43, 45
Pre-Socratics, 28, 51–2, 122–3, 124, 126
primal waters, 43–4
principle of the excluded middle, 132
Proferes, T. N., 55–6
psuchē, 214
psyche, 5, 73, 79, 81, 82, 275
puruṣa, 21, 22, 158, 165
relationship with *ātman*, 59, 65, 76, 79, 202
Pythagoras, 25
Pythagorean practices, 102–3
Pythagorean silence, 97–8
Pythagoreans, 42, 97–8

Radhakrishnan, S., 150
Ramanuja, 238n
Ranade, R. D., 149
Rangordnung, 270
rational soul, 108–9, 116
rational thought, 118, 118n
Rau, W., 199
reality, 135, 136, 141–2, 143
absolute, 7, 132; *see also brahman*
reason, 29, 80n, 99–100
rebirth, 83, 84, 85n
ethicisation theory, 9, 221–5
see also transmigration theories
rebirth eschatologies, 220, 222–3, 233
rebirth theory versus moral outlook, 229–30
recitational acrobatics, 197n
reconciliation, 238, 245, 246–9
Rees, A., 20
reincarnation *see* rebirth; transmigration
religious movements, typology of, 10, 235–6
Greek paradigm, 241–9
Indian paradigm, 236–41
'Remarks on Frazer's *Golden Bough*' (Wittgenstein), 230–1
Renou, L., 54n
Republic (Plato)
immortality, 125
justice, 254
knowledge, 98–9
mystic initiation, 214
reason, 99–100
ritual, 246n
societal divisions, 269
war, 274
retroversion procedure, 157
Ṛgveda (RV), 28
chariot allegory, 161
chariot metaphors, 198
concept of cow, 35–6
cosmonogy, 5, 30, 44–5, 46–7, 74–5, 76, 83–4
dawn, 31
evolutions of ideas from, 85–6

order in human life, 50–1
ritual, 32–5
rivers, 32
ṛtá, 4, 36–9, 53, 83–4
Rhetoric (Aristotle), 271
righteousness, 257
rite of succession, 231
ritual, 9, 30, 32–5, 212, 245, 249
fire altar ritual, 109–15, 156n, 198–203
see also karma-kāṇḍa; sacrifice
ritual correspondence, 204
ritual knowledge, 127
ritual tradition, 128
ritualism, 216
River God, 15
rivers, 15, 19n, 32
Romance of Alexander, 260–1
ṛtá
as dynamic and ontologically independent principle, 52–3
gods associated with, 46
meanings of, 1, 4, 40–1, 42–3, 47, 53n, 54n, 83–4
and natural phenomena, 48
and order in human life, 50–1
in the *Ṛgveda*, 28–9, 30–9
Rupa Goswami, 238n

sacred knowledge *see* highest knowledge
sacrifice, 30, 210–11, 258
interiorisation of, 9, 204–9, 215–19
philosophical rejection of, 245, 246–7
polis religion, 241–3
see also karma-kāṇḍa; ritual
salvation, 6, 119, 121
Salya Parva, 274
sam, 59
Samavedic chants, 197n
Saṁhitā, 197n
Sāṃkhya, 3, 20–3, 25
Śaṅkara, 134n, 142n, 196–203
freedom and compassion, 145–6
reasoning, 141–2
undivided being, 7, 135–6, 138, 138n, 139, 140
Sanskrit, 12
Sarama, 36
sát, 28, 44, 45, 46, 47
Śatapatha Brāhmaṇa (SB), 109, 111–13, 116, 208, 236
satyam, 67, 67n
science, 170n; *see also jñāna*
scientific knowledge, 142
Seaford, R., 69n
Sedley, D., 107–9
self, 104–5, 123, 128, 129, 131, 275–6
in chariot imagery, 90, 180, 182, 183
and immortality, 109, 115, 121
see also ātman
self-awareness, 136, 138, 140, 142, 145
self-care, 108
self-control, 102
self-desire, 132
self-divinisation, 107
selfhood, 7, 132, 133
self-immortalisation, 6, 107
self-knowledge, 79–80, 121, 122, 132
senses, 18, 22, 51, 63, 76, 182
transcendent, 24
separation *see* boundaries
shanti, 272
Shelley, P. B., 85n
signs, 29
silence, 97–8
slave morality, 266–7, 266–7n
slave values, 270
slavery, 263
Slaveva-Griffin, S., 196
Smith, B. K., 114, 115, 207
Smith, C. C., 150n, 151n, 156n, 157n
social change, 67–9
social justice, 254–5
social status, 270
societal divisions, 269–70
Socrates
chariot allegory, 154
chariot imagery, 178, 194, 196
honesty, 259
personal religion, 248
Platonic recollection, 96–7, 99, 102
societal divisions, 269
Soma plant, 110–11
Somic juice, 30, 33, 35, 36
soul, 80n, 124, 275
in chariot allegory, 164–5, 177
in chariot imagery, 178–80
in chariot metaphors, 180–3
cosmology, 73–4, 77, 82–3
human, 14, 108–9, 154, 155, 178–9, 222
immortality, 105–6, 108–9, 115–16, 154, 180
nature of, 149
tripartite structure, 81n
see also ātman; *brahman*
soul chariot *see* chariot allegory
souls of the gods, 155
source domain, 169, 170
sports, 173
Śrauta Sūtras, 205
śruti, 24
Staal, F., 110
state, 268–70
stillness, 98, 99, 101, 102
Strabo, 252n, 253n
subjugation, 161
subtle elements, 23
succession, rite of, 231
suicide, 262–3
sukhá, 37n
sun, 30, 33–4, 35, 36, 37, 199, 202
sun chariots, 174–6
supernatural cognition, 38, 38n
svadharma, 273
Śvetāśvatara Upaniṣad (SvU), 90
Symposium (Plato), 102, 214, 215

tadvana, 131n
Taittirīya-Brāhmaṇa (TB), 202
Taitttirīya Upaniṣad (TU), 77, 199–200, 257

tanmātras, 23
target domain, 169, 170
tattvas, 3, 21–2
taxonomy, 226, 227–9
technological metaphors, 184
technologies of self-immortalisation, 6, 105
  ancient Greece, 105–9
  early India, 109–15
'Technologies of the Self' (Foucault), 6, 105
techno-therio-anthropomorphisation, 175
tetracyts, 25, 26
Thapar, R., 256, 263
theoretical immortality, 126
theoretical life, 106–7
theōria, 6, 119, 124–5
theurgy, 249
thinkers, original, 266
thinking, 29, 141, 212
thought, 107, 118, 118n
Thus Spake Zarathustra (Nietzsche), 275n
Timaeus (Plato)
  cosmology, 5, 71–4, 75, 77–8, 79–80
  evolutions of ideas from, 85–6
  immortality, 81–2, 83, 107–9, 115–16, 116–17
  Platonic recollection, 100
  taxonomy, 227–9
tracks, 30–1
transcendent sense, 24
transmigration theories, 9–10, 220–1, 225–9, 230–2; *see also* rebirth
trembling, 213
trifunctional ideology, 3, 12–13, 20
truth, 7, 118–19, 130–3; *see also rtá*
Tsong Khapa, 92
Tull, H., 207–8
Turner, M., 170

ultimate boundary, 143–4
ultimate knowledge, 132
undivided being, 7, 138, 139, 140, 142, 143–5
undivided existence, 138
universe *see* cosmos
unshaken, 144
Upaniṣads, 196–7
  ātman, 4–5, 55–6
  chariot metaphor, 81
  cosmonogy, 5, 75–6, 76–8, 79–80
  cross-cultural contacts, 151n
  elements, 23
  evolutions of ideas from, 85–6
  knowledge, 120–2
  sacrifice, 216
  similarities with Parmenides, 186–7
  truth, 130–3
  universal identity, 207
  wonder, 128–30
  world-rejecting religions, 237
  yogic practices, 88–9
  see also individual Upaniṣads
upāsanā, 90n, 238
urbanisation, 26
Uṣa, 48
usury, 259–60
Utopia, 255

Vaishnava tradition, 239–41
value judgements, 226, 227–9
values, 232, 270, 273
van Binsbergen, W. M. J., 26
varnas, 270
Varuṇa, 46, 48, 50
Vedānta, 6
Vedanta Sūtra, 238n
Vedic sacrifice, 204–9
vegetarianism, 225–6, 227, 229, 260–1
vi, 5, 58, 66
Vicakṣaṇa, 16
vicāra, 93n, 95
victory, 121, 271
Vijarā, 15, 19n
violence, 260–1
virāj, 24–5
virtues, 90–1, 96
Viṣṇu, 158, 160
vitarka, 93n, 95
Vṛtra, 46–7

wagons, 171–2
Wallis, R., 235–6
war, 270–2, 274
water, 23, 24, 32
Weber, M., 223
West, M., 12
Western alchemy, 104
widow-burning, 262
wind, 23, 24
wings, 155
wisdom, 6, 96, 98, 102
Wittgenstein, L., 230–1
wonder, 7, 119, 128–30, 129
world, 30, 56
world soul, 73–4, 74n, 77, 83
world-accommodating religions, 10, 236, 238–9, 246–9
world-affirming religions, 10, 235–6, 236–7, 241–3
world-rejecting religions, 10, 236, 237–8, 243–6
worldly existence, 4–5
Wynne, A., 91

Xenophanes, 243–4, 245
Xuan Zang, 254

yajmāna, 202, 205
yakṣa, 129
Yama, 156
yoga, 182, 238
  chariot allegory, 156, 157–8, 159, 161
  Samkhya, 20–1
Yoga Sūtra (YS), 93, 94–5, 157n
yogic traditions, 6
  goals, 87
  methods, 87, 88–96
  principles, 88
yuj, 198
yukta, 157

EU representative:
Easy Access System Europe
Mustamäe tee 50, 10621 Tallinn, Estonia
Gpsr.requests@easproject.com

www.ingramcontent.com/pod-product-compliance
Lightning Source LLC
Chambersburg PA
CBHW061706300426
44115CB00014B/2584
* 9 7 8 1 4 7 4 4 2 7 1 4 2 *